LOVE
UNKNOWN

LOVE
UNKNOWN

THE LIFE AND WORLDS OF
ELIZABETH BISHOP

———

THOMAS TRAVISANO

VIKING

VIKING
An imprint of Penguin Random House LLC
penguinrandomhouse.com

Owing to limitations of space, text and image credits can be found on pages 411–12.

LIBRARY OF CONGRESS CATALOGING-IN-PUBLICATION DATA
Names: Travisano, Thomas J., 1951– author.
Title: Love unknown : the life and worlds of Elizabeth Bishop / Thomas Travisano.
Description: [New York, New York] : Viking, [2019].
Identifiers: LCCN 2019016018 (print) | LCCN 2019980677 (ebook) |
ISBN 9780525428817 (hardcover) | ISBN 9780698191624 (ebook)
Classification: LCC PS3503.I785 Z89 2019 (print) | LCC PS3503.I785 (ebook) |
DDC 811/.54 [B]—dc23
LC record available at https://lccn.loc.gov/2019016018
LC ebook record available at https://lccn.loc.gov/2019980677

Printed in Canada
1   3   5   7   9   10   8   6   4   2

Book design by Gretchen Achilles

For Elsa, as ever,

and

for my friends and colleagues in the Elizabeth Bishop Society

. . . Truly, Friend,
For ought I hear, your Master shows to you
More favour than you wot of. Mark the end.
The Font did only, what was old, renew:
The Caldron suppled, what was grown too hard:
The Thorns did quicken, what was grown too dull:
All did but strive to mend, what you had marr'd.
Wherefore be cheer'd, and praise him to the full
Each day, each hour, each moment of the week,
Who fain would have you be, new, tender, quick.

The Temple (1633)

FROM GEORGE HERBERT'S "LOVE UNKNOWN"

CONTENTS

Elizabeth Bishop's life is a great story. It is the story of a young girl who lost her father to Bright's disease when she was eight months old and lost her mother to an incurable mental breakdown when she was five. It is the story of a woman who struggled with shyness and self-doubt, with alcoholism and severe and lasting autoimmune disorders, with barriers imposed by gender, and—as Adrienne Rich noted—with "the eye of the outsider"[1] imposed by her lesbian sexuality. It is, at its core, the story of how a young girl who had grown up orphaned, abused, and isolated made herself, with determined effort, into a world traveler and into the creator of unforgettable poems.

Within this great story lies an intricate web of smaller stories—stories about Bishop's relationships with celebrated writers, artists, and composers, and with many lesser-known friends and lovers across the globe. Exploring Bishop's network of relationships with literati, glitterati, visual artists and musicians, locals, travelers, students, scholars, medicos, and politicos—along with an international gay underground then nearly invisible to the dominant culture—brings to life the varied mid-twentieth-century worlds on the three continents through which she moved. Bishop began writing self-exploratory letters that were vivid, funny, and sophisticated by the age of fourteen. Her later verse, prose, and letters depict her early experience, starting at the age of three, with extraordinary clarity. Family records, too, paint a remarkably lucid picture of Bishop's life *before* the age of three. Even if Bishop had not become a world-renowned poet, her life history would be worth exploring because it offers such a portrait of a distinctive human individual's lifelong struggle against adversity. But Bishop did make herself into an author of true greatness, and the record she left behind offers a compelling account of how a unique creative artist was first born and then made. In her self-deprecatory way, Bishop often maintained in interviews that the pattern of her life was the result of a series of sheer accidents. But her precocious adolescent writings make it crystal clear that from her middle teens she was already sketching out a life plan prioritizing travel, love, friendship, independence, observation, and the making of poetry. From adolescence onward, Elizabeth Bishop kept to the basic outlines of her plan, and as a writer and a person, she made the most of it.

The Elizabeth Bishop who has emerged for me, after forty years of engagement with her life and art, was a quietly determined individualist whose actions and choices were marked by a consistent willingness to accept risk, flavored by a keen eye for detail and a dry and distinctly wicked sense of humor. Bishop was a woman who struggled persistently against physical and emotional liabilities that might have disabled others. Yet she made a life that, for all its imperfections, was marked by wit, energy, courage, dedication, and lasting artistic achievement. As her friend and protégé James Merrill observed, "It was *du coté de chez* Elizabeth . . . that I saw the daily life that took my fancy . . . with its kind of random, Chekhovian surface, open to trivia and funny surprises, or even painful ones, today a fit of weeping, tomorrow a picnic." For Merrill, "Elizabeth had more talent for life—and for poetry—than anyone else I've known, and this has served me as an ideal."[2] One of the most famous recurring images in Bishop's writing is the rainbow, and she certainly viewed life in its full spectrum. Her openness to all kinds of experience, be it perplexing, bitter, funny, or invigorating, remains one of the chief attractions of her life and art. These characteristics also account, at least in part, for Bishop's profound and ongoing influence over her fellow writers and her steadily growing attractiveness to readers.

It has become an axiom among critics that Bishop's lifelong dedication to travel was determined in large measure by a search for "home." Yet travel was not simply a search for security or shelter. It was also a search for adventure, risk, and discovery, a search for friendship and lasting love, a search for artistic material, and, perhaps most important, a quest for freedom that found its basis in a childhood marked by loss, isolation, and constraint. The "art of losing" Bishop ruefully celebrated with such poignant irony in perhaps her most famous poem, "One Art," was linked in equal part to a life and art of *finding*—an art demanding the sort of encounter, appraisal, and understated epiphany that appears in such abundance throughout her work.

Bishop's uncanny knack for balancing depth and lightness in a completely natural and engaging manner helps her readers to see the world in new ways. As Merrill observed shortly after her death in 1979, "I like the way her whole oeuvre is on the scale of a human life; there is no oracular amplification, she doesn't go about on stilts to make her vision wider. She doesn't need that. She's wise and humane enough as it is."[3] Yet her quality of lightness, and the consistently human scale of her poetry, did not preclude profundity. As another friend and protégé, Frank Bidart, observed fifteen years after her death,

> *Bishop's life, idiosyncratic, seemingly marginal, was exemplary. Her masked but intense refusal to be anything but herself reveals like an X ray the contradictions and pleasures of twentieth-century culture. The tragedies at the root of her life were at the root of the mastery achieved by her art.*[4]

This unique combination of qualities—once undervalued but now widely appreciated—prompted David Orr to declare in the *New York Times Book Review* in 2006 that "nothing matches the impact of a great artist, and in the second half of the 20th century, no American artist in any medium was greater than Elizabeth Bishop."[5] As May Swenson wrote in an ecstatic letter of praise that offered the first detailed reading of Bishop's 1955 *Poems*, a book that would later win a Pulitzer Prize, *"Not to need illusion—to dare to see and say how things really are, is the emancipation I would like to attain*, as you have—but I guess you don't need to try, you just do see that way, being you."[6]

This biography hopes to show Bishop's life and art as a persistent, intricate, and ultimately successful struggle of speech against silence—a struggle in which her work remains persevering and curiously buoyant even as it grows out of and confronts isolation, suffering, and loss. Many of her most elusive or enigmatic poems can begin to seem almost transparent when biographical insights are sensitively applied, and her poems' magic only heightens as we witness the struggles out of which her work emerged, struggles that she distilled and transformed through the peculiar alchemy of her art. And at the core of her greatness as an artist lies her unparalleled re-creation of her experience as a child.

CHAPTER ONE

BETWEEN TWO WORLDS

When Elizabeth Bishop was three years old, she witnessed the Great Salem Fire—an event that took place on the night of June 25, 1914, and that she would remember for the rest of her life. The fire raged in the darkness, sweeping through nearly 250 acres of the historic Massachusetts harbor town of Salem and reducing to charred ruins the homes of more than twenty thousand inhabitants. The flames forced hundreds of Salem's residents to flee in small boats across Palmer Cove toward the relative safety of Marblehead on the opposite shore.

It was there, near the beach at Marblehead, that Elizabeth was sharing a summer house with her recently widowed mother, Gertrude Bulmer Bishop, and her father's family. In the posthumously published poem "A Drunkard," Bishop recalled that as the flames across the bay grew higher, "the sky was bright red; everything was red: / out on the lawn, my mother's white dress looked / rose-red; my white enameled crib was red," and she watched as boats filled with escaping people arrived on their beach. Yet the residents of Marblehead themselves felt anything but safe, for "the red sky was filled with flying motes / cinders and coals," and many citizens were hosing their roofs to prevent their houses, too, from bursting into flame.

In the midst of this chaotic scene, the child, in search of her mother outdoors, found Gertrude and various neighbors giving coffee and food to Salem's refugees. Her own cries for attention and reassurance went unnoticed. All Bishop could later recall receiving from her mother was a stern reprimand early the next morning, when the two were pacing the shoreline. As the child out of curiosity picked up a fragment of a woman's long black cotton stocking from a beach "strewn with cinders, dark with ash— / strange objects . . . blown across the water," her mother responded sharply, *"Put that down!"*[1] This rebuke for her inquisitiveness provoked deep embarrassment and guilt, feelings that would echo through the decades in her memory, only to reappear in a profoundly self-exploratory poem—linking this experience with her problem with periodic alcohol abuse—that Bishop still had on her desk at the moment of her death.

Bishop's mother, Gertrude, was in fragile psychological health when the Great Fire occurred in 1914. Her bouts of emotional disturbance had become acute following the death of her husband three years earlier, when the infant Elizabeth was eight months old. Two years after the fire, when the child was five, Gertrude would suffer a mental breakdown from which she never recovered. Bishop would continue to be haunted by her mother's disturbing outcries: "a scream, the echo of a scream" that, as she discloses in her 1953 story "In the Village," signaled her mother's mental collapse. This was the scream that became a part of Bishop's inner world and "came there to live forever—not loud, just alive forever."[2] Bishop would continue to suffer from these and other traumatic early losses—losses so extreme and so well remembered that she once told her friend and fellow poet Robert Lowell, "When you write my epitaph, you must say I was the loneliest person who ever lived."[3]

Yet there was another side to Bishop's personality that must be understood if we are to grasp the complex persona she presented to the world both in her personal life and in her poetry. Though her frequently traumatic past was very much alive for her, Bishop was also extraordinarily engaged with the present. When, approaching sixty, Bishop arrived to teach at Harvard University in the fall of 1970, the younger poet Kathleen Spivack noted that "she had the quality of surprised youthfulness in her eyes." Spivack also found her "quite unlike the austere public persona of 'Miss Bishop'" that Spivack had come to expect from the elder poet's reputation. In her second year at Harvard, Bishop set up a Ping-Pong table in the foyer of her small apartment on Brattle Street; playing the game was supposed to help the arthritis in her hands. Spivack recalls their weekly Ping-Pong matches where "Elizabeth dashed about on her side of the table, her charming face pursed with concentration, and bursting into laughter at her tricky shots."[4] Later in the evening, when guests arrived for dinner, they would be seated around the Ping-Pong table, now *sans* net and demurely graced by a tablecloth. As her friend and Harvard colleague Monroe Engel observed, Bishop didn't have space in her apartment for both her Ping-Pong table and a dining table, so she chose the former because, as she declared, "You could eat off the Ping-Pong table, but you couldn't play Ping-Pong on a dining table."[5]

According to her student Jonathan Galassi, Bishop had, in her college classroom, "almost willfully old-fashioned manners."[6] She addressed her students by their last names, a practice that had almost died out in American higher education by the early 1970s. However, she could also be unapologetically *herself* at moments where a little more decorum might have been expected. Bishop's blend of mannerly correctness and casual and cheeky unconventionality also plays out in her poetry, as does her seemingly contradictory fusing of spot-on accuracy with her uniquely homespun version of surrealism. She termed the latter quality "the always-more-successful surrealism of everyday life."[7] These paradoxical characteristics, plus her unquenchably youthful curiosity and her capacity for wit and droll amusement—which the late Nobel laureate Seamus Heaney termed her "dry, merry quality"[8]— helped attract a wide and distinguished body of friends, many of whom also became her devoted correspondents. These fortunate individuals became the recipients of a steady stream of Bishop's sharp and revealing letters, letters that are now widely regarded as one of the most brilliant and significant bodies of correspondence of the last century.

When Bishop began to teach writing and literature at Harvard University in 1970—and settled, the following fall, into that compact Brattle Street apartment just north of Harvard Square—she was very much a seasoned traveler. She had sojourned for most of the previous two decades in Brazil, and before and after that had lived for extended periods in Canada, France, Key West, Mexico, Washington, DC, Seattle, and San Francisco, punctuated by stopovers in locales as varied as coastal Maine, Cape Cod, Newfoundland, Spain, North Africa, Tuscany, and (most frequently) New York's Greenwich Village, where she kept for several years a "garret" on King Street as a pied-à-terre. But now, in her final decade, Bishop had returned to native ground. Her apartment on Brattle Street was just forty miles east of the residence (no longer standing) at 875 Main Street in Worcester, Massachusetts, where Bishop first drew breath. The sturdy granite gravestone in Worcester's Hope Cemetery under which Bishop's ashes lie buried—alongside the remains of her Canadian-born mother and her Worcester-born father—may be found just minutes north of the place of Bishop's birth. Yet Bishop's "there and back again" had been a long, eventful journey.

The Worcester of 1911, the year Bishop was born, was a bustling, prosperous, steadily growing industrial city—the third-largest urban center in New England after Boston and Providence, Rhode Island. Worcester was a community in which the Bishop family played a prominent role, but Bishop herself would not remember it fondly. Bishop claimed in a letter to Anne Stevenson, the author of the earliest critical book about her, that she had spent only a few miserable months in Worcester with her paternal grandparents. Between the ages of eight and sixteen, she had lived most of the year with a maternal aunt in a working-class neighborhood near Boston. These long and weary months, when she was mostly housebound due to illness, were relieved by summers with her maternal grandparents in

Great Village, Nova Scotia. Bishop's sense of her own national, regional, and familial identity was always complex and fluid. She was born in the United States to an American father and was thus legally an American citizen. However, Bishop described herself to Stevenson as three-fourths Canadian and one-fourth New Englander, because her paternal grandfather, like her mother's family, had been born in Canada. Yet even her Canadian roots were mixed with American; as she told Stevenson, "My maternal grandparents were, some of them, Tories, who left upper N.Y. State and were given land grants in Nova Scotia by George III."[9]

Bishop's father's family, the Bishops of Worcester, and her mother's family, the Bulmers of her beloved Great Village, Nova Scotia, were both respected within their communities, but the Bishops of Worcester were successful entrepreneurs and far more prosperous. In fact, the fulsomely titled *Historic Homes and Institutions and Genealogical and Personal Memoirs of Worcester County, Massachusetts*, published in 1907, extolled Elizabeth's paternal grandfather, John W. Bishop, as a living exemplar of the American Dream, and Bishop herself would later note, "His was an Horatio Alger story."[10] In the view of *Historic Homes*, Bishop's paternal grandfather was a man whose "rise from humble beginnings to a foremost place in the business world" contained "a valuable lesson" on the way to wealth and professional stature. *Historic Homes* records that John W. was born on Canada's Prince Edward Island in 1846, hence Bishop's claim that she was three-fourths Canadian. John W. migrated with his family to Rhode Island when he was eleven. After only a year of formal schooling, he was put to work in a cotton mill, where he labored hard until he was fourteen. He then shifted to the building trade—running away, according to Bishop, "with a box of carpenters' tools on his back."[11] He soon relocated to Worcester and worked his way up "with tireless energy and perseverance" until, in 1874—four years after an advantageous marriage—he went into business for himself as a builder. Over the next quarter century John W.'s business grew steadily. While maintaining a center of operations in Worcester, J. W. Bishop & Co.

opened satellite offices on New York's Fifth Avenue, as well as in Boston and Providence—this last, in part, for its proximity to Newport. *Historic Homes* attributes the success of the Bishop patriarch's business directly to "the personal factor. He worked hard and he worked late, and he never ceased to learn and apply."[12]

J. W. Bishop & Co. did erect several of the summer cottages—or, as *Historic Homes* more precisely terms them, "costly palaces"—that line Newport's Millionaires' Row along the shores of Narragansett Bay. However, the firm was primarily focused, as Bishop would later recall, on "public buildings, college buildings, theatres, etc." These included "many in Boston, including the Public Library, the Museum of Fine Arts, etc."[13] These distinguished and still-popular edifices are known not only for their usefulness and their aesthetic appeal, but also for the thoroughness and soundness of their construction. It was frequently said in the trade that a J. W. Bishop & Co. building stayed built.[14]

Owing to his limited schooling, John W. Bishop became a builder, not an architect, but the *Architectural Record* asserts that his expertise in architecture and interior design was such that he was considered "like one of those master marble workers to whom the most eminent sculptor can entrust his plaster of Paris model with the perfect assurance that the finished marble, fashioned in its image, will need no retouching from his own hand."[15] Although all her life Bishop reserved her warmest feelings for her Bulmer relations, in one respect she was her Worcester grandfather's granddaughter. John W. Bishop's mastery of architectural form and the details of construction would be mirrored in Elizabeth Bishop's later mastery of poetic form and verbal detail. What he learned to build with stone, she would learn to build with words.

At the time of Bishop's birth, her grandfather's company was at the height of its success and was just completing, in the heart of Worcester, one of its most singular and appealing public buildings: the home of the American Antiquarian Society.[16] Because of the richness and uniqueness of its holdings, scholars of early American history and popular culture have been drawn for more than a century to this Colonial Revival building on Worcester's Salisbury Street, which stands just two miles from the place of Bishop's birth. The architecture of this building is so striking that it must reveal something of her father's and grandfather's minds and personalities. Its sturdy brick exterior hardly prepares one for the stately splendor of its interior, which centers on a reading room of arresting beauty. Graceful Ionic columns frame the open, octagonal atrium of this chamber, and "under its generous dome,"[17] light gently filters down on an aspiring scholar who may sit absorbing the history and popular culture of America's earliest centuries from periodicals once hot off the presses. The statement made by the Antiquarian Society's home and research library—and its remarkable reading room—is that printed words matter.

Elizabeth's father, William Thomas Bishop, served as first vice president of J. W. Bishop & Co. As manager of the company's Worcester business, he directly supervised construction of the Antiquarian Society library. Perhaps he was working so near to home because he had been recently married; during the latter stages of work on the Antiquarian project, his wife, Gertrude, was pregnant with the girl who would prove to be their only child. The Antiquarian building was completed and occupied in mid-January 1911,[18] less than a month before Elizabeth's birth on February 8, 1911. Tragically, this would be the last building whose construction her father would see through to completion.

William Thomas, born in 1872, was the eldest of the four surviving children of John W. Bishop and his wife, the well-to-do Sarah Foster of Holden, Massachusetts. Four other siblings had died in infancy or early childhood. One of William's sisters, Marion Edith (born 1877), married Thomas Coe of Worcester and had three children. Unfortunately, she—like her brother William—died in the same year that Bishop was born. Her father's two other siblings were Florence (born 1875), who never married, and John W. Jr. (born 1880), who married but had no children. This aunt and uncle would later figure heavily—and, from Elizabeth's standpoint, not always happily—in her life.

Four days after his daughter's birth, Bishop's father wrote a genial letter addressing his Bulmer in-laws, commenting cheerfully and a little proudly that his wife "has more milk than she knows what to do with, so we shall make butter probably. We started to have twins and when we changed our minds forgot to cut off half the milk supply."[19] Much of what Bishop knew of her father came from her mother's family. As Bishop recalled, both William's own unmarried sister, Florence, and the Bulmers "were devoted to him" and found him "very quiet and gentle."[20] He preferred staying home with a good book to engaging in the social whirl, but by all accounts, his shyness—a trait his daughter would later share—relaxed when among intimate friends and family. Elizabeth prized the half dozen books from her father's extensive collection that were eventually handed down to her. These included "his very elegant edition of [Ruskin's] 'Stones of Venice,' with his bookplate, given him by two of his sisters for Christmas, 1898."[21] Any lingering vestige of the father she never knew was something she would hold on to for life.

Gertrude's background was very different from her husband's. Although both had roots in the Canadian Maritimes, hers were far deeper and more immediate. She was born in August 1879 in Great Village, Nova Scotia. As Sandra Barry has written, "Great Village in the early twentieth century remained essentially as it had been in the late nineteenth century. Horse-drawn wagons still rumbled along dirt roads, and oil lamps still lit the interiors of homes (and consequently Bishop's memories and imagination)."[22] Bishop would always vividly recall the "rich farming country" of Great Village, with its "dark red soil, blue fir trees—birches," and "a pretty river running into the bay through 'salt marshes.'"[23]

Bishop's mother Gertrude was the third of five surviving children of William and Elizabeth Bulmer. Her siblings included an elder sister, Maud (born 1874); an elder brother, Arthur (born 1877); and two younger sisters, Grace (born 1889) and the much younger Mary (born 1900). Another sister, Lizzy, died stillborn. Each of Bishop's Bulmer aunts and uncles would figure importantly in her life, and each would make significant appearances in her poems and stories. Bishop would later term herself a "country mouse," and her attachment to the beautiful yet homely rural world of Great Village lay very deep. Her conscious identification with the Bulmer line never flagged. Bishop attributed most of her personal and artistic character to the Bulmers, yet Bishop's mode of artistry found parallels on both sides of her family. Her sensitivity, wanderlust, and modesty had strong antecedents in the Bulmers, just as her reticence, her deep sense of artistic form and structure, and her acute attention to detail reveal important links to the Bishops. Her love of reading and contemplation, her devotion to art, and her wry sense of humor had precedent on both sides.

Her maternal grandfather, William Brown Bulmer[24] (born 1848), the owner of the local tannery, was a gentle, hardworking, civic-minded, and widely respected citizen. He owned a compact house in the center of the village, and like most of his neighbors, he worked a small farm. Elizabeth always insisted that William Bulmer was her "favorite grandparent. He was a darling; sweet-tempered, devout, and good with children." She also recalled that on Sundays, when he served as a deacon of the Baptist church, "he passed the collection plate [and] he would slip me one of those strong white peppermints that say (still, I think) CANADA on them."[25]

Bishop's "For Grandfather," her wry and affectionate elegy for William Bulmer, is among the finest of her many posthumously published poems. In it, she pictures her grandfather's ghostly yet tangible form in death, "stocky, broad-backed and determined / trudging on splayed snowshoes" toward the North Pole, and she imagines that "if I should overtake you, kiss your cheek, / its stubble would feel like hoar-frost / and your old-fashioned walrus mustache / be hung with icicles." The poem concludes with a cry of protest and anguish, attempting to halt his inevitable march: "Grandfather, please stop! I haven't been this cold in years."[26] Here is a powerful yearning for closeness and affection, even as reality intrudes and the object of that affection grows ever more frozen and remote.

William's wife, born Elizabeth Hutchinson in 1850, was the sister of George Hutchinson, a then-popular artist and illustrator whose work—although she "never knew him"[27]—would figure in two notable Bishop poems. Bishop remembered her maternal grandmother as a sometimes querulous woman. Her favorite saying was a half-groaned "*Nobody knows—.*" Still, as Bishop trenchantly observed in her fragmentary, posthumously published poem "The Grandmothers," "It was true. Nobody knew."[28] However, she also saw her Bulmer grandmother as an observant, hardworking woman, one who laughed and cried easily, was a skilled housekeeper, and remained deeply devoted to her husband, children, and grandchildren.

Bishop's mother worked briefly as a schoolteacher in rural Cape Breton. Then, as did her younger sister Grace, she trained as a nurse in Massachusetts General Hospital. When Gertrude met her future husband, William Bishop, in 1907, she was twenty-seven years old, seven years his junior. Even then, William's health was unsteady—a few years earlier he had given up on a business venture because of ill health—and there is reason to believe that the couple met while he was a patient in Massachusetts General.[29] Gertrude's youthful appeal is confirmed by a comment made to Bishop by her uncle Thomas Coe, who had married William's sister, Marion. Bishop's uncle Thomas told her, late in his own life, "Your mother was the most beautiful skater I ever saw—I fell in love with her, too, when I saw her skate." Bishop confessed in a letter to Anne Stevenson that, "These bits of information always surprise me very much, since I know so little."[30]

There is reason to suspect that differences in wealth and social status prompted some degree of resistance on the Bishop side to the marriage of William to Gertrude Bulmer, especially since the couple's June 22, 1908, wedding occurred not in Worcester but in Lower Manhattan's elegant, neo-Gothic Grace Church, the first major commission of noted architect James Renwick Jr. The soaring arches and lofty stained-glass windows of this Episcopal place of worship aligned, to be sure, with William's penchant for fine architecture. The choice of such a venue might also suggest a willingness on

Gertrude's part to be led away from her humble Baptist origins. Gertrude's younger sister Grace was then working as a nurse in New York. Grace may have been the only family member on either side to attend the ceremony.

The newlyweds honeymooned in Jamaica and Panama before returning to Worcester, where William resumed his duties in the family business. Any initial coolness toward the marriage on the part of William's parents appears to have been set aside upon the couple's return—though it was never completely erased. Gertrude Bulmer Bishop had risen far above her station, and her mother's anxious preoccupation with the need to dress and act the part of a patrician lady was noted repeatedly by Bishop in her extensive studies of their early years. This preoccupation with fine clothes, which appears ultimately to have crossed the line into mania, is further corroborated in surviving medical records—records whose content Bishop herself would never see. Bishop would later explain the complex balance between her two families with an allusion to her paternal grandfather's own humble origins on Prince Edward Island: "The Bishop grandparents came to visit in Canada several times, apparently—twice that I remember. Although my father had married a poor country girl the older generation were still enough alike, I think that they got along in spite of the money difference—it was the next generation [of Bishops] that made me suffer acutely."[31] Indeed, one measure of shared sensibility may be discovered in the fact that while her Bishop grandfather kept a chauffeur-driven car at a time when automobiles were still a rarity, and although he could have easily afforded a much grander home, he and his wife elected to live in what Elizabeth's cousin Kay Orr Sargent describes as "a sprawling beautiful farmhouse, at 1212 Main Street, [that] was in the country, a couple of miles from the center of Worcester." There were always farm animals about, and while an elderly farmer did the actual farmwork, "Grandpa knew what needed to be done."[32] Bishop's uncle John W. Jr., who took pride in his horses and dogs, would similarly choose to reside with his wife, Mabel, in a farmhouse located a few miles beyond the western edge of Worcester.

———

The earliest account of Bishop's life is inscribed in her parents' copy of a once-popular volume styled *The Biography of Our Baby*. The adult Elizabeth always wished to keep this volume close to her, although in later years she was no doubt amused by the post-Victorian sentimentality of its language and imagery.[33] Yet the book holds its fascination. This initial account of the life of the poet-to-be proves intriguing as much for its gaps and elisions as for its disclosures, for it tells a story that began in pride and joy, then took a sharp turn toward unanticipated tragedy, while fresh losses lurked in its shadows and empty spaces.

The details of Bishop's birth appear on the opening page of the volume, where handwriting (indicated here in italics) fills in the blanks left open between passages of the *Biography*'s quaintly grandiloquent prose.

Be It Known by these
presents
that on this the *8* day of *February*
in the year *1911*
Elizabeth Bishop
was born at *875 Main St, Worcester Mass.*
unto Mr. and Mrs. *William Thomas Bishop*
at *10:45 am* o'clock.

Just to the left of the newborn Elizabeth's name was an image of a winged and tousle-haired fairy-child, proffering a large bouquet of roses tied with a long, flowing pink ribbon. The blanks left for the mother's and father's names bear no signatures, but although the baby was born at home, the signatures of an attending physician and nurse are duly affixed.

On a following page, one encounters an idealized lithograph of a dapper young father in a summer suit and a lovely young mother in a flowered housedress sharing the delightful enterprise of weighing their baby. Under the title "Baby's Weight," Elizabeth's own weight is recorded "At Birth" as a healthy "7 lbs." By the third month that weight has advanced by regular stages to "10 lbs. 12 oz." Then, in Elizabeth's fourth month, an ominous note enters the chronicle, and fills lines left open for the five advancing months. That note reads, "Mother had to / go away with / Father & leave / Elizabeth for / three months." The timing of this departure corresponds exactly with the observation in William's obituary that "he gave up active work in the middle of June, and failed steadily from that time. The cause of his death was Bright's disease." Bright's disease (now termed glomerulonephritis) is an excruciating form of kidney failure that was then incurable and that even today remains difficult to treat, and it drove Bishop's father and mother to seek medical attention outside Worcester, leaving her in the care of her Bishop grandmother for several months. On October 13, eight months after his daughter's birth and just one month after he and his wife returned to Worcester from their fruitless journey, William died. The interrupted progress of Elizabeth's weight resumes with only one more entry, made two months after her father's death: "17 ½ pounds at 10 mos." Then the chronicle of "Baby's Weight" abruptly ceases. A new and more difficult life for Gertrude and Elizabeth Bishop was about to begin.

The obituary in the *Worcester Magazine* that recorded Bishop's father's death was pasted into her baby book, and it remained one of her few tangible records of her father. The obituary's photograph of William Thomas Bishop reveals a solidly built, broad-shouldered man in a tightly buttoned business suit. He sports a sober mustache, and as he gazes off into the middle distance, he holds his hands clasped firmly behind his back. One can imagine Bishop contemplating this seemingly confident yet sober image, endeavoring to read its secrets. The obituary begins, "The death of William T. Bishop, vice-president and manager of the Worcester business of the J. W. Bishop Company, on Oct. 13, at the early age of 39 years, 8 months and 8 days, removed one of the ablest men among the contractors and builders who have made Worcester famous in every part of the United States." His fundamental reticence is confirmed by the statement that he was a "self contained man, intensely interested in his work and the welfare of the company with which he was connected," and by the further observation that "his love of home and quiet environment kept him from becoming very well known socially." Reading these words, Bishop would feel a kinship in his reticence, as surely as she would identify with the statement that he was "a wide reader of solid literature." This was not much to go on for a child seeking to know her vanished father. Her Bishop relatives, observing their own form of reticence, later spoke of him only rarely—one of the many silences that would surround Elizabeth Bishop's life. Yet one principal difference between father and daughter lies latent in this obituary notice, for while her father displayed a deep "love of home and quiet environment," Bishop would become a famous traveler.

Yet there can be no doubt about the depth of the attachment Elizabeth's mother formed for her husband during their all-too-brief marriage. Indeed, the balance of Gertrude's life and widowhood—she would live until 1934—was centered on her grief over her lost husband.

In the years following William's death, Gertrude, along with her daughter, shuttled frequently between the environs of her late husband's family in Worcester and her own family home in Great Village. Such travel, whether by rail or via a direct ferry service between Boston and Yarmouth, Nova Scotia, was considered easy and commonplace in those days, and the Bulmers were long accustomed to journeys between Great Village and the prosperous region to the south they referred to as "the Boston States." Photographs in her baby book show the two-year-old Elizabeth in the summer of 1913 enjoying a picnic in the Great Village sunshine, surrounded by the many children of her family's friends, the Des Brisays. Photos taken in August 1915 show her playing happily in bathing costume upon the weathered Tidnish Shore in Nova Scotia, then bobbing neck-deep in the water as she looks back at the camera with a beaming smile. In a series of four photos taken in October of that year, an alert and healthy Elizabeth looks straight at the camera and reveals a series of what would prove to be characteristic moods: first playful, then acutely focused, then serious, then—as she perches alongside an extremely fluffy white cat—positively mischievous.

Bishop's earliest recorded memories of her mother are fragmentary, and nearly always seem fraught with uncertainty, tension, and pain. The most extensive of these memories was the incident on the beach following the Great Salem Fire, but another incident reappears in various forms throughout her writing, both in prose versions and in various unfinished poems. As Bishop recalled it, she and her mother were paddling in one of the famous Swan Boats at Boston's Public Garden in the summer of 1914. When her mother offered a peanut to an actual swan swimming alongside, the aggressive bird bit her mother's hand, drawing blood through her black mourning glove. The fragmentary poem "Swan-Boat Ride" conveys, in its telegraphic style, a sense of the traumatic nature of this incident for the young Elizabeth, for her mother, and also for the adult poet who would one day try to come to terms with this incident and its much more tragic aftermath. In her draft version she cries out to the "ungracious, terrifying bird!" She then acknowledges that although she and her mother remained "afloat, afloat . . . suspended," for her "the whole pond swayed"; for her mother, perhaps, the event "descended" into "madness and death." In any case, Bishop can factually report, "I saw the hole, I saw the blood."[34]

A less cataclysmic version of this scene appears in "A mother made of dress-goods," an unfinished poem opening with an image of a mother who is hard to discern or identify through the layers of widow's weeds she continually wears: "A mother is a hat / black hat with a black gauze rose / falling half open." Here her accoutrements of mourning include simply "a long black glove / that the swan bit / in the Public Gardens."[35]

Gertrude suffered her first recorded onset of mental illness in 1914 while living with Elizabeth in Massachusetts. According to her sister Grace's deposition, she "jumped out a 2nd story window." Following that incident, with grandfather Bishop covering all expenses, Gertrude "was treated in Deaconess Hospital, Brookline, then sent to Dr. Morton's private Sanatorium, Norwood, Mass." Once in the sanatorium, according to Grace, she was "not suicidal or homicidal, but morbid and depressed. Remained in the Sanatorium about three months and came out practically well."[36] It must have been following this hospitalization that Bishop faced the reprimand from her mother after the Great Salem Fire.

In 1915, Bishop and her mother relocated to the family home in Great Village, and there an event occurred that led, nearly five decades later, to one of Bishop's most masterly creations, "First Death in Nova Scotia." This poem explores a four-year-old child's contemplation of the mysteries of death. It grows out of Elizabeth's loss of her first cousin, the infant son of her mother's brother, Arthur. The poem begins, mostly in a child's language, with a portrait of the scene from the child's point of view as her mother quietly leads her into the experience of mourning. The atmosphere of the scene is deeply Canadian, with its many testimonials to Canada's emotional ties to the English monarchy. There, "in the cold, cold parlor," the white corpse of her cousin Arthur had been laid out under a series of chromographs adorning the wall: an image of Edward, while he was still prince of Wales, beside his neglected royal consort, Princess Alexandra, and the reigning royal couple, King George flanked by his queen, Mary.[37]

The prevailing atmosphere, as in "For Grandfather," is one of piercing cold. Chromographs are artificially colored images built on black-and-white photographs, and here these representations of living and departed British royalty offer not-quite-convincing simulacrums of a more majestic form of life. These would confuse a child trying to reconcile whatever boundaries might separate the living from the dead. When the child's mother leads her to confront the motionless form laid out in her cousin's coffin, her words are gentle. Yet silence surrounds the scene, and no explanations are forthcoming about the reality of death:

"Come," said my mother.
"Come and say good-bye
to your little cousin Arthur."

As Bishop presents the scene, she was "lifted up and given / one lily of the valley / to put in Arthur's hand." At that moment, her four-year-old self confronted more than a few sources of amazement, and more than a few perplexing facts that she found difficult to explain. The pallor of death on her cousin's face reminds her of "a doll / that hadn't been painted yet," but the surprising shock of red in his hair makes her think that Jack Frost had tried "a few red strokes" on her cousin's hair and then had "dropped the brush / and left him white, forever." The child keeps trying to reach for familiar corollaries, but none will quite suffice. As a last straw, the child conjures a delightful fantasy: her cousin Arthur will live on in a fairy kingdom alongside the colored shadows, "warm in red and ermine," of the regal figures who surround him in the cold, cold parlor. Yet as the poem concludes, Bishop's childhood self finds that this comforting fantasy cannot be sustained, for she asks herself how Arthur could ever get there, "clutching his tiny lily, / with his eyes shut up so tight / and the roads deep in snow?" Just as Gertrude had been forced to face the death of her husband in 1911, her child, Elizabeth, is compelled to confront the finality of the death of her young cousin, a haunting loss culminating in a poem published in *The New Yorker* forty-seven years after the event.

Bishop did indeed lose a first cousin, the son of her uncle Arthur, though his gravestone in Mahon Cemetery tells a story that differs from the poem in more than one important detail. His small, heart-shaped stone identifies the lost child not as Arthur, son of Arthur, but as "F[rank] Elwood / Son of Arthur & / Mabel Boomer / Died June 29, 1915 / Aged 2 Mos." In "First Death in Nova Scotia" Bishop intensified the identification between father and son by giving them the same name. Perhaps more significantly, she centers the imagery of the poem not in the halcyon sunshine of a Great

Village June, but in a world of frigid whiteness that emphasizes the starkness, finality, and mystery of death.

What is impossible to know for certain, from this distance, is whether Bishop misremembered the name of her infant cousin, or the season of his death, or both—or whether she deliberately altered these details to create a more effective poem. In Bishop's poetry, such changes are important because her poems contain so much fact. Either way, through a blending of fact and imagination in "First Death in Nova Scotia," Elizabeth Bishop has led us gently into her own emotional world as a four-year-old, a girl who finds herself face-to-face with the mystery of loss that the adults around her are unwilling or unable to explain.

CHAPTER TWO

THE COUNTRY MOUSE

In June 1916, when Elizabeth was five, her mother was placed in a mental institution, the Nova Scotia Hospital in Dartmouth. Bishop's mother would never emerge from this hospital alive—and Bishop would never see her again. Ten years later, Bishop's paternal uncle and legal guardian, John W. Bishop Jr., in the process of enrolling his niece at Walnut Hill School, made the following claim about Bishop's awareness of her mother's mental illness and hospitalization: "These facts are either unknown to Elizabeth or, at most, only surmised by her, since no one has ever spoken to her about her mother and she has never mentioned her." These words were recorded in notes made at a meeting between Bishop's uncle Jack and the staff at Walnut Hill in July 1926. The record continues: "Elizabeth's guardian is most anxious that no mention of these facts shall be made to Elizabeth. She has been a 'lonely little girl' and he anticipates much happiness for her at Walnut Hill."[1] Bishop's own writings throughout her long career indicate just how little her uncle Jack Bishop understood his niece and ward, and how greatly he underestimated the young Elizabeth's powers of observation and recollection. Her work in verse and prose returns again and again to the moment of her mother's climactic mental breakdown in the summer of 1916—a moment that her family surrounded in silence. Her work returns as well to the escalating series of losses and dislocations that preceded Gertrude's breakdown and to the further—and, if possible, still more painful—series of such losses that followed hard upon it. Each of these events occurred before her seventh birthday.

Bishop never attempted to construct a continuous autobiographical narrative of these life-altering events. But if her writings in prose and verse that record these early years are placed in chronological order and explored with sensitivity, a story unfolds in intricate detail, and at times almost moment by moment. Existing documents, along with recorded recollections by neighbors and relations, confirm the essentials of Bishop's narrative, as well as many of its more surprising details. Such records also reveal occasional minor inconsistencies or deviations from fact in Bishop's accounts. Significantly, while Bishop sometimes altered or suppressed an individual's true name, every figure in Bishop's writings about this early period may be traced to an actual person. She herself acknowledged that while she condensed the timing and rearranged events to better serve the narrative, her landmark autobiographical story "In the Village" was mostly factual. Bishop alerted *The New Yorker*, noted for its scrupulous fact-checking even of poems, that "In the Waiting Room," written more than four decades after the event, conflates two 1918 issues of the *National Geographic* into one.[2] Still, by writing about her past with such persuasive specificity, Bishop became, in effect, the archaeologist of her own history. At the heart of that story echoes the unforgettable sound of her mother's scream: "It was not even loud to begin with, perhaps. It just came there to live, forever—not loud, just alive forever."[3]

In the spring and summer of 1916, the five-year-old Elizabeth Bishop and her widowed and distressed mother, Gertrude, found shelter in the home of Gertrude's parents in Great Village. Gertrude, still dressed in black, remained in deep mourning for her husband who had died four years before.

Following her return to Great Village, Gertrude displayed escalating symptoms of psychological disturbance, while her daughter, Elizabeth—a self-described "little pitcher with big ears"[4]—watched and listened intently from the sidelines, striving to make sense of a world charged with enigmas. In a letter written from Great Village in 1925 to Louise Bradley, Bishop's first great epistolary friend, the fourteen-year-old Elizabeth would describe the Bulmer domicile as "a homely old white house that sticks its little snub nose directly into the middle of the village square. It is an inquisitive house."[5] But perhaps it was the young Elizabeth who was so inquisitive, as she struggled to parse the language and gestures she witnessed in that mysterious realm ruled by adults. For her, this was a realm of nervously whispered phrases and sidelong glances.

Before her culminating breakdown, Gertrude had made occasional trips away from Great Village to Boston or elsewhere, seeking distraction and emotional relief. During these excursions, Elizabeth often remained behind in Great Village in the care of her maternal grandparents, William and Elizabeth Bulmer. By the early summer of 1916, as Gertrude's psychological condition grew more dire, a family assembly had gathered to meet it. In her autobiographical story "In the Village," Bishop dramatized what she would always recall as the defining moment of that crisis. She speaks, in the opening pages of the story, from a child's point of view. "It was a hot summer afternoon. Her mother and her two sisters were there. The older sister had brought her [mother] home, from Boston, not long before, and was staying on, to help. Because in Boston she had not got any better, in months and months—or had it been a year?"[6] The child's next comment, in the story, records and carries forward the tone of desperation she must have registered in the voices of these aunts—in actual life her aunt Maud, her mother's elder sister, and the younger aunt, Grace. "In spite of the doctors, in spite of the frightening expenses, she had not got any better." The mother's confusing cycle of departures and returns is briefly summarized: "First she had come home, with her child. Then she had gone away again, alone, and left the child. Then she had come home. Then she had gone away again, with her sister; and now she was home again." The child, it would seem, is left to wonder to whom she actually belongs, and remains uneasy about her role in the present scene. "Unaccustomed to having her [mother] back, the child stands now in the doorway watching."[7] Does this child, trapped in the third person, feel so distanced from her only surviving parent—and so distanced from her own identity—that she can find no way of speaking the pronoun "I"?

The events leading up to this family's gathering over Gertrude Bulmer Bishop's emotional crisis may be understood more clearly with the benefit of a document that Bishop herself never had the opportunity to read, a "Statement" that accompanied Gertrude Bulmer Bishop's committal to the mental wards of the Nova Scotia Hospital in Dartmouth in June 1916, authored by Bishop's aunt Grace, her mother's younger sister. Bishop always referred to Grace as her favorite aunt, finding her alert, kind, levelheaded, keenly intelligent, and more openly communicative than any of her other relatives on either the Bishop or the Bulmer side. The statement delivered to the medical superintendent of the hospital offers no attempt at diagnosis, but Grace was a trained observer, and described her elder sister's behavior in response to a multipage printed questionnaire. Her handwritten answers to these questions, despite their tone of clinical objectivity, offer a moving account of the escalating sequence of events that led to Gertrude's committal, words and actions that Bishop herself must have witnessed, at least in snatches, during the first five years of her prodigiously observant lifetime.

Grace noted the breakdown by her sister in 1914, observing that Gertrude emerged on that occasion from a private sanatorium in Massachusetts "practically well." But she remained in deep mourning and—as would soon become clear—in continuing emotional distress. Grace reported Gertrude to have been "mild" and "steady" before the onset of her illness, and described her sister, in the years before her husband's death, as neither impulsive, fanatical, passionate, jealous, nor contrary—though she did add, unprompted, the words "but very headstrong."[8] Grace indicated that her sister "was not very religious when well. Went to church when she felt like it. During this last attack has been more religious."[9] Events took a turn for the worse in March 1916, when she received a business paper that upset her. Although her husband's will provided generously for Gertrude and her daughter, her responsibilities toward the estate appear to have weighed heavily upon her, and Grace linked her sister's March attack to a sharp spike in anxiety about her financial well-being and physical health, claiming that these worries left her often "very much upset" during this period. She also had heart and kidney disorders deemed to be imaginary, as well as bouts of religious mania. Grace, who was living in Boston, could report her own observations of Gertrude's various journeys to that city.

> When she travelled to Boston, imagined she saw people she knew, & that she was watched as a criminal. There at times she would be greatly excited and talk about the war, equality of labor, Catholicism, being hung, burnt as a witch, or electrocuted, etc.[10]

One of Gertrude's deepest fears regarded the potential loss of her only daughter: "Has always been afraid someone would take her child away from her." The tragic irony is that the force of this anxiety over the loss of her daughter surely contributed to the separation that both mother and daughter would endure.

Gertrude's emotional symptoms were frequently bound up with physical ones. She complained of being unable to hear and suffered from nervous chills. She had weak spells. She began to imagine that she was being hypnotized, and became suspicious that the medicines given to her contained poisons. When asked "Has the patient shown any appreciation of the changed mental condition?" Grace's answer quietly underlined the situation's pathos: "Yes at times wonders why she has to suffer so, and then again thinks she is doing it for someone else." When asked if "suicide or violence to others [has] been threatened or attempted," Grace confirmed that, unfortunately, such had been the case: "In March of this year, after receiving business letter, tried to hang herself with the sheet, and caught her mother about the throat."[11] Despite Gertrude's previously mild and steady disposition, her early life had contained at least one premonition of future breakdowns, for when she was about fifteen or sixteen years old, her father found her making for the river after becoming nervous and depressed over failing her examinations at school.

Bishop would later deny to Robert Lowell—who in 1957 was making a poem of his own, "The Scream," out of "In the Village"—that her mother had ever threatened *her*. At least Bishop didn't recall any direct threats, asserting that her mother's danger for her was only implicit in "the things I overheard the grown-ups say before and after her disappearance." She added that she didn't want the situation to appear "any worse than it was."[12] Bishop's telling word "disappearance" parallels what occurs in her story "In the Village": one day her mother was simply gone, and Bishop gradually came to understand that she might never return. Her uncle Jack Bishop's 1926 testimony to Walnut Hill authorities confirms that the circumstances of Gertrude's committal to a mental institution were never explained to Bishop as a child. Such was the fear, shame, and anxiety associated with the stigma of mental illness at that moment in history. As a child growing into adolescence, Bishop remained haunted by the apprehension that her mother's mental illness might be hereditary. Having received no explanation of what had happened, she had no opportunity to share in a grieving process with her family over their common loss. Instead, she faced a vast emptiness.

Although Gertrude's family made every effort to shield Elizabeth from her mother's most disquieting behaviors, this observant child could not help but notice many disconcerting things, one reason why she claimed that "amazement"[13] was perhaps her infancy's chief emotion. One crucial source of that amazement was the scream—or, in another version, the series of screams—that her mother uttered when she attempted to emerge from the formal garb of mourning four years after her husband's death. In the opening of Bishop's story "In the Village," the cry of anguish or surprise or fear or protest that issued from her mother is understated. Yet it is also pervasive in its lingering presence, as "a scream, the echo of a scream," that still hung, at least for her, about this little Nova Scotian village. In her ears, and perhaps those of others, the scream "hangs there forever," staining the "pure blue skies" above the church's steeple.[14] Dr. Richard Famularo has suggested that one of the characteristics of post-traumatic stress disorder is the way that "traumatic experience is followed by recurrent or intrusive recollections." These include "frightening dreams, reenactment of the trauma, and the intense reaction to symbolic reminders of the trauma."[15] Here, the scream lingers as a symbolic reminder in the speaker's memory. In fact, in Bishop's story, the scream assumes an independent life, becoming not merely a sound but a color—one that alters all it touches, for her and also those who share a memory of the event. This color is always tinged with a faint shade of blue: "the color of the cloud of bloom on the elm trees, the violet on the fields of oats." As Bishop was writing "In the Village," she was living in Brazil. She was already well versed in Freudian psychology, and she was reading through her romantic partner Lota de Macedo Soares's vast collection of psychoanalytic literature, from Freud to Melanie Klein. She had experienced, six years before, a period of probing psychoanalysis with Dr. Ruth Foster, a therapist who served as a crucial figure in her development as both a person and an artist. Thus, Bishop was well prepared to hear the echo of her mother's scream as a return of the repressed, an almost tangible manifestation of Bishop's pain over the sudden disappearance of her mother. It also functions—paradoxically—as her most potent means of keeping that memory alive.

In both her 1953 story "In the Village" and the earlier account of the scene in "Reminiscences of Great Village"—an uncompleted story draft that Bishop worked on in 1936, not long after her graduation from Vassar College—the fitting was at her mother's request. The ceremonial fitting of her mother's new purple dress—which curiously mimics the fitting of a bridal dress—took place in "the large front bedroom with sloping walls on either side" in her grandparents' home. More than a century later, the walls of that room still slope symmetrically, just as Bishop described them.

Gertrude had not had a new dress fitted since 1914, the year of her first breakdown and her committal to the Massachusetts sanatorium. In the published version of the story, Gertrude's mother-in-law sent her a bolt of elegant purple fabric—traditionally the color worn by a woman emerging from deep mourning. As events unfolded, however, it was clear that Gertrude felt deeply conflicted about leaving behind her widow's weeds. Significantly, the child of "In the Village" consistently confuses the meanings of the words "mourning," which she overhears but doesn't quite understand, and the more familiar, and more hopeful, "morning."

The sprawling 1936 draft "Reminiscences" and the finely honed and compressed 1953 "In the Village" vary sufficiently in detail to allow students of her past to compare how Bishop at different times remembered— or chose to reshape for artistic purposes—these vital moments. Bishop's mother, who was "very thin," wasn't "at all sure she was going to like the dress," and she kept asking, "Is it a good shade for me? Is it too bright?"— and then, "Should it be black? Do you think I should keep on wearing black?"[16]

Both versions of the dressmaking scene suggest that Gertrude could not cope with the emotional stress of the shift away from mourning clothes that she herself had initiated. In the 1953 published version, the mother's growing anguish and her climactic outburst are handled briefly and elliptically, in three short sentences:

The dress was all wrong. She screamed.
The child vanishes.

Not long after, the mother simply disappears, without any explanation— even as an unspoken sorrow permeates the Bulmer household. Soon the child, now referring to herself in the first person, as an "I," catches her grandmother crying into the potato mash, "which tastes wonderful but wrong. In it I think I taste my grandmother's tears; then I kiss her and taste them on her cheek." At least in Bishop's version of events, her family's tears of loss may be tasted or felt, but they must never be explicitly shared or acknowledged. Such unacknowledged tears run as a leitmotif from Bishop's earliest phase as a writer to the very end.

In Bishop's 1936 draft of "Reminiscences of Great Village," the dressmaking scene is rendered with considerably more emotional violence. The dressmaker, at the decisive moment, picks up a large pair of shears in the process of fitting the dress "& takes hold of the extra cloth." In this version the child's mother, curiously named Easter, falls to her knees and snatches the cloth away from the dressmaker.

"No, no, take the scissors away. Grace! make her stop, it will bleed. I shall bleed."

Grace's attempts at soothing words go unheeded, and soon the child's distressed mother is shouting, "You won't take my dress away. The only dress I have in the world. You want to bare me naked. It's mine, it's mine. You can't have it. You want to make me all naked." Issues of clothing and nakedness were always central to Bishop's memories of her mother. During an intensive process of psychoanalysis with Dr. Ruth Foster, when she was thirty-six years old, Bishop created for her therapist a detailed written account of her past, produced in a series of ever-more-revelatory installments. In the fourth installment of these recollections, dated February 24, 1947, Bishop reminded Foster that in a home and village with no running water, she used to watch her mother bathing. "My mother would stand by the wash stand & I remember hanging my head over the foot of the bed to watch her—and upside down too sometimes I think." Although she remembered her mother as very pretty, she also saw her as somehow threatened, noticing, as she recalled it, the vulnerability and defenselessness of "that small white body."[17] Here, as in the unfinished poem "A mother made of dress-goods," the bathing scene is located in the same front room of the Bulmer house in Great Village, with its sloping walls. In the poetic fragment, dating likely from the 1970s, Bishop sees "a naked figure standing / in a wash-basin shivering." This naked, uncomfortable figure is in a "half-crouch," like the "sloping-ceilinged bedroom."[18] This bedroom is the very chamber that would serve as the site of the traumatic dressmaking scene. In nearly every one of Bishop's recurrent visualizations of her mother, Gertrude appears either as vulnerably naked or as wrapped in and shielded by the traditional attire of mourning. Never does her mother appear at rest or wearing casual clothes.

When "In the Village" first appeared in *The New Yorker* in 1953, it was attentively read and actively discussed in Great Village. Several neighbors recollected Mate Fisher, the village smith, and his affinity for children, and for the young Elizabeth in particular. In her story, Bishop presents the blacksmith's shop as a place of magic where the horseshoes "sail through the dark like bloody little moons" and "drown in the black water, hissing, protesting." In this shadowy haven, all creatures, human and animal, appear at ease, unhurried, and—unlike her mother—comfortable in their own skins, including two men who stand watching, chewing or spitting tobacco, and the horse being shod. "Manure piles up behind him, suddenly, neatly. He, too, is very much at home. He is enormous. His rump is like a brown, glossy globe of the whole brown world. His ears are secret entrances to the underworld." The child studies this equine creature, and there is something soothing, almost heroic, about him, for he wears "medals" on his chest, and on his forehead, and "the cloud of his odor is a chariot in itself."

The male horse in the smithy has his female equivalent in Nelly, the family's Jersey cow, who on an errand the child leads, or rather follows, up a road lined with the homes of familiar neighbors, alternately friendly or persnickety, to a rented pasture some ways off. Lowell, reading the story when it first appeared in 1953, and aware of the mournful context surrounding it, observed of this endearing passage, "I could weep for the cow." As Bishop wrote to her friends Kit and Ilse Barker from Brazil shortly after the story was published, "Cal Lowell said it reminded him of a 'ruminating Dutch landscape'? and then, after that, the Dutch mistress of Brazil's best poet, (I've never met her) with the incredible name of Madame Blank, wrote me how it was so much like Holland, and sent me a large

Dutch gingerbread: I think that the idea of a cow must just remind some people of Holland, that's all." Nelly, also completely at ease with herself, makes her presence felt as a somewhat willful companion who is at the same time almost a friend. Nelly's cow-flops land with a fascinating "Smack. Smack. Smack. Smack," as the Jersey continues her stately, unperturbed procession, leaving behind her a trail of aromatic circles, "fine dark-green and lacy and watery at the edges."[19] Once Nelly reaches her pasture, the five-year-old narrator wonders whether she, too, might linger there. "For a while I entertain the idea of not going home at all, of staying safely here in the pasture all day, playing in the brook and climbing on the squishy, moss-covered hummocks in the swampy part." But such a fantasy is not to be fulfilled, for as Nelly wanders off to join a bovine friend, the child finds that "a great sibilant, glistening loneliness suddenly faces me."[20]

"In the Village" leaps over the family's decision to send her mother to a sanatorium. The fact of her mother's disappearance is presented obliquely, as a matter of inference by the child. "Now the front bedroom is empty. My older aunt has gone back to Boston and my other aunt is making plans to go there after a while, too. . . . The front room is empty. Nobody sleeps there. Clothes are hung there." It seems that no one in the family now wishes to inhabit the chamber that witnessed her mother's culminating breakdown, even though it is the finest bedroom in the house.

Bishop's mother's committal to the mental wards of the Nova Scotia Hospital was by no means without its tangible signs. Every week a package was sent off. In these packages her grandmother nestled such items as cake, fruit, preserves, and chocolates, along with the occasional handkerchief, New Testament, or "calendar, with quotations from Longfellow for every day." As Bishop watched her arrange these parcels, she noticed how her grandmother inscribed "the address of the sanitarium . . . in purple indelible pencil on smoothed out wrapping paper. It will never come off." This color, of course, is the same as her mother's purple dress. The child's job was to carry this parcel to the post office. Having picked up a sense of shame and secrecy from those around her, she did not want others to read the address on the parcel as she proceeded on her errand. In Bishop's story "In the Village," her journey takes her past the village smithy, and on this particular journey she feels compelled to hide that telltale address: "I walk far out in the road and hold the package to the side away from him." Even when Nate, the blacksmith, calls out cheerily, "Come here! I want to show you something," shame prevails and she pretends not to hear him. One of Bishop's relatives, Hazel Bowers, who later lived in Bishop's grandparents' house for many years, recalled in 1985 that when the story appeared in *The New Yorker*, Mate Fisher confirmed to her that whenever Bishop was carrying a package to the post office, "she never did stop on the way over. She always stopped on her way back." Bowers added, "The grandparents didn't want anybody to see the address where the parcel was going."[21]

Bishop would arrive at the small post office finding "no one except the postmaster, Mr. Johnson, to look at my grandmother's purple handwriting." In her account, the "very old, and nice" postmaster greets her with the words, "Well, well. Here we are again. Good day, good day." After examining the address and carefully weighing the package, he observes, "Yes. Yes. Your grandmother is very faithful."[22] Hospital records confirm that Gertrude frequently received packages from home, at least in the early years of her confinement. The postmaster's remarks make quite evident that he, and no doubt nearly everyone in Bishop's small village, knew where Bishop's mother now resided. Most, if not all, were surely saddened by this loss and sympathetic toward Gertrude's child.

Bishop evoked a scene from shortly after her mother disappeared in a poem she composed forty years later, the 1956 "Sestina." Bishop's maternal grandmother is pictured as struggling to maintain an aura of normalcy while "September rain falls on the house."[23] There, in the failing light, her grandmother shares the kitchen with her grandchild, reading jokes from the farmer's almanac and laughing and talking to hide her tears. Bishop here invents new psychological and narrative use for the sestina form, which dates back to the troubadours of Provence in the thirteenth century. In a series of six-line stanzas, six end words reappear, each time in a different order: "child," "tears," "house," "stove," "almanac," and "grand-mother." These words function, as did the scream of her "In the Village," as a Freudian return of the repressed. Bishop noted later that her grand-mother cried easily, and here the child traces the migration of her grand-mother's salty tears, as they dance like mad on the hot, black stove, lurk in her tea, and stand out like the buttons on the shirt of the man standing in front of the crayoned house she herself has drawn. Now the tears enter her imagined flower bed like curious seeds. A sestina traditionally ends with an envoy, a three-line stanza comprising all six of her end words. Here Bishop announces the source of her vocation as an artist—an artist who translates silence and loss into enigmatic, singing, and articulate words: "*Time to plant tears* says the almanac. / The grandmother sings to the mar-velous stove / and the child draws another inscrutable house."[24]

The "September rain" of Bishop's "Sestina" locates the poem's action in the fall of 1916, three months after her mother's committal to the sanatorium in Dartmouth, and at the start of Bishop's on-again, off-again career as a student of grade school and high school. For a five-year-old growing up in Canada, Bishop's first academic experience was to attend primer class (the Canadian counterpart to American kindergarten) at the nearby regional school, a short walk from the Bulmer home that took her over the cast-iron bridge, past the blacksmith shop and post office, and up a gently sloping hill, toward a tall, white, cupola-crowned building of three stories. Bishop recalled this all-too-brief educational experience in Canada in her story "Primer Class."

She begins with an evocation of what was, for her, the visceral nature of memory. "Every time I see a long column of numbers" clumsily handwrit-ten, "a strange sensation or shudder, partly aesthetic, partly painful goes through my diaphragm." The effect on her is a sharp shock, like seeing the "dorsal fin of a large fish suddenly cut through the water." Being con-fronted two decades later with similarly wobbly numerical columns in the grubby account books of Key West milkmen, lottery ticket sellers, and bar-keeps could make Bishop feel suddenly short of breath. As Bishop explained it, "The real name for this sensation is memory. It is a memory I do not even have to try to remember or reconstruct; it is always right there, clear and complete."[25] For Bishop, as her work consistently demonstrates, memory was not just visible or auditory. It was also somatic—that is, of the body. She saw memories in her mind's eye and recollected them in her ear, but she also felt these memories, through involuntary shudders in her body, particularly in the diaphragm, a fact of no little importance given her life-long susceptibility to asthma. In "Primer Class," Bishop tied this somatic effect of memory to what she called her "summer of numbers," those months when, before she entered primer class, she learned to form these mysterious numerical figures on a slate in the Bulmer kitchen under her grandmother's watchful eye. It was a difficult task for Bishop, as the numbers, like words, were felt as well as heard and seen.

While mathematics, especially in its higher forms, would always remain a challenge for Bishop, she immediately took to reading, saying of her Canadian primer, "I loved every word of it." In her Great Village school, she experienced some of her earliest encounters with the elusive playfulness of words, as when she mispronounced the name of classmate Muir MacLaughlin, as "Manure MacLaughlin."[26] Bishop's was not a one-room schoolhouse—there were several classrooms on the first two stories of this tall, wood-framed building—but Bishop's teacher, Georgie Morash, did educate a body of students from primer class through fourth grade in a single large classroom. Miss Morash, as Bishop recalled her, conducted her classes with authority, but also with kindness and respect for her students. Bishop associated primer class not only with her lifelong engagement with the mysteries of words but also with the mysteries of maps and with her lingering uncertainties about national identity. The five-year-old Elizabeth listened in on the geography lessons conducted for the higher grades, and from her seat near the rear of the classroom, she also studied the maps on the classroom's front wall, which could be pulled down like window shades. Bishop recalled, "I wanted to snap them, and pull them down again, and touch all the countries and provinces with my own hands." She was particularly taken with the map of the land in which she was now residing: "I got the general impression that Canada was the same size as the world, which somehow or other fitted into it, or the other way around, and that in the world and Canada the sun was always shining and everything was dry and glittering. At the same time, I knew perfectly well that this was not true."[27]

What Bishop recalled as "the most dramatic incident of Primer Class"[28] might appear, on the face of it, trivial. Still, this incident leads us into the heart of Bishop's mind and character. Bishop's sixteen-year-old aunt Mary was the child of her grandparents' old age and was much younger than Bishop's mother or her other aunts. Aunt Mary, too, was attending Bishop's nearby school, in a higher class on the second floor. Mary had teasingly caused the five-year-old Elizabeth to be a little late for class. When she heard the second bell, the one that "really meant it," Bishop was terrified because until then she had never actually been late. She ran as fast as she could, and could hear her aunt behind, laughing at her. Bishop rushed into her classroom and threw herself, "howling, against Miss Morash's upright form." Her teacher drew her into the cloakroom and responded kindly that "being only a few minutes late wasn't really worth tears, that everything was quite all right, and I must go into the classroom now and join in the usual morning songs."[29] Such an incident in which—to echo Bishop's poem "The Map"—the "emotion too far exceeds its cause" indicates the weight of anxiety and uncertainty under which the young Elizabeth was living following the unexplained disappearance of her mother. Earlier in the story, Bishop had stated matter-of-factly, "My father was dead and my mother was away in the sanatorium." Then she added, "Until I was teased out of it, I used to ask Grandmother, when I said goodbye, to promise me not to die before I came home."[30] In Bishop's psyche, her earliest losses were tied to an ongoing state of disquiet and to a reflexive fear of abandonment. These feelings were tied as well, or so this incident with lateness appears to suggest, to deep-seated guilt and a sense of responsibility that required her to maintain, or at least appear to maintain, a state of perfection in her life as well as in her writing.

In the winter of 1917, as she later recalled, Bishop suffered severe bronchitis. On February 14, 1917 (six days after her sixth birthday), the *Truro Daily News* noted that "Little Miss Elizabeth Bishop, who has been ill for some weeks, is rapidly convalescing."[31] This was the first of many health-related interruptions to her early schooling. Still, Bishop was able to return to primer class and complete her first year, and she recalled that she "enjoyed this first experience of formal education." In particular, she discovered the *"artistically* enjoyable" experience of playing with words. According to her own perception, "the letters had different expressions" and "the same letter had different expressions at different times."[32] Most important, as her primer class year approached its close, she felt she had "the 'First Grade' to look forward to, as well as geography, the maps, and longer and much better stories." She would remain in the same classroom, with the same understanding teacher. She could imagine herself continuing in the same school for many years, and perhaps even mastering one day "those mysterious numbers."[33]

But such was not to be. In mid-August 1917, as noted in the *Truro Daily News*, Bishop's aunt Maud; Maud's husband, George Shepherdson; and Bishop's aunt Grace arrived to "spend a few weeks with Mr. and Mrs. Boomer." Grace returned to New York by September 5. A week later, not long before she was to begin first grade with her admired Miss Georgie Morash, Bishop's wealthy paternal grandparents arrived by train and stayed at the village hotel, the Elmonte House—attempting to book a room with a bath, only to learn that such a room was not available anywhere in Great Village. This visit would turn out to be fateful for the girl the *Truro Daily News* referred to again as "Little Miss Elizabeth Bishop." According to that newspaper's notice, Bishop and her grandparents returned to Massachusetts by train as of October 11, 1917, in the company of her aunt Maud. Bishop memorialized leaving Nova Scotia in the autobiographical story

"The Country Mouse," which was completed as a polished draft in 1961 but not published until five years after her death, perhaps because she did not wish to make public her negative assessment of her Bishop family. As this memoir begins, the six-year-old Elizabeth is ensconced in a sleeper car on the old Boston & Maine railroad, heading south from Great Village to the home of her Bishop grandparents in Worcester. As Bishop recalled it resentfully many years later, "I had been brought back unconsulted and against my wishes to the house my father had been born in, to be saved from a life of poverty and provincialism, bare feet, suet puddings, unsanitary school slates, perhaps even the inverted *r*'s of my mother's family." Bishop noted that "with this surprising extra set of grandparents, until a few weeks ago no more than names, a new life was about to begin," a life that pointed toward "a strange, unpredictable future."[34]

Her "new" grandmother, Sarah Bishop, appears throughout the memoir as an emotionally distant, formidably proper matriarch who thinks nothing of disposing of her small grandchild's dolls ("I was quite fond of one or two," said Bishop) because she "found them all in no condition to go traveling in Pullmans." These are replaced by a new, more proper, and "totally uninteresting" doll that the grandmother insists on naming Drusilla ("I couldn't stand that name"). An elegy unpublished until after her death begins, "Where are the dolls who loved me so, / when I was young?" and concludes with a glance at the unflinching sunniness of their unchanging visages: "Their stoicism I never mastered / their smiling phrase for every occasion."[35]

As Bishop later remembered it, the rangy old Worcester farmhouse where her Bishop grandparents lived, which hung on the edge of a fast-growing city, seemed utterly gloomy. Its several inhabitants—including her grandparents, her aunt Florence, her uncle John W. Bishop Jr., and their various servants—seemed nervous and unsettled. Once, sent to fetch her grandfather's eyeglasses from his empty bedroom, Bishop caught a glimpse of herself in a long mirror and was shocked by what she saw: "my ugly serge dress, my too long hair, my gloomy and frightened expression."

The creature in her grandparents' house with whom she most identified was a dog, a Boston bull terrier belonging to her aunt Florence (Aunt Jenny in this story) who was "oddly named Beppo." Bishop added, "At first I was afraid of him, but he immediately adopted me, perhaps as being on the same terms in the house as himself"; neither felt that he or she quite belonged. Beppo seemed in many ways unsettled, and Bishop presents him as almost an alter ego of herself: "He had a delicate stomach, he vomited frequently. He jumped nervously at imaginary dangers, and barked another high hysterical bark. His hyperthyroid eyes glistened, and begged for sympathy and understanding."[36] When members of the family felt he was being "bad," he was exiled to a large closet for half an hour. Bishop once discovered Beppo "punishing *himself*" after creating a "smallish puddle of vomit." She observed that "no one had ever before punished him for his attacks of gastritis, naturally; it was all his own idea, his peculiar Bostonian sense of guilt." This was a sense of guilt that Bishop herself shared, intensified by her residence in the Bishop household.

One of the numerous challenges Bishop faced following her unwilling transfer to Worcester was the necessity of attending an American rather than a Canadian first grade. This meant she had to follow American patriotic rituals, rituals given more intensity by the climate of the First World War. As she recalled it, "Most of all I hated saluting the flag. I would have refused if I had dared. In my Canadian schooling the year before, we had started every day with 'God Save the King' and 'The Maple Leaf Forever.' Now I felt like a traitor. I wanted to win the War, of course, but I didn't want to be an American."[37] When she confessed these feelings at home, to her Bishop grandmother, the militantly conventional matron was horrified and forced her granddaughter to engage in a daily recitation of "The Star-Spangled Banner." Bishop recalled of "this endless poem," "Most of the words made no sense at all. '*Between his loved home and the war's desolation*' made me think of my dead father, and conjured up strange pictures in my mind."[38]

Bishop was disturbed by the atmosphere of her paternal grandparents' dinner table, so different from the Bulmer kitchen in Great Village. What troubled her most were the words and actions of her uncle Jack Bishop, who would one day become her guardian. Bishop recalled twenty years later, for her therapist Dr. Ruth Foster, that her uncle Jack would argue constantly with her Bishop grandparents and would frequently say, regarding Bishop herself, "that someone needed a spanking or a whipping." Bishop recalled, "I hardly ever spoke at the table,"[39] because she was terrified.

She further recalled to Dr. Foster, "Uncle Jack would keep going on about why didn't I laugh and play etc. what he used to be like at my age, etc. and I was so scared of him." The Great Village pleasures of Mate Fisher's blacksmith shop, her journeys to pasture with Nelly the cow, and her companionable porridge breakfasts with Grandma Bulmer now seemed far out of reach. Bishop added that "Aunt Florence also contributed her share of remarks about whippings too—they must have taken a real pleasure in talking that way."[40] Although her Bishop grandfather was apparently not unkind, he *was* emotionally reticent, and as the founder of a successful building company, he had acquired a terse habit of command. Bishop found this new grandparent "intimidating": "He was another grandfather and I already had one I loved." She began to fear this new grandfather as well, though most of the moments of family kindness that she remembered were related to John W. Bishop. One was a gift from her grandfather of two golden bantam hens and one rooster. About these creatures Bishop joyfully exclaimed, "They were reddish, speckled, with tiny doll-like red combs; The rooster had long tail feathers." Heightening the appeal of these colorful domestic fowl was the special henhouse constructed by her grandfather's handyman. A second bright moment came when her grandfather asked if a certain little girl wouldn't like to have piano lessons. Bishop eagerly assented and thus began what would turn into a long career as an amateur keyboard player. The third such moment came when her grandfather held her up to a window one night to view the light of the streetlamps glistening off the trees after an ice storm. As Bishop recalled it, she said, "'Squint your eyes up, Grandpa . . . tight!' and he did." For Bishop, "it was one of the few unselfconscious moments of that whole dismal time."[41]

When a beloved family servant, Agnes, decided to return home to Sweden to get married, Bishop considered this the last straw. "I wept and clung to her skirts and large suitcase when she kissed me good-bye. After that, things went from bad to worse. First came constipation, then eczema again, and finally asthma. I felt myself aging, even dying."[42] And Bishop was indeed becoming dangerously ill. Bereaved, uprooted, intimidated, deeply unhappy, and with her lungs weakened by that severe case of bronchitis suffered the year before, Bishop experienced a violent case of eczema and what doctors feared might prove to be a fatal case of asthma, soon followed by the symptoms of Saint Vitus's dance (now known as Sydenham's chorea), a condition defined by rapid, involuntary jerking motions that affect the face, hands, and feet.

"The Country Mouse" closes with a scene that also appears in Bishop's "In the Waiting Room." Both versions of the story present Bishop as a girl about to reach the age of seven, accompanying her aunt Florence (under the guise of a pseudonym) to a dentist's office, where Florence is scheduled to undergo an examination. In each version, Bishop seats herself in the dentist's waiting room and begins studying the February 1918 *National Geographic*; the difference between the two versions is that the prose treatment in "The Country Mouse" shows Bishop suffering from eczema and asthma. And the crisis of identity dramatized in the climax of both versions is rendered in the prose account in a way that is both darker and more explicit: "A feeling of absolute and utter desolation came over me. I felt . . . *myself.* In a few days it would be my seventh birthday." And she adds, "I was *one* of them too, inside my scabby body and wheezing lungs. 'You are in for it now,' something said. How had I got tricked into such a false position?" In her late poem, the speaker recovers from the effects of vertigo, and settles back into an everyday reality that remains familiar, even though, on a psychic plane, it may have been altered forever. But the 1961 prose version, "The

Country Mouse," closes more abruptly and far more darkly: "It was like coasting downhill, this thought, only much worse, and it quickly smashed into a tree. *Why* was I a human being?"[43]

At last it became clear that Bishop could not endure life much longer in her Bishop grandparents' home. In fact, her Bishop grandfather belatedly acknowledged that his wife had little talent for raising children, since three of their own had failed to survive childhood. In May 1918, three months after the events presented at the end of "The Country Mouse," the seven-year-old Elizabeth was delivered to the apartment of her aunt Maud Bulmer Shepherdson and her husband, George, on a working-class street in Revere, Massachusetts. Elizabeth, struggling for life and breath, was carried into the apartment by her Bishop grandfather's kindly chauffeur. "I couldn't walk," she recalled, "and Ronald carried me up the stairs—my aunt burst into tears when she saw me." Elizabeth Bishop was just seven years old, but she had been on the move for most of her early life.

Along the way, Bishop had acquired, in compensation for her losses, a sharp sense of humor, a keen ear for language, a love of natural beauty, a decided skepticism toward received opinion, an understanding of the value of freedom, and a keenly developed sense of the ridiculous. Perhaps most important of all, at least for her development as a writer, she had learned to watch, to wait, to listen, to keep her own counsel, and to miss almost nothing as she quietly studied and absorbed the encoded language and mysterious behaviors of the adults who surrounded her.

CHAPTER THREE

WERE WE ALL
TOUCHED BY MIDAS?

Elizabeth Bishop would later describe the neighborhood in Revere, Massachusetts, as "a medium-poor section of a very poor town."[1] The Shepherdsons' second-floor apartment, in a two-family dwelling at 55 Cambridge Street, was located just a half dozen miles northeast of the gilt-domed Massachusetts State House that stands on Boston's Beacon Hill, overlooking the famed Public Garden.

The street was steep and unpaved. Bishop would later recall that if her aunt and uncle's apartment had stood just a bit higher on that hilly street, she might have peered out of the front bay window and glimpsed the apex of the Boston Custom House Tower, "then a landmark in Boston."[2] Six decades later, while teaching at Harvard in her final years, Bishop would find herself living in a pleasant, book-lined, art-filled, and manuscript-crammed condominium at Lewis Wharf, where she enjoyed what Elizabeth Spires described in a 1978 interview as "a spectacular view of Boston Harbor."[3] Bishop, when she could, always lived near the water. This spacious condominium, her last home, was located on the fourth floor of a newly renovated warehouse just off Atlantic Avenue and merely a ten-minute walk north of that historic Boston Custom House.

Yet as a child in Revere, the dream of such a life seemed far away indeed. Bishop continued to suffer from the asthma and eczema that had overwhelmed her brief and unhappy stay with her paternal grandparents, and for years following, she continued to suffer so acutely from autoimmune disorders that she could attend school only sporadically. She lived through her early teens in a state of near isolation, playing with the children in her aunt and uncle's ethnically diverse, lower-middle-class neighborhood when she was well enough to venture out, but she had no purposeful activity beyond the confines of the Shepherdson apartment except reading and thinking and exercising her considerable powers of close observation. Of necessity, Bishop found ways to occupy herself indoors. "I could draw the floor plan now,"[4] she later wrote of the domicile where she always felt more like a guest than a person who fully belonged.

The Revere apartment was full of books, and piled high with back issues of the *National Geographic*. Perhaps it was while studying these that Bishop first imprinted on her memory the kind of graphic images of strange lands and unfamiliar peoples that she later found in the February and March 1918 issues of the *Geographic*, images that would make such a memorable appearance in her late landmark poem "In the Waiting Room." As she acknowledged to Anne Stevenson, "I went to school on and off but remember chiefly lying in bed wheezing and reading—and my dear aunt Maud going out to buy me more books."[5] Confined by illness to this apartment with its "tiny kitchen" and "tiny dining room"[6] for much of her early life, Bishop found in reading, imagination, and close observation of what was near at hand her primary means of exploration, refuge, and escape. Many years later, in a letter to Robert Lowell, she would explain her "passion for accuracy" by saying, "Since we do float on an unknown sea I think we should examine the other floating things that come our way very carefully; who knows what might depend on it?"[7]

When Elizabeth Bishop first arrived at 55 Cambridge Street, her childless aunt Maud, her mother Gertrude's elder sister, was forty-four years old.[8] In her unfinished but extensively detailed memoir "Mrs. Sullivan Downstairs," a crucial source of insight into her life in Revere, Bishop characterized Maud as "small, worried, nervous, shy."[9] Aunt Maud had given up her career as a nurse and was focused on her housekeeping, her marriage, and the needs of her husband, George. As Bishop later noted to her psychiatrist Ruth Foster in February 1947, "I resented Uncle George frightfully—everything was done for his comfort and enjoyment, nothing for anyone else."[10] Even so, Maud did find time for reading, painting, and sessions with her sewing machine. Aunt and niece spent a great deal of time together. Maud was a painter not without talent who "did beautiful sewing," and Bishop fondly recalled how "she'd sit down at the piano and we'd waste an afternoon singing World War I songs. She had 'a beautiful alto voice' and we sang hymns in parts sometimes, too—While I polished the endless brass pipes in the kitchen."[11] A few years later, Bishop would find herself singing hymns in a local church choir, an experience that led her to note wryly in a letter to a friend that "one always thinks the soloist looks very soulful and good from the audience. And when you sit *beside* her it gives one rather a shock to see her take a *huge* piece of gum from her mouth just before she rises to sing 'The garden of prayer.'"[12]

Although her aunt's tiny kitchen smelled of coal gas and lighting gas, "it was warm and cozy." Of this scene, Bishop concluded, "My aunt and I loved each other and told each other everything and for many years I saw nothing in her to criticize."[13] Bishop had an affinity for cast-iron stoves. The stove in her maternal grandmother's Great Village kitchen was a wood-burning Little Marvel. The stove that dominated Maud's kitchen in Revere was a blackish-green coal-and-gas-burning Magee Ideal, the name of which she "read for years and years and made a rubbing of it and its cast iron flowers once in a while when it was cold."[14] On bitter-cold New England nights Bishop frequently suffered asthma attacks, and as she gasped for breath her aunt Maud "probably never slept for nights and nights, getting me injections of adrenaline."[15] Dr. Bessel van der Kolk, the author of

The Body Keeps the Score: Brain, Mind, and Body in the Healing of Trauma, has suggested that Bishop's childhood history represents "a textbook case of the kind of traumatic childhood experience that would lead to lifelong auto-immune disorders and alcoholism." According to van der Kolk, "After such extensive traumatic experiences, the body feels that it is under attack, and that it needs to fight back."[16] This could encourage the release of excessive antibodies, which would turn the immune system against itself and produce effects such as the chronic asthma and eczema that she experienced, especially when exacerbated by weakened lungs resulting from the severe bronchitis she had experienced. Van der Kolk associates Bishop's life history and symptoms with C-PTSD, complex post-traumatic stress disorder, and suggests that the timing of Bishop's breakdown in the winter of 1917 and the lifelong nature of her autoimmune afflictions are consistent with the disorder. Psychiatrist Alice Miller makes a similar point when she asserts that even when an individual is encouraged to hide the sources of her trauma from the adults surrounding her, or from herself, "the patient never stops telling us about [her] reality in the language of [her] symptoms."[17] Yet Bishop would never allow her own symptoms to define or limit her, and Bishop's struggle to turn silence into speech would remain a central preoccupation of her life and art.

When the young Elizabeth felt well enough, her aunt Maud would sometimes treat her to an outing at a genteel amusement park known as Salem Willows, located a few railway stops to the north on a small finger of land just beyond the city of Salem. Salem Willows looks out upon the sea, toward Beverly Harbor, Salem Sound, and the Atlantic. One of the park's chief attractions was a large carousel, designed by a famous maker, boasting an array of brilliantly carved and painted animals for children of all ages to ride upon. "Salem Willows," Bishop's poem on this experience, went through thirteen surviving handwritten and typescript drafts and was moving toward completion—and still on her desk—at the moment of her sudden death in 1979. Had Bishop lived to see "Salem Willows" through the editorial mill at *The New Yorker*, it would have become her first-ever published treatment of her difficult years with her aunt Maud and uncle George.[18]

The poem begins with a flash of excitement and power: "Oh, Salem Willows, / where I rode a golden lion, / around and around and around, / king of the carrousel." Indeed, of all the carousel's enticingly carved and painted figures—camels, elephants, horses, tigers—"above all others / I preferred the lion, / and I mounted him astride." And how could she not prefer the lion: "His wooden mane was golden," and his tongue was "enameled red," while his eyes were magical, "brown glass with golden sparkles."[19] Yet this brilliant creature is capable of no real action: "His right forepaw was lifted / but the others wouldn't budge." The child speaker begins to recognize that the carousel of which she fancies herself king offers only illusions of power and forward motion, for her lion and the other brilliant figures revolve "around and around and around, / sumptuously, slowly, / to the coarse, mechanical music / of the gold calliope!"[20] All the enchanting objects in the poem prove not quite real.

The plaster musicians at its center are merely "front halves" who can't perform on their instruments. "From time to time to the music, / they'd raise a flute, but never / quite to their lips, they'd almost / beat their drums, / they'd not quite / pluck their upheld lyres." Like Tantalus of Greek myth, they can never quite touch or taste the satisfactions lying just beyond their grasp. "It was as if that music, / coarse, mechanical, loud, / discouraged them from trying." Beyond the carousel "glitters a glassy sea"—hinting at the lure of a more expansive life of travel and discovery. But for now, as the carousel slows to a stop, the child recognizes that she must return to the less-than-satisfying confines of her life in Revere, conducted there by her meek though kind aunt Maud, who throughout her niece Elizabeth's adventure quietly "sat and knitted / and knitted waiting for me."[21] The suspended animation of the carousel's wooden and plaster painted figures seems to mirror the state of suspension and incompletion defining the life of deferral she was now compelled to live.

As Bishop circled "around and around and around" on that brilliantly carved carousel, her mother, Gertrude, was enduring a far more severe state of suspension not quite four hundred nautical miles to the north and east along the Atlantic Ocean's long, sandy shelf. For in Dartmouth, Nova Scotia, just across a deep harbor from the provincial capital of Halifax, stood the tall brick confines of the Nova Scotia Hospital for the Insane. Bishop's paternal grandfather, John W. Bishop, continued to pay all of Gertrude's medical expenses while she remained in the Nova Scotia Hospital,[22] and according to Bishop, her paternal grandparents made repeated attempts to have Gertrude transferred to a private hospital in the United States, only to be defeated by US immigration laws. As she put it to Anne Stevenson in 1964, "The tragic thing is that she returned to N.S. when she did, before the final breakdown." Bishop explained, "At that time, women became US citizens when they married US citizens,—so when she became a widow she lost her citizenship. Afterwards, the US would not let her back in, sick, and that is why she had to be put into the hospital at Dartmouth."[23]

Had Gertrude Bishop been allowed to return to the United States, she might have found treatment at the renowned McLean Hospital in Belmont, Massachusetts (whose later patients included poets Robert Lowell, Sylvia Plath, and Anne Sexton), or at the progressive Worcester State Hospital. Sigmund Freud had visited the latter hospital in 1909—the year in which Freud, in the company of his colleague Carl Jung, gave his historic "Five Lectures upon Psychoanalysis" at Clark University in Worcester, just a few blocks west of grandfather Bishop's homestead. Among the dignitaries in attendance at these lectures was Dr. Ernest Jones, whose three-volume *Life and Work of Sigmund Freud*, completed in 1957, Bishop would one day devour and enthusiastically recommend to her friend Lowell.[24] Freudian psychoanalysis, which had received such a warm reception in Worcester in 1909, was by no means accepted in provincial Canada at the time of Gertrude's decisive breakdown in 1916, nor would it be acknowledged there for many years to come. There is no evidence that Gertrude Bulmer Bishop ever received either any form of psychiatric diagnosis or analysis or any form of drug therapy.[25] Today, an assessment of the symptoms carefully detailed by Grace Bulmer in her statement for the Nova Scotia Hospital, as well as those chronicled in the hospital's own clinical record, might lead to a diagnosis of severe bipolar disorder with depressive features—or, to apply somewhat earlier parlance, manic-depressive insanity. But such diagnoses were not yet widely recognized. Effective drug treatment of bipolar disorders—employing such mood stabilizers as lithium or other agents—remained decades in the future. In her 1964 letter to Stevenson, Bishop continued to reflect on her mother's might-have-beens. "One always thinks that things might be better now, she might have been cured, etc." Bishop added, "I have several friends who are, have been, will be, etc. insane." These friends, who included, among others, Robert Lowell, "discuss it all very freely and I've visited asylums many times since. But in 1916 things were different. After a couple of years, unless you cured yourself, all hope was abandoned."[26]

Bishop's aunt Grace continued to be involved in the oversight of Gertrude's care in Nova Scotia. Bishop recognized in Grace Bulmer an "active, strong, humorous woman" who lived in the present. But while she found Grace forthcoming on many subjects, Bishop had trouble extracting from her aunt specific information about her mother because, "being the kind of woman she is, her technique is to bury it, not speak of it." Still, the observant Bishop no doubt gleaned significant details about her mother's condition, for as she acknowledged to Stevenson, "children do have a way of overhearing *everything*."[27] But while Bishop almost certainly managed to make more or less accurate guesses about her mother's condition, a full understanding of her mother's fate and—perhaps more important—a shared experience of mourning over that fate with her mother's and her father's families were lost behind a veil of silence, shame, anxiety, and dread.

In later life, Bishop read extensively in the literature of psychoanalysis, but she never had the opportunity to study the clinical record of her mother's long confinement, attempting unsuccessfully to gain access to this record during a 1946 visit to Nova Scotia.[28] The first of the clinical record's observations was made on July 6, 1916, less than a month after aunt Grace

Bulmer's sworn deposition for the asylum. This first observation is largely favorable, perhaps even hopeful: "Patient has been very well behaved since coming to the hospital, acting in a very ladylike way." In the early days of her confinement, Gertrude's caretakers in the asylum observed her reading in her room or doing light sewing—although "at times she acts a little peculiarly and gives way to mild delusions." Even so, "she has parole, and so far has always behaved very well." A comment a few days later noted only "slight delusions."[29] Perhaps they were hopeful that the much-to-be-desired self-cure would actually take place.

Unfortunately, the hospital staff's next observation, dated September 18, 1916, shows Gertrude's condition taking a turn for the worse: "Patient at present on ward 2.—she was more or less destructive on ward 7." Even so, three months into her confinement, Gertrude continued to take an interest in her appearance and to write "a great number of letters to her people. . . . She still has delusions, but does not speak of them very often." But as Christmas 1916 approached and Gertrude was entering her sixth month in the hospital, she was becoming increasingly—and understandably—morose and withdrawn. A December 13 comment notes what might now be understood as a severe depressive episode in her bipolar cycle: "Patient's mental condition not so good. She sits on a bench all day long in ward 1, and does not speak to anyone. She does not care to write letters now, nor take as much interest in personal appearance as she did. She has delusions of persecution." An observation three weeks later noted ominously, "She has given up writing letters," and an observation after Christmas noted, "No improvement."

Gertrude did return to writing occasional letters home in the early spring of 1917 and, according to the hospital's account, was "fairly rational" when visited by family, although this visit did not include her only daughter. No doubt the six-year-old Elizabeth's ears were sharply attuned to what she could overhear about that visit. In July 1917, the hospital staff acknowledged that they found Gertrude "very troublesome" and that she was keeping to her room "in more or less seclusion."[30] There follows then a lapse of almost *two years* in the staff's written observations of Gertrude. Not a single comment appears for the remainder of 1917, nor is there any comment at all in 1918, when crucial decisions were being made about her daughter Elizabeth's life and future, including her removal from Nova Scotia and her delivery into the hands of her paternal grandparents.

Perhaps one cause of this lapse in the hospital's commentary was the Great Halifax Explosion, which occurred on December 6, 1917, when the French freighter *Mont-Blanc*, laden with explosives and highly flammable materials slated for delivery to the Western Front in support of the Great War in France, collided with another vessel in Halifax Harbor and caused the largest man-made explosion of the pre-nuclear age. More than two thousand residents of Halifax were killed in the blast, and hundreds of buildings in Halifax were destroyed. Across the harbor in Dartmouth, where the hospital stood and looked out over the water, there was also widespread devastation. Gertrude's response to these events went unrecorded, but Bishop herself must have surely wondered how her mother was affected by this traumatic conflagration.

In "The Country Mouse," Bishop describes herself in the winter of 1918 telling a Worcester friend and classmate in a *"sentimental* voice" that when her mother "went away and left me . . . she died too." Bishop noted that her friend was "impressed and sympathetic"—but also relates her own horror at having lied "deliberately and consciously," asserting that this untruth made her aware for the first time of "falsity and the great power of sentimentality— although I didn't know the word." Bishop added, "I didn't know then, and still don't whether it was from shame I lied, or from a hideous craving for sympathy, playing up my sad romantic plight."[31] Surely her craving for sympathy seems understandable, rather than hideous, under the circumstances.

When the Dartmouth clinical record broke its silence about Gertrude on May 6, 1919, it was to refer—tragically—to "homicidal tendencies," which led to long periods of isolation in her room. This May 1919 observation also shows that apparel remained a vexed and vexing issue for Bishop's mother. The clinical record remarked that Gertrude demanded all sorts of fancy clothes, but that "when any clothing is given to her she soon destroys it or throws it out the window." Gertrude's conflicted attitude toward clothing—which may have been driven, at least in part, by anxiety over the fact that in marrying William Bishop, she had moved decidedly upward in the social scale, and that following his death, she was left in a socially anomalous position—closely parallels Bishop's account of her mother's relationship with apparel. Although Bishop never saw her mother after the age of five, she had somehow intuitively grasped the importance of and ambivalence toward elegant clothing in her mother's psyche—an insight that is quite consistent with a series of observations in hospital records that she never had the opportunity to review. The hospital also reported troubling "auditory hallucinations."[32] Distressing as the May 1919 observation might seem, it offers the only detailed description of Gertrude's mental and emotional health to be found in the clinical record for more than a decade.

Fifteen months would pass between this May 1919 observation and the next, on August 31, 1920. This merely noted "little change since the last report," adding that Gertrude had again stopped writing letters to home. Another nineteen months would pass until the staff's next comment, which reads, in full, "No change." An observation a year later found Gertrude in a guarded room, suffering hallucinations. From then on, year after year, throughout the entire decade of the 1920s, observations of Gertrude Bishop's status read, in full, either "No change" or "No change since last report."[33] These records make it clear that the hospital's staff had given up all hope of their patient's recovery. Meanwhile, for good or ill, Bishop's Bulmer family consistently demurred from bringing Bishop into any contact with her mother.

In later years, Bishop struggled to express in verse her understanding of her mother's bleak existence in the Nova Scotia Hospital. The most compelling of these efforts is the evocative but fragmentary poem "The walls went on for years and years," alternatively titled "Asylum."[34] This uncompleted poem struggles, over the course of many drafts, to enter the perspective of her mother and express what Bishop could only guess might be her experience through all those "years and years." Still, Bishop surely deduced or overheard enough to form a mental image of her mother's decades of solitary confinement. Drafts of the poem depict Gertrude desperately studying every detail of a room in which she is isolated, as she strains to discover something—anything—that might serve as a source of interest or engagement: "The ceiling was tiresome to watch / overburdened with fixtures & burning lights / but the floorboards had a nice perspective. / They rose a little here, sagged there / but went off alas under the wall."[35] Bishop, too, knew of confinement, as, too ill to attend school for more than brief periods, she remained sequestered in that Revere apartment. It was no doubt during her time in Revere, as she studied every detail of the Magee Ideal stove and read through stacks of *National Geographic*, that Bishop formed her own determination to engage in a life of travel.

Crucial also to this determination—and decisive in her development as a poet and a person—were the long summers Bishop spent with her maternal Bulmer grandparents in Great Village. These Nova Scotian summers were part of an arrangement for her care worked out between the Bishop and Bulmer families. Bishop's health was generally better in the summer, and due to her ongoing seasonal exposure to Great Village at its verdant best, the Bulmer home and its surroundings would become the center of indelible memories. Bishop's writings from mid-adolescence until her death demonstrate over and over her attachment to the great natural beauty of her mother's native place. She would never forget its unique blend of landscape and seascape, nor the rhythms of its quietly industrious village life. Her writing would memorialize many images from the place: "the cloud of bloom on the elm trees" and "the violet on the fields of oats."[36] A nearby water meadow grazed by munching cows alongside irises "crisp and shivering" would lodge deep in her imagination—a mental image that emerged with startling force some decades later as, in "Poem," she studied a small good picture dashed off "in an hour, 'in one breath,'"[37] by her great-uncle, the artist George Hutchinson. She would remember, too, the shifting tides of the Bay of Fundy and its easternmost inlet, Cobequid Bay, whose moving waters nipped at the irregular shoreline of her village. The Bay of Fundy empties itself completely twice a day with each retreating tide, leaving behind only vast flats of "lavender rich mud / in burning rivulets." As a child, and later as a returning adult, Bishop witnessed on occasions the outward ebb and then the returning flow as the Fundy tide came roaring back and the bay in its recovered fullness became a sea "silted red," over which a red sun set.[38] For her, this quiet yet distinctive Nova Scotian community—with its broad, flowering fields, its dusty roads, its tidal rivers, salt marshes, and fens—would live in memory both as a locus of irrecoverable loss and as a realm of inexhaustible consolation.

The Bulmer home where she nestled during her seasonal returns still stands "along the dark seam" of the Great Village River, which "breathes deep with each tide."[39] The family lot is narrow as it fronts the village but boasts a considerable depth of property behind, lying close to the Great Village River and reaching back toward the salt marshes adjoining the Minas Basin. Bishop recalled, "We made yeast from the hopvine on the barn; [we] had no plumbing," and remembered how they would light the house "with oil lamps, etc."[40] Oil lamps—and cast-iron stoves—would figure prominently in Bishop's later writings, and her experience with these domestic objects would return during her early years in Brazil. Alongside her maternal grandparents' home, the elm trees "hung heavy and green," and the straw matting inside the house "smelled like the ghost of hay," while "along the matted eaves, painstakingly, sweetly, wasps go over and over a honeysuckle vine."[41] This world of interwoven sights and smells and sounds functioned very differently in her imagination from the straggling semi-urban neighborhood in Massachusetts that she shared with her aunt Maud and uncle George. But while her annual summer returns to Great Village served to keep her imagination and affections alive, her poetic roots were planted not only in Great Village but also in Revere and Worcester.

By her own testimony, Bishop struck off her first poetic spark when she was eight years old, while listening to the buzz of activity in her maternal grandmother's kitchen. Her best white shoes required cleaning for Sunday school, and Gammie Bulmer was daubing gasoline on the shoes' soiled white tops and applying Vaseline elsewhere to their patent leather. Bishop was entranced by the interplay of these sounds: "I went around all day chanting 'gasoline/Vaseline'. . . . It may not have been a poem, but it was my first rhyme."[42] Years later, Bishop would rhyme the three-syllable "suspension" with the four-syllable "comprehension."[43] She dared to end a signature poem with the tongue-twisting slant rhymes "jawful," "awful," and "cheerful."[44] She had the audacity to rhyme "extraordinary geraniums" with "assorted linoleums," and, in her "Roosters," to produce such awful but cheerful triple rhymes as "making sallies / muddy alleys / marking out maps like Rand McNally's."[45] In perhaps her most widely read poem of all, the villanelle "One Art," Bishop rhymes the recurring "master" and "disaster" with such words or phrases as "fluster," "last, or," "vaster," and finally "gesture." This precocious eight-year-old's delighted appropriation of the found rhyme "gasoline / Vaseline" was merely the first step on a lifelong journey involving verbal play, experimentation, and discovery.

In "Manners," Bishop's affectionate 1955 tribute to her maternal grandfather, William Bulmer, she builds a world out of a far simpler and more decorous sequence of rhymes. Subtitled "For a Child of 1918," "Manners" opens with a series of perfect, monosyllabic rhymes. As they sit together on the "wagon seat," her grandfather advises her to "Be sure to remember always / speak to everyone you meet." Her elder's gentle directives espouse communal sharing and mutual responsibility—and soon their horse-drawn wagon starts to accumulate additional wayfarers, since, as her grandfather advises, one must always offer a ride to anyone one meets. These include "a boy we knew" and the boy's big pet crow, who alights from her friend Willy's shoulder and hops from fence post to fence post just beyond the advancing wagon, but not beyond his master's call. Bishop admits, "I was worried. / How would he know where to go?" But crow and boy remain in easy accord, for whenever "Willy whistled he answered." Grandfather Bulmer praises this "well brought up bird" who answers when spoken to.

But times are changing, and her grandfather's generous counsel confronts a challenge when automobiles speed by, for then "the dust hid the people's faces" and loud shouts of "Good day!" go unheard. Yet her grandfather Bulmer's world soon returns to its familiar pattern where good manners between man and beast still prevail, after they arrive at the steep Hustler Hill: he said "that the mare was tired, / so we all got out and walked, / as our good manners required." Bishop's poem serves not only as an affectionate tribute to her grandpa Bulmer, but also as an elegiac farewell to the social code he had grown up with and continued to espouse, a code already under duress in 1918 as the car began to displace the horse-drawn wagon. Future generations of parents and grandparents would *not* be advising their offspring to speak—let alone offer rides—to every stranger they observed along the roadside.

In her series of 1947 letters to her psychiatrist, Bishop drew a sharp contrast between her beloved Bulmer grandfather and her uncle George Shepherdson, the primary male presence in her aunt Maud's home in Revere, and a figure who ruled the roost in Revere most decidedly. Her uncle had met her aunt Maud in Great Village, and later they had moved to Massachusetts, where George became a bookkeeper, at a modest salary, for General Electric. Bishop's exploration of her painful relationship with her uncle forms the concluding segment of her last letter to Dr. Foster, dated February 24, 1947. This segment runs three closely typed, single-spaced pages under the heading *"Uncle George."* Bishop's entire multipage self-exploration with Ruth Foster appears to have been working up to these final disclosures regarding her uncle's abusive treatment of her aunt Maud and herself. When Bishop wrote to Dr. Foster, Maud had already died, but her uncle was still living.

She describes George Shepherdson as a tall and very powerful man, and she observed that on two or three occasions he had broken her aunt Maud's ribs. "I saw it happen once—he was just lifting her off a table or something and she said Oh my ribs and fainted." Bishop recalled another occasion where her uncle "lowered me by my hair over the second story verandah railing—all in the spirit of good clean fun." She also recalled a prolonged period when he talked about beating her almost every evening, it seemed. Bishop tried to ignore these discomfiting monologues, but they ended only after she threatened to tell her Bishop grandfather about it—which had its effect, since John W. Bishop was paying his granddaughter's expenses in Revere. These remunerations likely had formed a significant slice of the Shepherdson family income. Uncle George's aggressiveness was not limited to members of his own family. Bishop recounted to Dr. Foster, "He was a real sadist you know—gloats over violence, despises any other race but his own, hates colored people, etc., believed in the Ku Klux Klan and the protocols of Zion, etc." Yet Bishop concluded, characteristically, "What I dislike more than the streak of cruelty is his dreadful sentimentality—I guess they often go together. His eyes are always filling with tears, etc."[46]

Bishop also recalled incidents of inappropriate fondling when Uncle George was giving her a bath, shortly after her arrival in the apartment at the age of seven. "In my innocence I guess I just thought it was an unusually thorough washing but then I remember feeling suddenly very uncomfortable and trying to pull away from him. This may have happened more than once." She also recalled other episodes that were "certainly sexual—just his way of holding me, etc"—incidents that escalated as she passed through puberty and reached the age of fourteen or fifteen. Characteristically, Bishop asserted that she did not see Uncle George as entirely at fault for his behavior, which she tied to the brutal conditioning her uncle had received from his own parents. "The father was apparently an old devil. He would never let [his children] say a word or ask questions and he used to horsewhip them brutally. Aunt Maude told me this once as a reason for why he behaves the way he did with me. The mother *is* an old devil. . . . She is 92 now, and just as wicked as wicked can be."[47]

Bishop, attempting perhaps to exculpate the caregiver, insisted to Dr. Foster, "I shouldn't make out that life with Uncle George was unmitigated hell, because it wasn't and a lot of the time I felt fond of him—there were just some stretches that were worse than others." But she did recall one particularly haunting occasion: "I woke up and found my aunt Maude on her knees beside my bed. I think she may have been praying. Anyway I pretended to be asleep. . . . She may possibly have gotten in with me I don't know." She added, "It made a deep impression on me and although I was quite ignorant of matters of sex I somehow immediately felt that that brute of a man had been mean to her in some way." Perhaps Aunt Maud was praying both for herself and for her niece, but as Bishop noted, "My aunt 'put up with him' as they say," and Maud's tone about her husband "was always 'Oh you know how men are.'" Bishop noted in "Mrs. Sullivan Downstairs" that she and her aunt "told each other everything"—but her letter to Dr. Foster suggests that she *didn't* tell Maud quite everything. The Foster letters also imply that one feature Bishop ultimately did see to criticize in her shy and worried aunt was her meekness toward her husband. This, while understandable given the physical power and threat that he represented, left Maud in no position to defend either herself or her niece.

Bishop's only direct communication with her family about Uncle George's behavior came in the form of hints she later dropped to her aunt Grace. Maud died in 1940 while staying in Grace's Nova Scotian home. Grace became so disturbed by George's hectoring behavior toward his dying spouse that she sent him away a few days before Maud's passing, so that George was not present when his wife died. Grace told her niece, "You know I've never felt the same about George since Maude died." According to Bishop, Grace added "that she had sometimes wondered if it weren't partly [George's] fault that I hadn't married—though I'm not sure how she meant it. She's a smart woman."[48] In this final letter to Dr. Foster, Bishop explicitly attributed her long-standing distrust of men—excluding only her maternal grandfather and her exceptionally gentle Key West neighbor, the philosopher John Dewey—to her uncle George Shepherdson. Although her uncle was not a blood relative, his inappropriate touching must certainly be regarded as incestuous.

In a consideration of post-traumatic stress disorder, Dr. Richard Famularo argues, "The traumatic experiences of childhood often involve maltreatment by parents or other caregivers. The resulting loss of protection, sense of betrayal, daily fear, and overwhelming sense of helplessness may color all of the child's later personal relations."[49] According to Dr. van der Kolk, clinical tests have demonstrated that "the bodies of incest victims have trouble distinguishing between danger and safety." This is likely to provoke severe autoimmune disorders, since the immune system is rendered "oversensitive to threat, so that it is prone to mount a defense where none is needed, even when this means attacking the body's own cells."[50] Bishop was *already* suffering severely from asthma, eczema, and Saint Vitus's dance as a result of traumatic losses before she entered the home of her uncle George Shepherdson. Now was added the lasting burden of incestuous emotional and sexual abuse visited upon her by her uncle.

Bishop's earlier sequence of losses has been documented beyond question. Among the many factors that make Bishop's disclosure of her uncle George's behavior seem credible are the very detailed and specific nature of her allegations, the reported corroboration of her aunt Grace, and her efforts to extenuate her uncle's actions by seeing them as the product of his own traumatic past. We also find corroboration in the language of symptoms: the fact that even into her mid-thirties Bishop displayed a visceral wariness toward men. Her relatively few male friends were chiefly the husbands or partners of close female friends, with these female friends serving as a buffer. One example would be the married couple Lloyd Frankenberg and Loren MacIver. Perhaps the cathartic effect of Bishop's disclosures to Ruth Foster about Uncle George may have wrought a significant change in this condition. Although her anxious stance toward a perilous world did not undergo a magical transformation, three months after offering her series of painful disclosures to Ruth Foster about her traumatic relationship with George, Bishop formed a deep and lasting friendship with Robert Lowell. She would later find close and trusted male friends in James Merrill, Ashley Brown, Wesley Wehr, David Kalstone, Lloyd Schwartz, Frank Bidart, and many others. Such a change can be confirmed very simply by a scan of Bishop's selected correspondence, the 1994 *One Art: Letters*. This volume features very few letters addressed solely to male friends before her February 1947 analysis by Dr. Foster—but many, many letters to male friends written after that date.

Bishop was an avid reader from an early age. She worked diligently on her own at the art of poetry, beginning with those first experiments at the age of eight. Her earliest poems that can be dated with certainty, published at the age of fourteen, already reveal a musical ear, an eye for distinctive detail, a grip on traditional rhyming patterns, a notable command of rhythm and meter, a clever deployment of wit and allusion, and a deft handling of figurative language. One crucial example of this early poetry is an undated and untitled ballad beginning with the line "Once on a hill I met a man. . . ." This crucial but neglected poem was first published many decades after its composition in *Edgar Allan Poe & the Juke-Box*, and now almost demands to be read as an allegory of Bishop's own situation of confinement in a narrow world—the world to which she was exiled by her Bishop grandfather, to be ruled by her abusive uncle, and to which she was further confined by the chronic illnesses brought on by earlier and still ongoing traumatic stress. While the emotions in the poem are very real, its details are translated into the realm of magic. Like many voracious young readers, Bishop was drawn to fairy tales, perhaps because—as her friend Randall Jarrell would later observe—"the ogre of the stories is so huge, so powerful, and so stupid because that is the way a grownup looks to a child."[51] The dominating male figure in *this* poem is not an ogre but a malevolent sorcerer who is powerful, devious, and utterly pitiless.

The poem, which exists in a single handwritten copy in the Vassar archive, begins with a description of a powerful male wizard—"With silver beard and starry cloak / And pointed shoes"—who promises to show her a wonderful, faraway fairy-tale kingdom. Editor Alice Quinn finds this sorcerer reminiscent of grandfather Bishop, but his outright cruelty would seem to align more strongly with her uncle George; for despite the wizard's promise to show her the magical "Babylon or Shadow-land," he locks her in a tight enclosure, "a tiny house" amounting to just "four walls, a little door, a roof." Having secured his victim, and cackling with glee, this evil figure recites the Lord's Prayer "wrong way round!"—an ancient curse long associated with satanic rituals. Then, without a further word, "the lock clicked twice; a little wind / Sobbed once, and he was gone like mist."[52]

The imprisoned child tries to peer outward through a window, but in a manner reminiscent of Tennyson's "Lady of Shalott"—a poem the young Elizabeth surely knew—she cannot view nature directly. She can see only a projected image on an interior wall—"Of shadow people, shadow beasts"—and trace pale faces on the walls; despite these glimmers of humanity, the imprisoned child cannot make contact with any real human counterparts. She seems trapped in a perpetual loop of isolation, with the "small, sobbing wind" as her only companion. Still, perhaps she *does* hear a human voice outside the walls, for soon the child asks uncertainly, "Who are you out there with the wind?" Could the flickering image of a face "that palely gleams / Among the throngs upon my walls" be a real person and perhaps even a potential friend? Yet this yearned-for voice outside the door—or is it just the sobbing wind?—entails some danger. At last, the imprisoned speaker concludes despairingly that the shadowy friend who lurks in the periphery outside her prison had "better go away," as she fears the reprisals that might be visited upon her if her powerful captor came and found that she had temporarily escaped his thrall.[53] A decade later, in the mid-1930s, Bishop would compose an extensive series of fables of enclosure that revealed her ongoing struggle with a sense of imprisonment, and an experience of being silenced, that had dominated her youth and adolescence. These fables include another riff on Tennyson, the witty "Gentleman of Shalott," a poem that deftly and assuredly balances comic and tragic viewpoints of its narcissistic gentleman. None of the fables of enclosure she composed just after college is nearly so dark, or so nearly despairing, as this heartbreaking early ballad.

This ballad articulates not only Bishop's desperate need for sympathetic friends but also her yearning for travel. As she would one day prove, when she did find sympathetic friends, she held on to them—often for decades and frequently for life. Bishop would maintain these friendships in part through the alluring power of the written word. She would come to define herself as one of the most enthralling letter writers of her age. And if Bishop's career as a poet started early, so did her career as a correspondent, her epistolary career beginning with a series of revealing and often even enchanting letters that she wrote to an aspiring female poet nearly her own age, a talented and empathetic young woman named Louise Bradley.

CHAPTER FOUR

WADING IN THE MUD OF THE CELESTIAL GARDENS

We live but once *and I'm going to live*!
BISHOP TO LOUISE BRADLEY,
OCTOBER 16, 1926

One afternoon in July 1924, the thirteen-year-old Elizabeth Bishop found herself seated in a railway car on a branch line of the New York, New Haven and Hartford Railroad, traveling south from Revere toward the eastern shore of Cape Cod. She was on her way to begin the first of many summers at Camp Chequesset, a private sailing camp for girls. When her train pulled into the Wellfleet station and she stepped onto the platform, she noticed many longtime campers eagerly greeting one another. For a moment she felt out of place. Then something surprising occurred that took her breath away. As she wrote two years later to Louise Bradley, her first great epistolary friend, "I remember the first time I saw you—in the dirty station. You were very excited over seeing all the campers again—and when you came to me you said, 'I don't know *you*, but I'll kiss you, too.'"[1]

Bishop had lived a life of extreme isolation, scarcely able to find any friend her own age with whom she might share her numerous interests and passions. All that was about to change, at least for a few golden weeks each summer. As Bishop summed it up in the chronology she constructed for her psychiatrist Ruth Foster, "I went to summer camp on Cape Cod and made my first real friends."[2] Some years later she recalled to Anne Stevenson, "When I was 13 I was well enough, summers, to go to camp, and it wasn't until then, briefly, and then at Walnut Hill, that I met girls who were as clever or cleverer than I was, and made friends, and began to cheer up a bit."[3]

Bishop was surprised to discover that she was suddenly popular. She further noted the presence of "several slightly emotional friendships" among the female campers. Indeed, she told Foster that a few years following her own camp experience, a crisis arose when it turned out that "all the little girls were falling in love with each other right and left," causing the staff, on the advice of a psychoanalyst, to close the camp for that summer and start over the following year.[4] The young Elizabeth, known there as "Bishie," would continue to attend Camp Chequesset over the course of six summers, typically spending July as a camper and August with her Bulmer grandparents in Nova Scotia. One emotional friendship that the thirteen-year-old Bishop herself formed during her first year at summer camp was with the girl who had bestowed that unexpected kiss of greeting on her. Louise Bradley was a somewhat older girl, a rising high school junior who was then in her final year at Camp Chequesset. After that first summer together, their friendship would be maintained for more than a decade in the form of frequent letters and much less frequent meetings, a pattern that reappears in many of the numerous epistolary friendships that Bishop would maintain in later life.

Camp Chequesset had been selected for her by her uncle Jack Bishop. Elizabeth's grandmother Sarah and her grandfather John W. Bishop died within a few days of each other in 1923. John Bishop left Elizabeth ten thousand dollars in his will. This bequest, combined with the more substantial sum she had inherited from her father, made her an heiress on a minor scale. Her uncle John W. Bishop Jr., her late father's younger brother, now became her legal guardian, as well as manager of her finances until she came of age. Although Bishop resented her uncle Jack for the bullying language she had absorbed from him in her grandparents' home as well as for the emotional distance he displayed toward her in later life, Jack did take his duties as her guardian seriously. And he showed some adroitness at finding supportive placements for his ward, first at summer camp, and later at boarding school. These experiences were funded by income from the trusts it was Bishop's good fortune to inherit. And the first fruit of that inheritance was this initial summer at Camp Chequesset.

In his detailed exploration "Elizabeth Bishop at Summer Camp," William Logan describes Camp Chequesset as overlooking "the shellfishing fleet in Wellfleet Harbor. . . . The camp stood across the bay from the town pier, on some forty acres of ground once inhabited by Chequesset Indians, whose shell heaps could still be found along the beach." Logan notes that "girls at this saltwater camp were expected to excel in swimming and sailing—the counselors kept detailed records of their progress." Campers also learned to chronicle their encounters with nature in lined notebooks— the beginning of Bishop's lifelong habit of writing down her observations and sketching her literary projects in notebook form. Bishop came to be regarded as a strong swimmer and a particularly skilled sailor. Describing the camp's open-ended daily routine, Logan observes, "The girls might sail to Billingsgate Island to dig clams, or take a day trip on the Mouette to Plymouth or Provincetown (where at fourteen Bishop discovered a book of George Herbert's poems), or a three-day cruise through the Cape Cod Canal to Buzzards' Bay and Nantucket."[5]

Bishop formed a close friendship with Louise Bradley during her first year as a camper. They shared not only an enjoyment of camp life but a passion for sailing. They also shared a strong interest in poetry and a desire to achieve a career as a poet. Since Bishop's first year at camp was also Bradley's last, Bishop strove to keep the relationship alive by writing letters. Bradley's letters in response to Bishop's do not survive, but Bradley carefully preserved her letters from Bishop, and they now reside in the archives of Wylie House at the University of Indiana. Bishop's first letter to Bradley was written from Great Village in early August 1925. Bishop had completed her second year at camp and was visiting her Bulmer grandparents. Her first letter to Bradley opens with the announcement that "I have never been homesick but just at present I feel awfly campsick and as I know you will understand my feelings I am going to write to you." She wrote of the "inquisitive house" in which she was now residing and added, "I have been swimming several times in the lovely red sandstone rockhole. It is so pretty[,] for little yellow leaves float all over the top and make little brown and gold shadows on the bottom. I wish I was a fish, sometimes, so I could stay under longer and watch them." In this, her first surviving letter to any recipient, Bishop also announces one motivation that would carry her through a long and prolific career as a writer of letters: "I feel immensely better already[,] for writing does make one feel better. . . . You know what a relief writing is when one is gloomy." This letter extolling the emotional safety valve of correspondence is signed "With ever so much love / Bishie Bishop."[6]

Bishop's earliest published poem appeared in the fall of 1925 in volume 18 of the *Camp Chequesset Log*, which Logan aptly characterizes as a "fairly transparent sales organ." Bishop's "The Call" fit right in with the *Log*'s agenda while also demonstrating that she had picked up some of the salt-air savor and rhythmic swing of her New England predecessor Henry Wadsworth Longfellow. "The Call" proclaims that even in Revere, "the wind, as it blows through the foggy streets, / Has a taint of the tangy spray," and that despite her distance from camp, "the odor, though faint, seems to my heart / To come straight from Wellfleet Bay."[7] The nostalgia-laden effort of this fourteen-year-old literary aspirant might smell distinctly like camp spirit, but it also shows Bishop's youthful command of traditional poetic language, and her capacity to get tactile experience into her work as she evokes "the tang of the sea."

Following her second summer at the camp she referred to in the final line of "The Call" as "old C. C.," Bishop was at last judged well enough to attempt to complete her first full academic year since primer class in Canada eight years before. At first, she found the transition into this new environment quite difficult. In response, she began writing to Bradley with some regularity, starting in a September 17, 1925, letter lamenting that "School has commenced and is just terrible! I do hate it so. The teacher raves at me and says I don't pay attention. Probably I don't but I don't like to be told so." She had begun to keep secrets from her aunt Maud, and she would put these thoughts and ideas down in a notebook—a habit she had begun at summer camp and would maintain throughout her life. She told Bradley, "Auntie found my little black notebook hidden under a chair seat. I think she wanted me to show it to her but I wouldn't. I won't be laughed at. *You* know. It is hidden behind the fairy tales in the bookcase now." She also lamented, "Louise, my hair is turning curly all over!! Won't it be awful. Why did God give *me* such hair and *you* such a perfectly wonderful wig."[8] This lament was accompanied by a comic line drawing of her own curly locks.

In Bishop's later years as a letter writer, she discovered a tone blending intimacy and directness with more than a little dry humor and self-irony and an aura of modulated emotional control. But these early letters to Bradley, while always observant and frequently funny, display what can only be described as adolescent mood swings, as they frequently gyrate from one intensely expressed attitude to its opposite, sometimes in the span of just two or three sentences. Thus, in a January 5, 1926, letter to Bradley, after commencing with the complaint "I really intended not to write for ever so long, to pay you back" (for not replying more promptly to an earlier letter), she immediately continues, "But I feel as you used to say 'terribly confiding,' so I will be real forgiving and answer your letter now." She observes of Bradley, "You must be an awfully noted personage at your school—senior, editor of the Poetry department and all that." Then she laments, "Here I am, just a poor freshman and famous for nothing but a terrible dumbness in Algebra. Louise, I got C in deportment, for 'inattention'!" Then, her spirits shoot skyward: "I have just made a wonderful discovery! Walt Whitman!" She concludes, based on a huge volume of Whitman she had brought home from the local library, that "his poems make one feel like singing and shouting." Bishop's aunt Maud and uncle George had recently moved a few miles to the north from their apartment in Revere, to a small house in Cliftondale, a section of Saugus. This new domicile at 20 Sunny-side Avenue stood behind a ridgeline not far from the sea. Bishop exclaimed, still in high spirits, "Isn't it a beautiful world, Louise? I have just found it out and in spite of the numerous mud puddles and D's in Algebra, I have been fairly walking on tiptoe." She added, "I have made some lovely friends in my new home, a little mussy old library, a dear little brook almost beside my house, a delightful family of eight pine trees and best of all, the cliff." Of course, none of these new "friends" is an actual person. Bishop added, of the local geography, "The Cliff is a real one, very high, and just a little beyond the brook." If one climbed to the peak of the ridge above the house in Cliftondale, one could look out over the cliff and toward Broad Sound, Nahant Island, and Massachusetts Bay, whose waters stretched in a widening vista eastward toward the Atlantic. Bishop told Bradley, "It gives one an awfully farseeing feeling to stand there and look way off at the islands and lighthouses and little ships." Then, her spirits come crashing downward and she closes the body of her letter with the words "Please write to me though as I am so awfully lonely."[9]

Bishop added a postscript apologizing for the "nightmares of poems" she had sent to Louise, and asked eagerly of a promised poem by Bradley: "What was *yours* about? I would like to see it." Research by Michael Hood into Bishop's school records confirms that she did earn a C in deportment during her first marking period at school in Saugus. However, she earned A's in the subject later in the year, suggesting that she had begun to achieve a more comfortable accommodation with her new experience of formal schooling.[10]

With the approach of spring in the month following her fifteenth birthday, Bishop penned an upbeat letter to Bradley suggesting what appears to be a desire for further intimacy with her slightly older friend. This March 30, 1926, letter begins with the salutation "Dearest of all dear Kindred Spirits," after which Bishop announces with elfin good cheer, "Flowers have such delightful names I think. Delphinium like your eyes, daffodils like a laugh and petunias like fairys petticoats hung up to dry." Then she adds, "I love to get out and dig in 'the good brown earth,' and also I like to go in my bare feet! It feels so nice but I guess it is impossible until I get to heaven." Then she offers an extraordinary invitation to her friend and confidant: "Will you join me in wading in the mud of the celestial gardens?"[11] Marianne Moore, who would one day become Bishop's mentor, had suggested just a few years before, in "Poetry," one of her most widely quoted works, that good poems should be "like imaginary gardens with real toads in them." Bishop did not discover Moore's work until her final year at Vassar College, but Bishop's proposal to go "wading in the mud of the celestial gardens" uncannily prefigures both the similarities and the differences of Bishop and Moore as poets. Moore would prove a masterful handler of the interplay of diverse poetic figures, including toads, frigate pelicans, pangolins, and the jerboa, but she tended to avoid the messy actuality of mud. On the other hand, Bishop felt a strong impetus toward the literary exploration of the tattered, the battered, the neglected, and the soiled—elements that she characteristically handled with delicacy.

Bishop continued to worry about what seemed to be turning into chronic bad hair days, complaining that her looks hadn't improved and that her increasingly curly hair had grown much worse—to the point where she was contemplating shaving her head. She now combed her hair straight back and looked "something like a lady Paderewski in a very bad temper." She enclosed a romantic poetic nocturne in which "the cold moon has turned to my mother," along with a mock-heroic ode, "To Algebra," which begins with a denunciation of that subject's resistance to ambiguity. "You," it declaims, "are the workings of a fixed rule." She acknowledged in a postscript to Bradley that this poem had forced itself upon her after she earned what she termed the "remarkable" grade of 37 on an algebra test.

In many ways, Bishop's first year of full-time schooling since her Great Village primer class remained a struggle. Nine days after her remarkable algebra grade, Bishop wrote to Bradley of a scolding she had received at the principal's office: "I have a good mind but I will not use it—I am lazy and indifferent—I look out the window and dream—etc. It would be lovely if they were wrong so that I could feel martyred but alas! It's the truth." She claimed, perhaps with some exaggeration, that she had only avoided being expelled because she lied so convincingly to the principal. She was also suffering that night from "a *little* asthma." She then asked her friend Louise, "Did you ever feel like a cat? I do tonight. Like a battered old alley-cat with chewed ears wandering around in the dark. It's a very strange feeling—so *alone*. Did you ever think—no matter how many friends you have—no one can really reach *you*? I feel sometimes like a person on another planet—watching someone on this world. Good-night!" Then, upon reflection, she added, "Isn't that an awful paragraph! You better not take it seriously."[12]

But if her reality was often troubling, there was always the realm of dreams, and there, her friend Louise was often the central figure: "I had a lovely dream the night before last. I dreamed that you and I were walking in a most beautiful green field. Suddenly, hundreds of little birds flew down and lighted on my head and arms and fluttered all round. It was so real—more real than getting up at half-past six and dressing in the dark." Bishop added, "It is awfully weird so early in the morning—but I see the sun rise—behind pine trees."[13] Despite her struggles with mathematics, the fifteen-year-old Elizabeth Bishop closed this first full year of formal schooling on a more than respectable note. She had earned no less than an A in deportment and a final grade of 82 out of 100 in algebra.

In July 1926 Bishop began her third year at Camp Chequesset, and she wrote to Bradley right away about an early challenge to her artistic vocation that she faced even in this camp's supportive environment: "Night before last there was the most beautiful mist. It came in in long trailing banners like ghosts. I wrote a poem about it. I rather wish I hadn't because I forgot & left my notebook out." While her aunt Maud might have sought permission to read Bishop's notebooks, in this case a fellow camper nicknamed Brownie seized on the assemblage of poetic drafts while Bishop was outside the cabin. "When I came in she told me I was crazy—'No rhyme—Bishie what do you write such stuff for?'" Bishop added, "I do not care what *she* thinks, but all the same—And others might think so too." The admonished Bishie concluded, "I fear I am crazy to even think of being a poet."[14] Toward the end of her life, Bishop would insist that becoming a poet had occurred more or less by accident, but her letters to Bradley make clear that by the age of fifteen she already yearned passionately for a poetic career. These letters, along with other corroborating evidence, allow us to trace the ongoing efforts, challenges, and doubts she had to overcome in the process of learning her craft. And they also suggest the reasons she might have had to dissemble about the depth and early origins of her poetic vocation. Thirty years later, assessing Bishop as a mature poet, Robert Lowell would affirm that "in all matters of form: meter, rhythm, diction, timing, shaping, etc., she is a master." Bishop had conquered these elements of form in part because she had started so early at public school in Saugus. Into this letter from camp Bishop tucked the free-verse "Mist Song," inspired by her recent nocturnal observations. This early poem picked up and developed phrasing from her letter, as she sees clouds of mist moving over the "austere flats" that hug the shoreline of the camp; as, like "a troop of silver ghosts," they trail "fragile grey garments"; as they "tread slowly, proudly, shoreward."[15]

But while her poetic vocation might have faced occasional challenges at Chequesset, when she returned to Cliftondale each fall, Bishop felt even more like a fish out of water. In a letter from August 1926 she lamented, "Oh, why aren't you here to talk with me! I am eaten up with dust and dullness—and Auntie says 'Elizabeth—if you don't take that bored superior look from your face no one will like you.' What do I care—I only want certain people to like me anyway." Then she asked a question that stood, more or less, at the core of her future life. "Louise—is it right for a *young woman* to trail off to the ends of the earth—Norway—India—alone? And live in strange places and do strange things—or two young women." She added, "Men can do it, but is it OK for women? Perhaps it would be better if there were two." Then, in one of the many invitations Bishop would extend to Louise to share with her a romantic life in an exotic land, she added, "*You* come with me."[16] One persistent fantasy, returned to in many letters, was that she and Bradley might "live on a South Sea island" like Robert Louis Stevenson. "One can live entirely on cocoanuts . . . and think what a savings that would be. We could spend all our money on books."[17] Bishop's letters to Bradley show that by the age of fifteen, if not before, she felt a passionate and unapologetic attraction to other women. She was ready to express this attraction to Bradley in words that could scarcely be regarded as ambiguous.

Bishop's uncle Jack had arranged for Bishop's attendance at Walnut Hill School, a private boarding school in Natick, Massachusetts, for the fall of 1926, but Walnut Hill required that all students receive vaccinations and her doctors had determined that Bishop was not well enough to be vaccinated on account of her asthma, eczema, and general physical condition. So her matriculation at Walnut Hill was deferred for a year. In the interim, Bishop attended the private North Shore Country Day School, which she described to her friend Louise as "a perfect *Hades*—*with* modern improvements." Both school life and home life, Bishop admitted, were challenging for her: "I haven't any family whatever—excepting a few aunts and uncles who are all trying to bring me up a different way." She would sometimes claim the advantages of not having affectionate but demanding parents, but surely she was protesting too much when she declared, "It's glorious not to feel you'll have to turn out well or you'll break someone's heart." It is notable that Bishop was never formally adopted by any of the relatives who, by turns, oversaw her care. In her own view, as she told Bradley, "they'd peacefully let me slide to my doom." In the face of this, Bishop might seem justified in exclaiming, "I would give everything I own for one hour of complete—*understanding*."[18]

Meanwhile, she repeated her invitations to run off with Bradley to a remote setting—perhaps India, perhaps Ireland, perhaps even the shoreline of Nova Scotia—where they might share a cottage and a sailboat and "do all sorts of crazy—delightful—things." In spite of her traumatic childhood and the seemingly impenetrable barriers imposed by her difficult health, Bishop made a momentous declaration that would color her entire future: "We live but once *and I'm going to live*!" Bishop added, by way of a closing to this fateful letter, "Good Luck—and snatch what ever you can, while you can."[19] Thenceforth, she would live her own life according to these dictums.

In the spring of her only year at North Shore Country Day in Swampscott, Bishop wrote of her continuing struggles with mathematics—perhaps offering such a struggle because it was the one subject she couldn't teach herself during her long, sequestered hours in the Revere apartment. She queried Bradley, "Have you ever had *logarithms*? And aren't they *terrible*! I have a beautiful, slim brown book and on the inside it is just rows and rows and rows of numbers! I could weep—it looks almost like poetry from the outside. This June I take a college exam in Algebra and oh—I just *know* I'll flunk!" Then she added, "Oh, you know that old thing—'To Algebra'—I had to write blank verse in English, so I handed it in with a few corrections. Made quite a sensation. . . . I don't think the teacher understood it though—she's such a smug-ass." The opening stanza of Bishop's blank-verse expression of disaffection with the world of numbers sums up mathematics as an orderly, unvarying universe that may be governed by logic and grounded in truth:

> *You are the workings of a fixed rule.*
> *The pivoting of wheels of law and order,*
> *The simple, set foundations of many truths,*

For her, the symbolic language of mathematics seemed like an unfathomable conundrum:

All these are in your cabalistic signs
And yet I find you as mysterious and indefinite
As the wheelings of the worlds through space.[20]

Bishop's free-verse ode to the encroaching mist off Wellfleet contrasts sharply, and appropriately, in form and style with her strictly pentameter protest against the fixed rules of mathematics. This shows that even in her mid-teens, Bishop had attained a clear understanding about the alignment of sound and sense. She could write freely about the incoming fog and strictly about the laws of mathematics, exciting by turns the displeasure of a fellow camper at Chequesset over her free verse and the amazement of a classroom of fellow English students over her adept pentameters.

Although Bishop disparaged the smugness of her English instructor in her letter to Bradley, she later came to appreciate this teacher as an influential and inspiring guide. In fact, she told Ruth Foster in 1947 that this North Shore Country Day English teacher, with the unlikely name of Mrs. Littlefinger, was the first good teacher she had ever had, and the first to actively encourage her writing.[21] At the end of her year under Mrs. Littlefinger's tutelage, Bishop published five pieces in her North Shore Country Day literary magazine, the *Owl*. These included a wry short story, more or less in the O. Henry mold; two brief exercises on Tennyson's *Idylls of the King*, one of which astutely critiques the subordinate role of women in the poem; and a prose piece in Latin titled "Commutatio Opinionis." But the gem of her offerings in the *Owl* is "The Ballad of the Subway Train," a bold and charming poem. This not only provides a compelling allegory of Bishop's early development but stands as an extraordinary piece of work in its own right. "The Ballad of the Subway Train" sets out confidently to create a primordial world:

Long, long ago when God was young,
  Earth hadn't found its place.
Great dragons lived among the moons
  And crawled and crept through space.

These great dragons lived "ten thousand thousand years" in a world of innocent pleasure, power, and play. With eyes that "were as the whizzing suns" and tails like "sharp flails of light," these creatures "bunted meteors with their heads / While unseen worlds dropped by; / And scratched their bronzy backs upon / The ridges of the sky." This ballad, with its confidently cheeky tone and its balance of lightness and grandiloquence, reveals a sixteen-year-old poet who is taking pleasure in her own literary powers, cleverly deploying assonance and alliteration to create ballad stanzas that are metrically correct and at the same time jazzy and fun. Her playful dragons seem, through these years, to be gamboling through their own celestial gardens. Despite their tremendous size, the demeanor of these "great dragons" remains curiously childlike, even infantile. The primordial world they inhabit, at a time when even "God was young," is expansive and apparently free of law or restraint. But then, abruptly, they are caught out in a calamitous if inadvertent crime, when "one day / they chanced to eat / A swarm of stars new-made." Without any prior warning, this provokes God's fury, and with anger that "made the planets shake," he pronounces these unexpected and extraordinary words of damnation:

> "*You have been feeding, greedy beast,*
>   *Upon the bright young stars.*
> *For gluttony as deep as yours—*
>   Be changed to subway cars!*" [22]

This climactic turn in Bishop's ballad offers nothing less than a precocious tragicomic remaking of the story of Adam and Eve and their lost paradise. In John Milton's epic version, Adam and Eve deservedly suffer their loss of Eden, because they have been duly warned against eating the fruit of the Tree of the Knowledge of Good and Evil. The crime of Bishop's dragons, by contrast, when they eat that swarm of new-made stars, resembles the instinctive impulse of a child. Nonetheless, God's anger is swift and final—no hope here of "paradise regained." Yet comedy remains alive in the sheer incongruous surprise of the event and in the surprising congruence of the long and sinuous shape of a dragon with the creature's future life as a train of subway cars. Bishop's texture is lucid, her imagery precise. Yet the arbitrary and punitive judgment of the poet's "God" recalls the opening scene in Bishop's "The Country Mouse" and that other early ballad "Once on a hill I met a man."

Already, by the age of sixteen, Bishop had shown that as a poet she could deploy allegory and humor to explore her deepest emotional concerns. She had proven that she could exploit traditional poetic forms in surprising ways. And she had published at least one truly excellent and original poem, while drafting many further examples during a promising, self-imposed apprenticeship. Moreover, she had demonstrated a determination to be guided by the motto "We live but once *and I'm going to live!*"

CHAPTER FIVE

WALNUT HILL

W hen sixteen-year-old Elizabeth Bishop arrived at Walnut Hill School in Natick, Massachusetts, in the fall of 1927, she made an immediate impression on her fellow students.[1] Walnut Hill was then a conservative private boarding school for women with a commitment to high academic standards and the stated goal of placing its graduates in elite women's colleges. "It is hoped," the school's sober admissions pamphlet declared, "that the graduates of Walnut Hill may be recognized as women of fine scholarship, cultivated and womanly manners, and Christian character."[2]

Yet as Bishop entered Walnut Hill, she perhaps did not bid fair to meet these expectations. Rhoda Wheeler, who would become a lifelong friend and later teach English on the college level, wrote to her mother in her first letter after their arrival, "There is a girl, Elizabeth Bishop by name, who does not believe in Christ or the Supreme Power who was the only girl in the school who didn't sign the pledge [of the Christian Association]."[3] A week later Rhoda Wheeler noted, "Additionally she is a vegetarian. All this is on her own hook too. She is full of the old harry and awfully nice but hard to get to know well. She loves poetry and has loads of volumes of it." Wheeler added, "Last night she and two others (not I!) were caught climbing all over the Stowe roof by way of the fire escape."[4] The following spring, in a sketch titled "Roof-Tops," Bishop would reflect on the creative atmosphere at Walnut Hill, seeing in the Victorian rooftops on campus "these many-slanted, many-shingled planes as things like kettle covers, or corks, beneath which we boiled and fermented."[5] Bishop soon dropped her vegetarianism, but she never lost her sense of adventure, nor her readiness to view the world from unusual perspectives.

Stowe was one of the school's main academic buildings, but during each of her three years at Walnut Hill, Bishop lived in the picturesquely gabled Eliot House, the school's primary residence hall. By no means a common-place dormitory, it boasted a sunny living room equipped with a large fire-place and window seats, which were designed for informal social and intellectual gatherings. It also offered the school's 120 students "four din-ing rooms of moderate size with small tables, so that the quiet and order of a family are enjoyed at meal times."[6] Even though Bishop sometimes chafed against her school's strict regimen and expectations, she found an authenti-cally homelike environment as well as a close circle of friends at Walnut Hill. Frani Blough, who became another lifelong friend and who would later serve for many years as the managing editor of *Modern Music*, would one day recall her own first encounters with "a most remarkable girl. She looked remarkable, with tightly curly hair that stood straight up, while the rest of us all had straight hair that hung down. And she was remark-able in many ways besides." For one thing, "she had read more widely and deeply than we had. But she carried her learning lightly." Moreover, "she was very funny."[7]

Joan Collingwood, too, commented more than sixty years later on Bishop's memorable presence: "She had an almost oval face, beautiful blue eyes, and frizzy hair. You couldn't look then look away."[8] It was not just Bishop's wit, learning, or appearance that impressed Collingwood and Blough; they were similarly dazzled by Bishop's ability to perform, imag-ine, and create. They were beguiled by the large repertoire of stories that she "could tell, not read," and her fund of lively songs and Nova Scotian sea chanteys. What's more, Blough recalled many years later that "if some school occasion called for a new song, or a skit, it would appear overnight like magic in her hands." Not only did she impress with her distinctive identity; she also acquired a distinctive name: "We called her 'Bishop,' spoke of her as 'the Bishop,' and we all knew with no doubt whatsoever that she was a genius."[9]

Bishop was soon writing for the school's literary magazine, *The Blue Pencil*, an elegantly produced publication that put out three issues a year: one in the fall term, one in the spring term, and a senior number in June. A high proportion of the 120-member student body had to contribute simply to fill this periodical's annual quota of pages. In this welcoming venue Bishop would publish throughout her three years at Walnut Hill a steady stream of poems, reviews, sketches, essays, short stories, and even a one-act play. Bishop received early recognition of her writing skill when four pieces, two in prose and two in verse, were selected for the fall number of *The Blue Pencil* during her first term. Bishop later told an interviewer that as a young reader, she "went through a Shelley phase, a Browning phase, and a brief Swinburne phase."[10] Bishop's very personal essay "In Appreciation of Shelley's Poems" brings her Shelley phase to life, linking her love of his poetry with her previous summer on Cape Cod at Camp Chequesset: "I . . . finally ended up devoting all of my reading time to Shelley."[11] Bishop's appreciation not only affirmed the intimate connection between life and art but led her to offer the following sound advice: "The best way to understand Shelley is to read a part of his biography and then read his poems that were written during the same period of his life." Bishop pictured herself seated by the shoreline of her sailing camp "with his poems in one pocket and *Ariel*, his biography by Andre Maurois, in the other, and the clouds and sailboats that he so loved around me." Situated thus, Bishop felt that she had a window into the mind of this Romantic precursor who, she felt, burned as "a bright, steadfast flame that by disillusionment and tragedy was strengthened and given deeper colors."[12] Some months earlier she had acknowledged to Louise Bradley, "[Shelley's] poems make me feel half like an angle worm and half like a god."[13]

Bishop never forgot her early affinity for Shelley. In a 1975 final examination given to a poetry class at Harvard, Bishop invited students to agree or disagree with Shelley's claims in "A Defence of Poetry" for the power of empathy, which Shelley described as the power of putting oneself "in the place of another and of many others." Bishop requested as well that her students respond to Shelley's claim that the imagination is "the great instrument of moral good."[14] In Bishop's early boarding school writings, she was already making her own claims for the value of empathy and the power of imagination. At the same time, she was facing—as Shelley had done before—the frustrations and challenges imposed on her by "ignorance and convention."[15]

In a late editorial for *The Blue Pencil*, Bishop further developed her thoughts on the powers of imagination and the value of resistance to conformity. Starting with a notion picked up in Miss Ellis's chemistry class, Bishop asserted that the hard work, discipline, and routine demanded by Walnut Hill would not turn herself and her classmates into tedious drones because "we have in ourselves, not the boiling lava of the earth, but a kind of burning, unceasing energy of some sort that will not let us be finished off and live in the world like the china people on the mantlepiece." She felt it was "this energy, this fire," which was always there, "ready to explode," that would drive them toward individuality and distinction.

During her Walnut Hill years, as in later life, Bishop always sought others who burned with their own unique energy and fire.

One such intimate friend was Barbara Chesney, who later became a professional painter and teacher of art, and whose forte in her later years was a bold mastery of expressive color. Chesney recalled that she and Bishop developed their friendship while attending concerts and plays in Boston. On one such occasion, Bishop "began confiding in me. She told me about her mother and the dressmaker and the whole story in 'In the Village.' It made me want to protect her. Elizabeth needed somebody then, and apparently I was it. I probably was the closest friend she had at that time." Perhaps unaware of Bishop's Camp Chequesset confidant Louise Bradley, Chesney added, "I don't know that she'd ever had a friend that close before."[16] Certainly Bishop saw and spoke to Chesney much more frequently than she did the elusive Bradley, with whom Bishop's relationship would remain, for the most part, epistolary.

Over the course of their relationship, well beyond their Walnut Hill years, Bishop made frequent visits to Chesney's family home in Pittsfield, Massachusetts. Yet even surrounded by Barbara Chesney's supportive family circle, Bishop remained to some degree a person apart. Always ready to blossom with wit and energy among kindred spirits, she "didn't fit in," as Chesney recalled, "with general conversation and small talk. . . . When I'd go back home, my friends didn't understand why I preferred seeing her." Yet for Chesney, "Elizabeth was far more interesting and had a lot more to offer and to learn from than other students at Walnut Hill," including "a catching sense of humor" and an instructive talent for "seeing the little offbeat thing."[17]

Chesney said that theirs was not a lesbian relationship, "though I do know that some people were concerned that it might be. Ruby Willis, the math teacher, once called me into her room and asked me if this was a 'normal relationship.' I don't remember what I said, but fortunately I ignored it." Within her circle of friends at Walnut Hill, Bishop found acceptance and encouragement because, as Chesney put it, "Elizabeth was different and I perceived and appreciated this."[18] Frani Blough agreed, recalling, "I had a fine time at Walnut Hill mainly because I knew Elizabeth and some people like her."[19] Joan Collingwood, who later became a teacher of literature, would observe, "The experience of Walnut Hill to me was the experience of knowing Elizabeth."[20]

Yet Bishop's social difference—born not only out of her history of childhood isolation and abuse but also out of the Calvinist reticence or taciturnity of her Bishop and Bulmer forebearers—proved challenging and enticing to her friends. As their first Thanksgiving holiday approached, Rhoda Wheeler enclosed a photo of Bishop in a letter to her mother. She noted, too, that her new friend was planning to remain at Walnut Hill during the Thanksgiving vacation—a mark of Bishop's growing disaffection from her nearby maternal and paternal aunts and uncles. Wheeler struggled over whether to invite Bishop, who remained uneasy with family holidays throughout her life, to share her family's Thanksgiving festivities. "I am sure we could have a good time but if there was a party she doesn't like to dance or do things like that. For instance, she would enjoy walking up the beach to the third beach or so and not stick around the house unless reading. Of course she wouldn't be impolite or anything but I'd be anxious to give her a good time. Shall I be selfish or have her? I suppose it's for me to decide. I guess I'll end up not having her."[21] As their relationship matured, Bishop did make several future visits to the Wheeler family, to which she responded appreciatively. Yet Bishop's reticence would continue to haunt her relationships. Joan Collingwood recalled, "There was this big gap in her life. Elizabeth didn't talk much about her childhood. It was too difficult." And her friend added, "I remember exactly how she looked one time when she was leaving our house in Plymouth Massachusetts, after a visit. It was a very sad look and stayed with me. Maybe the right word would have called her back." Still, according to Collingwood, Bishop never lost her humorous touch, "a general attitude of amusement toward the foibles of the human race." Just as important, Bishop never lost "her own sense of rightness" as an artist. "She was absolutely sure of that in a way which at that age not many people are."[22]

Walnut Hill emphasized a sound mind in a sound body. Along with academic, spiritual, and cultural pursuits, the school placed a strong emphasis on athletics, and Bishop would one day recall with a certain fondness the energetic physical activity of her boarding school years. The school also insisted on maintaining a healthful diet. Candy, even if sent from home, was not just discouraged but strictly regulated. The Walnut Hill admissions brochure claimed that student health frequently improved under their disciplined regimen, and for Bishop, at least, this proved to be the case. In her first year, however, even though she had been cleared at last to receive the vaccinations required for matriculation at Walnut Hill, Bishop continued to suffer acute outbreaks of chronic asthma and eczema.[23]

That first fall term, Bishop was such a frequent patient in the school infirmary that she had to take incompletes in algebra and French. Bishop's captious aunt Ruby, the wife of her uncle Jack Bishop, penned a letter to the school in February 1928, complaining of what she saw as her niece's lack of progress. Ruby observed, "Elizabeth is rather spoiled and has not been made to do many things. . . . She was always a sort of pathetic child having to fight asthma and eczema ever since she was a baby. I can only hope that she will do better as time goes on." Later in the spring of that first year, Ruby did note an improvement in the demeanor of her niece. She wrote to the school's principal, Miss Bigelow, "As we see her only occasionally, we can see a big change in her . . . , and believe she is on the right track."[24]

Bishop's course of study included Latin, English, chemistry, and ancient history, along with courses in French and mathematics. She did well in most of these subjects but continued to struggle with algebra. This did not endear her to math teacher Ruby Willis, the same instructor who had questioned the normality of Bishop's relationship with Barbara Chesney. As Frani Blough remembered it, Willis was "a real tough nut, very severe and large, a lot of white hair. She kind of glared at you and glowered." Willis and Bishop never got along because, according to Blough, "Elizabeth was inclined to be a bit fresh. Elizabeth couldn't stand Miss Willis because she was such a dragon."[25] Since Bishop studied math all three years at Walnut Hill, this battle carried right on through to graduation.

On the other hand, Bishop was a special favorite of her English instructor, Eleanor Prentiss, who later went on to teach at Wellesley College. Bishop explained to Anne Stevenson that Miss Prentiss "was an excellent teacher of English *for that age* (hopelessly romantic!)." Along with their work together in the classroom, Bishop felt that Prentiss "helped me even more, probably, by lending me all her books I took a fancy to and admiring my early verse—too much, no doubt."[26] Blough recalled that Prentiss "would sigh over things" and "write sentimental notes," but that she also had good taste in literature and was eager to bring along "anyone who showed a sign of any talent." Blough admitted, though, that Prentiss was "a kind of trial because she was so spiritual."[27] Bishop's correspondence with Blough contained more than a little eye-rolling over moments of post-Victorian spirituality on the part of this encouraging but hopelessly romantic literary mentor.

The poems Bishop published at Walnut Hill do show marks of Miss Prentiss's guiding hand—to the point that Bishop later adopted a dismissive attitude toward poems that appeared in *The Blue Pencil*. While it is true that few of them show anything like the irreverent verve of "The Ballad of the Subway Train," written at North Shore Country Day, these poems do reveal a precocious mastery of traditional verse forms, along with distinctive flashes of language or observation that give hints of what was to come.

The opening stanza of "Behind Stowe," which accompanied Bishop's appreciation of Shelley in that initial fall *Blue Pencil* number, melds the fairy-tale world she loved in the early days of her correspondence with Bradley with hints of the keen eye and ear that would later appear in her mature work. Here she declares, "I heard an elf go whistling by," one that whistled "sleek as moonlit grass." Following the elf, she finds the place "where dusty, pale moths fly" and hears the crickets sing. Moths retained a particular fascination for Bishop. And the notable simplicity of language, specificity of observation, linear development of thought, quietly modulated pacing, and absence of maudlin self-involvement in "Behind Stowe" all remain impressive in the work of this still-adolescent poet.

Along with her fascination with moths, Bishop had a strong affinity for climbing trees, which she loved to shinny up to gain a point of vantage on the world below, a characteristic that carried well into her college years. In her second poem in the first *Blue Pencil* number, Bishop explored, in direct and straightforward language, the link she felt with a neighbor-like tree adjacent to her room in Eliot House. "To a Tree" begins, "Oh, tree outside my window, we are kin." "Sufficient bliss," the poet concludes while gazing out her window:

> For me, who stand behind its framework stout,
>   Full of my tiny tragedies and grotesques grieves,
> To lean against the window and peer out,
>   Admiring infinites'mal leaves.

Characteristically, Bishop minimizes the significance of her own losses and tragedies, while she hints at being continually haunted by them. She follows romantic conventions by articulating the search for solace through a personal bond with a living thing in nature. But the poem goes well beyond convention, at least in its handling of musical sound, in its final line, where an intricate play of consonants, vowels, and multilayered alliteration rustles through that closing phrase, "Admiring infinites'mal leaves."

Walnut Hill began as a feeder school for Wellesley College, which was then a women-only college. Its dorms and classrooms stood just two miles from the Wellesley campus, a manageable walk and an even more manageable bike ride. Boston, too, was readily accessible. A short trip on the Boston and Albany Railroad would deliver students to Boston's South Station. Off-campus excursions were regulated and sometimes chaperoned, but permission to attend cultural events at Wellesley or in Boston was generally granted. In 1929, Rhoda Wheeler wrote her mother of her plan to attend one such event with Bishop, a "Wellesley concert to hear some Russian people, a singer and pianist whose names I have entirely forgotten."[28] The pianist was Sergei Prokofiev, who performed his own compositions, and the singer was Prokofiev's wife, soprano Lina Llubera. Bishop would later tell Anne Stevenson that she shook hands with the great composer after this performance, adding that Prokofiev's wife sang excerpts from 'The

Love of Three Oranges.' She declared that Prokofiev's compositions "and his way of playing I remember as giving me a whole new idea of music.—Possibly the idea of 'irony' in music was a revelation."[29]

Bishop studied piano throughout her years at Walnut Hill and became a capable performer. At a student recital in the spring of her final year, she led off the program with two preludes by Chopin and the *Solfeggietto* by C. P. E. Bach. She followed with the droll and rhythmically spiky gavotte from Prokofiev's op. 32.[30] Prokofiev's gavotte was easily the music program's most avant-garde work. The previous spring, she had ventured Debussy's "Clair de Lune."[31]

While making new friends at Walnut Hill, Bishop maintained her intimate correspondence with Louise Bradley. In a January 3 letter to Bradley during her first year, Bishop acknowledged the difficulty of putting her thoughts into words. "Sometimes I think words are wonderful things and they dance attendance, but I can't find the right ones tonight." Bishop may have been responding to a Bradley letter that was more directly affectionate than usual, because she added, "But you know how you have made me feel—as happy as when we once had three precious days together." Bradley must have also confessed insecurities about their relationship, since Bishop added reassuringly in a postscript, "Don't be silly—of course no one has taken your place! God bless you."[32]

Yet in the same letter, Bishop worried too about whether Bradley's attentions might be wandering, and she struggled also with her own progress toward adulthood under the strenuous Walnut Hill regimen. "Louise," she exclaimed, "I am a little afraid. . . . I've done a lot of growing up." She added, "I change so often that I fairly spin—and so I really keep some stability—like a gyroscope, I guess." Then, as she so often did in letters to Bradley, Bishop deprecated herself in the process of exalting her friend: "I am so afraid that you won't be able to like me as much as you used to. . . . I'm nothing but a dreamer and a useless rebel—and you're a poet." Bradley had transferred from the University of Indiana, where she had been quite unhappy, to Radcliffe College in Cambridge, Massachusetts, which was nearer to both her home and Walnut Hill. In another postscript, Bishop urged Bradley, "Couldn't you come down to see me some Saturday afternoon? School is so lovely I must show it to you. It's only about a half an hour from Boston."[33] Yet there is no evidence in their letters that they met at Walnut Hill, even if she insisted in her signature, "I love you always— always, / Bishie."[34]

When Bishop wrote to Bradley two months later, in March of her first academic year at Walnut Hill, it was to describe to her confidant the experience of a recital given at the New England Conservatory's Jordan Hall by the renowned English pianist Myra Hess. Bishop confessed in her letter to Bradley that she found this concert's effect on her "impossible to describe." She was overwhelmed, in particular, by the haunting impact of Hess's performance of Charles Tomlinson Griffes's rippling impressionist fantasy *The White Peacock*. The experience of this dreamlike work—in a style not unlike Claude Debussy's—left her "so exhausted that I managed to get a *Don't Disturb* sign" placed on her Eliot House door. This granted Bishop license to "stay in my room and have dinner here and watch everyone else go to church and write till five o'clock. Write is right—I owe eighteen letters and I have to produce some sort of lengthy article on *Northanger Abbey* and an editorial for *The Blue Pencil* before Tuesday! But all this is very unimportant."[35]

During this sanctioned hiatus from school routine, Bishop focused most intently not on any of these requirements but on a poem, written out by hand, that she enclosed in her letter to Bradley. This March 1928 letter offers much more than a finished draft of a Bishop poem in the making. It reveals, as well, the process of creation of the poem from inception to completion. Bishop's opening lines convey her yearning to reproduce the richly atmospheric musical moment she had experienced through the hands of a master pianist: "I am in need of music that would flow / Over my fretful, feeling finger-tips, / Over my bitter-tainted, trembling lips, / With melody, deep, clear, and liquid-slow." Perhaps Bishop felt that this was an experience she might never hope to reproduce by means of her own, less skillful touch on the keyboard. In the succeeding lines, the tune lifts into the realm of the human voice, as she hears "a song to fall like water on my head, / And over quivering limbs, dream-flushed to glow." In the course of a few feverish hours, the seventeen-year-old Bishop had crafted in her opening lines the perfectly formed octave of a Petrarchan sonnet.

Bishop concludes with an exactly rendered Petrarchan sestet that makes a subtle turn toward generalization, declaring, "There is a magic made by melody." Although her own initial response to Myra Hess's performance had been feverish, here Bishop stresses that an intense musical experience offers "a spell of rest, and quiet breath" in which the "cool / Heart" sinks to "the subaqueous stillness of the sea," and is "held in the arms of rhythm and of sleep."[36]

In these closing lines, the listener's spirits, lifted at first beyond the keyboard into song, settle dreamily downward toward slumber. In the closing lines of her January letter to Bradley, Bishop declared, "I'm going to try to sleep and dream of warm sunlight in some lovely place and a pale green sea and you."[37] Here, inspired by Hess's artistry at the keyboard, Bishop discovered in words, and shared with an intimate friend, a yearning to transform bitterness and pain into a state of calm.

Bishop's "Sonnet," which began as a private meditation to be shared with a special friend, soon made its appearance in *The Blue Pencil*. The text then slumbered in the Walnut Hill archives until it was reprinted for a new audience, four years after Bishop's death, in a section—"Poems Written in Youth"—incorporated into Bishop's *Complete Poems: 1927–1979*. But during her Walnut Hill years, Bishop was also composing a more irreverent kind of verse altogether, of a style that could never have found a place between the covers of her school's literary magazine. One such effort appeared in another Bishop letter to Bradley, sent from Camp Chequesset in July 1928. Bishop was trying to inveigle a promised poem out of Bradley that the latter had not yet sent. She then urged teasingly, "However, just to prove to you that I can write *beautiful* poetry—here is my only brainchild in a month." What followed was a limerick that might have shocked Miss Prentiss.

There was a young woman named Russle
Who wore an enormious bustle.
  On a gay buggy ride
  A snake dropped inside—
How Miss Russle's bustle did hustle.[38]

Bishop resumed her letter with the wry admonition, "After which vulgar limerick how can you refuse me?" Bishop would later require students in a Harvard poetry writing class to memorize a poem by the limerick's Victorian popularizer, Edward Lear.[39]

Earlier that summer, after her first year at Walnut Hill, Bishop wrote to Louise Bradley from Cliftondale to express again a recurrent yearning, inspired in this case by a magazine piece she had recently read. She told Louise, "And oh there is an article in this month's *Atlantic*, Louise, about a man who lives on a little South Sea Island. We simply must—we could get a job as traders for some steamship company, I know, and then we could live in a grass-roofed hut with palm trees and sun on top and the ocean all around and write and read and dream and write some more. . . . For heaven's sake what are we young for if not [to] do the impossible things we want to, to give us pleasant . . . recollections for our old age?" Bishop made every effort to enlist Bradley as an intimate partner in her exotic plans. "I'm going to be a quahog fisherman and a truck-driver and a farmer, and we're going to live in the South Seas."[40] Although Bradley's responses to Bishop do not survive, one often gets the sense that in the face of Bishop's persistent effort to urge Louise to one northern coastline or tropical island nest after another, Bradley's replies show her ever-so-gently backing away. Having received Louise's response to one of these invitations, Bishop replied, "I sometimes have a horrible feeling that you take a motherly interest in me—no more nor less. And when you send me *Best Love* it sounds like 'Best bib and tucker.'" Perhaps this is one reason why, although they corresponded frequently, they seldom met.

But if intimacy with Bradley remained ever just out of reach, her classmate Judy Flynn was nearer at hand, if never quite attainable. Bishop described for Ruth Foster the strong personal and physical attraction she felt for this Walnut Hill classmate: "I fell really in love with a girl named Judy Flynn. She was one of the most beautiful adolescent girls I've ever seen. Very Irish . . . , very tall with dark red hair, almost black at a distance and eyes that were a slightly lighter shade." Bishop added that she "had a beautiful deep voice," and that "she was as nice as she was beautiful, too." She confessed, "I was scared of her at first but quite suddenly she seemed to reciprocate my feelings pretty much and I was really crazy about her for the two years she was there. We got talked about." Even so, the vice principal, Harriet Farwell, who always kept a protective eye on Bishop, was supportive of the relationship and took them on outings.

Bishop's family life continued to be a challenge as she approached her final year at Walnut Hill. Her Bishop grandparents had died in 1923. Bishop's now quite elderly Bulmer grandparents had moved away to Montreal to be cared for by their daughter Mary, so for the first time in years, Bishop did not make her annual summer trip to Great Village following her stay at Camp Chequesset. This meant that she did not see her favorite aunt, Grace, who was living on a farm outside Great Village that summer. Instead, she passed an uncomfortable stay with her uncle Jack and aunt Ruby Bishop, with whom she continued to experience a difficult relationship. As she wrote to Louise Bradley in August 1929, "I wonder why I'm not made for family life. I *feel* made for it, but perhaps my relations don't." And she added, "I think I lead a double life—school and camp—and the in between times are only the periods of interment while I await the latest resurrection."[41] She later told Ruth Foster, with reference to her Walnut Hill years, "I tried to avoid visiting all my relatives as much as possible."[42] In a post-college notebook, she recalled telling her college friend Margaret

Miller, "Families seem to me like 'concentration camps'—where people actually let out their sadistic natures."[43]

Following her unhappy stay with Jack and Ruby, Bishop traveled to Stockbridge, Massachusetts, where plans had been made for her to visit her aunt Florence Bishop, her late father's unmarried sister. Then, in mid-September 1929, she would proceed to Walnut Hill School to begin her senior year. In her late masterwork "In the Waiting Room," Bishop would characterize Florence, under the name Aunt Consuelo, as "a foolish timid woman." In a 1956 letter from Brazil, Bishop told her beloved aunt Grace that Florence "is really impossible, poor thing, and always manages to get under one's skin and say *the* most unkind thing of all, whatever it may be, sooner or later—though she doesn't want to: you can almost see her trying to be nice, and then out it comes, some horrible, mean remark!" Bishop added, "One of her favorite cracks to me is that being a writer makes a woman coarse, or masculine."[44]

During her visit with her aunt Florence, her aunt decided to host a party with boys and girls of Bishop's age. Many girls of eighteen might have found this prospect appealing, but Bishop was terrified at the very idea, and particularly by the prospect of having to talk to strange boys. This phobia appears to have been rooted in her experience with her abusive uncle George. Bishop related to Ruth Foster that after earlier experiences of verbal abuse and inappropriate touching dating back to her preteens, "Later on when I was 14 or 15 or so he was always trying to feel my breasts and I'd try to get away from him and never let on to myself exactly what it was he was doing, but he was so very large and strong I would get caught sometimes."[45] As the evening for the party involving strange boys approached, Bishop was in town on errands with her cousin Nancy Orr. Then she simply disappeared, and nobody knew where she had gone. As she told Dr. Foster much later, "I tried not to get panicky but I got scareder & scareder." So while her cousin was inside a store, she "just started walking, almost uncontrollably."[46] Soon, she found herself hitchhiking toward Walnut Hill

School. There, she hoped to meet Harriet Farwell, the vice principal who had always treated her so sympathetically. Finding the school locked up when she arrived that evening, Bishop slept in the woods nearby in a slight rain and woke to find her face being licked by a friendly hunting dog. As she approached the school that morning, wet, dirty, and bedraggled, she was spotted by Miss Mulligan, an English teacher who lived across the street from the school's entrance and who treated her with understanding.

Bishop recalled to Foster that Miss Mulligan "took me to her house and put me to bed and made me scrambled eggs herself and didn't ask any questions at all for a long time. So finally I began to think of how worried my aunt must be etc. and told her what I'd done & she called Aunt Florence—neither of them could figure out why though and I wouldn't say."[47] Perhaps the eighteen-year-old Bishop felt that if she broke her silence, she would have had to explain her fear of boys, and this might have led almost inexorably to uncomfortable disclosures about her uncle George.

While in her unexpected place of refuge, Bishop witnessed a very different form of family life than what she had known in the home of her abusive uncle or her carping aunts. "That night was Miss Mulligan's old father's birthday and I remember thinking how pleasant and peaceful it all seemed and how wonderful it must be to have a nice family." Miss Mulligan, knowing of Bishop's friendship with Judy Flynn, arranged to have Bishop stay with Judy and her family until school opened a few days later. As Bishop recalled for Foster, "Judy and her brother drove down from Manchester NH and got me." Significantly, Bishop recalled of the journey back to Manchester, "I was terrified of the brother of course but at least Judy was along and I didn't have to talk to him." Bishop's "of course" when mentioning her terror of her friend Judy's presumably inoffensive brother is surely telling. When Bishop arrived at Judy's home, she was surprised when Mrs. Flynn asked her, "Why are you so unhappy?" Bishop later said of her desperate flight from Aunt Florence's party, "I don't believe I've ever told this story to anyone before." But the event did not go unnoticed by Bishop's teachers and friends at Walnut Hill, where it became a matter of school record. Nor did it go unnoticed by the members of her family, who continued to regard Bishop, in her own words, as "hopelessly queer."[48]

Just after this incident, she wrote to Bradley, saying, "Dear Louise—you are really my family, you know. I belong to you and I'll do whatever you tell me—honestly." In her imagined scenario, Bishop's slightly elder friend would play the controlling role: "It's a sort of fairy relationship. I suspect you will surprise me any minute and turn into a bird or lock me up in a small brown house until I behave." Bishop added, "You do know so much more than I do. I wish you would tell me whether to do one's duty is right or to do what one wants." Bishop remained at the Flynn home, rather than returning to her aunts, until she began her senior year at Walnut Hill. Flynn, who had graduated the previous June, herself proceeded to Wells College, where she would begin her undergraduate career.

Just as Bishop found a way to render comically her feelings of enclosure in "The Ballad of the Subway Train," she turned her disquiet over family life and the threat posed by male suitors into a mordantly funny verse performance, "I Introduce Penelope Gwin," a poem Bishop wrote while at Walnut Hill and gave to Judy Flynn. In January 1975, Flynn returned this and other comic poems to Bishop, along with, as she told Blough, "a whole batch of *Blue Pencils*, 1928-29," and a note that offered both an apology for being unable to attend a Bishop reading and a tribute to Bishop's "special genius."[49] Perhaps Bishop shared the poem with Flynn because she knew the background under which Bishop had created it. Bishop told Blough that she thought her comic performances in couplets were "a lot better" than her more serious, published Walnut Hill poems, though she confessed that she hadn't "the faintest recollection of having written them."[50] Editor Alice Quinn relates in her notes to *Edgar Allan Poe & the Juke-Box*, "The heroine of this poem makes a lively drama out of two imperatives: avoiding aunts . . . and forswearing marriage."[51] In the looping handwritten script of her teen years, the words are surrounded and illustrated by a series of cartoonish children's colored stickers that Bishop had somehow laid hands on. Each of these daft-looking stickers has written underneath it the name of an important figure in the poem, beginning with "Our Heroine," a comic penguin—hence, of course, her name. Penelope is "a friend of mine through thick and thin." Just as Bishop would in future years, she travels "much in foreign parts / Pursuing culture and the arts." Also like Bishop, Penelope concludes, "This family life is not for me." Transparently functioning as Bishop's alter ego, this assertive fictive penguin declares, "I will not let myself be pampered / And *this* free soul must not be hampered." Each of the figures pictured in her carefully chosen colored stickers is surrounded by unlikely accoutrements. And although she travels light, Penelope playfully explains the usefulness of these accessories as the poem unfolds. Her blue balloon prompts her to "lift my eyes, / Above all pettiness and lies," while a compact potted plant is all she needs to "hide from a pursuing Aunt." Here, in these playful rhymes, the irreverent teenage Bishop was laying out her future life plan with remarkable prescience.

Bishop's alter ego, Penelope, insists, "My aunts I loathe with all my heart / Especially when they take up art." But hatred is no sufficient protection, since "anything in the shape of one. / Can make me tremble, turn, and run." In quest of freedom and adventure, and in flight from the entanglements of family life, Penelope embarks on a career of travel that takes her "through country lanes and sixty states / At really quite astounding rates." She soon finds her way to Paris and Rome. But as Penelope recalls, it is in Russia that she makes her biggest find: "A Russian Aunt-Eater it was— / Large appetite—and lovely jaws." This curious "aunt-eater" might turn the tables on her intimidating aunts since "an Aunt will look at him and faint, / Even the kind that sketch or paint." This ferocious Russian carnivore is represented in sticker form by a large but smiling and cuddly St. Bernard who sports a stuffed toy monkey on his back.

While traveling in "Romantic France," as Bishop did shortly after graduating from college, Penelope dallies with heterosexual love in the form of a "handsome German tutor," whose cartoon avatar takes the form of a quacking male mallard. However, Penelope quickly concludes, "But no! I would be no man's wife," and indeed, on closer examination, the charms of this male mallard prove overrated, for "his mouth hung open all the time," and it gave her senses "quite a jolt / To find he had begun to molt." At last, with the enigmatic adage "What is not is and what is not," Penelope bids her audience a quick "Adieu"—and the poem ends abruptly with the approving couplet "I'm sure we all admire Miss Gwin. / How very sweet and kind she's been." This genteel characterization of dear Penelope seems to anticipate Bishop's later persona as the well-mannered lady poet who pursued her own course while quietly subverting traditional norms in her life and art.

After an incident in which Bishop and a friend dressed in grotesque outfits and paraded around Natick, the sympathetic vice principal Harriet Farwell decided that the time had come to try to get at the root of Bishop's emotional issues. When Bishop was admitted to Walnut Hill, her uncle Jack had insisted to school officials that his niece and ward knew nothing about her mother's mental breakdown, and that her mother's institutionalization must not be mentioned or discussed with her. Miss Farwell disagreed, and she requested—indeed, almost demanded—permission from Jack to have Bishop consult a psychiatrist in Boston, a certain Dr. Taylor. Farwell reported to Bishop's guardian that this psychiatrist "did not seem to be worried at all about Elizabeth's heredity. The fact, however, that Elizabeth probably has repressed within her a certain amount of information about her mother, she did consider to be very serious." Farwell added, "I feel very sure myself, in fact, I may say positively that Elizabeth does know some if not all of the truth about her mother." This would be enough, in Farwell's assessment, "to make her very unhappy and keep her in an abnormal state of mind." She added, "Dr. Taylor feels very decidedly that submerged facts of this kind are dangerous and should be brought out into the open."[52] At last, with Jack Bishop's permission, a therapy session with Dr. Taylor was arranged. But such was the family code of silence she had lived under throughout her life that Bishop found it impossible to open up to Dr. Taylor. As she later told Dr. Ruth Foster, "The analyst got no where with me at all—I wouldn't talk, although I really liked her." Bishop added, "On the way home Miss Farwell remarked that she thought I probably worried about my mother a lot." Bishop confessed, "I hadn't even realized she knew about it," adding that she was "so overcome . . . that I burst out crying."[53]

Bishop felt a very strong attraction to Judy Flynn, though Judy was more or less engaged through this period to a young man named Dave, and Judy's mother herself thought that Judy might actually prefer her relationship with Bishop. However, when Flynn graduated and went off to Wells, Bishop must have been conscious that her young friend was leaving her sphere of influence and that the risk of losing Judy was very high. In the last semester of her senior year, Bishop published in *The Blue Pencil* a long-neglected poem that explores the loss of Judy to the world of men, titled "Dead."[54]

More than any of Bishop's other *Blue Pencil* poems, "Dead" is a risk-taking experiment that raises more questions than it answers. Even its one-word title remains grammatically unsettling, as does the poem itself. In this poem, Winter is a powerful male figure—"The Winter is her lover now, / A brilliant one and bold"—and he is in the process of stealing the affections of a female beloved from the poem's speaker, for "she has gone away from me, / Estranged and white and cold."[55] This poem is clearly an allegory of Bishop's own painful experience of attraction and potential loss. The lesbian associations of "Dead" were expressed so obliquely as to have passed under even the censorious eye of Miss Willis, Bishop's dragonish math teacher. In describing the lost beloved as "estranged and white and cold," Bishop anticipates by more than twenty years the cold moon goddess of her 1951 "Insomnia," a pale white figure who "looks out a million miles" but never at the forlorn and lonely estranged lover who speaks the poem. By the close of "Dead," the poem's aspiring lover must admit defeat: the object of her desire has been carried off by the seductive male figure, and all that remains is a single telltale token of her submission to Winter: "This frost upon the grass." The poem suggests just how risky the prospect of love appeared to Bishop, then and later.

Bishop's "Dead" deflects attention from its theme of lesbian love and loss by the simple expedient of applying no gendered term to the poem's speaker. This tactical withholding of a gendered term, for either the lover or the beloved or both, was a technique Bishop would continue to employ throughout her career. The unspecified gender of the narrator is even more important in her compressed and compelling *Blue Pencil* story "The Thumb." Bishop's last creative effort at Walnut Hill, this story uses Poe's technique of gradually shifting a narrator's tone from cool detachment to manic obsession, and also interweaving elements of unearthly ideality with a strong whiff of the perverse. The story centers on the narrator's growing obsession with an attractive and intelligent woman named Sabrina, with a subtly erotic undertone that builds to almost frantic intensity as it unfolds.

Sabrina is identified from the start as a woman of delicate femininity. She lives in "one of those silk-hung apartments, with sunlight coming in at the windows through pale lime-colored curtains, and clear fragrant tea running out of a silver teapot all day long." Sabrina's physical charms balance idealized beauty with a cool undercurrent of sexuality. "If you could think of a Madonna whose face was thinner about the cheek and chin, with a look of humor and something subtly emotional about it—well, that would be Sabrina."[56] Perhaps Bishop was modeling Sabrina on aspects of her friend Judy or was thinking of a girl from summer camp nicknamed Happy, whom she wrote about to Bradley. This was a girl who "looks like a myth and a Valentine and a fairy tale." She admitted to Bradley that this new camp friend's good looks "frighten me. Why does everything agreeable frighten me so?"[57]

Bishop's narrator soon discovers something frightening in Sabrina. "Good God—the woman had a man's thumb! No, not a man's,—a brute's— a heavy, coarse thumb with a rough nail, square at the end, crooked and broken." This thumb, on the hand of a woman of unearthly beauty, excited an intense reaction in Sabrina's suitor: "It was a horrible thumb, a prize fighter's thumb, the thumb of some beast, some obscene creature knowing only filth and brutality."[58] The question of gender ambiguity lies at the center of the story. Sabrina's suitor, the narrator, is neither named nor identified by gender, and may be experiencing either a heterosexual or homoerotic attraction to Sabrina, and at the same time, Sabrina's almost preternatural representation of traditional femininity is controverted by her masculine prizefighter's thumb. The conflicted desire that drives the story escalates with the obsessive narrator's admission, "My mind dwelt upon what it would be like to touch her—to take that hideous hand and hide it in my own." The speaker adds, "I realized that all this was bound to lead me into something wrong, but I couldn't seem to escape it." When finally sure of Sabrina's love, and grasping for the first time the hand with the hideous thumb, the suitor is unable to face the consequences of this successful wooing. Instead, the suitor simply flees the scene, and the story abruptly closes with the words, "I got up and left her without a word and I never went back."[59]

B ishop's final year at Walnut Hill was in several ways a triumph. Following in the footsteps of her friend Frani Blough, Bishop served as editor in chief of *The Blue Pencil*. She was accepted to both Vassar and Wellesley, and chose Vassar—perhaps because Blough was already there and friends such as Rhoda Sheehan would also be attending with her, or perhaps because, located in Poughkeepsie, New York, it stood at a further distance from her sometimes disquieting Bishop and Shepherdson aunts and uncles. By the time she graduated from Walnut Hill, Bishop was already becoming a published writer of considerable experience. And she had begun to develop a body of friends who would stick to her for life. She was also very clearly setting off on a course of her own choosing. Her class picture shows her in full profile, staring intently off into the distance. The motto beneath this striking photo reads, "The locks of the approaching storm." This phrase from her beloved Shelley's "Ode to the West Wind" appears to predict a tempestuous future for this promising Walnut Hill graduate, but it also makes humorous reference to Bishop's conspicuously frizzy locks. Beneath that intent profile, and that Shelleyan motto, Bishop's native place is given as Great Village, Nova Scotia. Bishop was not only announcing here her ongoing allegiance to that favored place, but also quietly suggesting her disaffection from her relatives in Cliftondale and Worcester. Elizabeth Bishop, as her class photo and motto clearly suggest, was now setting forth, at the age of nineteen, on what would prove to be an adventurous and often stormy journey through life.

CHAPTER SIX

CON SPIRITO

A short stroll north of the Vassar College Library leads the wanderer to a curving, shaded footpath flanked on either side by twenty stone benches hewn from black Laurentian granite. Carved on the broad, flat, polished surfaces of each of the benches are a series of poems or poetic excerpts crafted by Elizabeth Bishop. These include some published only after the poet's death, drawn from the manuscripts housed in the library's climate-controlled Special Collections wing. These granite benches, and the poems incised upon them, are meant to celebrate what a college publication terms "the genius of one of Vassar's most distinguished alumnae."[1] They honor, too, the twenty-year tenure of Vassar College president Frances Fergusson, a notable proponent of the arts, dedicated to her on her retirement in 2006. Conceptual artist Jenny Holzer, who created the installation, explains that "I make benches when I want to find a certain way to bring text and people together."[2]

One seeking the lingering presence of Elizabeth Bishop at her alma mater—or any unsuspecting Vassar student, parent, or alum seeking nothing more than a place to sit and rest in the dappled shade—might encounter lines such as these, extracted from Bishop's "Sandpiper," a poem she published twenty-eight years after her graduation: "The world is a mist. And then the world is / minute and vast and clear." Bishop's sandpiper is "looking for something, something, something." Yet for all of her later fame as a Vassar alumna, by the time she reached the end of her freshman year, Bishop was by no means certain that she would find what she was looking for at Vassar College.

To begin with, Bishop encountered roommate troubles. She recalled in a 1978 interview with Elizabeth Spires (Vassar '74) that because she had registered for college a little late, "I had a roommate whom I had never wanted to have. A strange girl named Constance. I remember her entire side of the room was furnished in Scotty dogs—pillows, pictures, engravings and photographs." This was not Bishop's notion of a congenial decorating style. On the other hand, Bishop conceded, "I probably wasn't a good roommate either, because I had a theory at that time" that as a stimulus to poetic inspiration, "one should write down all one's dreams."[3] So she kept a pot of pungent Roquefort cheese at the bottom of her bookcase because she felt that "if you ate a lot of awful cheese at bedtime you'd have interesting dreams."[4]

Three months earlier, the summer before college, Bishop had written to Louise Bradley of an altogether different approach to managing one's dream-life: "I have discovered a way to go to sleep—soothing and resulting in sweet dreams. You say all the names of flowers you can remember over and over and over. Larkspur and Zinnia and Ragged Robin and Marigold, etc."[5] Bishop's nocturnal shift from soothing larkspur to redolent Roquefort as she drifted toward slumber suggests a shift, as well, in her attitude toward poetry. She would diverge from Eleanor Prentiss–approved, late-Victorian lyricism in the direction of something sharper, edgier, and perhaps even more dyspeptic—in short, something more distinctly modern.

Bishop's dormitory during all four of her years at Vassar was Cushing House, a U-shaped brick structure that stands not far off from the broad stones on which her poems are now inscribed. When Bishop arrived at Cushing, it was the college's newest and largest residence hall. In their 1978 interview, Spires asked Bishop about an oft-repeated Vassar legend—handed down from generation to generation for more than forty years—that Elizabeth had once spent the night in a tree outside her dorm. Bishop confirmed the truth of this bit of Vassar lore, adding that she had embarked on this arboreal adventure because "those trees were wonderful to climb. I used to be a great tree climber. Oh. We probably gave up about three in the morning." Then Bishop asked pointedly, "How did that ever get around?"[6]

James Merrill famously remarked of Bishop that "she gave herself no airs. If there was anything the least bit artificial about her character and her behavior, it was the wonderful way in which she impersonated an ordinary woman. Underneath, of course, was this incredible fresh genius who wrote the poems that you adored."[7] However, upon entering Vassar, Bishop stood out as different—even if, as she suggested to Spires, "I think everyone's given to eccentricities at that age."[8] Bishop had established a close bond with Walnut Hill English teacher Eleanor Prentiss, despite the latter's penchant for flowery verse. But she did not hit it off with Barbara Swain, her first-year English instructor at Vassar. Indeed, Swain described their relationship as "purely a classroom one, and very distant at that." Swain found Bishop "an enormously cagey girl who looked at authorities with a suspicious eye and was quite capable of attending to her own education anyway." For a midterm evaluation of her intractable student, Swain "wrote on Bishop's card that she was evidently doomed to be a poet."[9]

Bishop may have been doomed to be a poet, but she entered Vassar in September 1930 with the avowed intention of becoming a musician. Bishop had performed regularly and creditably at the keyboard in Walnut Hill recitals, frequently playing challenging material. But in the more competitive setting of Vassar College, even a comparatively simple Bach three-part invention proved hard to master, and her dreams of a career as a musician were quickly dashed. Bishop's close Walnut Hill friend Frani Blough, who was a year ahead of her at Vassar, observed that when Bishop appeared at her first of the monthly recitals required of college music majors, "Elizabeth came to play her best piece, and she got stuck. She started again, and she got stuck. Then she got up and left. Elizabeth never played in public again. She had too much stage fright."[10] As her friend Frani would later observe, "You can stretch writing poetry over any amount of time to perfect a word, but you have to have a carefree abandon when playing."[11]

Bishop's Walnut Hill piano teacher, who knew her to be an effective performer, was so distressed by this crisis in her former pupil's musical development that she asked Bishop's Vassar instructor, Miriam Steeves, to provide an account of what had gone wrong. Steeves noted with approval that Bishop "apparently had done, and was capable of doing, both musical and intelligent work." However, she observed that Bishop was "technically handicapped by an unusual amount of muscular tension, which I believe to have been one phase of an overtense . . . nervous organization." Steeves claimed that she had worked hard to help Bishop overcome this handicap but concluded, "I am sure it was too deep-seated to be altered easily."[12]

Trauma specialist Dr. Bessel van der Kolk's observation that under such pressure "the body feels that it is under attack, and that it needs to fight back,"[13] is consistent not only with Bishop's ongoing autoimmune disorders but with the deep-seated muscular tension Miriam Steeves observed, and is consistent, too, with Bishop's lifelong struggle with performance anxiety; it would take years for her to grow comfortable giving poetry readings. It may have also played a role in her perfectionism as a writer. Bishop's mind and body were braced in a defensive state, and one mark of her achievement as a writer was her discovery of ways to turn these emotional challenges to artistic advantage. She learned how to deploy her active curiosity and sense of humor as a tonic in the face of these afflictions. And she discovered that when she encountered places that most resembled her beloved Nova Scotia, especially places on a river or by the sea and particularly if they featured oil lamps or woodstoves, she could find a temporary haven against the anxiety that usually haunted her.

Bishop's piano instructor at Vassar was unlikely to have known about Bishop's traumatic past. Even so, the commentary offered by Miriam Steeves suggests she sensed a linkage between the challenges Bishop faced at the keyboard and "the difficulty which she seemed to have in adapting her quick and imaginative, but too self-conscious self to college conditions."[14]

While the evaluations Bishop received from the first-year instructors in her favored fields, English and music, proved insightful and even prophetic, they fell far short of the warm and sympathetic encouragement Bishop had enjoyed from the faculty at Walnut Hill. At Vassar College, Bishop would need to find her own way of adapting.

Along with roommate troubles, and the arm's-length treatment Bishop received from key instructors, Bishop found difficulty that first year in making friends in the larger and more cliquish environment of her new school. In 1947, she noted to her psychiatrist that in her freshman year, "I hadn't many friends at first except old school friends, Rhoda Wheeler, etc. Saw very little of Frani."[15] And after the intimate, family-like dining room at Walnut Hill's Eliot House, Bishop found the noisy dining hall in Vassar's Cushing House most unsettling. One new friendship Bishop did form in her first year was with Eleanor Clark, who would later become a distinguished essayist. Eleanor's sister, Eunice, was a year ahead, and Eunice Clark (Jessup) would one day recall humorously of Bishop, as well as her sister and herself,

> We had an acute case of happy-few-ism. My sister Eleanor arrived at Vassar—after a year studying literature, music, and Italian in a rarefied atmosphere in Rome—at the same time as Elizabeth Bishop, probably the most erudite freshman since John Stuart Mill. They shuddered constantly at the company they found themselves in; dining in a bedroom by candlelight rather than braving the raucous Philistines in the college dining room.[16]

Bishop memorialized her discomfort with the Cushing dining hall in "A Word with You," a poem published in April 1933 that captures a common feature of student life at a small liberal arts college: the experience of living in a fishbowl—or as this poem aptly frames it, a zoo. In a college dining hall, anything one says or does might be witnessed or overheard, or might be aped, jeered at, or gossiped over by the speaker's classmates—or as the poem has it, the speaker's fellow inmates inside the college "zoo." "A Word with You" begins with a vigorous warning: "Look out! there's that damned ape again." Perhaps one might escape gossip or ridicule if one sits "silently until he goes / or else forgets the things he knows / . . . about us." Only then could one "begin to talk again."

The vehement, exasperated tone of "A Word with You," marked by the staccato rhythms that would remain characteristic of numerous later Bishop poems, continues in a poem whose abrupt and violent exclamations capture the feeling of being watched, harassed, and imitated. In its final line, the poem circles back to its beginning: even if one has shaken off the parrot and the monkey, one must still "be silent," for now "the ape has overheard."

After Bishop's death, her friend and fellow poet May Swenson discovered this example of Bishop's Vassar writing among the "Poems Written in Youth" collected posthumously in her 1983 *Complete Poems: 1927–1979.* Swenson's discovery of this unexpected bit of verse-revelation prompted her to compose a verse-reflection on her elusive friend, titled "Her Early Work." Swenson concludes:

> *"A Word with You"*
> *had to be whispered,*
> *spoken at the zoo,*
> *not to be overheard*
> *by eavesdropping ape or cockatoo.*[17]

Swenson showed that she had sensed in Bishop's early work a crucial characteristic of her later poetry: her desire to disclose her most intimate thoughts and feelings in a tone that might most be heard by her more alert and sympathetic readers. Bishop's most revelatory poems often begin by speaking quietly, and sometimes almost in a whisper.

At last, one winter evening in their freshman year, when the nervous strain in which they lived began to seem too much, Bishop and Eleanor Clark decided to make a break for it, heading off without a definite plan toward Eleanor's mother's closed-up house in Litchfield, Connecticut. As

Eleanor's sister, Eunice, remembered it more than forty years later, "After blowing their funds on an aimless series of trains, buses, and taxis, they found themselves at 3 a.m. in a blizzard in Stamford, [Connecticut,] penniless."[18] Eunice recalled, "They started to thumb their way north and were immediately pulled in by the police." The arresting officers, who suspected these two wayfaring college girls of being prostitutes, called on Bishop to disclose the contents of the bulging pockets of her navy pea jacket. These included a pad full of notes in ancient Greek and *The Imitation of Christ* by Thomas à Kempis. According to Eunice Clark, "The police figured they were the oddest floozies the force had ever caught, and finally consented to call my mother, who rescued them before dawn."[19]

After her difficult first college year, Bishop spent the summer of 1931 in coastal Plymouth, sharing a cottage and access to a sailboat with a Walnut Hill friend, while mulling over whether to return to college for a second year. Late in the summer, she traveled to the vicinity of Wellfleet, near Camp Chequesset. In an effort to think things through, she set out from Wellfleet on an adventure she described to Louise Bradley: "I walked the Back Shore from Nauset Light to Provincetown," a solitary, nocturnal hike along the beach of more than twenty miles. Bishop explained that she had impulsively set off "one night about eight o'clock . . . with a little tin lunch box containing a thermos bottle of black tea, a ham sandwich, a tooth brush & comb & a mouthorgan. It was a very nice little trip only I got to the end much too soon." She found it "wonderful along there in the middle of the night—the sky, stars and the water and sand all phosphorus. I went in my bare feet most of the time and stopped for a swim occasionally." She worried, however, that like her still-talked-about nocturnal adventure in a Vassar tree, "that's the kind of thing that makes most people think you're a sort of athletic freak."[20] Late that summer of 1931, still mulling over whether to return to college, she took a room alone in an upper-floor apartment in Boston. She told Bradley, "My lord, the landlady is shaking the rugs out the window below me and I'm getting all the dust." She added, "At present I'm living at 90 Pinckney Street, up three or four flights. I don't know exactly what I'm doing. Sometimes it's highly entertaining and others it's too much like crime and punishment." Musing with comic exaggeration on the possible parallels between herself and Dostoyevsky's Raskolnikov, she wondered, "Am I a social outcast or a Vassar girl? It must be decided."[21] Perhaps the decision might come down to a coin toss. She asked Bradley, "Where are you going to be this winter? I have to flip a penny about college pretty soon, I suppose. You might help me perform the ceremony."[22]

Bradley, who had bemoaned her own difficulties during her first year at the University of Indiana and thereafter transferred to Radcliffe, must have written Bishop a sharp reply, telling her, in effect, to cut out the nonsense and return to college. Bishop acknowledged in reply, "I think, on the whole, you did a wonderful piece of work in that letter"—a letter Bradley aimed, or so Bishop states, at "giving college its due." Bishop noted, "Your letters quite often terrify me." And she added, "I wish I could write letters like that—but then, no one needs to have them written to him or her that I know, except myself." Yet Bishop confessed to finding the result bracing: "If you will only do it again—keep it up at intervals during the winter months—ah, I'll be a PBK [Phi Beta Kappa] in my junior year, a friend to all, and a really delightful character besides." Ultimately, then, Bishop decided to remain at Vassar to mollify her friend Louise Bradley, and also to placate her uncle Jack Bishop, at least until she came of age at twenty-one and "he throws me over to the mercy of LIFE and the Stock Market."[23] Of Vassar she admitted, forlornly, "I think of it in terms of a bed, a peaceful, lonely breakfast, a swell library, and the faint chance of finding some interesting work or friends." Though Bradley's letter might have served as a bracing tonic, Bishop nonetheless voiced a plea: "Please write a letter entirely about yourself—never mind giving 'college its due.'"[24]

In the weeks following her reluctant return to Vassar College, Bishop very quickly found herself amid a circle of congenial friends, and she began to enjoy college a great deal more than she had expected. One new friend was the soon-to-be-distinguished author Mary McCarthy. McCarthy recalled of her relationship with Bishop, "At Vassar I was class of '33, and she was class of '34. I entered the fall of the crash of September '29 so we lived through college in the Depression, and so we were rather, I think, more rebellious, more different, though not perhaps in conventional ways."[25]

McCarthy recalled that "Elizabeth had a very amusing face. She had amusing hair, which was very, very electric and kinky—alive. She looked like somebody from the last century." McCarthy further observed, "I think we had more sense of her as a comic writer," and added, "I think of a poem that she wrote about living next to the toilet." More than fifty years after the fact, McCarthy was able to recite this poem from memory for a PBS television documentary, with a look of evident glee on her face:

> *Ladies and gents, ladies and gents,*
> *Flushing away your excrements,*
> *I sit and hear beyond the wall*
> *The sad continual waterfall*
> *That sanitary pipes can give*
> *To still our actions primitive.*[26]

McCarthy declared emphatically, "Now, *that* poem was well known in the smoking room of our hall."[27] During their Vassar years together, McCarthy had become a close friend of Frani Blough. Bishop now felt reconnected to Blough—and she, Mary McCarthy, the Clark sisters, Blough, and others began to come together as a circle of writers, artists, and social critics who shared common interests and a similarly satiric outlook. Together, they could observe the world of Vassar and beyond, each from her own not-so-conventional point of view.

One of the closest, most complex, and most enduring bonds that Bishop formed at Vassar College was with a brilliant fellow student, Margaret Miller, who became an art historian, a student of literature, and a painter. As Bishop told Ruth Foster, one of the highlights of her sophomore year at college was that she "became very good friends with Margaret Miller almost right away."[28] Rhoda Wheeler considered Miller to be Bishop's "intellectual equal."[29] Another friend, Gretchen Keene, described Miller as "thin, birdlike, with bright eyes and a nice, sharp sense of humor. She was innovative, academic, and had a lively mind." Harold Leeds, who knew Bishop and Miller in New York some years later, recalled that "Margaret was special in many ways. She and Elizabeth had a very similar curiosity about things and words." And like Bishop, Margaret was "extremely expressive."[30] Bishop's feelings toward Miller soon developed into passionate attachment, but while they remained extremely close friends throughout college and into later life, Bishop sensed early on that her romantic attraction was not reciprocated, and she tried to remain silent about these feelings. When Bishop did, on very rare occasions, make even the mildest overture, she met with a sharp rebuff. Still, their close friendship continued, though not without its challenges, and always, it would seem, on Margaret Miller's terms.

On February 8, 1932, Elizabeth Bishop turned twenty-one years old. She was now more at liberty to make her own decisions than most young women were when they came of age. She was, of course, extremely fortunate to enjoy a modest but sufficient independent income, particularly in the heart of the Great Depression. But when it came to family, she was almost completely alone. She did make occasional visits to her uncle Jack and aunt Florence Bishop, and to her aunt Maud and uncle George Shepherdson, but she more frequently spent college holidays alone at Vassar. Instead of family, she chiefly focused on her friends from Walnut Hill and Vassar, making frequent visits to Barbara Chesney in Pittsfield as well as school-year forays from Poughkeepsie south to nearby New York City. Bishop enjoyed a lively and companionable vacation in the summer of 1932, renting a cabin at familiar Wellfleet with Chesney, which they shared with other school friends who later joined them. Then, in August 1932, Bishop embarked on a walking tour of Newfoundland with classmate Evelyn Huntington.

Bishop kept a journal of her Newfoundland travels, an informal travelogue that makes clear that these two young women journeying together along the Newfoundland coast were the object of great local curiosity. In addition to hitchhiking rides on gravel trucks and having lively, incongruous conversations with indigenous innkeepers, they mastered the art of making codfish chowder and consumed huge breakfasts featuring "*wonderful* coffee and toasted rolls."[31] Near the start of her journey, in an August 20 postcard to Frani Blough from St. John's, Bishop wrote, "This place is far beyond my fondest dreams. The cliffs rise straight out of the sea 400-500 feet. I wish, and not just conventionally, that you could see them. The streets and houses all fall down to the water—apparently supported on the masts of the ships."[32] When their tour of Newfoundland came to a close, Bishop had enjoyed a lively and strenuous several weeks, involving the kind of activity that she always found both energizing and therapeutic. She had also observed fragments of material that would one day find their way into two important later poems, "Large Bad Picture" (1946) and "Over 2000 Illustrations and a Complete Concordance" (1948).

By mid-September 1932, Bishop found herself back at Vassar College for the fall semester of her junior year, where she began to hatch a scheme, with several of her literary classmates, whose result has become Vassar legend. Bishop's friend and editor Lloyd Schwartz once remarked that "the fascinating thing about Elizabeth Bishop as an undergraduate was how accomplished a writer she already was."[33] During her first five semesters at Vassar College, however, Bishop had little opportunity to display these accomplishments. From the fall of her first year at Walnut Hill, Bishop's contributions to *The Blue Pencil* had been eagerly accepted. In her senior year, Bishop had followed Frani Blough as *The Blue Pencil*'s editor in chief. But by the end of her fall term as a junior at Vassar, not one of her contributions had been accepted by the *Vassar Review*, whose conservative editorial board formed a rival clique that opposed Bishop and such friends as Blough, Mary McCarthy, Eleanor and Eunice Clark, and Margaret Miller. As Bishop recalled the situation for Elizabeth Spires, "Most of us had submitted to the

Vassar Review and they'd been turned down. It was very old-fashioned then. We were all rather put out because *we* thought we were good." Stymied by the *Vassar Review*, in the fall of her junior year Bishop joined the editorial staff of Vassar's semiweekly newspaper, *The Miscellany News*. The editor in chief of the *Miscellany News* was Eunice Clark. Frani Blough appeared regularly as music critic. Mary McCarthy was designated "Star Reporter." Bishop served as editor and, in recognition of her comedic skills, as regular contributor to the widely read humor column, "Campus Chat." While Bishop and her friends worked together on the *Miscellany News*, they plotted to launch a renegade literary magazine of their own. Meeting at a downtown speakeasy and drinking what Bishop called "ghastly" red wine out of teacups, these stifled authors fleshed out their plan for a magazine rivaling the *Review*. It would seek adventurous writing in all genres—to be authored chiefly by themselves—while encouraging submissions from like-minded contributors. The first issue would appear in the spring of Bishop's junior year, in February 1933, with another following in April 1933. Publication would be anonymous. Advertisers would be sought. The practical details of production posed few problems, since the editors were already experienced at putting out a semiweekly paper. Mary McCarthy proposed calling it *The Battle-Axe*. But Bishop's subtler suggestion, *Con Spirito*, with its punning title alluding to the journal's conspiratorial roots and to its aspirations toward a spirited style of performance, wisely carried the day.

As the planning for *Con Spirito* approached fruition on December 30, 1932, Bishop wrote to Bradley from her Vassar dorm, "I'm enjoying college far too much for my peace of mind."[34] Mary McCarthy recalled that when the first issue appeared in February 1933, "it created a sensation."[35] Coverage of *Con Spirito* and the interest and controversy it provoked appeared regularly in Vassar's *Miscellany News*, and it was noticed in the literary press in New York and elsewhere. The *Miscellany News* coverage included letters to the editor, pro and con, as well as interviews with members of the (mostly sympathetic) faculty. Since the editorial staff of the

Miscellany was dominated by such coconspirators as Eunice Clark, Bishop, Blough, and McCarthy, this semiweekly paper's extensive coverage of *Con Spirito*, a barrage of free advertising, can hardly have been accidental. Remarkably enough, even visiting dignitaries such as noted literary scholar Herbert Grierson and the great T. S. Eliot himself were cited as speaking favorably of *Con Spirito* in the pages of the *Miscellany News*.

Eliot had arrived at the Vassar campus in early May 1933, just after the appearance of the second issue of *Con Spirito*. He was present to participate in the world premiere of his first play, *Sweeney Agonistes*. For the *Miscellany*, Bishop was assigned to report on a reading and talk Eliot would give on his work before his play's debut performance. Bishop's lead article on Eliot's performance reported that the renowned poet made the implausible claim, "My poetry is simple and straightforward," and that "the audience laughed wholeheartedly in reply."[36] Bishop interviewed Eliot himself shortly thereafter. Both were sitting on formal and uncomfortable upholstery in a Vassar salon during the course of what Bishop later described as a "blazing hot day." Bishop observed in her interview with Spires that the exceedingly correct Eliot "finally asked me if I would mind if he undid his tie, which for Eliot was rather like taking off all of his clothes."[37] Bishop's 1933 interview for the *Miscellany* cited Eliot's claim that on a college campus, he favored "short-lived, spontaneous publications" over long-established school organs. Eliot added that such magazines were "more interesting and had more character the fewer the editors and the fewer the contributors."[38] Since these observations exactly matched *Con Spirito* to the disparagement of the *Vassar Review*, surely Bishop had been asking the great man a carefully calibrated series of leading questions.

One of Bishop's most intriguing *Con Spirito* pieces is "The Flood," which appeared dead center on the front page of the magazine's first issue, flanked by a stirring manifesto declaring the new magazine's guiding editorial principles, the first of which was the rejection of condescending journalistic misogyny and the second of which was the abjuration of the *Vassar Review*'s seemingly incurable literary stodginess. The first poem Bishop published at Vassar, after an outpouring of poems at Walnut Hill, "The Flood" features what her later poem "Roosters" would call an "active / displacement in perspective," for it imagines a community that finds itself slowly but steadily submerging under a mysterious rising tide of water. A world where all had once appeared normal or stable finds itself strangely transformed. Somehow, a kind of underwater existence continues, even as the water quietly immerses the entire community. The poem begins by describing the movement of the flood, which "finds the park first" and makes the trees "turn wavery and wet." Under the pressure of these changes, man-made conveyances undergo a strange metamorphosis and come to seem alive. The cars and trolleys are "goggle-eyed" and look like "gaping fish" as they "drift home on the suburban tide."[39] What once were hills are now submerging islands. The church steeples, projecting above the waterline, now function as bell buoys, with ships passing above them, not below. But how can there be anyone alive down there, somehow ringing out those bells of warning? "The Flood" leaves such questions unanswered.

As Eliot had predicted, such a "spontaneous publication" as *Con Spirito* would indeed be short-lived. Three of the most important coconspirators, Mary McCarthy, Frani Blough, and Eunice Clark, graduated in the spring of 1933. The magazine managed to push out one more issue in November 1933, the fall of Bishop's senior year. By then, as Bishop told Spires, "the *Vassar Review* came around and a couple of our editors became editors on it and then they published things by us."[40] Still, this short-lived outlaw publication had made a lasting impact. It had helped to launch the careers of several significant writers and editors, and it soon become a part of Vassar lore. As Bethany Hicok, author of *Degrees of Freedom: American Women Poets and the Women's College, 1905–1955*, has observed, "A reading of the three issues of *Con Spirito* reveals not only specimens of high-quality writing, but also a critical edginess that places these women at the forefront of the literary and political debates of the 1930's."[41] Bishop herself began sending her *Con Spirito* pieces out to national journals. Two were accepted and published before her June 1934 graduation, and others received encouraging responses inviting her to "keep sending us your work." On January 30, 1934, Bishop proudly announced to Frani Blough the receipt of a check for $26.18, her first payment as a professional writer, for the publication in *The Magazine* of a *Con Spirito* short story, "Then Came the Poor."

Bishop put the capper on the "marriage" between Vassar's rival literary enterprises with her jaunty "Epithalamium," which appeared in a November "Campus Chat." Bishop's first line invokes the Greek god of marriage. Her second line deploys a rhyme that might have made Cole Porter blush. And her fourth line turns a popular adage about marriage on its head.

Hymen, Hymen. Hymenaeus,
Twice the brains and half the spaeus.
Con Spirito *and the* Review
Think one can live as cheap as two.
Literature had reached a deadlock,
Settled now by holy wedlock,
And sterility is fled.
Bless the happy marriage bed.[42]

The union of Vassar's two warring literary magazines may have been a marriage of convenience, but it still proved fruitful. During Bishop's first two and a half years at Vassar, not a single literary submission of hers had appeared in any Vassar venue. Over her final three semesters, she published eighteen, including nine poems, five stories, three essays, and a book review.[43] In the process, Bishop indeed demonstrated just how accomplished a writer she already was. She had gained confidence in herself and in her friends as authors. And as Bishop herself recalled, "We had a wonderful time doing it, while it lasted."[44]

In her junior year at Vassar, Bishop developed one important relationship that was not tied to her efforts on *Con Spirito*. This was her friendship, later a romantic partnership, with Louise Crane. Some of Bishop's Vassar friends, including Mary McCarthy, relied on scholarships, but many others, including Blough, Miller, and the Clark sisters, were the daughters of well-heeled parents. The wealth of Louise Crane's family was on an entirely different scale. Louise was the product of her father Winthrop Crane's second marriage, to Josephine Boardman. Louise was the youngest of four Crane siblings, and—since the family patriarch was sixty when Louise was born—she was the child of her father's old age. Winthrop Crane developed his own father's Crane Paper Company into a literal money machine when in 1879 he secured an exclusive contract to print Federal Reserve notes, the currency of the United States. At just the right moment, Winthrop Crane made significant investments in the Otis Elevator Company and AT&T, and he served in succession between 1897 and 1913 as the Republican lieutenant governor, governor, and United States senator for Massachusetts.

Louise Crane's father died in 1920, when Louise was seven. Thenceforth, Louise remained under the watchful eye of her mother, Josephine, who was twenty years her husband's junior but even so was forty years old when her youngest child, Louise, was born. Josephine B. Crane, known to Louise as "Ma," was a formidable figure in her own right. Josephine Crane demonstrated a keen interest in the arts, and became the influential co-founder of the Museum of Modern Art. She maintained an artistic salon on Thursday evenings in her dazzling eighteen-room co-op apartment on Manhattan's Fifth Avenue, a base of power from which she exercised considerable sway over the art scene in New York.

Growing up in such a heady and privileged world, Louise Crane developed a character all her own. She was two years Bishop's junior and entered Vassar in 1931, a year behind Bishop. Louise was an indifferent student, and she would never graduate. As the youngest of four children, Louise had learned to be something of a provocateur. Like Bishop, she had a sense of adventure, a love of risk, and a keen sense of the ridiculous. Crane also displayed a taste for what Bishop called "slumming,"[45] and an uncanny knack for judging the intrinsic quality of works of art.

As Bishop confessed with a sense of shame to Ruth Foster in 1947, she often felt acutely uncomfortable when well-off friends from Walnut Hill or Vassar dropped in on her at the Shepherdson home in Revere, and later in Cliftondale. Bishop admitted, "For years I was intensely ashamed of Aunt Maud, all that part of my life, I concealed it pretty much from everyone." Nor was it Bishop alone who felt embarrassment. "In my Aunt's case she was simply terrified of my friends to start with & I was aware of her fear as well as my own." No doubt some of Bishop's anxiety was tied to the transference of her deep shame over the abusive treatment she had suffered from her uncle George, which she felt compelled to hide. Of course, as Bishop observed to Foster, "a lot of children go through periods of being ashamed of their parents without any such provocation as I had." Bishop credited Louise Crane as the person who helped her get over those feelings, because she "was so nice to my aunt and Uncle . . . When I first knew her she had really . . . quite an extraordinary knack for a girl of her age for getting along with all different kinds of people and putting them at ease."[46] During her years of travel with Crane after college, Bishop would find herself moving seamlessly across a wide range of economic and cultural levels, and she even achieved a degree of reconciliation between herself and her aunt Maud and uncle George.

While she was developing relationships with a range of Vassar friends, cofounding a successful if short-lived literary magazine, and launching a career as a published author outside her undergraduate confines, Bishop was also working out a series of artistic principles at college that would continue to inform her writing for the rest of her career. One of the defining works for her future development that Bishop produced at Vassar was "Gerard Manley Hopkins: Notes on Timing in His Poetry," which she published in the *Vassar Review* in the spring of her senior year. Hopkins, an English poet and Jesuit priest who died in 1889, has been aptly described by Christopher Ricks as "the most original poet of the Victorian age."[47] Hopkins's poetry was far ahead of its time, and very little of it appeared in print until three decades after his death. When at last, in 1918, a collected edition of

Hopkins's poetry was published by his friend Robert Bridges, then England's poet laureate, it created a sensation in advanced literary circles. An expanded edition, the version Bishop would have read, appeared in 1930. Bishop was profoundly influenced by Hopkins's radically inventive use of poetic language and by the provocative theories on poetic rhythm and imagery that Hopkins unfolded in his posthumously published letters to Bridges.

Bishop's Vassar essay focused particularly on the way Hopkins "times" the articulation of his idea, by which Bishop meant the moment he chose to stop his movement toward "the poem; unique and perfect," which "seems to be separate from the conscious mind, deliberately avoiding it, while the conscious mind takes difficult steps toward it." In Bishop's view, Hopkins chose "to stop his poems, set them on paper, at the point in their development where they are still incomplete, still close to the first kernel of truth or apprehension that gave rise to them."[48] In her essay on timing in Hopkins, Bishop also cites a noted essay by M. W. Croll, "The Baroque Style in Prose." Bishop seized on Croll's assertion that the purpose of Baroque prose writers, such as John Donne in his sermons, was "to portray, not a thought, but the mind thinking." The goal of these writers was to capture not a state of settled certainty, but that moment "in which the idea first clearly objectifies itself in the mind," so that "each of its parts still preserves its own peculiar emphasis and an independent vigor of its own—in brief, the moment in which the truth is still *imagined*."[49] These principles, which Bishop articulated in the work of Hopkins and then appropriated and reconfigured for her own use, would continue to guide the development of her poetry in years to come. As she described it in a 1966 interview, the purpose of the poet is to "dramatize the mind in action rather than in repose."[50] Bishop, who was right on the brink of proving herself a mature artist, would in less than a year after her graduation begin to deploy these principles in such breakthrough poems as "The Map," "The Imaginary Iceberg," and "The Man-Moth." She would continue to find original ways to "dramatize the mind in action," right on through to such culminating creations as "One Art," "Santarém," and "Pink Dog."

One of the more unusual by-products of her early absorption in Hopkins's poetry and poetics was her "Hymn to the Virgin," which appeared in the second issue of *Con Spirito*. Hopkins was noted for his jagged-sounding sprung rhythms and his startling use of alliteration, which he drew from his explorations of Anglo-Saxon poetry. Bishop puts these Hopkins-like effects together with a distinctly un-Hopkins-like verbal assault on a neglected statuary image of the Virgin Mary discovered behind a curtain in a poem that displays Bishop's exploration, as an undergraduate, of the artistic possibilities growing out of violence of tone; in a poem that describes Mary's effigy as a "wax-faced, wooden-bodied one" who might, in a flippant and convoluted phrase, "have us to worship us-wise?" Indeed, this carven image of the Virgin is taunted with the words "Turn not aside Thy pretty-painted face, parade and meet our audience-eyes you must."[51] While by no means one of Bishop's subtlest or most satisfactory creations, "Hymn to the Virgin"—along with "A Word with You," which appeared in the same issue of *Con Spirito*—shows that Bishop was experimenting with effects of tone and sound in her undergraduate writing, a source of energy in her work that she would bring under full artistic control within the course of just two short years. And when her "Hymn" was selected for the April 1934 issue of *The Magazine*, within weeks of its appearance in *Con Spirito*, it marked Bishop's first paid appearance as a poet at the age of twenty-two.

While Bishop was exploring the original poetics of Gerard Manley Hopkins, she was also reading whatever poems she could lay her hands on by Marianne Moore, an equally distinctive poet who lived in Brooklyn. In "Efforts of Affection," Bishop's posthumously published memoir of their long friendship, Bishop recalled her efforts at Vassar to find more than a handful of Moore's poems to read. Having "read every poem of Miss Moore's I could find, in back copies of *The Dial*, 'little magazines,' and anthologies in the college library," she realized that Moore's one book to date, *Observations* (1924), "was not in the library and I had never seen it." When Bishop asked Fanny Borden, the soft-spoken college librarian, why "there was no copy of *Observations* by that wonderful poet Marianne Moore in the Vassar Library," Borden was "ever so gently taken aback." Borden then inquired, with apparent surprise, "Do you *like* Marianne Moore's poems?" Borden then revealed she was a friend of Moore's mother, had known Marianne as a young child, had found her singular, and was still her friend. Borden lent Bishop her own copy of *Observations* (stuffed with clippings of negative reviews) and arranged a meeting between Bishop and the elder poet. What Borden failed to answer was Bishop's initial question: why indeed was the work of an American poet as renowned—at least among her fellow poets—as Marianne Moore not represented in the "swell library" of a women's college such as Vassar? At a time when T. S. Eliot was so lionized that his plays might be premiered with considerable fanfare on the Vassar campus, and at a time when jokes about the transparency of his work would be instantly understood by a Vassar audience, Moore herself was living in comparative obscurity, with her work almost inaccessible. One year after Bishop's interview with the college librarian, Moore's *Selected Poems* was issued by Faber & Faber and Macmillan, with an introduction by Eliot himself. No doubt, the Vassar library would one day find a home for this slim volume.

One Moore poem that Bishop mentions discovering in Fanny Borden's copy of *Observations* was "Marriage." Bishop declared that such poems as these "struck me, as they still do, as miracles of language and construction. Why had no one ever written about things in this clear and dazzling way before?" In Moore's "Marriage" Bishop found a contemporary poem that was not only extraordinary in its construction but that dramatized the mind in action, portraying "not a thought, but the mind thinking." Moore's poem opens with a seventeen-line-long sentence that considers the concept of marriage, "This institution, / perhaps one should say enterprise," from one skeptical perspective after another. This curious yet pervasive institution or enterprise of marriage (perhaps haven, perhaps prison) is an entity alive with contradictions, "requiring public promises / of one's intention / to fulfill a private obligation."[52] After a series of such wary legalisms, Moore suddenly leaps toward the question, "I wonder what Adam and Eve / think of it by this time." Perhaps marriage does offer some temptations—"this firegilt steel / alive with goldenness"—yet all in all, it seems a "circular" or self-perpetuating tradition, perhaps even an "imposture." And for such a one as Miss Moore herself, it remains an institution or an enterprise "requiring all one's criminal ingenuity / to avoid."[53] Still, on the face of the gravestone Marianne Moore shares with her mother in Gettysburg, Pennsylvania's Evergreen Cemetery, a blank space under the poet's name may be found—on which her husband's name, had she ever had one, would have been embossed.

Perhaps not everyone would find this multidirectional poem "clear"; that Bishop claims she did shows her and Moore's parallel skepticism toward marriage. Both women exercised all their ingenuity, criminal or otherwise, to avoid it.

When these singular women met outside the New York Public Library in March 1934, they immediately discovered a connection, despite Bishop's shyness and a difference in age of well over twenty years. Bishop soon wrote to her friend Frani, saying that Moore "is simply amazing. She is poor, sick, and her work is practically unread, I guess, but she seems completely undisturbed by it and goes on producing perhaps one poem a year and a couple of reviews that are perfect in their way. I've never seen anyone who takes such *'pains.'*"[54] The younger poet soon hit on the inspiration to invite Miss Moore (the name by which Bishop would address her elder for several years to come) to the Ringling Brothers Circus. Circuses, it turned out, were Marianne Moore's favorite amusement (as perhaps Bishop had guessed from Moore's many poems devoted to exotic animals), and she recounts how Moore smuggled in a bag full of stale brown bread to feed to the elephants ("one of the things they liked best to eat"), while the elephants trumpeted their pleasure.[55] After such bonding moments as these, their friendship, despite occasional artistic flare-ups, never flagged over the many years to come.

Elizabeth Bishop did face at least one prospect of marriage during or just after her Vassar years. She met Robert Seaver, who was four years her elder, while visiting her Walnut Hill friend Barbara Chesney in Pittsfield during a school vacation in 1931. Seaver had majored in chemistry, but he had studied literature in college and was keenly interested in modern poetry. After a brief stint at teaching, he was now living with his family, working in a local bank, and feeling some frustration with his lot. Seaver had been stricken with polio in his teens, and moved around on crutches, but his sister, Elizabeth Seaver Helfman, recalled that "he compensated for this by becoming so charming, that, for instance, girls would sit out with him rather than dance." She wrote in her October 1, 1931, journal, "What a continually amazing and interesting person is Bish. It's fun to have her here: a person with unique ideas and no insipid gush." One Christmas holiday during Bishop's time at Vassar, Bishop went to Nantucket with Seaver, where they shared a room in a local inn. Because they were unmarried, they worried this might produce trouble with the innkeeper, but one evening she pleasantly surprised them by sharing with them a tray of hot grog. Seaver would occasionally visit Bishop at Vassar, and they remained in touch throughout her college years. Bishop was drawn to Seaver's intelligence and appreciated his obvious interest. He must also have had an intuitive understanding of her sexual preference, once lamenting to Bishop, "I think you would like me better if I was a girl."[56]

Not long after Bishop's exciting first meeting with Marianne Moore, a traumatic event lay in store for her. According to the Dartmouth hospital's clinical record, the assessment of Bishop's mother Gertrude's condition throughout the 1920s and well into the 1930s continued to be dispatched with the cursory words "no change" or "little change since last report." As those years ticked by, and nothing passed between mother and daughter except the lingering echo of that "frail, almost-lost scream," Elizabeth Bishop had matured into an inquisitive twenty-three-year-old woman who was on the verge of completing college and launching herself into the literary world. Her mother, on the other hand, had remained in a condition of nearly perpetual stasis.

Although Gertrude Bishop remained stable for nearly two decades, on May 16, 1934, a month before her daughter's Vassar graduation, Gertrude Bishop experienced the rapid onset of dangerous medical symptoms, including loss of consciousness, "severe seizures" on the right side of her body, and paralysis on her left. On that date, the hospital noted, "Her condition is rather poor and her relatives have been notified that she is quite ill and possibly may not recover." On May 17, Gertrude began running a very high fever. Reports on subsequent days showed no improvement. Early on May 29, the clinical record states that Gertrude's "relatives have been notified that she will not live very long." Bishop likely received an alert to this effect either directly from the Nova Scotia Hospital or from her Massachusetts relations. Hospital records on that same day, May 29, state, "Patient passed away at 4 p.m." Gertrude Bulmer Bishop, aged fifty-five, was dead. She had spent the last eighteen years in a sanatorium, living mostly in confinement on a solitary ward.

Gertrude Bulmer Bishop had been barred from a return to the United States during her lifetime, but her body was now to be "forwarded to Worcester, Mass for burial." Her mortal remains were buried beside the husband she had mourned so long, under the same gravestone. The letters on the outward-facing side of that granite marker in Worcester's Hope Cemetery read:

WILLIAM T. BISHOP

1872–1912

HIS WIFE

GERTRUDE BULMER

1879–1934

There is no evidence that Bishop was encouraged to attend the interment. Bishop wrote to her friend Frani Blough rather flatly on June 4, "I guess I should tell you that Mother died a week ago today. After eighteen years, of course, it was the happiest thing that could have happened."[57] But as her subsequent writings suggest, Bishop's feelings about her mother had not come close to reaching a resolution.

Bishop correlated the onset of her lifelong troubles with drinking to the death of her mother. Prohibition had been repealed in December 1933, and at the time of her mother's death, she was over twenty-one, so Bishop could now drink openly. In her senior year, Bishop and Margaret Miller were sharing rooms, and they had served as coeditors of the college yearbook, the *Vassarion*, which had recently been published to warm plaudits. Bishop recalled a moment for Foster that may have been "just before or just after my mother's death, but anyway she was constantly on my mind, when Margaret wasn't, that is—and I got very drunk downtown with Louise Crane, who did it on purpose." Although her recollections of this traumatic moment remained fragmentary, Bishop described herself to Foster as entering her dorm, sitting on the floor, "and I was howling away about my mother," while her friend Margaret patted her head.[58]

Two weeks after losing the mother she had not seen since she was five, Bishop was faced with the same questions confronting nearly every graduating college senior: What shall I do? And where shall I live? In her case, there could be no question of returning "home," wherever that might be. And with marriage also seemingly out of the question, she found herself contemplating the uncertain career that others had pegged her for since at least her freshman year at Vassar, if not before: that of becoming a poet. Bishop graduated from Vassar on June 11, 1934, and on June 20, Bishop told Louise Bradley, "The sad fact is that I've decided to live in New York." Bishop and Margaret Miller briefly contemplated renting an entire house in Manhattan, with rent to be shared by Margaret and her mother; Mary McCarthy and her new husband, Harald Johnsrud; Louise Crane; and perhaps a few others. But such a communal scheme proved impractical.[59] Miller and her mother instead found an apartment near the Brooklyn Bridge, and the recently wed McCarthy and her spouse would also find separate accommodations. Still, even living in New York, Bishop would have several Vassar friends nearby, and would be able to improve her acquaintance with Marianne Moore, while living at the center of the American literary and publishing industry. Perhaps she was also influenced to choose Manhattan over Boston by the insulating distance it would offer from her Massachusetts relatives. In mid-October 1934 Bishop's paternal uncle Jack died quite suddenly. In the course of a few months, Bishop had lost her mother, had graduated from college, had settled into a new career in a new place, and had lost her longtime legal guardian. Her only surviving elder Bishop relative was her ever-critical aunt Florence, who had recently spent time at the Austen Riggs sanatorium in Stockbridge, Massachusetts, for what appears to have been bipolar disorder and who was now running a bookshop in Stockbridge on her doctor's advice. On the maternal side, her mother's sister Maud still lived in Cliftondale with George, and Bishop visited them only infrequently. Bishop's beloved aunt Grace was far away in Great Village.

On June 30, Bishop took a room at the Hotel Brevoort in Greenwich Village. Not long after, she moved into a small apartment at 16 Charles Street, a few blocks west of Washington Square. On her many subsequent returns to New York City, she would frequently reside within a close radius of this famed Greenwich Village landmark. Bishop set up housekeeping on a modest scale in the Charles Street flat—at first she felt like she was "camping out in an apartment devoid of furniture, gas, ice, and hooks to hang things on."[60] After briefly contemplating and rejecting the pursuit of a PhD in literature, Bishop turned seriously to a career in writing, even as she told Frani Blough, "My affairs are all very much up in the air."[61] At age twenty-three, Bishop had full control over a modest independent income, and she was no longer beholden to her Bishop or her Bulmer relatives. Instead, she could embark on the life and career she had long prepared for through her many years of reading, writing, and extensive publication in school magazines. She would be a poet, she would soon become a world traveler, and she would be no man's wife.

Not long after the death of her uncle Jack, Bishop completed "The

Map," a remarkable poetic achievement that would become the lead poem in her first book, *North & South*. The fruit of more than a decade of prior effort and preparation as a poet, it marked a sudden breakthrough into her mature style. Bishop always claimed that she composed this poem at a single stroke while sitting alone on New Year's Eve in 1934, as she contemplated a map covered in glass. But this claimed date of composition cannot be quite correct, since Bishop sent a beautifully typed, completed version of the poem, including an apt revision suggested by Marianne Moore, in a letter to Louise Bradley dated December 23, 1934—in which she called it the only poem she had written recently in which she had any confidence.

"The Map" begins with a curiously teasing, probing quality. Like Marianne Moore's "Marriage," it looks at a single familiar object or subject from a variety of unpredictable angles. Yet it has a cool quality that is unlike Moore's more insistent, assertive approach. No one would mistake Bishop's "The Map" for the work of the elder poet. It begins with a series of assertions that modulate into inquiries and lead us almost to the margins of surrealism. For in this map, "land lies in water; it is shadowed green." But are these really shadows, or could they be shallows, standing at the water's or the map's "edges / showing the line of long sea-weeded ledges / where weeds hang to the simple blue from green"? Already, in her first four lines, Bishop has raised more questions than she has answered. She blends what she sees on the map's abstracted, two-dimensional surface with her memories of the Atlantic shoreline along which she had spent so many summers. Then, in a sudden turn, a portion of the map rolls out of its seeming slumber and becomes, or appears to become, a scene of action: "Or does the land lean down to lift the sea from under, / drawing it unperturbed around itself? / Along the fine tan sandy shelf / is the land tugging at the sea from under?"

Bishop became known for the accuracy of her observation, but this accuracy always involves an element of imaginative transformation. So many of the assertions in this poem turn into queries or posit contrary-to-fact propositions. In later life, one of Bishop's favorite books would be E. H.

Gombrich's classic *Art and Illusion*, which argues that the mind's cultural conditioning shapes much of what we see and understand. And from such early poems as "The Map" onward, Bishop would engage in the continuous, productive enterprise of interplaying art and actuality, with the purpose of encouraging herself and her readers to look at the world from fresh perspectives.

"The Map" flirts back and forth with questions that it never quite asks. Is a map a representation of the world, a fact, or an abstraction? Yet as these questions hover in the background, the two-dimensional map seems to spring to life before our very eyes, for soon "the names of seashore towns run out to sea" and "the names of cities cross the neighboring mountains," which might lead a viewer to posit the emotions of the map's creator, almost as one posits the emotions of the author of a poem. Is "the printer here experiencing the same excitement / as when emotion too far exceeds its cause"? Certainly more than a few of Bishop's poems of the next half decade would dramatize characters experiencing exactly such a state of elevated excitement. Every feature of her map—the land, the water, the printed names, the neighboring mountains, the yellow surface of Labrador, "oiled," or so we are playfully told, by "the moony Eskimo," and even, it would seem, the excitable mapmaker himself—has become animated, giving them all away, as she would put it in her slightly later poem "The Monument," as "having life and wishing." As the poem moves toward its close it poses the unexpected question, "Are they assigned, or can the countries pick their colors?" "The Map" makes no attempt to answer this question, or indeed to answer any of the other provocative questions it poses along the way. Instead, Bishop closes with a most ambiguous assertion: "More delicate than the historians' are the map-makers' colors." From the moment of this poem's composition onward, Bishop's life and work would also fluctuate freely between real and vicarious travel, just as her art would fluctuate freely, as it does here, between representation and abstraction.

During the year she spent in New York, Bishop would study art and history in courses she attended at the New School for Social Research. She would begin to draft many of the poems that now define her early mature style. Several of Bishop's poems, including "The Map" and four other poems that she later chose not to collect, would appear with an introduction by Moore, titled "Archaically New," in a 1935 volume titled *Trial Balances*. Moore had only a handful of Bishop's early poems to work with, but she put her finger on more than one signature characteristic of Bishop's style. Using her own distinctive diction, Moore observed that "the rational considering quality in her work is its strength—assisted by unwordiness, uncontorted intentionalness, the flicker of impudence, the natural unforced ending."[62] Over thirty years later, John Berryman would recall for Bishop just how keenly he had "admired and loved" her work since he had first encountered it in *Trial Balances* while still an undergraduate at Columbia University.[63]

While in New York, Bishop would also reject a marriage proposal by her admiring suitor, Robert Seaver, telling him, according to Seaver's sister, that "she didn't ever want to marry anybody."[64] Then, in July 1935, she would set forth on a steamship to Europe with a friend from Vassar College, planning a brief stay at a fishing village in Normandy and, as it turned out, a much longer stay with Louise Crane opposite the Luxembourg Gardens in Paris.

CHAPTER SEVEN

THIS STRANGE WORLD
OF TRAVEL

Thirteen months after her graduation from Vassar College, Elizabeth Bishop put the bulk of her earthly goods in storage—not for the last time—and embarked from New York on the SS *Königstein* en route to Antwerp and France. She set forth on this transatlantic voyage following a trail blazed by previous generations of American artists and writers. Longfellow, after graduating from Bowdoin College, spent three years in Europe mastering modern languages, and later, the novelist Henry James—who had been largely raised on the Continent—would make a career out of exploring the quandaries of Americans in Europe and of Europeans in America. In the first two decades of the twentieth century, such poets as T. S. Eliot, Robert Frost, Ezra Pound, and Hilda Doolittle (H. D.) built their reputations on work published in London. Soon after, the center of gravity for Americans in Europe shifted to Paris, with Gertrude Stein and Alice B. Toklas exercising a magnetic pull on a younger generation of American writers and artists. Sherwood Anderson, Ernest Hemingway, and Scott and Zelda Fitzgerald found themselves rubbing elbows in Stein's salon at 27 Rue de Fleurus with Picasso, Braque, James Joyce, Matisse, Juan Gris, and Marie Laurencin. With the exception of the Fitzgeralds,

Bishop would one day cross paths with each of these American sojourners to Paris and London, beginning with her interview of T. S. Eliot at Vassar in 1933. A year later, in the fall of 1934, when Bishop and Louise Crane learned that Gertrude Stein was to be driven to her first American lecture at the New School by Alec, the chauffeur in the employ of Crane's mother, Louise amused herself, as Bishop told Frani Blough, by describing Stein to Alec "as a simply ravishing young lady, a sort of movie star." Bishop added mordantly, "He will be considerably disappointed this evening."[1]

Bishop's traveling companion on the SS *Königstein*, her friend and fellow Vassar writer Harriet (Hallie) Tompkins, later remarked that "Paris just seemed to be the place that everybody headed for in those days."[2] But in choosing Paris, Bishop herself was not merely running with the current pack. She was following an itinerary laid out years before by her alter ego Penelope Gwin, the seriocomic penguin heroine featured in that Walnut Hill–era poem highlighted with stickers. Like the irreverent and perky Penelope, Bishop aimed to travel "much in foreign parts / Pursuing culture and the arts." As she embarked on a steamer for the Continent, leaving Worcester and Cliftondale behind her, Bishop was taking flight from her own "pursuing aunts" and confirming the truth of her previous assertion, "Family life is not for me."[3]

Bishop's voyage to Antwerp with Hallie Tompkins was not uneventful. The attractive Hallie found herself surrounded by numerous masculine admirers, including, as Bishop told Vassar classmate Frani Blough, "the male-model for Lucky Strikes ('I'll Never Let You Down,' 'I'm Your Best Friend')."[4] Both Bishop and Tompkins were shocked to discover that they had unwittingly booked passage on what Tompkins termed "a Nazi boat."[5] Bishop told Bradley that the ship flew "a small Nazi Swastika,"[6] and in a postcard scribbled on board and posted to Frani Blough on their August 3, 1935, arrival, Bishop lamented that, "The German tourists have so trampled on my person & intellect that I'm afraid I haven't much to say. I just hide away and moan and sail to Antwerp. They are simply IMPOSSI-BLE**@@."[7] Yet as Bishop noted to Frani a few weeks later, "Somehow the intense discomfort of train-trips and boat-trips fades out as soon as you get where you're going"—a state of mind that would stand her in good stead over the course of a long, nomadic lifetime.[8]

Tompkins had been finishing her last semester at Vassar and serving as editor in chief of the *Miscellany News* when the trip to France was proposed, so she left all of the planning to Bishop, whom she did not then know well. Tompkins appears to have deemed Bishop something of an airy aesthete, so she was surprised to find that her new friend's plans were all "quite practical. . . . Bishop knew exactly what to do in a very quiet and unofficious way."[9] Bishop had never previously crossed the Atlantic, but she was already a seasoned traveler, having quietly managed her own journeys around and about New England, New York, Nova Scotia, and even Newfoundland since her middle teens.

After a brief stay in Brussels (where the pair attended an exposition that "seemed to be mostly the dregs of the World's Fair, including Dillinger in effigy"[10]), Bishop and Tompkins made a five-day stop in Paris. Then they journeyed by rail to the eastern tip of Brittany, arriving by mid-August 1935 at the small fishing village of Douarnenez, a locale far off the standard tourist maps that Frani Blough had recommended. There Tompkins and Bishop settled in, as Frani had done before, at the grandly named, but in fact both cheap and modest, Hôtel de L'Europe. Hallie Tompkins enjoyed Douarnenez, staying on for a fortnight before returning to Paris. Bishop planned to linger longer, awaiting the arrival of her Vassar friend and romantic partner Louise Crane, who was then exploring Europe with her mother, Josephine. Tompkins described this coastal setting as "like Nova Scotia. It was pure Bishop terrain, a place she would naturally love."[11]

Bishop had brought with her a small library of French literature, including the poetry of Rimbaud and the French surrealists, and she began a daily routine of writing, reading, and study. She asked Frani, "Do you remember the slab of cement behind this hotel which they sometimes call the 'terrace'? It is very nice out there in the morning, lots of sun and several cats." There she would seat herself, "with a bottle of ink and a pen from breakfast till lunch every day."[12] Bishop remained throughout her life a morning writer, as her many dawn and morning poems and her frequent renderings of dreams attest. With an eye toward spurring on the literary productions of Blough and their *Con Spirito* coconspirators, Bishop urged Frani to consider placing her music reviews in Bishop's own currently favored venue, *Life and Letters Today*, an avant-garde British little magazine recommended to her by Marianne Moore. Bishop added, "We must all burst, blossom, and burgeon into print from now on."[13]

Bishop's letters to Moore were alive with the sort of imagery she knew her mentor would enjoy: "The fishnets (it's a center of sardine fishery) are an aquamarine blue, so the fish can't see them when they sink in deep water." She added, "A small circus came to town last night; the acrobats and the woman who trains little ponies stayed here. . . . Everyone in town, in full Breton costume, attended." Then, knowing Moore would share her feelings, she exclaimed, "I particularly liked it when one of the seals climbed his stepladder carrying a lighted lamp with a red silk shade and bead fringe on his nose."[14] To her old Camp Chequesset friend Louise Bradley, Bishop relayed certain less wholesome activities that she had shared with this Breton community, explaining, "The whole town is drunk every evening— you can get cognac for as little as 3½ cents a drink—and they troop up and down the docks singing at the top of their lungs."[15]

With her friend Hallie now in Paris, and Crane not yet arrived, Bishop told Bradley, "At present I am all alone in [Douarnenez]—at least I am the only English-speaking person for miles and miles. (With my French this is about equal to casting oneself out of an aeroplane with a parasol.)" For the moment, her health was holding up admirably—perhaps aided by the sea air—and she announced, "I have a regular battery of adrenaline with me, but I am getting quite proud of my adaptable System now—it takes just two nights wherever I go."[16] This long letter proved to be Bishop's last to Bradley, aside from two or three brief and friendly notes exchanged much later.

Louise Crane arrived in Douarnenez alone, and she and Bishop soon relocated to Paris, where Bishop's standard of living became decidedly more upscale. Crane and Bishop rented an apartment at 58 Rue de Vaugirard. Even so, Bishop wrote to Frani Blough, "In spite of the fact that we have *seven* rooms, five fireplaces, and a cook, it will not cost me as much as living on Charles Street did." Perhaps this is why so many American writers and artists seemed to be finding their way to Paris in the mid-1930s. As Bishop explained, "The house is right at the corner of the Luxembourg Gardens, where we walk and look at the fountains and dahlia and babies—and the violent croquet matches going on among cabdrivers and professors at the Sorbonne, I think, from appearances." Bishop then reflected on a phenomenon that would become a part of her life as a writer and traveler: "I just realized that undoubtedly in a country where everything has to be *observed*—just to make sure it isn't what you're used to—of course you get tired."[17]

Crane and Bishop's landlady was Clara Longworth de Chambrun, an American from a prominent Ohio family who had married the French count Aldebert de Chambrun. The Comtesse de Chambrun, whose own residence stood nearby, had earned a doctorate in literature from the Sorbonne and had established the American Library in Paris. As Crane characteristically explained the setup to her mother, "Comtesse de Chambrun (who's supposed to be a great authority on Shakespeare, I think—a homely, horse-faced, blunt woman, the bossy type, with all kinds of decorations in her lapels) is our landlady, and this apartment is furnished with her wedding presents, I guess—though it isn't so bad."[18] The comtesse offered Bishop and Crane a particular window into Anglo-French culture. After a visit to their landlady, Bishop insisted to Frani Blough, "I am not, never, never, an EXPATRIATE." She added by way of explanation, "We went to tea at Comtesse de Chambrun's and I met a few men—so languid, whimsical, so *cultured*—youthfully middle-aged, and reminding me of nothing so much as a flourishing fuzzy grey *mould*." But if Bishop found some transplanted Americans not quite forceful enough, certain young French gentlemen in the vicinity leaned too far, perhaps, in the other direction. "Some of the French Army lives in this house, and I am always squeezing into the elevator with a dashing young thing all spurs, swords, epaulets, and a headdress of red white and blue feathers, honestly about 18 inches high."[19]

Louise Crane's mother did not entirely approve of her daughter's relationship with Bishop. As Monroe Wheeler, a leading figure at the Museum of Modern Art, where Louise's mother was an important trustee, and also a close friend of Bishop's good friends, recalled, Mrs. Crane felt that "Louise had been carried off by her first affair with Elizabeth." Yet she pretended not to know the true nature of the relationship between her daughter and Elizabeth Bishop. As Wheeler recalled it, "Mrs. Crane always spoke about it lifting her eyes to the ceiling and professing ignorance." For Wheeler, "Mrs. Crane could only avert her eyes to its romantic overtones."[20]

While Bishop was living in Europe, she published "The Man-Moth," the first of what would prove to be a long series of notable poems set in Manhattan. "The Man-Moth" was inspired, Bishop claimed, by a misprint for "Mammoth" that appeared in the *New York Times*.[21] The poem begins by imagining a creature who is half man and half moth and who divides his life between a mothlike nocturnal existence among the skyscrapers "here above" and a cocoonlike existence riding the subway down below. As the poem begins, the Man-Moth emerges from his subway world "from an opening under the edge of one of the sidewalks / and nervously begins to scale the faces of the buildings." A figure for human anxiety in all its forms, his understanding is guided by neurotic fears:

He thinks the moon is a small hole at the top of the sky,
proving the sky quite useless for protection.
He trembles, but must investigate as high as he can climb.

Yet this Man-Moth is incapable of flight, so he pulls himself "up the façades" of the tall buildings, imagining that he will somehow reach the moon without wings and "push his small head through that round clean opening / and be forced through, as from a tube, in black scrolls on the light." His aboveground existence is driven by a single, instinctive imperative: "what the Man-Moth fears most he must do." But in his effort to reach the moon, "he fails, of course, and falls back scared but quite unhurt." The Man-Moth seems to replicate in fable form a version of Bishop's own instinctive wrestling with her anxieties and compulsions. What the poet fears most, *she* must do. Bishop's early work constantly presses against the limitations imposed by such neurotic fears.

Through her half-comic, half-serious presentation of her Man-Moth, Bishop finds a way to explore herself. After his brave, recurrent, inconclusive adventure in the realms above, the Man-Moth has no choice but to re-enter "the pale subways of cement he calls his home." When he boards a train, the doors close swiftly behind him and he "always seats himself facing the wrong way," and this train of his imagination reaches its "full, terrible speed" all at once.

Suddenly, in the poem's final stanza, the mood lightens, and its terms abruptly change, when the reader is addressed directly and given a surprising role, almost as the friend or analyst of the subterranean Man-Moth:

> *If you catch him,*
> *hold up a flashlight to his eye. It's all dark pupil,*
> *an entire night itself, whose haired horizon tightens*
> *as he stares back, and closes up the eye.*

"The Man-Moth" curiously recapitulates and transforms Bishop's early poem "The Ballad of the Subway Train," which had appeared in a school magazine a decade before. In both poems, a mythic creature or creatures move from a life on the earth to a life of enclosure in the subway. The tone of each poem is tragicomic. But while Bishop's early "Ballad" may be taken as an allegory of unmerited damnation or imprisonment that mirrors in emblematic form the most painful features of her early life, the allegorical details of "The Man-Moth" are far more ambiguous, offering the prospect of an unexpected reclamation, perhaps of vulnerability and inner purity or innocence, but only if the right kind of disclosures can be brought about. Robert Lowell said of "The Man-Moth," "A whole new world is gotten out and you don't know what will come after any one line. It's exploring and it's as original as Kafka. She has gotten a world, not just a way of writing. She seldom writes a poem that doesn't have that exploring quality; yet it's very firm . . . , it's all controlled."[22]

A companion poem to "The Man-Moth" is her "Gentleman of Shalott," published that same spring in James Laughlin's *New Democracy*. In "Sonnet," a late poem published in *The New Yorker* just three weeks after Bishop's death, the poem's central figure is described as "a creature divided." Such self-division is certainly the condition of the protagonist in her "Gentleman of Shalott." This tragicomic figure—dominated, characteristically, by neurotic fears—judges that because of his bilateral symmetry, he must be only half real and half mirror image. He imagines that "the glass must stretch / down his middle, / or rather down the edge," but he isn't sure which side of him is real—that is, "which side's in or out / of the mirror."

Bishop's short, jerky lines, with their nervous slant rhymes, comically evoke the precarious balance of the gentleman's existence. Still, he seems almost to enjoy his situation: "The uncertainty / he says he / finds exhilarating. He loves / that sense of constant re-adjustment." He certainly seems to be enjoying his apparent celebrity when he states, as if to the newspapers, that "he wishes to be quoted as saying at present: / 'Half is enough.'"[23]

Bishop's "Gentleman of Shalott" creates its own surreal universe, but Bishop also found surrealism in her immediate surroundings as she explored the strange world of travel. In "Paris, 7 A.M." Bishop turns the elaborately furnished Paris apartment she and Louise Crane shared into a peculiar environment in which time itself seems to have gone berserk. On a literal level, she and Louise were inhabiting an apartment full of ornate clocks, very few of which had been wound and were keeping accurate time. Bishop turns this into an elaborate drama not unlike that experienced by her Gentleman of Shalott, describing one early morning: "I make a trip to each clock in the apartment / some hands point histrionically one way / and some point others, from the ignorant faces." But what time is it, really? The poem embarks on an elaborate, speculative journey. Then we are at last brought back down to earth as we look out the window at the gray dampness of a Paris winter morning, where "the short, half-tone scale of winter weathers / is a spread pigeon's wing." In Paris for her, it would seem, time has begun to lose its meaning, and "winter lives under a pigeon's wing, a dead wing with damp feathers."[24] Her "Paris, 7 A.M.," with its disoriented sense of time and evocation of an oppressive climate, is surely inspired, at least in part, by a serious illness Bishop suffered during the winter of this first visit to Paris.

Likely as the result of an unresolved ear infection, Bishop began suffering from acute mastoiditis, a bacterial infection of the mastoid air cells that surround the inner and middle ear, leading to extensive swelling; in an age before antibiotics, the condition often required surgery.

Bishop became a frequent visitor to the Paris bookstore Shakespeare & Company, which was not far from the apartment at 58 Rue de Vaugirard. Hallie Tompkins recalled that Sylvia Beach, the proprietor of Shakespeare & Company, was quite impressed with "The Man-Moth" when it appeared in *Life and Letters Today* in 1936, and she arranged for Bishop to be invited to a party in honor of André Gide. Bishop accepted, but in the end she felt too shy or intimidated and backed out of attending. This would not be the last time she felt overawed at the prospect of meeting a writer or group of writers whom she admired, though in this case, or so Tompkins felt, Bishop was also intimidated by the prospect of having to depend on her limited French.[25]

After Bishop's uncle Jack died suddenly in October 1934, she learned that she would be receiving an unexpected inheritance. She decided to put this money into a clavichord from the workshop of Arnold Dolmetsch, the famous builder of replicas of early classical music instruments. Dolmetsch had been celebrated in essays and poems by Ezra Pound, and in more than one way, the clavichord was an ideal keyboard instrument for Elizabeth

Bishop. Johann Sebastian Bach appreciated the clavichord because, unlike a harpsichord, it could play both loud and soft. But the volume this instrument produced, even at its loudest, was very small, so it was used not for public performance but for private study or for the enjoyment of a few friends listening together in a quiet room. Moreover, it excelled at the work of the baroque masters—a period style to which Bishop was strongly attracted. Perhaps most important of all, it was comparatively small and portable. A frequent traveler could transfer it from one location to another with appropriate planning. When the Dolmetsch clavichord was completed, Bishop had it shipped to her apartment in Paris. Bishop, Louise, and their servant, Simone, engaged in a series of contortions as they struggled to extract the clavichord from its case for the first time. The readily amused Simone, who was frequently heard tittering at the peculiarities of her American employers, exclaimed that "it was just like pulling a body out of a coffin."[26] The instrument was green, and Bishop was pleased that unlike some Dolmetsch clavichords, it was not painted with excessive elaboration. Throughout Bishop's later travels, the transportation of her clavichord to her current place of residence continued to be a matter of some concern.

While remaining in Paris, Bishop continued writing. She explored not only her European experience, writing chiefly in a surrealistic vein, but also her memories of Nova Scotia, for which she used a more realistic style. She had hopes of turning her "Reminiscences of Great Village," which ultimately became the basis for the story "In the Village," into a novel, but such was not to be. She did, on the other hand, produce a short story, "The Baptism," for *Life and Letters Today* that presents a fictionalized version of her mother's mental breakdown. In the story, three unmarried sisters, Lucy, Emma, and Flora, attempt to weather a harsh Nova Scotia winter together in a small cabin. In this enclosed environment, Lucy, the youngest, begins to suffer from religious mania, as Bishop's mother, Gertrude, did during her 1916 mental breakdowns. At last, Lucy feels born again and insists on being baptized in the nearby river, just after the ice begins to break. Her health is fragile and Lucy's sisters fear for her life. After Lucy is baptized in the freezing water, a cold settles into her chest and she rests on a couch in the kitchen. As the story puts it, "One afternoon they thought she had a high fever. Late in the day God came again into the kitchen. Lucy went toward the stove, screaming." Lucy is badly burned as she embraces the stove, and dies the next day, calling her sisters' names as she passes. Ironically, "the day she was buried was the first pleasant day in April."27 Had Lucy been able to wait a few days for her baptism, she might have survived. The parallels between the religious mania of the fictional Lucy and that of Bishop's mother are unmistakable. And the fact that Bishop published this story three years after the sudden death of her mother suggests that she was continuing to brood over the link between her mother's breakdown and her death.

Even as Bishop was working busily on published and unpublished writings in prose and verse, her travels across Europe continued. She sent a postcard image of Piccadilly Circus to Frani Blough in March 1936 while aboard a paquebot (or mail ship) heading for North Africa. Bishop had not entirely enjoyed her first visit to England, and she remarked on her card, "Since last week your fondness for England has made me feel a little suspicious of you." In May 1936, Bishop wrote to Moore at a moment when evidence of the coming Spanish Civil War loomed over their travels. A priest commented to her and Louise that Holy Week processions were being held for tourists, "but not for *God*."28 By July 1936, not long after they had left Spain, the first shots of the Spanish Civil War were being fired. Soon, Crane and Bishop were on a liner heading back to the United States. They arrived in New York in June.

While in New York, Bishop continued to improve her acquaintance with Marianne Moore. Living in Lower Manhattan, Bishop was just a short subway ride from Moore's apartment at 260 Cumberland Street, which she later described as an "ugly yellow brick building with a light granite stoop," within which Moore led a rich but circumscribed life.[29] In "Efforts of Affection," a memoir Bishop composed near the end of her life, she describes in detail the world that Moore had created for herself in this apartment, watched over by her intelligent but old-fashioned mother with her protective instincts. She enjoyed "the peculiar way Marianne had of pronouncing my Christian name, coming down very hard on the second syllable. E*liz*abeth. I liked this, especially as an exclamation, when she was pretending to be shocked by something I had said."[30] Moore was guided by a very personal set of moral dictates and obligations, rules she imposed upon herself that others might not see the need for. One of these rules was that her visitors should be reimbursed the cost of the subway fare to Brooklyn, so she had a dish of nickels sitting out and all her visitors were expected to take these as they departed. Bishop did as she was told, and Moore announced to other guests that Elizabeth "is an aristocrat. She takes the nickel." The parallels and differences between Bishop and Moore were extensive. Both were completely dedicated to their art. Each had evolved her own technique and worked according to her own particular standards, and both were keen observers of animals and devoted chroniclers of the natural world.

Both were also original moralists. However, Moore's private rules were at once stricter and more eccentric than Bishop's, both as she applied them to herself and as she measured people, objects, and animals against them. Moore was also totally involved in her family life—tied for good and ill to her relationships with her mother and brother. Moore, too, as Bishop said, had little time for "the tender passion," whereas love and its complications remained a powerful concern for Elizabeth Bishop. Indeed, Bishop learned to her dismay that her former suitor, Bob Seaver, in the grip of a deep depression, died on November 21, 1936—an apparent suicide. A few days following his death, as she told Barbara Chesney, she received a postcard in the mail from Seaver bearing the words, "Go to hell, Elizabeth."[31]

In January 1937 Bishop set out on an adventure to Florida with Louise Crane, who loved fishing. She wrote to her mentor, from the Keewaydin Fishing Camp near Naples, Florida, "From the few states I have seen, I should now immediately select Florida as my favorite . . . it is so wild."[32] There she met a pair of newlyweds who would become her lifelong friends, Charles and Charlotte Russell (known to Bishop as Red and Sha-Sha), owners of the Keewaydin Fishing Camp and experts at sailing and fishing. Bishop wrote of a memorable excursion she took from this camp: "The purpose of my trip to Fort Myers was to see Ross Allen wrestle with an alligator and give a lecture on, and exhibit of, snakes." She wished Moore could have witnessed this: "I'm sure you would have liked it. [Allen] had two tremendous diamond-back rattlers; they popped balloons with their fangs, and you could see the venom springing out—it was in a floodlight." Then, in a sentence that Moore might have written almost as easily as her protégé, Bishop noted, "the rattling sounded like a sewing machine."[33] Bishop added, again correctly reading her audience, "Did you know—I didn't before—that when the puff adder plays dead and rolls on his back, a little blood actually trickles from his mouth?"[34]

While Bishop was exploring the fauna of Florida with the help of local experts noted for their showmanship, she was also offering an ambivalent response to the politically centered poetry of her time. Having recently returned from Spain at a time when it was about to explode into civil war, she volunteered to help the poet and translator Rolfe Humphries by translating poems emerging from the Republican side of the conflict. But having scanned some of the poems in question, she felt she could not proceed because the items she had been given didn't work sufficiently as poems. She said, in fact, "I feel that a simple obituary notice would be more moving."[35] Bishop herself would frequently engage political issues in her work, but characteristically, she embedded these in a detailed web of vivid natural or cultural observation, and she never wrote a single poem that could be termed polemical.

Bishop's own poetry of the mid-1930s was dealing not so much with the immediate present as the subterranean effects of her own past losses and traumas. And a poet to whom she felt particularly drawn as she explored these experiences was the great seventeenth-century religious poet George Herbert, who was, from Bishop's adolescence onward, one of her personal favorites. Bishop rarely traveled without Herbert's verse collection *The Temple* close at hand.

When Bishop, along with fifty other living poets, was asked by the poet and critic Richard Howard, the editor of the volume *Preferences*, to pair one poem by herself with a poem from the past, she selected her own "In the Waiting Room" and George Herbert's "Love Unknown." Herbert's poem involves a speaker who has passed through a series of uncanny religious trials, and who now complains of his sufferings to a friend. His heart has been twice removed from his body, once to be cleansed in a flowing font and once to be rendered in a fiery cauldron. When he takes to his bed to try to recover from these ordeals, he finds that the bed is stuffed with thorns. His interlocutor then interprets the significance of these trials—trials that have been imposed on him by his master (God) to help him achieve spiritual redemption. "Truly, Friend," the interlocutor replies, "For ought I hear, your Master shows to you / More favour than you wot of." This favor takes the form of suffering that leads to moral purgation and, ultimately, toward salvation, for "the Font did only, what was old, renew" and "the Caldron suppled, what was grown too hard." Likewise, "the Thorns did quicken, what was grown too dull." This interpretation is consistent with the Calvinist view that God visits the most intense trials as acts of grace on those he wishes most to save, and Herbert's poem expounds the point that each of God's trials "did but strive to mend, what you had marr'd." And so, as the poem concludes:

> *Wherefore be cheer'd, and praise him to the full*
> *Each day, each hour, each moment of the week,*
> *Who fain would have you be, new, tender, quick.*[36]

Bishop's lifelong affinity for Herbert is a natural one. She shared with him a sense of the emblematic significance of common things. Although Bishop was no churchgoer, Christian motifs appear throughout her poetry. She had a religious nature and education, and the foundations of her work are recognizably Christian. Her writing stresses the virtues of humility, patience, and renunciation (and it exposes false pretenses to those virtues). Like Herbert's "Love Unknown," Bishop's "The Weed" takes inspiration from the emblem of the tortured heart. Herbert's emblem fits into a well-established tradition illustrating a painful yet ultimately reassuring moral: the value, in Christian terms, of purging the heart's sins through the refining fires of divine love. Bishop was drawn to the idea that suffering had meaning, but she was in no way certain such meanings could be discovered. The enigma the heart presents in "The Weed" is consistent with the bitter mystery of *human* love. Herbert's "Love Unknown" ends with a definite Christian moral; Bishop adopted the last three words of "Love Unknown" as a kind of talisman. In 1964, she wrote to Anne Stevenson, "My outlook is pessimistic. I think we are still barbarians, barbarians who commit a hundred indecencies and cruelties every day of our lives, as just possibly future ages may be able to see. But I think we should be gay in spite of it, sometimes even giddy—to make life endurable and to keep ourselves 'new, tender, quick.'"

Like Herbert, Bishop suggests that only a lively and disciplined spirit can see aright. And she reconfigured Herbert's message in her own terms in her poem "The Weed," which was written during her year of travels, and which she worked over carefully with Marianne Moore before it was published in February 1937. Suffering has value, the poem suggests. If there is a moral in "The Weed," however, it is more uncertain. Bishop's weed, which grows in a severed human heart, seems triumphant.

> *The weed stood in the severed heart.*
> *"What are you doing there?" I asked.*
> *It lifted its head all dripping wet*
> *(with my own thoughts?)*

and answered then: "I grow," it said,
"but to divide your heart again."[37]

Given the moribund state of the speaker at the poem's opening, and the speaker's growing, uneasy consciousness of the weed's invasive progress, it is not impossible to read the weed's presence as a call for the sleeper to awaken and take the chance of life.

When Bishop and Crane set sail in late May 1937 aboard the *Britannic*, they agreed to make a return trip to Paris via the British Isles. They stopped briefly in Ireland, disembarking in Cork on June 5 and spending a night in Dingle Harbor, a setting that would emerge more than a decade later in a published poem. Journeying then to London, Bishop and Crane caught up with Margaret Miller, who had planned to meet them in England and to accompany them to France. Together the three of them crossed the channel. Crane acquired a car, and they drove on to Paris.[38]

Using Paris as a base, the three toured France together in the course of a halcyon summer, with Crane driving. They were having what Bishop described to Frani Blough as "an extremely nice time"—that is, until an accident occurred on July 19 that would change the course of Margaret Miller's life and haunt Bishop's, too, for years to come. As Bishop described it to Blough, "We were going quite fast, but" as they entered a curve, "we were overtaken and passed by an enormous heavy sedan that pushed us away off the narrow road." The car then skidded on a patch of sand. Bishop explained, "There was really nothing Louise could do—for a second it seemed just like an ordinary skid, and she said 'Hold tight!' and then we hit a deep grassy ditch." Bishop explained that their car turned over, throwing them all out, then righted itself. Bishop and Louise were unhurt, but they were terrified to discover that Margaret's right arm, which may have been hanging over the edge of the car, had been completely cut off halfway between wrist and elbow.

Bishop lamented, "It was absolutely the most gratuitously cruel and freakish accident I have ever heard of, and why in God's name it had to be *Margaret*——." As each of them stood in shock, the other car was quickly backing up to help them, and two men working in a field came running over as well. Bishop felt that the younger of them "undoubtedly saved Margaret's life. In half a minute he made a tourniquet." Then they got Margaret and Louise into the other car, and started for the doctor in the next town. Margaret was hospitalized, at first locally, then at the American hospital in Paris. It was a slow and difficult recovery. Bishop recalled her experience after Margaret, Louise, and the French drivers set off in search of the doctor: "I sat at the roadside for about an hour, surrounded by the morbid crowds." When the village priest arrived, "he looked at me, over his regular drunkard's nose—and I was really covered with blood—and said 'Were you all women?' I said 'Oui,' and he said 'That explains it—no man along,' and turned on his heel and walked off."[39]

Margaret Miller insisted that her mother not be told the whole truth. It therefore fell to Bishop to wire Mrs. Miller only that Margaret's right arm had suffered a fracture. She enjoined Frani Blough to strict secrecy about Margaret's actual loss of her right arm, but Bishop appears to have suspected that the full truth might somehow leak out. When she met Mrs. Miller at the dock in Le Havre in early August, "I discovered only after 15 minutes conversation . . . that she still thought it was only a broken arm." So it was she who had to break the truth to Margaret's mother. As she observed to Blough, "I now know what it feels like to be a murderer. Poor Mrs. Miller fainted, and I had an awful time bringing her to (although she thinks it was just for a second) but immediately afterwards she was very good and brave, and has tried to be so ever since, although we are terribly worried about her." In her letter to Blough, Bishop, still passionately in love with Margaret despite her affair with Crane, sounded almost jealous toward Margaret's mother and possessive toward her friend. "I am so afraid Mrs. Miller is bad for her—although she (Mrs. M.) tries very hard." Still, Bishop added, perhaps implausibly, "Her absolute devotion and her solicitude make poor Margaret feel worse, I think." Was Bishop displaying wishful thinking about her own absent mother, who was not available to drop everything and cross the Atlantic when her daughter was in need, when Bishop wrote "'Mother love'—isn't it awful"? Still, her following comment to Frani was surely at least partly true, in the wake of recent events: "I long for an Arctic climate where no emotions of any sort can possibly grow,—always excepting disinterested 'friendship' of course—."[40]

Margaret Miller stayed with her mother near the Seine River in Paris while she was recovering, and when she and Bishop walked in the city, they often stopped at the Quai d'Orléans, on the Île Saint-Louis, which looks out over the Seine in the direction of the nearby Cathédrale Notre-Dame de Paris. But in Bishop's poem "Quai d'Orléans," which she later dedicated to Margaret Miller, she focuses not on the cathedral but on the pattern of images in the moving waters of the Seine, as the river traffic stirs the water's surface. The poem might be called a reflection on reflections. The poem offers a series of teasingly contrary-to-fact statements that nonetheless capture the experience of watching water traffic move in its stately progress down the Seine toward the sea. "Each barge on the river easily tows / a mighty wake, / a giant oak-leaf of gray lights / on duller gray." The barge may seem to be towing a wake, but it isn't really, and the shimmering lights on the water may look like oak leaves, but they are really just reflections. Still, just behind these reflected images, "real leaves are floating by, down to the sea." Some of these leaves or ripples "make / for the sides of the quai, to extinguish themselves / against the walls." Bishop closes her poem with the cryptic words "but for life we'll not be rid / of the leaves fossils."

Bishop is suggesting to her friend Margaret Miller that they may never forget all the unspoken feelings and thoughts that have passed between them—remaining like fossils in Bishop's own memory, at least, even as they appear to be melting away so quietly. Bishop's Greenwich Village friend Harold Leeds would later recall that "We went with Margaret to spend the day at Vassar. Margaret would talk about such things as the marble on the toilet stall and she and Elizabeth would disagree about what the figuration in the marble resembled." Leeds's partner, Wheaton Galentine, added that an image that Bishop and Miller debated "was a fossil they had fantasized on the toilet wall."[41] The men's and ladies' bathrooms underneath the stairs on either side of the entrance to the Vassar College library, where Bishop's papers are now held, still have marble walls streaked with brown patterns that look much like oak leaves. Bishop's "Quai d'Orléans" depicts more than just a scene in Paris; she includes the "giant oak-leaves" on the wall of a Vassar College lavatory that Bishop and Miller had studied and tried to interpret in a less august setting, but under happier circumstances.

During Margaret Miller's long recovery, the legal case connected to her accident dragged on. As of August 21, Bishop was writing to Blough, "I think we will be in Paris forever." She added that there would have to be a trial "and the possibility of Louise being sent to jail!"[42] Crane's lawyers believed it would be easy to prove that the car that had pushed Crane's off the road was really at fault. However, Miller needed to collect her considerable medical expenses from Crane's insurance company. So, as Bishop explained, "Louise has to be convicted of negligence, etc., and take whatever the French law does to her."[43] After a closely managed trial, the judge cried out "Guilty!" However, Crane was not jailed. Instead, she paid only a small fine. Following this courtroom drama, the slowly recuperating Margaret Miller appears to have become restive in the presence of her anxiously attentive friends, and at her insistence, she was left in the care of her mother, while Bishop and Crane made a brief trip to Arles en Provence.[44]

After a return to Paris, Bishop wrote to Blough from the Hotel d'Angleterre in Rome: "You see we finally did get off to Italy, leaving Margaret & her mother at the Hotel de Seine, where I hope to God they are all right."[45] Bishop herself had been far from well in Paris, being hospitalized this time for asthma: "The asthma got worse and worse until my limbs were quite sievelike with needle punctures." Adrenaline is a short-acting form of relief that must sometimes be administered several times a day. The injections of adrenaline (and later of cortisone) that Bishop received or administered to herself over the course of a lifetime surely numbered in the thousands. Yet now, in Rome, she was suddenly "perfectly all right."[46] Bishop could never with certainty predict when or why asthma might strike her, how severe the attack might be, or when or why it might fade away.

Bishop and Crane planned to depart for New York from Rome in early December, but Bishop could still hardly bear to leave Margaret behind. No doubt her feelings involved a mixture of possessiveness, distress over her friend's suffering, anxiety, and survivor's guilt. Lingering with Crane in Genoa, she kept expecting Margaret to call her back to Paris, even on the day before the American ship SS *Exeter* was booked to sail. Once aboard ship, her sense of humor and sense of adventure returned. She wrote to Blough on December 10, "This boat is so *silly*. . . . It is all very American, and they seem to keep up so much 'tradition' about their exclusive services, etc., that it is in some ways like visiting Mt. Vernon." When the *Exeter* docked for a brief stay in Marseilles, she and Crane were "warned by the clean-cut, young, gum-chewing purser (everyone is awfully 'clean-cut') that, if we go ashore, to take a taxi immediately and not to go over there on the right because it is the toughest part of Marseilles. Of course we can hardly wait."[47] Within two weeks, she was home. On December 27, 1937, Bishop wrote to the poet and critic Horace Gregory from the Murray Hill Hotel in New York, "I have returned to my native land."[48]

CHAPTER EIGHT

THE STATE WITH
THE PRETTIEST NAME

When they made their initial journey south to Key West from mainland Florida by water in early 1937, Bishop and Louise Crane, both avid fishermen, were lured by tales of the spectacular fishing. Bishop promptly wrote to Frani Blough describing Key West in glowing terms, adding, "I hope [it] will be my permanent home someday."[1] As Bishop later told an interviewer, "I liked living there. The light and blaze of colors made a good impression on me, and I loved the swimming." She noted, "The town was absolutely broke then. Everybody lived on the W.P.A. I seemed to have a taste for impoverished places in those days."[2] Along with cheap rents, Key West, with its warm and comparatively dry climate, offered Bishop a possible release from the struggle for breath she experienced due to chronic asthma.

The island of Key West is the largest and southernmost extremity of a long chain of small, elongated islands (or keys) arching gracefully southward and westward for one hundred miles off the lower tip of Florida and into the Gulf of Mexico. Though incorporated as a city in the early nineteenth century, Key West even now retains something of the character of a distinct and individualistic village. It is easy to feel uncertain about what sort of civic entity Key West actually is, for when Franklin Roosevelt visited the island in 1939, he made what Bishop facetiously termed "the awful mistake" of praising Key West as "this pleasant village."[3] Bishop was amused as well when the Key West *Citizen* diplomatically but firmly altered FDR's reference so that it read "this pleasant city." If one stands at the center of this city or village and walks briskly in any direction for fifteen minutes, one will find oneself facing the sea.

Far from Manhattan's madding crowd, Bishop found a quiet setting where she might concentrate productively. Here, too, almost uniquely in America, she found a place where authorship tended to be recognized as a genuine profession. Ernest Hemingway was then and still remains Key West's most famous citizen. An author's non-writing hours might be filled with outdoor activities or domestic observations that might lead, in Bishop's case at least, to notable poems. And for writers such as she, who shared a taste for funky nightlife, that too might be readily discovered in Key West.

Lynn Mitsuko Kaufelt, author of *Key West Writers and Their Houses*, has observed that the island draws writers who find it "reminiscent of some ideal childhood world where one can wear short pants, polo shirts, and sneakers all of the time and stay home from school."[4] The island also offered attractions for a woman writer with a preference for other women. According to lifelong resident Dave Gonzales, executive director of the Hemingway Home and Museum, there is an old saying on the island that "in Key West, even the one-way streets go both ways."[5] For Bishop, life in Key West offered a more relaxed, sunnier, and more tropical return to her cherished childhood world of Nova Scotia—a warmer and more bohemian Great Village, without the looming Presbyterian church steeple across the village common and almost free, perhaps, from the haunting echoes of her mother's scream.

When Bishop and Louise Crane made their first brief visit to Key West, they arrived after sailing southward from the Keewaydin Fishing Camp in Naples, Florida, where Bishop had formed a close friendship with the camp's owners, Red and Charlotte Russell. After their arrival, she and Crane enlisted the services of the now-legendary Captain Eddie "Bra" Saunders. Bishop fairly gushed to Frani Blough, "By good luck we happened to get the best Captain to take us fishing that there is." She added, "He has been Ernest Hemingway's, my dear, for years and years (Ernest lives here now) and Dos Passos (the BIG MONEY was *written* there)." Bishop added further, "Captain Bra (his rather odd name) told us a story that we recognized as having been taken down verbatim by Ernest in his last book of stories." Key West had been devastated by the Great Depression, and Julius Stone, Franklin Roosevelt's chosen director of Federal Emergency Relief Administration on the island, had orchestrated what would prove to be a highly successful effort to rebuild the island's faltering economy based on an increase in tourism.

Robert Frost and Wallace Stevens had independently arrived on the island in the winter of 1935 and were surprised to find themselves next-door neighbors. This famous pair of modernist masters spent many afternoons in a give-and-take regarding their very different notions of the theory and practice of poetry.[6] Stevens, unlike Frost, would soon find ways to turn the island into a source of inspiration for such major poems as "The Idea of Order at Key West," which appeared within a year of his first arrival. In 1936, during his second winter there, the fifty-seven-year-old Stevens and the thirty-seven-year-old Hemingway, each having had a few too many, engaged in a now-legendary fistfight that temporarily bruised the dignity of both authors. Following a morning-after apology session during which they swore one another to secrecy, each boasted about the event to their astonished friends just as soon as they got the chance. Given its density of authors per capita, what happened in Key West did not always stay in Key West.

In a contemporaneous essay, *Harper's* writer Elmer Davis compared Key West to Greenwich Village or Montparnasse because on adjacent barstools in its most popular nightspots one might find "a duke, an anarchist, and a fan dancer."[7] Still, Bishop insisted that from her point of view, "Key

West is nice, not because of all this sport and these he-men litterateurs, but just because it is so pretty, so inexpensive and full of such nice little old houses." The surrounding water she described as "the most beautiful clear pistachio color," adding that "it is so pretty when you have actually caught one of these monster fish and have him all the way up to the side—to see him all silver and iridescent colors in that blue water." Bishop concluded decisively of Key West, "It is NOT like Provincetown."[8]

Twelve months after her first arrival with Crane, Bishop returned and was declaring herself ready and willing to make the island her home. After returning to New York from France at the end of 1937, Bishop stopped briefly in Manhattan, then spent Christmas in Cliftondale with her aunt Maud and uncle George Shepherdson. When she arrived in Key West in January 1938, Bishop began a period of residence that, while never quite year-round, would keep her coming back, season after season, over the course of the next decade. Crane, who had been hospitalized for an illness after her return to New York from France, planned to return to Key West as soon as she was well. Upon her arrival, Bishop found a room in a boardinghouse at 528 Whitehead Street, run by a Mrs. Pindar, that cost her, as she boasted to her friend Frani, just four dollars a week.

One of the side benefits of her current rooming house, she told Frani, was the amusing view it offered from its upstairs veranda of her elderly landlady Mrs. Pindar's "pink bloomers, which she hangs on the tree every morning." She added, "I am doing absolutely nothing but work, scarcely even read, and the results, for quantity, anyway, have been quite satisfactory so far." Bishop was using these early days in Key West to complete and prepare for publication a sequence of poems and prose pieces she had drafted during her European travels. She worked to such effect that 1938 would prove, along with 1937, a banner year in Bishop's publication history. Bishop had been preceded on the island by her aunt Maud and uncle George, who came on their niece's recommendation to enjoy the sun and the low prices, and no doubt also because they already liked and felt comfortable with Bishop's partner, Louise Crane. Bishop added in her early letter to Blough that she ate dinner with her aunt and uncle every night, and that they liked the island very much. Just how far her reconciliation with her uncle George extended remains uncertain, given the undiminished intensity of the resentment she would express toward him a few years later in her letters to Ruth Foster.

One product of Bishop's intensive spate of writing during her early months on the island was "Late Air," Bishop's first Key West poem, which was published by *Partisan Review*, along with two important Paris poems, in the fall of 1938. "Late Air" reveals the poet musing on the nature of love as she sits on a Key West veranda late on a humid summer night, hearing the intermingled strains of recorded music wafting toward her from the wireless sets playing loudly through the open windows of her neighbors' houses, as if "from a magician's midnight sleeve," so that the singers on the radio sets surrounding her "distribute all their love-songs / over the dew-wet lawns." These randomly dispersed and interwoven songs of love touch a raw nerve since "like a fortune-teller's / their marrow-piercing guesses are whatever you believe." Her title, "Late Air," plays on multiple meanings. While "air" could refer to a song, it might also refer to the humidity of the warm night sky, laying a semierotic glaze of dampness over neighboring lawns. Bishop's experience of love known or unknown, returned or unrequited, included moments reaching back to her childhood—and also her romantic friendship with Louise Bradley and her never-quite-reciprocated passions for Judy Flynn and Margaret Miller. The experience of, or search for, love had often proved marrow-piercing in her own life, as the love songs wafting out from the radio sets had almost seemed to guess.

Even in these prewar years, the United States military maintained a significant presence at Key West, where its naval airfield was used, among other things, as a training base for pilots. The navy had positioned brightly lit warning lights at key points on the island, offering nocturnal alerts to low-flying planes. And Bishop's poem, likely written from a veranda looking out over an adjacent naval installation, declares, "On the Navy Yard aerial I find / better witnesses / for love on summer nights." These witnesses comprise "five remote red lights" that "keep their nests there; Phoenixes / burning quietly, where the dew cannot climb."[9] The fictive phoenix of Greek legend, clad in bright red feathers, was believed to nest on a remote and lofty peak for centuries before consuming itself in fire in order to be reborn. This poem's five electrified phoenixes, nesting on the navy's aerials, seem to promise a remote and cool yet passionate and lasting love—a love more lofty, pure, and permanent than any Bishop herself had ever known.

Bishop attempted to lure Marianne Moore to join her in Key West, touting the island's natural beauty as well as its quirky detail and its frugality. But Moore, never one to journey very far beyond the confines of her Brooklyn apartment, demurred. And so Bishop kept writing away busily and, for the moment at least, living almost alone. In a January 31 letter to Moore, Bishop apologized for submitting a story, "In Prison," to *Partisan Review* before it had received her mentor's vetting. Bishop had received an urgent request from *Partisan* to send in a short story to meet a February 1 prize deadline, and she had sent the only piece she had on hand.[10] Moore greeted Bishop's apology with the tart reply, "If it is returned with a printed slip [of rejection], that will be why."[11] Bishop lamented to Frani Blough that *Partisan Review*, which was in the process of establishing itself as a favored venue, had "almost forced a story from me . . . and now I wish I had it back." Far from being returned with a printed slip, however, Bishop's "In Prison" won *Partisan*'s one-hundred-dollar prize—enough to cover a half year's residence at her Whitehead Street boardinghouse. The first-person narrator of Bishop's Kafkaesque "In Prison" can't wait for the day when his self-imposed imprisonment, and with it "my life, my real life, will begin."[12] At the time that this story appeared, *Partisan* was offering in its pages some of the earliest translations of Kafka's stories into English. The story appeared promptly in *Partisan*'s March 1938 issue. From submission to award to publication, it had been only two months. Still, even as late as May 1938, Bishop continued to apologize to Moore over having submitted it without her mentor's approval. Even so, and perhaps in part due to her growing appreciation of Bishop's maturity as a writer, Moore at last—four years after their first meeting—invited her protégé to begin addressing her by her Christian name. Bishop replied in a July 12, 1938, handwritten missive with the salutation "DEAR MARIANNE," showing her mentor's capitalized first name surrounded by sparklers, as if illuminated by the lights of a theater marquee.

Perhaps Bishop could focus so intently on her work during her first months on the island because Louise Crane, described by Bishop as "a magnet for all odd people, animals, and incidents,"[13] had not yet appeared. When Louise at last arrived in Florida in early March, Bishop met her in Miami. As Crane detailed in a chatty letter to her mother, the pair rented a car and drove to Keewaydin for a few days, where they went tarpon fishing under the light of a full moon. Then they journeyed by ferry to Key West, and Crane took up residence with Bishop at the Whitehead Street boardinghouse, sharing what she described as "nice big rooms in a nice big house." Crane described Key West as a wonderful place, extolling its "row on row of the most fascinating old houses, mostly very dilapidated, & all in a very particular local style." She also mentioned that Mrs. Pindar, Bishop's original landlady, had moved on, and the house was now in the hands of a rotund, stone-deaf, older white woman named Miss Lula, who relied heavily on a black servant named Coochie, "who bossed her all the time; it's really a scream."[14] In 1941, Bishop would turn the relationship between Miss Lula and her servant into the poem "Coochie." By then, Coochie had died, and in her poem Bishop sadly notes that the deaf mistress failed to appear for her servant's burial ceremony, despite the fact that Coochie had spent her life "in caring for Miss Lula." Miss Lula's absence is made clear in the lines, "The skies were egg-white for the funeral / and the faces sable." And with reference to Lula's deafness, which seems both physical and moral, she asks, "But who will shout and make her understand?" Out of such unfolding everyday events, and often using the actual names of individuals involved, Bishop wove the story of the world she found on the island of Key West.

A fter Crane joined Bishop at Whitehead Street, the couple began to search for a house to buy together. They ultimately chose a two-story house at 624 White Street on the edge of Old Town, built in the island's signature eyebrow style that in Lynn Kaufelt's view "broadcast character and charm." Bishop, who all her life had been a guest in other people's houses, now found herself bursting with pride at sharing a home of her own with her romantic partner. Bishop reported to Moore in early June that she and Crane had moved into this dwelling and that "the house seems perfectly beautiful to me, inside and out." Knowing her mentor's passion for flora and fauna, Bishop added, "In the yard we have 1 banana tree, 2 avocados, 1 mango, 1 sour-sop, 1 grapevine (1 bunch of acid-looking grapes) and 2 magnificent lime trees, one loaded with large limes." She added that they had "all sorts of insects and lizards, of course," and observed that she was currently reading "a terrifying tract" titled *The Truth about Termites*.[15]

Crane had noted to her mother Bishop's discovery of "the most wonderful primitive" painter. The day after she was writing to Moore about her new house, Bishop told Frani Blough of her discovery of the work of this same talented primitive artist, one of whose paintings had caught Bishop's eye when she encountered it by chance in the window of a Duval Street cigar store. He was the Cuban-born Gregorio Valdes, whom Bishop described as "our Key West [Henri] Rousseau." Valdes was "very small, thin and sickly, with a childish face and tired brown eyes—in fact he looked a little like the *Self-Portrait* of El Greco." She and Crane commissioned Valdes to do "a big painting of the house" and were most pleased with the result, in part because it blended a plethora of actual details with appealing additions that went beyond the actual. These elaborations included, as Bishop described it, "a parrot and a monkey, several types of strange palm trees, and the sky 'all pinkee,' as he says."[16] Bishop explained that when Valdes delivered his finished painting, no one was home to receive it, so he had left it facing outward on the porch next to the front door. When Bishop approached her home, she felt she was recognizing multiple images of the house, each inside the other, receding perhaps into infinity "like the Old Dutch Cleanser advertisements."[17]

Not long after her discovery of Valdes, Bishop arranged to have this large painting of her house displayed along with a smaller one at the Museum of Modern Art as featured works in an exhibit, "Unknown Painters."[18] In part because of such recognition, Valdes began enjoying an increasing number of artistic commissions, and as a result he changed from the small palette in front of his studio advertising his skills as a "Sign Painter" to a much larger placard reading "Artist-Painter." Sadly, Valdes fell ill just a few months after his belated discovery as an artist-painter, and he died of double pneumonia in May 1939. In a memorial appreciation of Valdes published in *Partisan Review*, Bishop observed that Valdes was at his best painting something "that he knew and liked." In such paintings, he combined a meticulous level of close observation with the capacity "to make just the right changes in perspective and coloring" to give his work "a peculiar and captivating freshness, flatness, and remoteness."[19] This was exactly the direction in which Bishop's own art was moving as she sought to render her experience of Florida into words.

Bishop's aesthetic was also moving in sympathy with Valdes when she worked with the brush. An amateur watercolorist of genuine talent since her early years, Bishop often claimed that she would have preferred to be a painter rather than a poet. After settling in on White Street, Bishop began producing her own series of watercolor images of Key West. Each of her watercolors is notable for its distinctive point of view. Bishop created numerous images of the nearby and singular Key West Cemetery, including a colorful *Grave with Floral Wreaths* and the haunting *Graveyard with Fenced Graves*. Bishop's painting of a shack matter-of-factly offering "Tombstones for Sale" features a tree with bright red flowers in the foreground and, in the background, a lineup of gravestones lettered with the words "For Sale" in crude daubs of black. This image graced the cover of her posthumously published 1984 *Collected Poems*. She created numerous images of neighborhood buildings, including the sprightly *Harris School*, the structure set off with a seemingly abandoned bicycle sprawling in front and two kites soaring above. Her *Armory, Key West* depicts a large and striking bright yellow wood-frame building that stands just a few houses down the block from her home. In its current state of restoration, the building resembles Bishop's painting almost exactly, except that, as in all of Bishop's painted buildings, the structural lines are never quite square. (Valdes's buildings are even more asymmetrical.) William Benton, editor of Bishop's posthumously published volume *Exchanging Hats: Paintings*, notes of Bishop's watercolor, gouache, and ink *County Courthouse*, created after a local storm had wreaked a degree of havoc, "Downed power lines contribute to the sense of disorder. The scene is the exact opposite of what a Sunday watercolorist might select." Bishop had her own way of making just the right changes.

As Bishop and Crane made their home together, they began to develop an intriguing and diverse social circle as well. One neighbor who became a close friend was the distinguished philosopher John Dewey, a leading figure in the American pragmatist school and an influential proponent of progressive education. Bishop was very much taken by Dewey's simplicity and gentle manner, and his appreciation of and curiosity about the world around him. In a letter written shortly after meeting him, she described Dewey as "such a wonderful old man, and so *cute*." Bishop later told Ruth Foster that up until then, she felt really safe and comfortable in the company of only two men, her kindly Bulmer grandfather and John Dewey. Like Bishop, Dewey "loved little things, small plants and weeds and animals."[20] In a 1960s interview, Bishop noted that Dewey and Marianne Moore "are the only people I have ever known who would talk to everyone, on all social levels, without the slightest change in their manner of speaking."[21] She took pleasure in the way Dewey treated everyone around him with an equal level of respect and aspired to such behavior herself. When Tennessee Williams arrived in Key

West in 1941, he described the island to a friend—after a night at Sloppy Joe's—as "the most fantastic place that I have been yet in America," finding it "even more colorful than Frisco, New Orleans or Santa Fe." Williams soon found himself invited to a Bishop-Crane party on White Street, where this sometimes antisocial playwright spent much of his time looking away from the other guests. But Williams, too, was impressed with John Dewey. When introduced to him on the beach, Williams described him to a friend as "82 years old and spry as a monkey."[22] Bishop came to know Williams, though not intimately, and she also became friends with Dewey's brilliant if sometimes acid-tongued daughter, Jane, a specialist in military ordnance who would put her skills to work soon enough for the United States Army at the Aberdeen Proving Grounds during World War II.

One close observer of the social milieu in which Bishop moved in Key West was her fellow watercolorist Martha Watson Sauer, who lived on the island with her husband, Robert, a lawyer. Sauer remembered Bishop as "pretty, with beautiful eyes and lovely skin." Their friendship became rather intimate in part because they were "interested in each other's health." They were fellow asthmatics, and in Sauer's view, at least, it was Bishop's lifelong search for relief from asthma that had brought her to Key West. Sauer recalled, "Any time Elizabeth, who had access to much more advanced doctors than I had down here, would find a new medicine, she would write to me and tell me about it." Sauer found Bishop "delightful, quiet, fun, witty, not physically exuberant, but interesting."[23] By comparison, Sauer found Crane more outgoing and "a better organizer." She thought of Crane as being "brisk . . . managerial and frank" while remaining fun to be around.[24]

At the center of Bishop's social circle in Key West was Pauline Pfeiffer Hemingway, Ernest's estranged second wife. Hemingway had met journalist Pauline, a staff writer for *Vanity Fair* and *Vogue*, in Paris in 1927. Following an affair with her, Ernest had divorced his first wife, Hadley, and married Pauline. The couple then decided to return to the United States in order to have and raise children. John Dos Passos recommended Key West, and when they arrived on the island in 1928, they liked it and decided to stay.

Pauline's family had considerable wealth, and it was Pauline who, with Pfeiffer family funds, purchased the large house and property at 907 White-head Street that is now the Hemingway Home and Museum. Pauline gave birth to two sons, Patrick and Gregory. Political differences were a growing source of friction in Ernest's marriage with Pauline. She, an ardent Catholic, had backed Franco's Nationalists in the Spanish Civil War, while Ernest had enthusiastically backed the Republicans, as he made clear in *For Whom the Bell Tolls*. Nine years after the Hemingways' first arrival, Ernest began an affair with Martha Gellhorn in 1937 while in Spain covering the war. Ernest left Pauline in 1938, just as Bishop was arriving on the island, in order to pursue his relationship with Gellhorn, who then lived in Cuba— just a short sail away from Key West aboard Hemingway's storied fishing boat, the *Pilar*.

Hemingway married Gellhorn in 1940, shortly after his divorce from Pauline became final. As part of the settlement, Pauline Hemingway retained ownership of the Whitehead Street property, and she continued to live there, raising her two sons. One friend recalled that during Bishop's frequent forays to New York, she "was always buying clothes for Hemingway's boys in Macy's basement to ship to Pauline."[25] As Sauer remembered her, "Pauline was a very sociable, congenial kind of person. She was trim, neat, kind of birdlike with bright eyes and an inquiring look." Bishop later described her as "the wittiest person, man or woman, I have ever known."[26] The convivial Pauline hosted frequent parties at her home, inviting a circle of friends drawn largely from the island's growing literary and artistic communities. During the course of her many visits to the Hemingway home, Bishop studied what she called "that wonderful Miró *Farm* . . . with everything in it, trees, hens, fences, etc., and a dog barking at footprints."[27]

One regular attendee and special favorite at Pauline Hemingway's parties was a young man named Tom Wanning, who would become one of Bishop's lifelong friends. Wanning was a brilliant individualist from a good family who—though a voracious reader from childhood—had flunked out of Exeter, Andover, and Yale because of the scant attention he paid to each of these demanding schools' formal academic curricula. Wanning appeared in Key West in the mid-1930s, following his ejection from Yale, and he found a favored place in Pauline's social circle. According to one story, the young man had been delegated to make the rum punch at one of Pauline's parties. When guests noticed that they weren't feeling any alcoholic effect, Pauline asked Wanning which bottle on a nearby shelf he had used to spike the punch. He pointed to the bottle and Pauline, devout Catholic that she was, exclaimed, "Tommy, you've put in the Holy Water!"[28]

Wanning had sufficient family income to cover his modest needs, and he chose not to work. In order to dodge uncomfortable questions about his current state of employment, he would offer the poker-faced reply that he was writing "the definitive life of Millard K. Fillmore." Longtime friend Milton Trexler recalled that this gambit invariably proved "a good conversation changer." Trexler added, "Tommy was a good listener and talkers loved to be around him. In fact everyone he knew talked to excess. Pauline must have been no exception. He also told me that at the dinner table, Pauline talked, Ernest didn't, even though it was clear that Ernest was always in charge."[29] When Wanning's nieces and nephews—who found him an endearing if perplexing character—composed their uncle Tom's obituary, they found themselves stuck for a term to describe their uncle's profession, and they finally settled on the word "reader."[30]

Bishop enjoyed Wanning's intelligence, his irreverent attitude toward traditional social mores, his bibulous proclivities, and also, no doubt, his talents as a listener. In her Key West poem "Little Exercise," later dedicated to Thomas Edwards Wanning, Bishop invites her reader to engage in the mental exercise of considering a mild ocean storm "roaming the sky uneasily" off the Florida shoreline, "like a dog looking for a place to sleep in." Next, the reader is invited to "listen to it growling," and to think of the offshore mangrove keys receiving the storm's warm, gentle rain, as an unperturbed heron slightly bestirs itself and a boulevard lined with palm trees is freshened by the rain. The poem glides gently toward its conclusion, with the storm, visible from a great distance over the flat expanses of the Key West shoreline, having done much to entertain and revitalize the surroundings, and yet little to disquiet or unsettle the prevailing scene. "Think of someone sleeping in the bottom of a rowboat." As the gentle southern storm passes over this figure, we are asked to think of him, in his small boat securely tied to "a mangrove root or the pile of the bridge[,] / . . . as uninjured, barely disturbed."[31] This figure, detached from and safe amidst his life's storms, stands in stark contrast to the title figure of her poem "The Unbeliever," one of the last of her early fables of enclosure. Bishop's unbeliever does *not* sleep undisturbed in the bottom of a rowboat while a gentle storm passes by. Instead, he sleeps "at the top of a mast," like the unbeliever in a story by the Puritan author John Bunyan, and this unbeliever's recurrent dream centers on an anguished outcry: "I must not fall. / The spangled sea below wants me to fall. / It is hard as diamonds; it wants to destroy us all." When Bishop dedicated "Little Exercise" to Wanning, she was suggesting that she saw him as living in parallel to the sleeping figure in her rowboat. The tightly wound Bishop seems almost envious of this Wanning-like figure's capacity to allow life's storms to pass over him while remaining at rest and—at least for the moment—uninjured and barely disturbed.

In a brief memorial piece written just after Bishop's death, James Merrill recalled a Key West snapshot of Bishop that lingered in his imagination, showing her "with bicycle, in black French beach togs, beaming straight at the camera: a living doll."

After a day spent writing, fishing, swimming, bicycling, and observing, Bishop—along with many fellow Key Westers—enjoyed spending a night on the town. In May 1938, the twenty-seven-year-old Bishop thanked Frani Blough for the gift of a beautiful scarf, declaring, "I shall do the Rhumba with it at Sloppy Joe's—with a tight white satin evening dress—Saturday nights, and in between times, keep it draped on the wall."[32] Bishop explained to Frani that Saturdays and Wednesdays were rumba nights at Sloppy Joe's, adding that "one of Joe's 'girls'—there are six of them—is the Key West champion, and she is really wonderful, very very Latin, and fat, really more exactly like a [Gaston] Lachaise in the flesh than anyone I've ever seen." Bishop added, "The last time I saw her she wore baby-pink satin, skin tight, no undergarments, and used a small raspberry colored scarf."[33] Crane noted in one of her surprisingly frank letters to her "Ma" that she and Elizabeth had been introduced to these eye-popping rumba soirees by the seventy-year-old Hutchins Hapgood, a noted American author, journalist, and outspoken anarchist who in retirement was devoting himself to "investigating the low-life of Key West," and who, according to Crane, enjoyed performing this hip-swaying Cuban box-step with the enormous "Luisa, queen of the rumba."[34] It was surely from such tales that Merrill conjured his image of Bishop as a writer who might, of an evening, "jot a phrase or two inside the nightclub matchbook before returning to the dance floor."[35] When not participating in Sloppy Joe's rumba nights, Bishop and her friends frequented Pena's Garden of Roses, another popular Key West watering hole favored by the literati. As historian Maureen Ogle observed, friends would gather there "around five o'clock each day . . . to drink, talk shop, and gossip."[36] There were many moments on the island, too, where shifting cultural norms collided to produce startling incongruities. Short pants were only slowly gaining acceptance in Key West in the late 1930s, and Crane announced to her mother that at the grand opening of the Key West Arts Center, "it really was a scream; half of the people came in evening clothes, the other half in shorts."[37]

In line with Crane's voyeuristic penchant for "slumming," she and Bishop celebrated their first Christmas Eve in Key West "in a rather bizarre way," as Crane told her mother, "by going to a Holy Roller meeting" at a nearby church that she and Bishop frequently attended and found "really fascinating—it is very tiny & ramshackle & has colored & white adherents. There was one old colored lady who 'shouted' & 'demonstrated' so vigorously that the minister held her up as an example in contrast to us; 'Here is this old lady of 85 years who really demonstrates and there are two young ladies of about 25 who don't do a thing.'"[38] Another woman at the meeting testified that she used to demonstrate consumer goods in a Miami store window but was now much happier demonstrating salvation at these church meetings. Having been chided for their inappropriate gravitas and having listened further to parishioners talking in tongues, Bishop and Crane concluded their Key West Christmas Eve by shooting off fireworks on the beach.[39]

During her early years in Key West, Bishop's poetic style underwent a significant and lasting transformation. Bishop moved away from such introspective fables as "The Man-Moth," "The Weed," and "In Prison" and toward more representational poems that could directly respond to the exotic natural world she found around her on the island. Bishop discovered in this semitropical setting the "always-more-successful surrealism of everyday life" that she was always searching for. Bishop's earlier poetic palette had remained nearly monochrome. The mingled reflections in her "Quai d'Orléans," for example, are by no means iridescent. These watery reflections are distinguished only by subtly varied shades of gray, with occasional flecks of pale yellow from small leaves drifting down toward the sea. Though Bishop's earliest Key West poem, "Late Air," does offer piercing notes of red illuminating the night sky, these are not the colors of nature but represent the artificial glow of incandescent lamps.

Just over a year after these two poems appeared together in the August/September issue of *Partisan*, Bishop published "Florida" in the same venue, a breakthrough poem that marked a comprehensive and permanent change in her style. "Florida" grew directly out of Bishop's 1937 visit to the Keewaydin fishing camp, and it bursts with the exaltation of a discovery that is both geographical and artistic. In the poem, the "state with the prettiest name" seems to float "in brackish water." This state at least *seems* to be "held together by mangrove root," roots that when living seem to spawn on their surfaces "oysters in clusters" and that, once they have died, "strew white swamps with skeletons." The echo of Marianne Moore in the first line is unmistakable—almost as if Bishop were acknowledging her debt to Moore as she launches a style uniquely her own. This new style presents the reader with an unfolding collage of natural color and movement, while reveling in the same sort of verbal and intellectual play, including those unexpectedly juxtaposed slant rhymes ("oysters in clusters") that Bishop had begun to explore in her Bulmer grandmother's kitchen in Great Village at the age of eight.

Bishop's descriptions in "Florida" are full of playful hints at the way human observers bend their sense of nature in directions that they find familiar. Birds, for instance, may seem hysterical, embarrassed, or clowning. Bishop's flair for depicting familiar objects or actions in surprising ways— ways that link these with objects or actions just as familiar but from another realm of experience—displays itself throughout "Florida" in a manner that would become a permanent feature of her art. For example, Bishop tells us:

Thirty or more buzzards are drifting down, down, down,
over something they have spotted in the swamp.

She then suggests, with amusing precision, that this motion resembles nothing more than "stirred-up flakes of sediment / sinking through water." On the bark of a burnt tree "the charring is like black velvet." Hunting mosquitoes produce "ferocious obbligatos." And as night falls over the scene, effacing the bright colors that had proved so engaging, the coast of Florida becomes "the poorest" black-and-white "postcard of itself." Bishop's "Florida" closes with lines that seem to step directly out of a February 4, 1937, letter to Moore that Bishop penned from the Keewaydin Fishing Camp. She had gone to Fort Myers "to see Ross Allen wrestle with his alligator" and hear his lecture on snakes. Describing Ross Allen's edifying encounter with the alligator, Bishop observed that Allen "slid into the water, and went right on talking. It was quite a sight to see his solemn baby face apparently floating bodiless on the surface of the water, while from it came his imitations of the alligator's call: the 'bellow,' the love-call, the warning, and the social call." Bishop's poem compresses these details into a crisp series of declarations that bring to life the "alligator, who has five distinct calls." In her reimagining of her letter to Moore, Bishop playfully renders these calls in decidedly human terms: "friendliness, love, mating, war, and a warning." Although her 1939 "Florida" might appear at first to be a straightforward example of naturalistic description, on closer examination it proves to be permeated by verbal play, fictive gaming, and an ongoing meditation on the interwoven character of life and death. Published so soon after she had made a home in Key West, this poem demonstrated that Bishop had found a style that would allow her to represent her new experience of the semitropics—to reveal the mind in action while satisfying her mind's own cry for the exotic.

Throughout her years in Key West, Bishop remained a devoted fisherman, but not all of her fishing experiences took place aboard a charter boat in the company of Louise Crane or under the watchful eye of the celebrated Captain Bra. Bishop would often rent a small motorboat and go fishing on her own. Her 1940 "The Fish," a poem that was for many years regarded as her signature work, until it was displaced by "One Art," grew out of just such an experience. In a manner characteristic of her new style, "The Fish" begins with an economically descriptive opening, then slowly gathers intensity as it moves ever deeper toward an understanding of its subject—in this case, a "tremendous" and seemingly unknowable fish the speaker has caught and is now holding outside her "little rented boat" to examine more closely. She later identified her catch to Robert Lowell as a jewfish, a species (now appropriately renamed the goliath grouper) that can weigh up to four hundred pounds, although Bishop's catch was surely not quite so large. The poem's central mystery is why this tremendous fish was so easy to pull up alongside this small boat, by a lone fisherman: "He didn't fight. / He hadn't fought at all." Bishop offers a tour of this massive, big-jawed grouper, looking first at its brown skin, which "hung in strips / like ancient wallpaper." This skin is "speckled with barnacles," and "infested / with tiny white sea-lice." And it has become, apparently, so lethargic that "two or three / rags of green weed hung down" from its underbelly. The poem then begins a tour of the great grouper's interior, starting with "the frightening gills, / fresh and crisp with blood, / that can cut so badly." This leads her imagination deeper inside the fish, toward a consideration of "the dramatic reds and blacks" of the fish's "shiny entrails," and its pink swim bladder, "like a big peony." Then the observer steps back, to look the fish straight in the eyes, which are "far larger than mine / but shallower, and yellowed." These eyes "shifted a little, but not to return my stare."

The fish appears to be making his mark on the poet, but other fishermen have left their own marks on the fish—in the form of a series of hooks and broken fish lines, including one "fine black thread / still crimped from the strain and snap / when it broke and he got away." The speaker's mood up to this point has been inquisitive and comparatively calm, but it now becomes impassioned, and the fish and the hooks and lines begin to seem "like medals with their ribbons / frayed and wavering" or even like a "five-haired beard of wisdom / trailing from his aching jaw."

Only after the serial violence involved in hooking a fish has been confronted can the poem move to its culminating and ecstatic lines. For as she stares and stares, "victory filled up / the little rented boat / from the pool of bilge / where oil spread a rainbow." And from this oily bilge the rainbow seems to spread "around the rusted engine / to the bailer rusted orange" and across the thwarts, the oarlocks, and the gunnels

> —*until everything*
> *was rainbow, rainbow, rainbow!*
> *And I let the fish go.*

With the writing of "The Fish," Bishop was putting into action a new method of composition that she hinted at in letters to Marianne Moore but never fully explained. Her new style, melding her study of the method she found in Edgar Allan Poe's poems and stories and his essay "Philosophy of Composition" with her earlier ideas on Hopkins, baroque writers, and timing in poetry, would display the mind thinking while slowly building to an unexpected climax. Only in the poem's last lines would all of this accretive detail pull sharply together, often to uniquely powerful effect. And the monochrome of Bishop's earlier style was now decidedly replaced by "rainbow, rainbow, rainbow."

Elizabeth Bishop noted to Anne Stevenson that, "Pauline Hemingway . . . sent my first book to Ernest in Cuba. He wrote her he liked it, and said, referring to 'The Fish,' I think, 'I wish I knew as much about it as she does.'" She added proudly that even "allowing for exaggeration to please his ex-wife—that remark has really meant more to me than any amount of praise in the quarterlies."[40] Bishop remarked further to Stevenson, "I know that underneath it, Mr. H and I were really a lot alike. I like only his short stories and first two novels—something went tragically wrong with him after that—but he had the right idea about lots of things."[41] The view Bishop and Hemingway shared most closely is that profound knowledge of a thing—based on close and concentrated observation—is the backbone of literary art. Bishop makes this figure literal in her poem "The Fish," where she describes not only the surface of her "enormous" catch in remarkable detail, but also its interior, including its skeletal structure. Even at the moment of composition, Bishop saw a connection between "The Fish" and the work of Hemingway. As she wrote to Moore with characteristic modesty, "I am sending you a real 'trifle'"—a word that she interestingly places in quotation marks. "I am afraid it is very bad and, if not like Robert Frost, perhaps like Ernest Hemingway. I left the last line on it so it wouldn't be, but I don't know."[42] That last line, of course, is, "And I let the fish go." Bishop's remarkable "modesty" about her life and work, very much like Hemingway's equal immodesty, was a product of a deep-seated and ineradicable insecurity, making yet another point of connection.

Bishop shared Hemingway's obsession with presenting complex experience in simple words, and she also shared with him a sense of the value of what is left unsaid. In fact, what Hemingway states about prose in *Death in the Afternoon* applies exactly to Bishop's verse: "If a writer of prose knows enough of what he is writing about he may omit things that he knows and the reader, if the writer is writing truly enough, will have a feeling of those things as strongly as though the writer had stated them. The dignity of movement of an ice-berg is due to only one-eighth of it being above water. A writer who omits things because he does not know them only makes hollow places in his writing."[43] Bishop's masterly letters convey decisively the depth of what she knew through close observation—only a small fraction of which found its way into her poetry—and this helps to explain why there are so very few (if any) hollow places in her writing.

One of the prose writers most likely to have anticipated and influenced the famously "reticent" Bishop style in verse was Ernest Hemingway, as he'd come before her in articulating and putting into practice an artistic theory of omission. Bishop told an interviewer in 1978, "The greatest challenge, for me, is to try and express difficult thoughts in plain language. I prize clarity and simplicity. I like to present complicated or mysterious ideas in the simplest way possible. This is a discipline which many poets don't see as important as I do."[44] Yet Hemingway clearly shared that discipline, and on this level, too, the author of "The Fish" and the author of "Big Two-Hearted River," that "simple" tale of fishing and not fishing, are "really a lot alike."

A long with its waters and seascapes, the houses of Key West continued to hold a particular fascination for Elizabeth Bishop. In January 1938, she reported "a very small cottage I can look right into" belonging to a black maker of Cuban cigars. As Bishop was readily able to observe, "The only furniture it contains besides a bed and chair is an enormous French horn, painted silver, leaning over a pith helmet, also painted silver."[45] Bishop kept returning to this house to study it and also, in all likelihood, to get to know its owner. More than three years after her initial observation, Bishop published a poem about this cottage titled (after a series of changes) "Jerónimo's House." The poem is presented as a dramatic monologue, spoken by the owner, Jerónimo himself, and it presents, from the start, an ambivalent portrait of a home that is, in his eyes, not just "my house" but "my fairy / palace." This is no marble hall, however; it is made "of perishable / clapboards with / three rooms in all." In fact, the impoverished speaker describes his home as "my gray wasps' nest / of chewed-up paper / glued with spit." In these lines, lyrical phrases mix with an angry staccato to amplify the ambivalence about this domicile. Still, it is "my home, my love-nest," and its every detail seems open to the public eye. As Jerónimo notes himself, these passersby can see the fried fish on the table, ready for dinner, "spattered with burning / scarlet sauce" along with the dish of hominy grits and the bouquet of pink tissue paper roses.

In an early letter about her own house, Bishop told Moore that her landlady had reported a dramatic drop in the barometer, betokening the looming arrival of a hurricane—always a danger on this island near the Gulf Stream. Bishop may have been remembering this moment of risk in her closing of "Jerónimo's House," for she has him say, almost casually, of his perishable love nest that when he moves he takes "these things, / not much more, from / my shelter from / the hurricane."[46] Jerónimo's home, its windows wide in response to the island's fearsome heat, presents an open book for any passerby to read at will—or for an observant author to turn into a poem. But Bishop's own personal and emotional life could not be so publicly placed on display—not even in Key West and certainly not in the pages of the journals in which she published her work, especially when that work dealt with the themes of home and love.

Bishop's fascination with Key West's geography and topography, its flora and fauna, its cultural variety, and its array of daytime and nocturnal activities led her to a new style combining observed fact with exoticism, allowing her to project into verse what she called "the always-more-successful surrealism of everyday life."[47] Up until her time in Key West, she was always a guest or tenant, but she had now bought a home with her romantic partner. She had also found a congenial social circle and a culture with a range of diverse ethnicities and backgrounds, ranging from Cuban cigar makers and primitive painters to Pentecostal Christians to renowned pragmatic philosophers and onward even to septuagenarian, barhopping, rumba-dancing anarchists. In Key West, living among such casually associating diversity, she could enjoy a relationship with a same-sex partner while raising few, if any, eyebrows, at least among her immediate neighbors. But war clouds were gathering, and Key West's strategic location as an island capable of projecting defensive military power from the southeastern extremity of the continental United States would soon redefine its character entirely.

CHAPTER NINE

AS OUR KISSES ARE CHANGING

In a December 1952 letter to a friend, some years after her departure from Key West, Bishop enthusiastically greeted the appearance of Hemingway's late masterwork *The Old Man and the Sea*, observing that she "liked most of it—all except about six of his really horrible lapses—enormously. Such a wonderful sense of the sea and space." Eleven years earlier, Bishop demonstrated her own sense of the sea in "Seascape," one of her greatest Key West poems:

> *This celestial seascape, with white herons got up as angels,*
> *flying as high as they want and as far as they want sidewise*
> *in tiers and tiers of immaculate reflections*

Bishop offers a scene in which every shimmering object discovers and refracts color onto every other, so that "the whole region, from the highest heron / down to the weightless mangrove island" seems ablaze with sunlight, and among the mangrove islands one discovers "bright green leaves edged neatly with bird-droppings / like illumination in silver." She reveals a characteristic technique, serving to establish her early reputation as a master of delicacy while disguising her penchant for notes of indelicacy, and offering a framework into which she inserts a factually precise but incongruously indelicate detail that passes so quickly that it is easy to miss: her bright green leaves are *edged neatly with bird-droppings*.[1]

Bishop later claimed that accuracy, spontaneity, and mystery were "the three qualities I admire in the poetry I like best."[2] One source of mystery and surprise throughout "Seascape" is the way her representation flickers back and forth between actual things (herons or fish or mangrove roots)—familiar tropes from the realm of art—and opposing theological notions on concepts such as heaven or hell.

Bishop sees her scene partly in terms of a large-scale seascape painted by Raphael, *The Miraculous Draught of Fishes*, which shows large birds soaring above St. Peter as he stands upright and astonished in his fishing boat, which is laden to its very gunnels with a miraculous catch, as described in the Gospel of John. Reflecting water shines beneath the apostle and his fellow disciples, and behind them a pea-green expanse of sea reflects scattered clouds as it appears to melt into the receding blue horizon. The pope for whom Raphael created this large-scale cartoon was Leo X, and it served as a template for a Sistine Chapel tapestry that now only appears on special occasions. Poems made out of a work of art are termed ekphrastic, and Bishop's "Seascape" creates what might be called an ekphrastic surprise in that the poem discovers its relationship to a famous painting only after the scene has already been brought fully to life. Bishop, in a manner characteristic of her mature style, constructs a seascape that is celestial, naturalistic, and ekphrastic all at once, while at the same time dramatizing both sides of the internal conflict that she always carried within her.

Bishop embodies the other side of that conflict in what she terms "a skeletal lighthouse." Certain lighthouses in the Florida Keys are intended to stand in shallow water, not on dry, solid ground, and are not built out of masonry or concrete. Instead, they stand directly in the water on an exposed metal frame, and are often painted black-and-white. Bishop personifies a structure "standing there / in black and white clerical dress, / who lives on his nerves." This Puritanical figure, who has, it seems, but one way to look at the world, and one thing to say, "thinks that hell rages below his iron feet, / that that is why the shallow water is so warm." If this personified lighthouse is sure of anything, it is "that heaven is not like this." For him, "heaven is not like flying or swimming, / but has something to do with blackness and a strong glare." He waits patiently until night, for only then can he express himself by turning his glare into "something / strongly worded to say on the subject."

Although the lighthouse is presented as a kind of comic foil, it represented a part of Bishop, though Bishop's sympathies clearly lie with the light, beauty, and freedom of movement that she discovers in the sea and sky, pulled as she is toward the celestial beauty and pleasure of the natural seascape, which reveals its own, albeit non-Calvinist, theological and artistic authority, discovered in its parallels to an image Raphael designed for the Sistine Chapel.

Just before the paragraph in a 1940 letter to Marianne Moore in which Bishop offers her poetic "trifle," "The Fish," she observes what she calls a characteristic Key West story: "The other day I went to the china closet to get a little white bowl to put some flowers in and when I was rinsing it I noticed some little black specks. I said to Mrs. Almyda [her housekeeper], 'I think we must have mice' but she took the bowl over to the light and studied it and after a while she said, 'No, them's lizard.'"[3] Bishop's image as a quaint and ladylike master died hard, but it's difficult not to think that Hemingway would have enjoyed this piece of domestic scatology even more than Marianne Moore.

In fact, Bishop and Moore soon got into a dispute over the scatological references and other elements that Moore found dismaying in "Roosters." The argument erupted after Bishop submitted a copy of the poem for

Moore's review and Moore responded by sending back a complete rewrite of the poem, naively titled "The Cock," that Moore and her mother had written together. Bishop politely refused to accept this reworking and published "Roosters," one of her greatest poems, as originally written. They remained close friends and frequent correspondents, a token of the strength of their bond, but their relationship had reached a turning point. No longer would Bishop submit poems to Moore for her approval, as she had done for the previous five years. Bishop had discovered a new voice in which she had written a series of masterly poems. She was now on her own as a writer.

Neither Bishop nor Louise Crane lived in Key West full-time, which meant that they often spent weeks, and sometimes months, apart. Bishop enjoyed spending the fall of 1940 in a cabin in the mountains near Brevard, North Carolina, with her adventurous friends Charlotte and Red Russell. Red Russell recalled that "when Lizzie wasn't doing anything else, then she would sit and write. She was always writing something down. Lizzie liked the whole idea of the frontier kind of experience, getting away from cars and people."

Bishop would also make forays into New York, where she spent time with artists and writers such as the couple Loren MacIver and Lloyd Frankenberg, for whom she found a studio in 1941. When in the city, Bishop made her own definite impression. *Partisan Review* editor Clement Greenberg explained that Bishop was noticeable because she did not fit the standard literary pattern of the time: "I remember Elizabeth because she stood out. Elizabeth wasn't a yacking literary type all the time. She wasn't Delmore Schwartz." He added, "You felt with Elizabeth life came first." She was not concerned with presenting a marketable persona. In Greenberg's words, "She wasn't a celebrity figure, one whom journalism could catch hold of. Her poetry did it." He added, "She wouldn't have fitted in with the *Partisan Review* crowd." Perhaps most important, according to Greenberg, "I never felt Elizabeth belonged in any crowd."[4]

But Crane was spending even more time in New York, where she became extremely involved in both the art and jazz scenes of the city. And given her wealth, her engaging personality, and her mother's connections, she made for a different kind of impression. Crane was also drawn strongly to African American art and at one point had a relationship with Billie Holiday. Between 1935 and 1941, she had spent most of her time traveling with Elizabeth Bishop, and now she seemed ready to leave Key West behind and settle into her new role as a patron of the arts in New York, sponsoring musical and artistic events. Bishop picked up on this dynamic in her light verse "Letter to N.Y." published in *Harper's Bazaar* on September 15, 1940, and dedicated to Louise Crane. Since none of Bishop's early letters to Crane survive in prose, this verse letter is all we have of their early correspondence, but it is reasonable to assume that it captures the character of their correspondence, which must have been laden with droll banter. In "Letter to N.Y." Bishop refers to Crane's sowing her wild oats, and for Crane perhaps that is what her relationship with Bishop had meant.

Bishop's verse letter to Crane contrasts starkly with "The Soldier and the Slot Machine," a poem rejected by *The New Yorker* that remained unpublished until after her death. This study in compulsion explores a young soldier's addiction to gambling; he has been obsessively playing the Key West nickel slot machines, and is trying desperately to stop. The soldier claims he "will not ask for change again," and that "the barkeeper can see me dead" before he ever turns bills into coins to play the slots. The soldier remembers the "hundreds of times, thousands of times," he's added his nickels in an effort to achieve a row of winners. He associates the slot machine with compulsive drinking, a problem that increasingly troubled Bishop, insisting, "The slot machine is who is drunk / And you're a dirty nickel, too." Analyzing the interior of the machine, he wishes it could be thrown into the sea, but at the end of the poem he is still fighting his battle with compulsion.

Drinking was a major feature of the social fabric of Key West during Bishop's years on the island. Hemingway was a serious drinker, as was his wife Pauline, and so, too, Tennessee Williams and Tom Wanning. At least in her early years there, Bishop's own drinking seems scarcely to have stood out amid the island's imbibing culture. But increasingly, like the soldier at his slot machine, Bishop found her desire to drink difficult to control. She had become a victim of periodic alcohol abuse, or, in common parlance, a binge drinker. Her friend and protégé Frank Bidart would recall that much later, during her Harvard years, Bishop sometimes enjoyed moderate social drinking, and would even maintain long periods of complete abstinence. And yet at other times, she would take one drink and find herself unable to stop. Her bouts of periodic alcohol abuse could come on at any time, but most frequently they occurred when she was feeling abandoned or depressed. Heredity may also have been a factor. There are suggestions that Bishop's father, William Thomas, struggled with alcoholism, and her father's younger brother, Bishop's uncle Jack, had a severe problem but managed to quit entirely on his own. On her mother's side, Bishop would depict her uncle Arthur Bulmer, slightly fictionalized, in the affectionate story "Memories of Uncle Neddy" as "a lover, husband, father or grandfather, a tinsmith, a drunkard, [and] a famous fly fisherman."[5] Bishop recalled the temperance pledge "of the Iron Age Band of Hope" that her uncle Arthur could "recite to me years later, although he had broken it heaven knows how many times by then."[6] Bishop describes her uncle Arthur's drinking as taking the form, as hers did, of "periodic bouts." Family members claimed that Arthur's drinking would kill him, but Bishop observed that when he died at the age of seventy-six "it was of something quite different."[7]

Yet whether Bishop's accelerating issues with alcohol were brought on in part by childhood trauma or by heredity, they nonetheless had real-life consequences, one of which was the impact her bouts of drinking had on her romantic relationships. By mid-1941, Bishop's relationship with Louise Crane began to fall apart. Her drinking may have been one factor in the breakup. Crane may also have come under increasing pressure from her mother, Josephine, to end her lesbian relationship with Bishop and to return to a more conventional life in New York City. One hint of the wealthy Crane's future as a cultural doyenne in the metropolitan area may be gleaned from a comment made by a Williams College professor who attended a

concert Crane had sponsored. He told Crane that she was like a Medici—
and it would have been hard to play that role in Key West.[8]

Bishop surely knew that Crane was involved with other women during
her trips to New York, and gradually must have realized that she was losing
Crane altogether. She felt abandoned, and when Bishop felt abandoned, she
would enter a sustained state of extreme depression, which, as Crane told
friends, could involve suicide threats. The artist Mary Meigs, who became
one of Crane's lovers at a later date, only to find herself cast off as well, later
formed a bond with Bishop, since each could regard the other as one of
Crane's discards. This put them, according to Meigs, in the role of "friendly
conspirators who could freely discuss and laugh about the past and the
present." Meigs observed of the time she spent with Bishop, "I'd been
struck immediately by the fragility and delicacy of her mind and the sense
of her as a receiver of signals beyond human ears." Meigs added that "Louise was irresistible to women; she had blue eyes, full, it seemed, of innocent
candor and love of life. She adored people and parties; she wasn't an artist
herself, but she was able to spot unusual talent and to help artists with their
careers." Crane's earliest discovery had perhaps been Bishop herself, whose
career she had found ways to foster through the course of half a decade. But
now that relationship was over and Bishop would have to find a means of
moving on. As Mary Meigs commented in 1989, "Elizabeth and I belonged
to a generation of women who were terrified by the idea of being known as
lesbians, and for Elizabeth as a poet, the lesbian label would have been
particularly dangerous. One of the side effects of lesbians' fear of being
known to the world was our fear of being known to each other, so that a
kind of caution was exercised (certainly it was by Elizabeth) that no longer
seems necessary today." Yet, as would happen over and over in later years,
Bishop was soon able to identify a new lover with whom to begin again.

Without Crane, Bishop now found herself the sole owner of the house
on White Street, and she could not afford to maintain it on her own. Soon,
however, she met a woman named Marjorie Stevens who had become separated from her husband, a naval officer. Like Bishop, Stevens lived in Key

West at least partly because of her delicate health. Stevens liked to drink, too, and they began their relationship after Stevens helped Bishop up from a gutter into which she had fallen on their way home from a bar. Bishop told Ruth Foster that Marjorie Stevens had said to her that Bishop lying there with the streetlights playing on her face was "the most beautiful thing she'd ever seen." Perhaps Stevens was drawn to Bishop's apparent vulnerability. It was not long before Bishop was telling Stevens the story of the loss of her mother and other memories of her past.

Bishop rented out the house at 624 White Street and moved in with Marjorie Stevens at 623 Margaret Street in June 1941. She had her clavichord shipped there in December 1941. One crucial poem in Bishop's canon that might be located in the Margaret Street house is her posthumously published poem "It is marvellous to wake up together," an exquisite love poem that was discovered by Lorrie Goldensohn in Brazil in 1986 in the hands of Bishop's friend Linda Nemer. It is hard to be certain whether this poem describes Bishop's life with Stevens or with Crane. Brett Millier suggests the former, but Alice Quinn entertains both possibilities. The identification with Stevens may be supported by the fact that Bishop told Foster that she and Stevens were most often morning lovers. The poem describes an arriving electrical storm over Key West and the pleasure of knowing that despite the apparent threat, their house is protected by lightning rods, so that even if the house were struck by a bolt from the blue, they could "imagine dreamily / How the whole house caught in a bird-cage of lightning / would be quite delightful rather than frightening." This allows one to imagine other possible transformations from the "simplified point of view / Of night and lying flat on one's back."

The poem features one of her most beautiful endings. In this curious half world with its sudden lightning flashes and its "black / Electrical wires dangling," she finds that:

> *Without surprise*
> *The world might change to something quite different*

As the air changes or the lightning comes without our blinking,
Change as our kisses are changing without our thinking.[9]

When Bishop's lyrical exploration of lesbian eroticism was published with Goldensohn's introduction in the *American Poetry Review* in the winter of 1988,[10] it caused a sensation among readers and something of a revolution in Bishop studies.

Meanwhile, it was becoming ever more clear that the rising tide of war in Europe was going to have a lasting impact upon Key West, and the buildup began before the United States actually became a combatant nation. According to historian Maureen Ogle, "By December 7, 1941, the navy had either leased or purchased outright more than a hundred acres of land, most of it in or near downtown Key West." Bishop told Sha-Sha Russell in June 1941, "I feel so depressed," because "the Navy has bought all the land as far over as Whitehead Street." Pena's Garden of Roses, one of the favored nightspots of Bishop's crowd, was purchased and put out of business, and Bishop reported that the owner "cries and cries." Another mark of the changing times she mentioned to her friend Sha-Sha was that "Sloppy Joe [Russell] died very suddenly while he was visiting Hemingway in Havana. They closed the bar for a few days, and hung those awful palm branches and purple ribbons on the doors. Now young Joe is running it."[11]

Then, on December 7, war indeed descended upon Key West once more. The impact was almost immediate. Just two days later, on December 9, according to Ogle, "seventy-five trucks loaded with 1,500 troops rolled through the streets, heading for the army's facilities out near Fort Taylor."[12] Pauline Hemingway began to describe Key West as a "boom town," but the quiet island with its celestial seascapes that Bishop had sought and found was undergoing changes that made it difficult for her to remain. Another poem set on the island, "Full Moon, Key West," which was rejected by *The New Yorker* in September 1943, conveys Bishop's discomfort with the military presence. "The island starts to hum / like music in a dream."

What might be causing this sound? It is a crowd of sailors who, in the moonlight, look "paper-white":

> *Drunk,*
> *the sailors come*
> *stumbling, fighting,*
> *mumbling threats*
> *in children's voices.*[13]

Bishop and Stevens made a trip to Mexico in 1942, arriving in mid-April at the Yucatán city of Mérida, where they met the Chilean poet Pablo Neruda, who became a good friend. Neruda always claimed, implausibly, that they met on the top of the pyramid at Chichen Itza. On May 5, Neruda guided Bishop and Stevens to Mexico City, where he found them an apartment, and it was while observing the dawn in that city that Bishop found inspiration for her poem "Anaphora," which she later dedicated to Stevens. In August, Bishop and Stevens visited the Nerudas at their house in Cuernavaca. At the end of September, they left Mexico for New York, where Bishop remained while Stevens returned to Key West.

By the mid-1940s, Bishop was regularly shuttling up and down the East Coast, drinking more, and her relationship with Marjorie Stevens became increasingly troubled. Bishop's letters to Marjorie Stevens do not survive, but Bishop retained Stevens's extensive letters to her, which reveal an intensely anxious person and offer a concrete portrait of wartime Key West. Her letters are conversational and detailed, with much emphasis on the efforts of day-to-day living. Stevens was working as a bookkeeper in the naval station and she had monthly audits to do, which always placed her under considerable strain. In her long letters, Stevens constantly expresses deep concern for Bishop's health and welfare, though she also seems insecure about her own intellectual attainments relative to Bishop and her friends. The letters also reference rent controls imposed to manage wartime crowding, which placed limits on the rents Bishop could earn from her house.

It was difficult for the two to communicate by telephone, as long-distance telephoning was restricted during the Second World War and Bishop also seemed to feel considerable uneasiness about speaking on the phone at this time. Based on Stevens's letters, it seems that their rare, difficult-to-arrange, and expensive long-distance calls typically did not go well.

After 1941, Bishop published relatively little for several years, although her unpublished work—often on war or sexuality—continued to be of great interest. Bishop resumed publishing actively in the fall of 1944, when her four "Songs for a Colored Singer" appeared in the *Partisan Review*. A year later "Anaphora" appeared, a poem begun in Mexico, and also published in *Partisan*, that Bishop would later dedicate to Stevens. The year was marked by three more poems, "Little Exercise," "Chemin de Fer," and "Large Bad Picture." These were her second, third, and fourth poems published in *The New Yorker*, and they mark the beginning of a long and fruitful relationship between Bishop and the magazine that extended for more than forty years. With these new publications, Bishop had the material for a full book of poems, and she entered a contest held by Houghton Mifflin that received seven hundred manuscript submissions. The award included a cash prize of $1,000 and the publication of the submitted volume of poems.

Bishop's manuscript, with recommendations from the stellar trio of Marianne Moore, Edmund Wilson, and John Dewey, won the award, and her first book, *North & South*, appeared from Houghton Mifflin in 1945. The first half of the volume—mostly composed between 1935 and 1938 in the form of the surrealistic dream poems, troubled urban landscapes, and fables of enclosure characteristic of her early style—constitutes Bishop's northern pole. Her southern pole focuses almost exclusively on Florida and Key West.

During the course of 1946, two medical professionals who would have a lasting effect on Bishop's development entered her life: Dr. Anny Baumann and Dr. Ruth Foster. The first of these, Anny Baumann, would retain the

Elizabeth Bishop and her mother, Gertrude, Worcester, Massachusetts, February 1912.

Obituary photo of William Thomas Bishop, Elizabeth's father, Worcester, October 1911.

Elizabeth with her grandparents, William and Elizabeth Bulmer, Great Village, Nova Scotia, 1911.

Elizabeth, Worcester, September 1915.

Elizabeth and Margaret Miller, *Vassarion* staff photo, 1934.

"Bishie" at Camp Chequesset, Massachusetts, circa 1925.

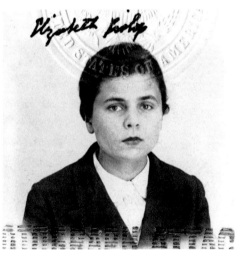

Passport photo, 1935.

Elizabeth and Louise Crane, circa 1940.

Elizabeth and bicycle, Key West, circa 1940.

Louise Crane and Elizabeth in New York, circa 1940.

Painting by Gregorio Valdes of house shared by Bishop and Crane in Key West, 1939.

Passport photo of Marjorie Stevens, 1941.

Elizabeth looking out on the roof of her "garret" apartment at 46 King Street, Manhattan, 1943.

Elizabeth at Yaddo with May Swenson and Beauford Delaney, fall 1950.

Lota de Macedo Soares and Mary Morse surveying the property at Samambaia, Brazil, 1940s.

Lota at Samambaia, 1950s.

Elizabeth relaxing at Samambaia with her cat, Tobias.

At Samambaia, 1954.

Swimming in the rock pool at Samambaia. Elizabeth noted that "I don't know whose legs those are."

I don't know whose legs those are

The granite peak from "The Mountain" looming over Samambaia.

Elizabeth outside the doorway to her studio at Samambaia, 1950s.

Elizabeth and Robert Lowell on the balcony of Lota's penthouse overlooking Rio de Janeiro, Brazil, 1962.

The view from the back porch of Elizabeth's Casa Mariana in Ouro Preto, Brazil.

Frank Bidart and Elizabeth boarding the ferry to North Haven, Maine, 1970s.

Elizabeth at "Driftwood," the seaside home of Louise Crane, Woods Hole, Massachusetts, 1970s.

role of Bishop's primary physician for the rest of her life, even when Bishop was living in distant cities. Baumann, who was born in Germany, later become a general practitioner in New York, and she had a definite gift for working with creative personalities. Baumann was willing to devote seemingly limitless time and attention to Bishop and to many fellow writers and artists, including Robert Lowell, who became Baumann's patients upon Bishop's recommendation. Robert Christ, a Bishop devotee who became Baumann's longtime patient in 1956, recalls discovering signed volumes of Bishop's poetry in Baumann's book-lined waiting room. These helped him pass waiting-times that often seemed interminable. Christ further recalled that once one finally entered the sanctum of Baumann's office, one's visits never lasted less than an hour. Baumann also willingly made house calls to Christ's West Side apartment, and she made similar frequent house calls to Bishop as well. Baumann was an expert diagnostician, and on many occasions she discovered the cause of a Bishop malady that had eluded other physicians. Baumann was equally concerned with Bishop's emotional health. Christ recalled that in moments of such concern, Baumann could adopt a tone that was: "severe, maternal," and he recalled hearing through Baumann's office door the distinctly audible words: "Mr. Lowell, for an intelligent man, how can you be so stupid?" But, Christ added, "you had to hear the compassion in that scolding, the understanding for what she didn't understand. Most times, I'll bet Elizabeth Bishop heard it all."[14] By mid-1946, Baumann had become so concerned by Bishop's depression and her compulsive drinking that, with the support of Margaret Miller, she prevailed upon Bishop to begin psychoanalysis with Dr. Ruth Foster. Bishop's work with Foster may not have resolved her drinking problem or her sense of isolation and depression, even when surrounded by admiring and supportive friends. But the start of her period of psychoanalysis can nonetheless be linked in time with the beginning of one of Bishop's great creative periods.[15]

Also correlating with the start of that great creative period is the unaccompanied journey Bishop made to Nova Scotia in August 1946, where she explored her past with her aunt Grace and made an unsuccessful attempt to gain access to her mother's medical records at the Nova Scotia Hospital. Her time there began a period during which she produced several of her greatest poems and stories. She was called back to the United States to sign papers to sell her White Street house in Key West, and would continue to return to Key West for the next several years, now as a visitor rather than a resident. Her quarrelsome long-distance relationship with Marjorie Stevens was coming to an end, and Bishop was drinking to a dangerous extent.

Bishop's *North & South* received for the most part very favorable reviews, although a few seemed notably condescending. The most enthusiastic of all was written by the most severe and exacting poetry critic in midcentury America, Randall Jarrell. His reviews could range from witty and euphoric to extremely harsh. He once wrote that a certain poet's work seemed to be produced "on a typewriter by a typewriter." But as Robert Lowell would later say, eulogy was the glory of Jarrell's criticism. When the often-prickly Jarrell liked a poet's work, he went all out, and he went all out for Elizabeth Bishop. He found "The Fish" and "Roosters," works that he considered "morally so attractive," to be "two of the most calmly beautiful, deeply sympathetic poems of our time." He felt that Bishop was "capable of the most outlandish ingenuity" but was also "grave, calm, and tender at the same time." He applauded Bishop's refusal to turn poetry into "gruesome occupational therapy" and appreciated the fact that her poems "are almost never forced." He added, just a year after the close of the Second World War, that "instead of crying, with justice, 'This is a world in which no one can get along,' Miss Bishop's poems show that it is barely but perfectly possible—has been, that is, for her." Perhaps, though, Jarrell's most insightful comment about Bishop as a person rather than as a poet is his observation that Bishop "understands so well that the wickedness and confusion of the age can explain and extenuate other people's wickedness and confusion, but not, for you, your own."[16]

Jarrell had intuited through Bishop's poems her own complex moral awareness. His emphasis on the calm in Bishop's work may have overstressed that side over the sometimes frantic or anxious elements that appear in poems such as "The Man-Moth," "The Weed," or "Love Lies Sleeping." But in his appreciation of the value of the decade of writing and further years of preparation that went into the making of *North & South*, Jarrell was for the most part uncommonly perceptive.

CHAPTER TEN

THE PRODIGAL

After her bus journey back from Nova Scotia to Boston and then New York, where Elizabeth signed papers closing on the sale of her much-loved Key West house, she took up full-time residence in her very small apartment at 46 King Street in New York. Now free from the pressure of completing her first book, she found herself busily working away at a series of new poems. And she continued to absorb the mostly favorable reviews that *North & South* had garnered. On January 14, 1947, the critic Arthur Mizener, later the author of notable biographies of F. Scott Fitzgerald and Ford Madox Ford, composed a laudatory review of *North & South* that he shared with Elizabeth, noting that he had been following Bishop's work since she was a senior at Vassar, and revealed shrewd insight into Bishop as a writer and a person. He spoke about how much her book had been worth waiting for, praised her for "how perfectly her poems balance devotion to fact and to memory and desire," and noted how "beautifully they combine toughness and elegance of mind."[1] Bishop would need both of those traits to carry her through the next half decade, which was among the most painful and uncertain, but also most poetically productive, periods of her life.

"Varick Street," one of the first poems Bishop produced after her return from Nova Scotia and the publication of *North & South*, grew directly out of the reality of her tiny Greenwich Village apartment, set on the edge of a round-the-clock industrial district beginning on the adjacent Varick Street. She later recalled, "There were printing presses across the street that kept going nights sometimes, using those pale blue daylight lights."[2] In addition, Bishop added that a Schrafft's candy factory and a pharmaceutical factory making antiphlogistine (a mentholated chest rub) stood on opposite sides of Varick Street, and when the aromas blended, it created effects "that were very strange."[3] Therefore, in an era before air-conditioning, "on summer nights, with everything going full blast and all windows open, the odors and sounds were something."[4] In Bishop's poem, these factories carry on their disquieting nocturnal life. The district's "wretched uneasy buildings / veined with pipes" seem to try, with quasi-asthmatic effort, to breathe through "elongated nostrils / haired with spikes" that take the form of tall chimneys. Within this nightmarish yet all-too-real environment, a sleeping couple are enclosed by the forces surging around their lonely room. A few years earlier, by contrast, in Bishop's "It is marvellous to wake up together," flashes of lightning playing over the Key West skies—and even, perhaps, striking the house of the poem's two central figures—become, through the protective magic of the lightning rod, not a threat but an erotic stimulant. But in an apartment adjoining Varick Street, the two sleepers—perhaps even the same two, Bishop and Marjorie Stevens—find themselves responding very differently, since:

> *Our bed*
> *shrinks from the soot*
> *and hapless odors*
> *hold us close.*

Bishop would tell May Swenson years later, "I dreamed that poem, all except two or three lines, and woke up one night saying the refrain in time to the printing presses."[5]

And I shall sell you sell you
sell you of course, my dear, and you'll sell me.[6]

She explained to other friends that this refrain, which appears in the poem three times, and closes it, "somehow seemed applicable to the commercial outlook and my pessimistic outlook on life in New York and in general at that time."[7] In that apartment, everything, including love, appears to be for sale. Bishop added dryly to Swenson that if the poem suffers from "any obscurity," that "is the fault of my dreaming procedure, I think. But I wish I could do it more often—it makes writing much easier!"[8]

"Argument," another dreamlike poem of 1947, gives expression to Bishop's increasingly troubled relationship with Marjorie Stevens—a relationship that could not exist comfortably either in Key West or in the King Street apartment. It is thus a relationship marked chiefly by separation, and an argument, which circles around itself without resolution, going back and forth between "Days" and "Distance," for the speaker faces "Days that cannot bring you near / or will not" and Distance, which is "trying to appear / something more than / obstinate." Distance is partly defined by "all that land / beneath the plane" following a coastline that carries her away from Key West, where Stevens chiefly resided while Bishop was living in New York. Days of separation seem marked on a "hideous calendar" such as those printed by the tens of thousands in a twenty-four-hour factory across from her apartment. The dedication on this giveaway calendar reads, with painful irony, "Compliments of Never & Forever, Inc." Perhaps such words on this calendar of days suggest that they might *never* come together and, further, that they might regret their looming loss of intimacy *forever*. These factors "argue argue argue" endlessly in Bishop's mind, "neither proving" her partner of the past five years "less wanted nor less dear." Despite strong emotional ties, this pair of lovers, perhaps because of an imperfect mesh in their personalities, cannot find a way to live either together or apart. Bishop brings her poem of self-argument about their continuing state of attachment and separation to a close with a sentence that finds, with appropriate syntactical challenges, "Days and Distance disarrayed again / and gone / both for good and from the gentle battleground."[9] "Argument" is characteristic of a series of jagged-edged love poems of this period. And its close, which suggests they might be "gone for good and from the gentle battleground," points apparently toward a domain where soon-to-be ex-lovers locate their differences.

At the same time that Bishop was composing such disquietingly personal lyrics as "Varick Street" and "Argument," she was also creating a series of nature lyrics—most often about the shoreline—that would enforce her growing reputation as a poet not of edgy self-exploration but of reserve, calm, meticulous accuracy, and humorous detachment—or as Marianne Moore would later term it, a "Modest Expert." On February 13, Bishop submitted what would prove to be one of her finest poems, "At the Fishhouses," to her friend and editor Katherine White at *The New Yorker*. Bishop suggested, in her usual self-deprecatory manner, that the magazine might find it "unusable," but White insisted that, "Far from being unusable it has given us a great deal of pleasure." Indeed, White promptly accepted it, describing "At the Fishhouses" as "a very beautiful poem and one that we are delighted to be able to buy and use when summer comes."[10]

Alongside such disquieting lyrics as "Varick Street" and "Argument," Bishop discussed the poem in minute detail with her psychoanalyst, suggesting that she might even dedicate it to Dr. Ruth Foster. Bishop's meditation on "At the Fishhouses" is dated simply "Feb 1947," and dominates the third of four such letters sent to Foster in February 1947. The poem begins quietly and beautifully, but most of Bishop's discussion of the poem with Dr. Foster focuses on the ending. This discussion is illuminating because Bishop seemed often to encourage only the most literal and impersonal readings of her poems, complaining, in fact, that the problem with critics is that they had "too much imagination." When pressed, she often claimed that a poem was merely descriptive, or she stated that events in the poem really happened and left it at that. Now, exploring one of her own poems in the safe space afforded by her analyst, Bishop engages in a reading that is both deeply imaginative and psychological, with a decidedly Freudian accent. She spins out the elaborate web of symbolic connections that she had woven into the poem, suggesting that perhaps she had symbolic implications in mind for many of her other works. Similarly, when she was defending the language and imagery of the 1941 "Roosters" from Marianne Moore's proposed excisions, she made very distinct claims that certain lines had to remain because of their intended symbolic importance.

The ending of "At the Fishhouses" is one of her most famous passages. The setting is the seacoast of Nova Scotia, familiar terrain for Bishop, but now in sharp contrast to her seascapes in Key West. For her the sea here is:

> *Cold dark deep and absolutely clear,*
> *element bearable to no mortal,*
> *to fish and to seals . . .* [11]

Her attention is drawn to one particular seal, who studies Bishop evening after evening while, with reciprocal curiosity, Bishop studies him. Obviously, this seal is "curious" about her. He is also interested in music, and indulging in a pun reaching back to her Baptist roots, Bishop notes he is "like me a believer in total immersion," so, of course, "I used to sing him Baptist hymns." In her analysis of the poem for Dr. Foster, Bishop equates the seal with Foster herself. She notes the Christian implications of the word "seal," meaning a bond, and alludes to the fact that a seal can also be a kiss. Clearly, her reference to Baptist hymns is more than a passing joke. Part of the equation between the seal and Dr. Foster is that both are studying Bishop as Bishop is studying them. Then the language of the poem moves to a contemplation of the water, which Bishop again reads in symbolic terms:

> *Cold dark deep and absolutely clear,*
> *the clear gray icy water . . .*

Bishop sees the water as burning with a dark gray flame that seems miraculous, almost sacred. Yet it is also painful, leading perhaps to something like the transformative suffering in her favorite Herbert poem, "Love Unknown." The final lines of "At the Fishhouses," in which she characterizes the icy water she has been contemplating, rise to perhaps the greatest apotheosis in all her work. Taken all together, this dark and briny sea is:

> like what we imagine knowledge to be:
> dark, salt, clear, moving, utterly free,
> drawn from the cold hard mouth
> of the world, derived from the rocky breasts
> forever, flowing and drawn, and since
> our knowledge is historical, flowing, and flown.[12]

Bishop would later tell Frank Bidart that she wasn't quite sure what these final lines meant when she wrote them, but she knew they were right, and when she put them down on paper she "felt ten feet tall."[13] The rocky breasts have been associated with her mother, and in her analysis with Ruth Foster, Bishop engaged in an extended reading of them.[14] It is astonishing that when Bishop submitted "The Fishhouses" to Katherine White—a poem that she understood to be among her best and most profound, as shown in her contemporaneous analysis with Ruth Foster—she worried that *The New Yorker* editor might find it "another unusable poem."[15]

Elizabeth Bishop and Robert Lowell first met at a dinner party hosted by their mutual friend, the poet and critic Randall Jarrell, in New York in January 1947, so her analysis with Foster and her dawning friendship with Robert Lowell were virtually simultaneous. Jarrell had been Lowell's friend since their days together at Kenyon College in 1938, where they shared the upper story of the house of their mentor, John Crowe Ransom. Bishop had met Jarrell more recently. In her initial letter to Lowell, Bishop apologized for having missed a subsequent visit with him and the Jarrells due to illness, and she congratulates Lowell on three important awards he had won in April 1947: a Guggenheim Fellowship, a cash award from the American Academy of Arts and Letters, and the Pulitzer Prize for his first book, *Lord Weary's Castle* (1946). Since Bishop herself had recently received the Houghton Mifflin Poetry Award—resulting in a cash prize and the publication of her first book, *North & South* (1946)—and had received, like Lowell, a Guggenheim in April 1947 to work on her next book of poems, both poets had been recently and successfully launched into the world of letters.

In 1974 Robert Lowell mused in a letter to Bishop, who by then had been his intimate friend, correspondent, and poetic peer for nearly three decades, "I see us still when we first met, both at Randall [Jarrell]'s and then for a couple of years later. I see you as rather tall, long brown-haired, shy but full of des[cription] and anecdote as now."[16] Bishop, displaying that penchant for accuracy and humorous self-deprecation that would so define her, replied, "Cal dear, maybe your memory *is* failing!—Never, never was I 'tall'—as you wrote remembering me. I was always 5 ft 4 and ¼ inches—now shrunk to 5 ft 4 inches. . . . And I never had 'long brown hair' either!—It started turning gray when I was 23 or 24—and probably was already somewhat grizzled when I first met you." Bishop characteristically added in a marginal note, "So please don't put me in a beautiful poem tall with long brown hair!"[17] Bishop's self-image is verified in a famous 1962 photograph of the two poets on the balcony of the apartment overlooking Rio's Copacabana Beach that Bishop shared for many years with her Brazilian lover, Lota de Macedo Soares. Bishop's left arm is entwined with Lowell's right as she—short, grizzled, gray-brown haired—beams affectionately up at Lowell, while he—easily a foot taller and sporting his trademark black horn-rims—beams affectionately down.

What matters most in this exchange is Bishop's droll yet firm refusal to be romanticized, to be cast—even flatteringly—as a quasi-mythic figure in someone else's personal epic. In an unfinished and unpublished memoir of her earliest meeting with Lowell, Bishop, showing the flair for description and anecdote praised by her friend, dryly recalled his "rumpled dark blue suit," "the sad state of his shoes," and the fact that he was "handsome in a[n] old-fashioned poetic way." Then she confessed, "I loved him at first sight."[18]

In her response to Lowell's nostalgic 1974 letter, Bishop said,

> *What I remember about that meeting is your dishevelment, your lovely curly hair, and how we talked about a Picasso show then on in N.Y. . . . and how much I liked you, after having been almost too scared to go. . . . You were also rather dirty, which I rather liked, too.*[19]

In her way, Bishop turns Lowell into one of those individuals or objects characteristically found throughout her own writing: a curiously appealing, if somewhat tattered, figure that remains entirely and uncompromisingly itself. And despite the fact that Bishop's long-standing relationships were always with women, Lowell emerges as subtly eroticized. The thirty-one-year-old Lowell, six years Bishop's junior, received Hollywood screen test offers when his image appeared in *Life* magazine, and Bishop later told friends that when she saw the film *East of Eden*, James Dean reminded her of Robert Lowell as she first met him in 1947. More significant, perhaps, than any of these other Lowellian allures was her discovery that she and Lowell could speak quite naturally about the making of poetry, and that such discussions "could be strangely easy 'Like exchanging recipes for making a cake.'"[20] Lowell would later refer to Bishop, in a letter, as his "favorite poet and favorite friend."[21] Bishop almost certainly would have said the same. And he was clearly attracted to her as well. But even aside from the question of sexual preference, she feared instability on both sides. Over the years, their relationship, though extremely close, would remain for the most part epistolary.

As Lowell wrote his initial letter to Bishop, he was about to begin the first of several stays at Yaddo, the famous artists' colony in Saratoga Springs, New York. He would encourage Bishop to make a stay at Yaddo, something she would actually do twice, although she never stayed there when Lowell was present.

Writing from Briton Cove, Cape Breton, Nova Scotia, where she was vacationing with Marjorie Stevens on what would prove to be their last trip together, Bishop responded in her second letter to Lowell with thanks for his laudatory review of *North & South*. Lowell's review praises Bishop's poems as "unrhetorical, cool, and beautifully thought-out," noting that "the splendor and minuteness of her descriptions soon seem wonderful. Later one realizes that her large, controlled, and elaborate common sense is always or almost always absorbed in its subjects, and that she is one of the best craftsmen alive." He notes her "marvelous command of shifting speech tones," in which she "resembles Robert Frost." Lowell also observes a "symbolic pattern" in "at least nine-tenths" of the poems—a struggle between "two opposing factors," one being "motion, weary but persisting," and the other being "terminus: rest, sleep, fulfillment or death." When "At the Fishhouses" appeared in *The New Yorker*, Lowell told Bishop, in what was just his second letter to her, that he felt "very envious in reading it." Explaining that, "I'm a fisherman myself," he acknowledged ruefully, "all my fish became symbols, alas!" He praised the "great splendor" of the description, adding that "the human part, tone, etc., is just right."[22] Lowell could have suspected few, if any, of the many layers of Freudian symbolic reading that Bishop herself had brought to "At the Fishhouses" in the exploration of the poem she had shared with her psychiatrist Ruth Foster. In that second letter, Lowell also traced the many possible prototypes of his distinctive nickname, Cal, which Bishop would invariably use going forward. None of them, he said, were flattering: "Calvin, Caligula, Caliban, Calvin Coolidge, Calligraphy." Of these potential prototypes, Caligula remains the most commonly accepted.

That second letter of Bishop's to Lowell, from Briton Cove, suggests just how quickly their imaginations had become intertwined, for it contains phrases and images that would soon find their way into her poem "Cape Breton," published by *The New Yorker* in 1949. Bishop notes that as she looks out over Briton Cove, "off shore are two 'bird islands' with high red cliffs. We are going out with a fisherman to see them tomorrow—they are sanctuaries where there are auks and the only puffins left on the continent, or so they tell us." And "Cape Breton" begins:

> Out on the high "bird islands," Ciboux and Hertford,
> the razorbill auks and the silly-looking puffins all stand
> with their backs to the mainland
> in solemn, uneven lines along the cliff's brown grass-frayed edge. . . . [23]

Bishop added in her letter that there are "real ravens on the beach, too, something I never saw before—enormous, with sort of rough black beards under their beaks."[24] Of all the birds mentioned in her letter, only the alluring ravens fail to find a place in her poem "Cape Breton." Bishop continues to incorporate the ear, the eye, and an awareness of time, adding a touch of mystery to the ending of this poem:

> The birds keep on singing, a calf bawls, the bus starts.
> The thin mist follows
> the white mutations of its dream;
> an ancient chill is rippling the dark brooks.[25]

In September 1947, Lowell left Yaddo and arrived in Washington to assume his duties as Poetry Consultant to the Library of Congress (a post—today styled the Poet Laureate Consultant in Poetry—that he would later pass on to Bishop herself). One of Lowell's tasks as the new consultant was to begin a collection of sound recordings of notable visiting poets reading their work. A recording of Bishop was near the top of his list. Bishop visited Lowell in Washington to record her work. She then continued south by train to Key West.

Bishop stayed temporarily in Key West with her friend Pauline Hemingway at her extensive property on Whitehead Street before finding more permanent quarters. A letter to Lowell contains a postcard of "Home of Ernest Hemingway, Key West, Florida," with the inscription from Bishop, "X marks my quarters." Bishop wrote to Lowell as well of the Hemingways' famous illuminated swimming pool, in a passage that very nearly qualifies as a comic prose poem:

> *The swimming pool is wonderful—it is very large and the water, from away under the reef, is fairly salt. Also it lights up at night—I find that each underwater bulb is five times the voltage of the one bulb in the light house across the street, so the pool must be visible to Mars—it is wonderful to swim around in a sort of green fire, one's friends look like luminous frogs.*[26]

Much to Ernest Hemingway's annoyance, the property he shared with Pauline had been listed on a 1935 map of Key West put out by FDR's Federal Emergency Relief Administration in order to encourage tourism, and Bishop found herself shooing eager Hemingway fans off a property that in actuality had always belonged to his wife. Bishop herself may be said to have lived in Key West for much of a decade in almost total obscurity. Despite the many poems Bishop published with Key West settings, including several in prominent journals such as *Partisan Review*, *The New Republic*, and *The New Yorker*, local historian Tom Hambright testifies that Bishop received nary a mention in the Key West newspapers during her lengthy stay on the island—and it was only in 1993, forty-seven years after she sold it, that her beloved house at 624 White Street received a historical plaque in her honor. Yet Bishop's comparative obscurity on the island had its advantages. She not only enjoyed more of the quiet peace many writers require, but the intensely private Bishop could see Key West life from a different, perhaps more intimate, and surely more domestic perspective than could the intensely public and decidedly masculine Hemingway. In any case, Bishop experienced (along with many other Key West writers) the extraordinary awareness not so much of living in Hemingway's shadow as of following in his wake.

In 1947, Bishop wrote to Robert Lowell, also a fisherman, about her experiences with the fishing boat captain Eddie "Bra" Saunders:

> He has "failed" a great deal and almost before we were out to sea the boat started smoking, the engine got red hot, we were in danger of blowing up, etc—in the midst of it all, Capt. Bra lit up a cigarette and looked very remote. We finally got in safely but it was quite exciting.

Bishop noted a friend's observation that "Oh Bra would like to do nothing better these days than take on a large good-paying party and head out to the gulf and never come back." Her own mordant response was, "But I don't want to be in on his Viking funeral."[27] As ever, her survival instincts remained strong.

In December, Bishop relocated from Pauline Hemingway's house to the apartment lent to her by Jane Dewey. There she wrote "The Bight," which might be read as her farewell tribute to Key West. Bishop's poem describes the active fishing trade and harbor life going forward in Key West Bight, the unostentatious marina that was only a five-minute walk from her current address at 630 Dey Street.[28] "The Bight" begins at a specific moment in this small harbor's daily cycle, and words from a letter to Lowell ("The water looks like blue gas—the harbor is always a mess, here") find their way directly into her poem, which begins, "At low tide like this how sheer the water is." Each image has a slight hint of incongruity, and image by image, a picture of the bight slowly accumulates. Here is a setting where "white, crumbling ribs of marl protrude and glare / and the boats are dry, the pilings dry as matches." Bishop's study of Key West Bight reveals a small working harbor full of paradoxes, in which the laws of nature sometimes seem to operate in reverse, because, or so we are told, "absorbing, rather than being absorbed, / the water in the bight doesn't wet anything," and in an echo of her letter to Lowell, the color of that water is "the color of the gas flame turned as low as possible." She claims that one can smell the water "turning to gas," though the smell more likely comes from one of the small engines operating in this workaday nautical setting. Of course, "if one were Baudelaire / one could probably hear it turning to marimba music." Bishop immediately redefines her times by citing the actual source of that music: a "little ocher dredge at work off the end of the dock," which "already plays the dry perfectly off-beat claves." In this peculiar, perfectly offbeat realm, human beings and the creatures of nature go about their business without paying each other much attention. But if one looks closely, one discovers unexpected visual rewards that searchers for the conventional sublime might overlook, for here "the birds are outsize," and

> *Pelicans crash*
> *into this peculiar gas unnecessarily hard,*
> *it seems to me, like pickaxes,*
> *rarely coming up with anything to show for it,*
> *and going off with humorous elbowings.*

Yet the place is not without its lyricism, either, because variegated man-o'-war birds "soar / on impalpable drafts" and one can watch them "open their tails like scissors on the curves."

As the birds crash and soar, the boats move along in their own unpretentious way:

> *The frowsy sponge boats keep coming in*
> *with the obliging air of retrievers.*

And soon, another line from Bishop's letter to Lowell slides seamlessly into her poem. In that letter she told Lowell that the harbor was now full of "junky little boats all piled up, some hung with sponges and always a few half sunk or splintered up from the most recent hurricane. It reminds me a little of my desk."

In verse form, this becomes:

Some of the little white boats are still piled up
against each other, or lie on their sides, stove in,
and not yet salvaged, if they ever will be, from the last bad storm,
like torn-open, unanswered letters.
The bight is littered with old correspondences.

Moving toward the conclusion, Bishop shifts our eye and our ear back toward that little ocher dredge that has been chittering away all this time—but now she observes it more closely:

Click. Click. Goes the dredge,
and brings up a dripping jawful of marl.
All the untidy activity continues,
awful but cheerful.[29]

When this poem was being prepared for publication by *The New Yorker*, some discussion ensued about the unconventional punctuation of the line that ended up reading, "Click. Click. Goes the dredge." Bishop hoped to capture, with this unconventional punctuation, the dredge's distinctive staccato rhythm. Her editor for this poem, William Maxwell, sympathized humorously with Bishop, suggesting that defying grammatical convention—to which his style editor had raised objections—might "rock the foundations of the magazine."[30] His letter ended with the plea regarding copy editors' alterations, "I hope you won't mind our leaving them the way they are," and in this case, Bishop left it at that. Discussions of the minutia of punctuation, with Bishop stretching the limits of convention in order to achieve the sound and sense she was looking for and *The New Yorker*'s resident grammarians attempting, with varying degrees of success, to rein her in, would form a staple feature of the discourse between Bishop and the principal venue of her later years, resulting in the elegant 2011 volume *Elizabeth Bishop and* The New Yorker: *The Complete Correspondence.*

In the fall of 1948, Bishop and Lowell would attend what became a famous poetry conference at Bard College in Annandale-on-Hudson, New York. The event was organized by Theodore Weiss and featured William Carlos Williams, Louise Bogan, Jean Garrigue, Lloyd Frankenberg, Richard Wilbur, Richard Eberhart, Kenneth Rexroth, and Joseph Summers. Summers, who became a close friend of Elizabeth Bishop's, along with his wife, U. T. Summers, recalled that "Lowell came because he heard Elizabeth was coming, and Elizabeth came because she heard Lowell was coming," although Lloyd Frankenberg and his wife, Loren MacIver, also served as attractions. Joseph Summers recalled that Williams was speaking about how "we'd have to write the American beat and the American line" and insisting that "nobody could write heroic couplets anymore, nowadays." At this, Bishop said, "Oh, Dr. Williams, you're just so old-fashioned! Cal's been writing marvelous heroic couplets recently." When Williams asked Lowell if this were true and Lowell replied, "Yes, I've been trying," Williams looked stricken. In Summers's eyes, "It was a wonderful moment." In a final session, each poet was invited to read from his or her poems and Bishop was too shy to read from hers, so Lowell read them. Joseph Summers felt that Bishop and Lowell "seemed very much in love" that weekend. Bishop told the Summerses some time later that "she loved Cal more than anyone she'd ever known except for Lota [de Macedo Soares, her companion in Brazil]." Yet she feared that because of his manic tendencies "he was a violent person and she knew he would destroy her." She added, "He wants to marry me and I just can't."[31] If Lowell's account may be trusted, in what has become a famous letter to Bishop written nearly a decade later in 1957, he never actually proposed. However, he did recall that he was tempted to during the Bard conference one night in the poets' dormitory: "I was so drunk that my hands turned cold and I felt half-dying and held your hand. And nothing was said, and like a loon that needs sixty feet, I believe, to take off from the water, I wanted time and space, and went on assuming."[32] Lowell was surely aware at that time of Bishop's preference for women, since he added regretfully, "Yet there were a few months. I suppose we might almost claim something like apparently Strachey and Virginia Woolf." He acknowledged that on the other hand, "our friendship really wasn't a courting" and "really led to no encroachments. So it is." Still, he also felt, looking back in 1957, "that asking you is *the* might have been for me, the one towering change, the other life that might have been had. It was that way for these nine years or so that intervened."[33] Bishop did not comment then on Lowell's account of these events from 1948, leaving his account unconfirmed but at the same time unchallenged. Despite such emotional ambivalences and complications, their friendship continued unabated in a series of letters evidently relished by both parties.

Participants at the Bard conference agree that it had involved some rather heavy drinking, and Lowell wrote to Bishop shortly after his return by train to Yaddo, with reference to the effect of consuming so much alcohol:

> *[The] next morning I felt wonderful at breakfast; but I noticed that I held on to my coffee cup with both hands, and when I got back to my room with the typed first draft of a stanza ugly and awful as life before me, after half an hour I discovered I was just staring at it, so I read the 3rd book of the Dunciad, where the Dunces contend in unmentionable contests and end by trying to see who can stay awake the longest over each other's books.*[34]

This, along with the balance of the letter, does not sound much like the language of courtship. Yet his attraction to Bishop, and his attentiveness toward her, remained strong, and Bishop returned it, though she generally contrived to maintain a certain measure of safe distance.

If Bishop was wary of taking on Lowell as her partner, she was also not quite sure she wanted any other woman to have him, either. Elizabeth Hardwick, too, had shown interest in Lowell during the Bard conference, and Bishop's first response to hearing that Hardwick would be arriving at Yaddo during a Lowell stay was to say in the postscript to a 1948 letter, "I forgot to comment on Elizabeth Hardwick's arrival—take care." John Malcolm Brinnin recalled that in 1949, when Bishop herself was at Yaddo and he told her that Lowell was to marry Hardwick, "Elizabeth crumpled at the news."[35] Yet soon, Bishop and Hardwick were making efforts to build bridges. The two Elizabeths exchanged occasional letters, though the Bishop-Lowell correspondence remained central, and when Lowell and Hardwick were planning a trip to Europe in 1950, Hardwick wrote to Bishop, "Cal and I are going to Italy in September. Why don't you come with us? We got this marvelous idea of the trip just last week and now this idea today, which occurred to us simultaneously, that you might come along." Instead, Bishop saw them off to Italy at the pier in New York and then, before their return, made her own freighter trip in 1951 to Brazil.

While Bishop was meeting with and getting to know an array of poetic contemporaries who would remain important to her for years to come, she was continuing to produce poems that would serve as cornerstones of her literary canon. A few months before the Bard conference, Bishop's "Over 2000 Illustrations and a Complete Concordance," one of her richest and most complex achievements, appeared in *Partisan Review*. In this poem, Bishop creates a mosaic, piecing together fragmentary recollections from early travels reaching back to her first journeys to Newfoundland, Europe, and North Africa with Hallie Tompkins, Margaret Miller, Louise Crane, and other college friends, as well as later journeys with Marjorie Stevens. The poem alternates images, from an engraved family Bible, which seems "serious" but also artificial and a little dead, to the less serious or "engravable" but perhaps more vital travels that she recalls in glimpses from her youth. The poem skips and leaps about from the entrance to St. John's Harbor in Newfoundland to St. Peter's in Rome to Mexico. It then moves to Volubilis, a partly excavated Berber and Roman city in Morocco, before shifting to Dingle Harbor in Ireland, and then to the brothels of Marrakesh, no doubt a locale into which Bishop was conducted by Louise Crane on one of her expeditions in search of local color. There they observed "little pockmarked prostitutes" who would balance tea trays on their heads while doing belly dances, then fling themselves "naked and giggling against our knees, / asking for cigarettes."[36]

Having confronted aspects of the profane in this celebrated Moroccan city, Bishop and her companion now confront a series of disquieting versions of the sacred, in the form of "holy" Muslim graves that were not "looking particularly holy" because of the degradations visited upon them by sand and wind and time. One of these frightening images was "an open, gritty, marble trough, carved solid / with exhortation." Due to the ravages of time, these exhortations seem like yellowed cattle teeth, and the open tomb itself is "half-filled with dust," but "not even the dust" of the prophet once entombed there.

Bishop's search for the sacred, or even the serious, in the holy cities of Rome and Marrakesh seems, at first, to have reached a dead end in her unnerving contemplation of this empty and not particularly holy-looking grave, while "in a smart burnoose, their guide Khadour looked on amused." Is there no meaningful connection between all Bishop has seen on her travels, with "everything only connected by 'and' and 'and'"? But now the poem returns to the previously unsatisfactory family Bible for another moment of contemplation. And here she achieves an ecstatic ending that rivals that of "At the Fishhouses":

> Open the book. (The gilt rubs off the edges
> of the pages and pollinates the fingertips.)
> Open the heavy book. Why couldn't we have seen
> this old Nativity while we were at it?
> —the dark ajar, the rocks breaking with light,
> an undisturbed, unbreathing flame,
> colorless, sparkless, freely fed on straw,
> and, lulled within, a family with pets,
> —and looked and looked our infant sight away.[37]

When the twenty-two-year-old James Merrill first read this poem in *The New Yorker*, he was "just bowled over." He had met Bishop at the Bard conference and soon arranged a lunch with her. According to Merrill, "I naively thought that I could spend most of the lunch telling her how wonderful I thought the poem was. It only took a couple of minutes, and whatever we talked about from then on, we were on our own."[38] Merrill recognized Bishop's resistance to hearing praise of her work, and also understood that there would be no more shoptalk between these supreme craftsmen. In an elegy written several years after her death, Merrill asked, "What tribute could you bear / Without dismay?"[39]

Even so, Merrill added, "I think she knew how much she had put in her poems. She must have known that they were wonderful." Perhaps the steady disapproval Bishop had absorbed from the Bishop side of her family, and the abuse from her uncle George, made her shrink from openly acknowledging or accepting the approval she earned from the distinctive quality of her work. Bishop and Merrill would remain admiring friends for more than thirty years. John Ashbery, a year younger than Merrill, was similarly impressed with "Over 2000 Illustrations." In 1969 he called it "possibly her masterpiece," and noted how she "plies continually between the steel-engraved vignettes of a gazetteer and the distressingly unclassifiable events of a real voyage." The publication of this single poem, one of her most avant-garde, would set Merrill and Ashbery on the path to becoming enthusiastic proselytizers of Bishop's work among a younger generation of American poets.

Despite her support among a younger generation of poets, in the final three decades of her life, the literary networking resource most vital to Bishop's personal welfare was her friend Lowell. When Bishop met Lowell, despite the successful publication of her book *North & South*, she was unsettled by the ending of her relationships with Louise Crane and Marjorie Stevens and struggling with depression and alcoholism. Lowell himself, while enjoying the success of *Lord Weary's Castle*, was also recovering from a major manic episode and from the breakup of his first marriage, to the novelist Jean Stafford. Bishop, displaced in childhood, had persistent difficulty finding a place or home in adulthood, and Lowell set about trying to help her take greater professional advantage of her growing literary reputation. Lowell's networking skills were by any measure impressive, and he frequently turned them to the advantage of his friends, and to the advantage of Bishop in particular. With his urging and support, in 1949, when she was thirty-eight, Bishop began a year of service in a post Lowell had already filled, as Poetry Consultant to the Library of Congress. Her Walnut Hill classmates, in her yearbook, had suggested that she might become the "Poet Laureate of Nova Scotia." But if she had held her Library of Congress office under its current title, she would have been serving as the poet laureate of the United States (indeed, many sources currently list her as such). Still, the scholar and biographer Joseph Frank, who came to know Bishop in Washington, later recalled,

> *I didn't even know if Elizabeth was American or not. I wasn't quite clear because she spoke so much about Nova Scotia. I had the feeling that she didn't feel at home in this country somehow, that she was rather alien from that point of view because [these] early years had shaped her sensibility in such a way.*

In Frank's mind, "there was not this kind of American casualness about her at all as a person. She was aware of that." He added, "She was much more rigorous in some deep moral and social sense than the ordinary American. She was very formal in many ways."[40] Bishop's work as poetry consultant was rather like that of a glorified reference librarian, yet she did have a public role in a way that was not entirely familiar or comfortable for her. A reporter writing for the *Boston Post* in 1950, in what was to be the first of Bishop's many published interviews, described her as "an attractive . . . quiet, [and] self-effacing" young woman who was discovered by the interviewer at her desk "wrestling with the muse in her own unique way."[41]

Bishop mentioned that she and her secretary, Phyllis Armstrong, were "constantly asked for poems on love, horses, marriage, dogs and death."[42] She also favored one inquiring mind with the history of the limerick—a form of which Bishop had demonstrated an early mastery in the example sent to Louise Bradley. While living and working in Washington, DC, Bishop got a close-up view of American government and the exercise of power in the early days of the Cold War. And she continued to struggle with the problem of alcohol.

Bishop found her public role at the Library of Congress difficult, yet with her increasing prominence as a poet, she was now being asked to play public roles more frequently. Characteristically, her response was to insist on the autonomy of the individual poet and the unique demands of each particular poem. For example, when asked by anthologist John Ciardi to answer a battery of questions about her aesthetic theory and practice for his 1950 anthology *Mid-Century American Poets*, Bishop responded assertively that "*it all depends*. It all depends on the particular poem one happens to be trying to write, and the range of possibilities is, one trusts, infinite."[43] Bishop resisted a process of critical appropriation that, in the years since the mid-twentieth century, was well underway to becoming an almost inevitable consequence of literary fame. While her Vassar classmate Muriel Rukeyser, in the same Ciardi anthology, asserted a universal psychology of poetic composition, Bishop expressed grave doubts about the means by which theory might actually shape practice: "No matter what theories one may have, I doubt very much that they are in one's mind at the moment of writing a poem or that there is even a physical possibility that they could be. Theories can only be based on interpretations of other poets' poems, or on one's own in retrospect, or wishful thinking."[44] Of course, Bishop had formulated a quite sophisticated theory of poetic form, as well as a partial theory of creative psychology, as far back as the mid-1930s, while she was still at Vassar. She used the word "theory" when alluding to her approach in a letter to Moore—without describing the theory. Bishop quietly continued to follow the approach she had elaborated in her essays in *Con Spirito* and the *Vassar Review*, asserting the value of creating, in her poems, the effect of a mind at work. For Bishop, the fact that these articulations were securely sequestered in college magazines that few if any of her immediate contemporaries were likely to discover gave her more freedom to maneuver than if she had packaged these principles in an aesthetic manifesto and attempted to steer the literary world to follow the course of her entirely contingent "theory."

While Bishop may have known where she stood in regard to a poetics of contingency, as a practical matter her life remained in its own uneasy state of contingency. Her former apartment on King Street had been demolished in 1949, and her goods were almost all in storage. After repeated urging from Robert Lowell, Bishop agreed to accept a residency at Yaddo. Her first visit, during which she suffered from excessive drinking and anxiety, was not a success. But her second visit to Yaddo, in 1950, marked an important chapter in her life, for on that visit she established a circle of close friends and correspondents who would, along with Lowell, help to sustain her through each of her last three decades. One of these was Pauline Hanson, the assistant to Elizabeth Ames, the director of Yaddo. Another was Beauford Delaney, an African-American painter who would later develop a significant career in Paris as a singer. Yet another was Pearl Kazin, a writer and editor and the sister of noted critic Alfred Kazin. More important, perhaps, than any of these were the poet May Swenson and an artistic couple, Kit Barker, an English artist, and his wife, Ilse Barker, a fiction writer who had been born in Germany. Swenson, two years Bishop's junior, became a keen reader and observer of Bishop. Swenson grew up in Utah in a large and affirming Mormon family. She openly expressed her emotions and wrote poetry that vibrates with spontaneity. Swenson was fascinated and intrigued by Bishop's more contained approach to her emotions and her more oblique and controlled poetic style. They were both lesbians as well, and each remained intrigued with the other in terms of how they chose to represent or deflect their sexuality in their work. In the years to come Bishop and Swenson would engage in a long exchange of letters exploring themes of poetry, poetics, love, family, and nature. Meanwhile, the Barkers, and particularly Ilse, would emerge as two of Bishop's most dedicated and loyal supporters. Although they lived on a different continent, they remained among her most diligent correspondents. Over the course of nearly thirty years, they received hundreds of letters from her, in which she spoke of almost every aspect of her life in entertaining and sometimes touching detail.

One poem Bishop completed during her second stay at Yaddo was "The Prodigal." When she was visiting the farm belonging to her aunt Grace and Grace's husband in Nova Scotia in the summer of 1946, she was surprised one morning to be offered a swig of rum by one of Grace's stepsons while they were standing alongside the pigsty. This event lodged deep in her imagination, and five years later it produced "The Prodigal." Bishop's poem recalls the biblical story of the Prodigal Son, a figure she clearly associates with herself. After squandering his inheritance and becoming destitute, the Prodigal Son works as a swineherd, and finds himself starving while the pigs are being fed. When he finally swallows his pride and returns home, his father kills a fatted calf and celebrates his return. But the whole journey has been a painful one, if also one that resulted in self-knowledge. During the years since her Nova Scotia visit, Bishop had been suffering from severe episodes of alcohol abuse, and she felt that her life was no longer fully under her control. Bishop kept returning to this situation, and finally produced a poem, in "The Prodigal," that typified her whole experience. It is a double sonnet, a form favored by her beloved George Herbert, and therefore, by implication, and because of the context of the poem, it acts itself out in a Christian context of trial, suffering, and ultimate forgiveness. During these years, Bishop was surrounded by friends who cared about her and looked out for her both personally and professionally. Yet as early as the age of fourteen, she had written to Louise Bradley about sometimes feeling like a "battered old alley-cat with chewed ears wandering around in the dark."

And she asked Bradley then, "Did you ever think—no matter how many friends you have—no one can really reach <u>you</u>?" She felt like a person on another planet, looking down on the earth while feeling "so *alone*."[45] For reasons reaching back to her earliest childhood losses and isolations, Bishop continued to feel, in her darker moments—including now in her present state of clinical depression—so *alone*, much as she felt, in adolescence, when composing that bleak poem of enclosure, "Once on a hill I met a man."

In "The Prodigal," Bishop succeeded in producing a poem on alcoholism and alienation from family that she could sufficiently distance from herself to achieve a measure of self-protection and aesthetic calm. She also succeeded in producing a poem that *The New Yorker* would find acceptable, despite their on-again, off-again insistence that poems should not be too personal. She achieves some distance from herself by embedding her prodigal's struggles with alcoholism in the center of the poem and by drawing on the biblical parable of the Prodigal Son for her frame of reference:

> But sometimes mornings after drinking bouts
> (he hid the pints behind a two-by-four),
> the sunrise glazed the barnyard mud with red;
> the burning puddles seemed to reassure.
> And then he thought he almost might endure
> his exile yet another year or more.

Bishop had already endured, or enjoyed, a self-imposed partial exile from her family, one that was now stretching into its second decade, but while this exile might have been liberating in some ways, it also took its psychic toll, as the poem implies. The farmer for whom the prodigal works often shuts up the pigsty in which the prodigal sleeps. Then the farmer goes home, removing the light and leaving the prodigal to sleep in the shuttered sty in darkness:

> Carrying a bucket along a slimy board,
> he felt the bats' uncertain staggering flight,

his shuddering insights, beyond his control,
touching him.

The prodigal, at least according to the biblical story, could go home to an opulent welcome. But this would also involve a confession of error and a plea for forgiveness. For Bishop, this would be high stakes indeed, and thus she can empathize with her prodigal. She concludes:

But it took him a long time
finally to make his mind up to go home.[46]

Bishop had been passing through one of the most difficult phases of her life. But in spite of the challenges, much had been accomplished. She had gone through her sessions of therapy with Ruth Foster, had published a significant body of poetry and entered a new phase in her writing involving a great psychological intensity, and her circle of friends had grown considerably during her stints in New York and Washington and her two visits to Yaddo. These friendships would sustain her during the long separation from the United States that was about to come. Now she formed a plan to make a journey by freighter, circumnavigating South America in search of an escape from challenges in her past life and with an eye toward new discoveries.

May Swenson met Bishop at her hotel a week before she left New York for South America and wrote about it to their friend Polly Hanson at Yaddo. Swenson found that Bishop was "in good health—her asthma is under control (she herself says she's as strong as a horse—and I think it's true—maybe more like one of those sturdy little Nova Scotian ponies)." However, Swenson added that "she does need help with her drinking problem, and she recognizes it."[47] Swenson was impressed with "A Cold Spring," a poem that Bishop had written while visiting her friend Jane Dewey's rural home in Maryland, not far from the Aberdeen Proving Grounds where Dewey had helped to design weapons during World War II. The poem charts the oncoming spring in Maryland from its cold, uncertain beginning, where "the violet was flawed on the lawn," and the "trees hesitated" to set forth their leaves. But slowly and surely, the uncertain steps toward spring keep going forward. A calf is born "in a chill blast of sunshine." The mother, in a flash of that indelicacy so characteristic of Bishop's work, "took a long time eating the after-birth," but, in the sort of quick reversal of the indelicate again so characteristic of Bishop's style, the calf "got up promptly / and seemed inclined to feel gay." The next day is warmer, and two of Bishop's most characteristic lines follow:

> Greenish-white dogwood infiltrated the wood,
> each petal burned, apparently, by a cigarette-butt;

The play of vowel and consonant sounds in the first of these lines is extraordinary, and the second line exactly characterizes the look of a dogwood petal in the most surprising way possible. Soon spring's effect becomes unmistakable as "the hills grow softer" and tufts of tall grass mark the location of each cow flop. Nature even provides its own jazz rhythm section as the "bull-frogs are sounding, / slack strings plucked by heavy thumbs."[48] And the poem ends on a note of celebration as the cold spring of its opening transitions into full summer on evenings when the "fireflies / begin to rise" from the thick grass, and then, "lit on the ascending flight," in a moment betokening celebration, they appear to drift upward simultaneously "exactly like the bubbles in champagne."[49] Elizabeth Bishop still found in nature moments of pleasure, peace, and reassurance, even in the midst of these difficult years. She discovered something, in the words of "The Bight," to be cheerful about, despite aspects of her life that she found awful. And now, in mid-November 1951, she was about to embark on a journey that would forever change the course of her life and art.

CHAPTER ELEVEN

TOO MANY WATERFALLS

O n November 9, 1951, Elizabeth Bishop set forth on the merchant ship *Bowplate* of the Norwegian International Freighting Corporation line, beginning the first leg of a voyage around the South American continent. The ambitious itinerary she laid out for herself would be funded by the first-ever Lucy Martin Donnelly Traveling Fellowship, which Bishop had been recently awarded by Bryn Mawr College. She explained to Bryn Mawr's president, Katharine McBride, "The ticket is a sort of investment, and I am hoping to get a lot of work done on the long, slow trip."[1]

If Bishop's nautical adventure proceeded as planned, she would leave behind the disquieting challenges of her recent life in the United States while indulging a wanderlust that seemed to point her ever southward. Her plan involved a series of extended visits at the IFC line's South American ports of call. When ready to move on, Bishop would board the next available IFC freighter and continue her circumnavigation. Along the way, she would extend her geographical experience while absorbing fresh material for future poems and prose to send to *The New Yorker*.

Bishop's first stop was Brazil's Santos harbor, where, as an IFC brochure promised eagerly, "you'll watch coffee being loaded for shipment to the United States [from] the world's leading coffee port."[2] Bishop, a lover of good coffee, planned to debark at Santos, stop briefly in nearby São Paulo, Brazil's largest city, then travel by rail to Rio de Janeiro. There she would visit her Yaddo friend Pearl Kazin, who had recently relocated to Rio. She also planned a more extended stay with two friends she had known in New York some years before, the wealthy and talented Brazilian intellectual Lota de Macedo Soares—who Bishop described to Yaddo secretary Polly Hanson as "extremely smart and awfully nice"—and Lota's former lover and current companion and business partner Mary Stearns Morse, "a nice Bostonian staying with her whom I also knew before."[3] After a visit with Macedo Soares and Morse, Bishop planned to continue southward in January toward Montevideo, Buenos Aires, and Tierra del Fuego on later IFC freighters. She would pass through the Straits of Magellan, pause at Punta Arenas in Chile, and turn north up the Pacific Coast toward Peru and Ecuador, where she expected to linger through April and May.[4] She would report back to Bryn Mawr on the results of her expedition in the late spring of 1952.

But before Bishop arrived at Santos, she and the MS *Bowplate* had to cross six thousand miles of the open Atlantic. At a cruising speed of fifteen knots, half that of a Cunard liner, this first leg of the trip would take many days. As touted in the IFC brochure, Bishop would enjoy her meals aboard her "cruise home" as part of her inexpensive rate of passage.[5] And she would find ample leisure to bring her acute powers of observation to bear on the heterogeneous seagoing microcosm that surrounded her. On November 12, three days after boarding the *Bowplate*, Bishop began a letter to Hanson, acknowledging, "I won't be able to mail it for about two weeks." But this, she added, "I find, is the nicest thing about a long slow trip," because "it doesn't matter in the slightest in what order you work on things, this review or that poem or a letter that has to be answered—with the result that I feel so free that I've really done a lot already in 48 hours."[6] On board nearly any vessel, from fishing boat to oceangoing craft, Bishop felt released from the burden of anxiety she always carried with her.

As her freighter plowed southward toward Santos, Bishop paused in her letter to Hanson to admire one of her favorite sights, a rainbow—in this case one "that comes and goes in the spray as if it were being dragged along."[7] Laden with an enormous cargo of jeeps and combines,[8] the *Bowplate* also boasted a Norwegian crew and a passenger list of nine souls. These included, along with Bishop herself, "a pale thin young missionary (Assemblies of God, whatever that is) and his pale thin young wife, and their three pale thin little boys aged four, five & six," as well as a Uruguayan consul from New York "who is nice but I think a little mad,"[9] a "refined but seasick lady,"[10] and one other lady whom Bishop found "the only person at all interesting aboard." This woman, whom she referred to respectfully as Miss Breen, would shortly be immortalized in a Bishop poem.

Breen, she wrote, "turns out to have been head of the *Women's jail* in Detroit for 26 years. Just my type."[11] On the day before the *Bowplate* reached its Brazilian destination, Bishop described her further to Robert Lowell: "She's about 70; very gentle and polite—tells how she accidentally solved such and such a murder, in an apologetic way, & confessed she was written up in 'True Detective Stories.'"[12] Bishop noted in the journal she kept on the voyage that Breen, "with whom I share a bath, is almost 6 ft. tall . . . large blue eyes & bluish waved hair. There is something very appealing about her, though I can't quite place it." She added that during their extended conversations, "most of her stories hinge, in her muffled, apologetic way, on murder."[13]

Retired police lieutenant Mary E. Breen joined the Women's Division of the Detroit police force in 1921, where she served as head of the Women's Detention Home. The *Detroit Free Press* considered her good copy and recounted, among many exploits, her role in the 1928 capture of a dope ring, the "Silk Stocking Gang,"[14] and the 1936 breakup of the Black Legion, a murderous white supremacist group.[15] Breen received a special departmental citation—rare for a woman of that era—for apprehending "Mrs. Grace Scott, Chicago murderess,"[16] and the female accessory to another murder was "led to confess . . . by the sympathetic attitude of Sgt. Mary Breen."[17] One profile of Breen in the *Free Press* described her as "mild mannered, gentle-voiced," but also as a "steel-hard disciplinarian."[18] In her shipboard letter to Hanson, Bishop—thinking of how she had pulled through her harrowing years in the late 1940s—referred to herself as "made of pig iron."[19] Perhaps she found in Mary Breen a kindred spirit: a woman who—beneath a surface of modesty, delicacy, and good manners—maintained a sharp eye for detail, a steely toughness, and a steady determination to succeed in a male-dominated profession.

Bishop's journal observed that Breen "speaks a lot to me about her 'roommate,' for many years I gather—a woman lawyer named Ida." Breen and Ida Lippman arrived together in Detroit in 1921, intending, in the words of the *Free Press*, "to whip some law and order into the local Women's Police Division."[20] In 1928, "scorning male reinforcements," they conducted "week-end raids on alleged disorderly houses [brothels], making eight arrests."[21] Lippman soon secured a law degree and became a prosecuting attorney, but she and Breen still lived together, and their intimacy received more than one approving notice in the *Free Press*. One 1939 feature described Breen as Lippman's "bosom friend"[22] and outlined a planned vacation in the Caribbean. Brett Millier has suggested that Bishop saw in Breen and Lippman's relationship a parallel to the partnership she herself was unconsciously seeking.[23] Certainly, in Lota de Macedo Soares, Bishop would soon encounter a formidable, witty, determined, and innovative woman—not entirely unlike Breen's partner, Ida Lippman—who would change her life forever.

As the freighter *Bowplate* entered Santos harbor, Bishop found herself at a crossroads. She was forty years old—soon to turn forty-one. She had a solid reputation as a poet and an enviable first reading agreement with *The New Yorker*. However, several poets of her generation, including her friend Lowell, six years her junior, were far more celebrated. She had suffered a profound psychological crisis over the past half decade, with bouts of alcoholism, anxiety, and depression, and she had submitted to an intensive period of psychoanalysis. She was in a slow process of recovery, but she had not yet worked herself all the way back. During her period of crisis, Bishop had maintained her extensive network of lifelong friends and correspondents, yet it had been a half decade since her last steady romantic relationship. Moreover, since 1946, when she gave up her house on White Street in Key West, Bishop had lacked any stable place of residence. With many of her books and possessions locked up in storage, Bishop had shuttled up and down the Atlantic shoreline, rather like the sandpiper of a later poem, with stopovers in Washington, Yaddo, Key West, North Carolina, the Maine coast, Nova Scotia, Boston, and New York. She had dwelt in rooming houses and hotels, or as a guest of friends—most recently on the Maryland farm of her friend Jane Dewey, where she had written her soon-to-be-published poem "A Cold Spring."

Bishop's next poem, "Arrival at Santos," captured her present situation in all its layered complexity. It opens with a conversational yet seemingly impersonal voice. But for all the apparent distance and reticence of its initial stanzas, Bishop's urgent personal concerns—and her many unanswered questions—project onto the unfamiliar scene:

> Here is a coast; here is a harbor;
> here, after a meager diet of horizon, is some scenery:
> impractically shaped and—who knows?—self-pitying mountains,
> sad and harsh beneath their frivolous greenery,
>
> with a little church on top of one.

Self-pity, uncertainty, meagerness, impracticality. Are these features inherent to this harbor and its surrounding buildings and promontories, or are they characteristics the poet fears she might harbor in herself?

The speaker, addressing herself in the second person, makes no claims of being a bardic wayfarer—as a male poet might do—asking herself in-stead, "Oh tourist, / is this how this country is going to answer you // and your immodest demands for a different world, / and a better life, and com-plete comprehension / of both at last, and immediately, / after eighteen days of suspension?"[24] "A different world," "a better life," "complete com-prehension"? Immodest demands indeed—but claims that keenly pressed on Bishop at her moment of entry. Abruptly, though, the time for musing is over and the moment of debarkation has arrived. "Finish your breakfast," the speaker curtly directs herself. As the poem segues from meditation into action, its pronouns slide from the distancing second person into a more col-loquial first person—beginning with the plural "we" and then the singular "myself" (though never the simple "I"). So, "gingerly now we climb down the ladder backward, / myself and a fellow passenger named Miss Breen." Then, as she and the fellow passenger brought to life in her letters confront a transient peril, Bishop's powers of observation switch to full alert:

> Please, boy, do be more careful with that boat hook!
> Watch out! Oh! It has caught Miss Breen's
>
> skirt! There!

Phrases from Bishop's letters seem to flow by direct current into punchy staccato sentences where—one brief crisis averted—Bishop's eye settles onto Miss Breen herself, who had now retired and was living in upstate New York.

> Miss Breen is about seventy,
> a retired police lieutenant, six feet tall,
> with beautiful bright blue eyes and a kind expression.
> Her home, when she is at home, is in Glens Fall
>
> s, New York.

Just this once, Bishop permits herself a touch of e. e. cummings, her recent New York neighbor, as the *s* of "Glens Fall/s" drops visually and aurally from one quatrain into the next, while the debarking duo make that final, lunging step downward into the waiting tender. Then, in two quick sentences: "There. We are settled."

On the day of their arrival, Bishop and Mary Breen were met at the Santos pier by Mr. and Mrs. Britto, Breen's friends from Detroit, who saw them through customs—where, the poet hoped, the customs officials would "leave us our scotch and cigarettes." The poem ends portentously with the lines "We leave Santos at once; / we are driving to the interior." Curiously, the name of this new nation, Brazil, never appears in her intriguing, precise, yet elusive poem of arrival. And while Bishop often stressed the factual accuracy of her poems, the Brittos were driving Bishop and Mary Breen just fifty miles inland to São Paulo. Her interior explorations would happen later.

After two days in what she considered this "confusing" city, Bishop journeyed three hundred miles east by rail to another coastal destination, the fabled Rio de Janeiro. On the morning of November 30, 1951, Bishop was met at the Rio station by Pearl Kazin and Mary Morse, the friend of Lota de Macedo Soares. Kazin herself was no fan of Rio, complaining of its corruption and inefficiency, and confessing later, "I could not lose myself in the seductive, tattered beauty of the city, as some of my American friends were able to do."[25] But for Bishop, tattered beauty was always the ultimate seduction, and although her own northern expectations were unsettled by Rio, she found herself decidedly intrigued. Pearl was still job-hunting, and Bishop found herself wondering how she and her photographer husband, Victor Kraft—the once and future lover of Aaron Copland—could make a financial go of it there. By contrast, Bishop's Brazil hostess, Lota de Macedo Soares, could offer her an entirely different window onto Brazil than was available to her friend Pearl. Lota had significant inherited wealth, mostly in real estate, and owned a top-floor apartment with stunning views in the Leme section of Rio.

Lota's most important property, however, was ninety minutes north of Rio, just beyond Petrópolis, Brazil's former imperial summer residence. There, on a secluded mountaintop, surrounded by parcels of land that she was gradually selling off, she was building an ultramodern house. Like most Brazilian women of her time, she lacked an academic degree, but given her forceful and extroverted personality, her inquiring mind, and her wide range of artistic and cultural interests, she had developed an extensive network throughout Brazil's small but brilliant intellectual elite, including prominent poets, artists, architects, fiction writers, musicians, journalists, and political figures. When Macedo Soares visited New York with Morse in 1942—and in the process met Bishop—she developed a strong admiration for the energy and determination she found in American culture, as well as for the quality and plenitude of American manufactured goods. There, she established ties with leading figures at the Museum of Modern Art, where Bishop also had important connections. She also became close friends with musicians such as the noted piano duo of Robert Fizdale and Arthur Gold, and with major contemporary artists, including sculptor Alexander Calder. Lota was much impressed by Bishop's poetry, which was just appearing in her first book, *North & South*, and—as Fizdale and Gold recalled—by Bishop's connections with leading figures in the American poetry scene, connections about which Bishop herself often seemed to be more diffident than proud.

Bishop later recalled her first Rio encounter with Macedo Soares in a letter to May Swenson: "Lota has straight long black hair.—I hadn't seen her for six years or so when I came here and when we looked at each other she was horrified to see I had gone very gray, and I that she had two silver streaks on each side, quite wide. Once I got used to it I liked it—she looks exactly like a chickadee . . . & it's quite chic."[26] Bishop told Pearl's brother, Alfred Kazin, in a letter dated "December 10th or 11th or 12th," that Lota and Mary had been "extremely hospitable—they have just turned over their apartment in Rio to me, maid and all, and I sit surrounded by Calders, Copacabana, Cariocans, Coffee, etc.—& of course a dysentery drug, which also begins with a C." From Lota's balcony in Leme, Bishop could look out over Rio's uniquely beguiling geographic setting: the broad golden sands of Copacabana Beach, the glittering ocean beyond, and the rocky outcroppings and abruptly rising mountains that frame the beach and encircle and set off the city. Bishop told Alfred Kazin that she planned to leave Brazil on the next freighter, departing about "Jan. 26th," and she added, "It is all very luxurious, and I never felt like Rilke before."[27]

For Bishop, however, the real event was her first encounter with Lota's fazenda, which she had named Samambaia. Bishop saw it for the first time after two days of Lota-directed sightseeing in Rio. Their journey by car required a ninety-minute drive north of the city, ascending into the mountains of the Serra dos Órgãos. After passing through the historic Imperial City of Petrópolis, their Land Rover turned off the main highway and made its tortuous climb up a steep and rugged mountain road. What Bishop saw when she arrived at Samambaia, as she later told Polly Hanson, was that Lota, "who owns lots of land" nearby, was "building herself a large and beautiful modern house up the side of a solid granite mountain—it is all so unbelievable and *impractical*, the scenery, to a northerner—and yet," as she added in a characteristic note of qualification, "I suppose New England itself was more impractical looking to begin with."[28]

The home Lota was constructing, from plans drawn up in collaboration with the distinguished young Brazilian modernist architect Sérgio Bernardes, is now considered an architectural treasure. Lota functioned as her own general contractor, overseeing every step of the construction process as she worked to turn a skilled architect's drawings into a solid reality. This was exactly the role performed decades before by Bishop's father and grandfather. However, since this project was taking place in a remote and challenging locale, and since Lota was a talented and exacting amateur rather than a professional managing long-term employees and suppliers, the construction process was messier than the businesslike, orderly, and tightly budgeted procedures of J. W. Bishop & Co. of Worcester, New York, Providence, and Boston. Amid Samambaia's extraordinary topography and the inevitable jumble of life in a construction site, Bishop found herself, in a strange way, coming home. Here, she would soon discover much-missed aspects of the world of her mother's family, the Bulmers of Great Village, Nova Scotia.

On Christmas day,[29] Bishop experienced an acute allergic reaction to "two very sour bites"[30] of the fruit of the cashew tree—a fruit that travels poorly and is hence unknown in North America. Bishop would relate in a letter to Dr. Anny Baumann, "The next day I started to swell—and swell and swell; I didn't know one could swell so much."[31] That swelling, which occurred above the neck, obscured her vision and made her head seem the size of a pumpkin.[32] Baumann diagnosed these symptoms as the dangerous Quincke's edema. Had the swelling gone to Bishop's windpipe, it would likely have stopped her breathing and proved fatal. This dangerous inflammation was soon reinforced by Bishop's chronic companions, asthma and eczema. Bishop spent many days in a Petrópolis hospital, surrounded by Macedo Soares and an attentive swarm of Lota's Brazilian friends. Bishop, who had felt so often deprived of tender care during her loss-haunted Calvinist childhood, found herself strangely charmed by these demonstrative attentions. To Marianne Moore, Bishop would remark, "I looked extraordinary and it shows how nice Brazilian people can be that it seemed to endear me to them rather than otherwise."[33] To painter friend Loren MacIver, she observed that "Lota and Mary were so nice to me" during her illness that "it was almost a pleasure."[34]

Bishop's emotions may have rebounded quickly, but her recovery of physical energy and strength required a full month and caused her to miss the departure of that January 26 freighter on which she had planned to continue her voyage south toward Tierra del Fuego. After her release from the hospital, Bishop continued her recuperation at Samambaia, just as her first rainy season was coming on. In mid-January, she described this experience to Polly Hanson:

> The mts. are black, the parts that show, and after the rains they are streaked
> with miles of shiny streaks of water, and after the clouds come down very

low—I'm in one right now—and float around, and the waterfalls and orchids are just like in the books.

Such experiences left a deep impression on her, since phrases and images from this letter found their way into more than one of Bishop's later poems.[35]

At last, on February 7, 1952—the day before her forty-first birthday—Bishop settled down to reflect in a letter to her English friends Kit and Ilse Barker on the eventful two months she had spent in Brazil, a country that was intended to be only a stopping point on her South American journey. Yet as her birthday approached on February 8, Bishop began to feel capable of resuming her strenuous itinerary. She would later give out to interviewers that her allergic reaction to the cashew fruit was the decisive factor in her choice to remain in Brazil, but she remarked to the Barkers that while "I have liked it so much here, thanks entirely to my friends, that I've stayed on and on," she was "now planning to take off on my vague little freighter line around March 1st."[36] Bishop's letter was interrupted by her birthday celebration, where she received a surprising gift from an unlikely source, an event that deflected—as it proved, for good—her plans to continue her freighter voyage.

When Bishop excitedly resumed her letter to the Barkers on February 9, it was to announce, "Heavens—yesterday was my birthday and I am fonder of Brazilians than ever." She added, "A neighbor who I scarcely know—because we have no known language in common, for one thing—came bringing me my lifelong dream—a TOUCAN."[37] The Tomskas were Polish refugees who "ran the zoo in Warsaw, I think it was. He does a huge animal business throughout the world." These émigrés had recently purchased a nearby property from Lota, and Bishop had been a frequent visitor "to admire their birds and animals but I never dreamed that they would give me a toucan—they're quite valuable." It seems never to have occurred to Bishop that Lota, who was in a position to know her attractive guest's lifelong wish, might have engineered or at least encouraged the surprising fulfillment of that dream.

Bishop was truly enthralled. Her letter to the Barkers shows that in a single day, Bishop had already named her new companion Uncle Sam (Sammy, for short) and studied her prize so closely that she could regale her friends with a scintillating account of Sammy's singular physical charms. "He has brilliant, electric-blue eyes, gray-blue legs and feet. Most of him is black, except the base of the enormous bill is green and yellow and he has a bright gold bib and bunches of red feathers on his stomach and under his tail."[38] She was also pleased to report on Sammy's singular digestive habits: "He eats six bananas a day. I must say they seem to go right through him and come out practically as good as new—meat, grapes—to see him swallowing grapes is rather like playing a pinball machine."[39] One could hardly travel with ease accompanied by such a frisky and demanding cabinmate on a small freighter plugging resolutely around the Horn.

With the arrival of Sammy, all talk of her departure on the next freighter melted out of her correspondence with her American and British friends. On February 14, Bishop was writing to Marianne Moore about a visit to Rio "to see about extending my Brazilian visa."[40] As Bishop's friend Frank Bidart would later recall, "One morning, Elizabeth was in bed and Lota came into her room and asked her to stay with her in Brazil. Elizabeth said yes. She was surprised she had said yes. She liked Lota but she was not in love with her. Over the next few years, she really fell in love with Lota."[41] Perhaps what Bishop first fell deeply in love with was the secure and curiously intriguing world that Lota was able to offer her on her mountain.

Not every North American might have found the world of Samambaia equally attractive, particularly while the main house remained under construction. As Bishop told the Barkers, "We are sort of camping out in a third of it."[42] But Bishop knew that her friend Moore would understand, for here was "a sort of dream combination of plant & animal life. . . . Not only are there highly impractical mountains all around with clouds floating in &

out of one's bedroom, but waterfalls, orchids, all the Key West flowers I know & Northern apples and pears as well."[43] Again, more than one image in this letter would later appear in a published Bishop poem. To Moore, Bishop reported that "now the butterflies have come for the summer— some enormous, pale blue iridescent ones, in pairs. . . . And I've never seen such moths." Yet along with this extraordinary fauna came days and nights lived under comparatively primitive conditions and a stream of house- guests that most of Bishop's northern friends would have deemed unwel- come. Because the house was unfinished and lit by oil lamps, "of course we get thousands [of butterflies], and mice, and large black crabs like patent leather, and the biggest walking-stick bugs I've ever seen." Still, Bishop felt that Moore would understand that "it is all wonderful to me and my ideas of 'travel' recede pleasantly every day."[44]

According to James Merrill, Bishop related that Lota had assured her that she "could very, very easily add a little studio apartment for Elizabeth to the house she was building." Such a gift would provide Bishop with two rooms of her own where she could write in peace and solitude, with breaks to enjoy the intriguing natural world and the supportive social and cultural network Lota was able to provide. As Merrill recalled it, "That was really what began the tears. Elizabeth said, 'I've never in my life had anyone make that kind of gesture toward me and it just meant everything.'"[45]

Yet not all of Bishop's American friends approved of her decision to remain. Pearl Kazin, who was then planning her own farewell to Rio, felt a strong "disaffection" for Brazil and couldn't wait to leave the country— which she did shortly after Bishop determined to stay. For Kazin, it was not just her own dislike of Brazilian life that "made Elizabeth's decision to live there seem risky";[46] to her, Bishop appeared "fragile," and as Kazin would later observe, Bishop "knew hardly anything of this immense country, yet at the age of forty she was committing herself to a foreignness more com- plex than even this experienced traveler had ever known." Kazin was trou- bled by a swarm of doubts: "Would she be able to find the asthma medicine she couldn't live without? Learn Portuguese, a language that confounded me? And wouldn't the modest income she had inherited from her father's family be frighteningly inadequate against a rate of inflation that galloped more wildly out of control every day?"[47]

Still, Bishop saw her stay as a path toward salvation and potential fulfillment. Lowell queried, not altogether approvingly, from his own current abode in Amsterdam, "Why Brazil? That's what everyone asks us."[48] Bishop couldn't resist proclaiming, "I have a TOUCAN—named Uncle Sam in a chauvinistic outburst. He's wonderful, gulps down jewelry or pretends to, can play catch with grapes, and has brilliant blue eyes like neon lights."[49] She added, with an air of satisfaction, "I seem to have become a Brazilian home-body, and I get just as excited now over a jeep trip to buy kerosene in the next village as I did in November at the thought of my trip around the Horn."[50] What Bishop couldn't quite tell Lowell in so many words was that she was falling in love with Lota, and that this accounted, at least in part, for a settled feeling that was new to her.

As Lota's forty-second birthday approached—five weeks after Bishop's own February 8 celebration of her forty-first, and five days before her exuberant missive to Lowell—Bishop felt ready to express through her art her deepening attachment to Lota and Lota's world. She memorialized her decision to stay in the form of a unique birthday gift. Calling on her skills as a watercolorist, she crafted a still life featuring one of the kerosene lamps that provided the house with illumination. On that watercolor Bishop inscribed, in black ink, the first, briefest, simplest, and most direct of the series of love poems that she would dedicate to her newfound partner and protector:

> *For Lota:*
>> *Longer than Aladdin's burns,*
>> *Love, & many Happy Returns.*
>>> *March 16th, 1952*
>>>> *Elizabeth.*[51]

Elizabeth Bishop's unusually forthright gift of verse celebrates the comparatively primitive but comforting conditions under which they were living and hints at the bright prospect of their future union. Bishop also wryly alludes to Lota's predilection for America-made manufactured goods—here a leading brand of oil lamp named for that popular figure from *The Arabian Nights.* For all its brevity and understated wit, her couplet speaks to the luminous promise of a passionate and lasting love.

On March 14, 1952, two days before she proffered her gift of art and verse to her hostess and newfound love, Bishop sent Katherine White, poetry editor of *The New Yorker,* her first Brazilian poem, "Arrival at Santos." After minor quibbles over punctuation, the poem appeared in *The New Yorker*'s June 21, 1952, issue. Given Bishop's deliberate rate of poetic production and *The New Yorker*'s stately editorial methods, this was an almost journalistic rate of speed. The poem—and particularly that final line, "we are driving to the interior"—might be taken as an oblique announcement to her friends and colleagues of her decision to reside in and explore that never-named country, Brazil.

In the opening of "Arrival at Santos," Bishop refers to the promontories surrounding Santos harbor as "impractically shaped and—who knows?—self-pitying mountains." Perhaps Bishop was thinking more of her own Samambaia mountains, since she frequently dubbed these "impractical" in her letters to North American friends. In her second Brazilian poem, "The Mountain," Bishop comically dramatizes the inner emotional life of just such an impractical and even self-pitying mountain, no doubt thinking particularly of the exposed granite peak under which she now resided in her unfinished home. This mountain, voicing its own thoughts in a singular dramatic monologue, expresses a partly comic geologic crisis of identity, emphasized by the poem's alternating refrains: "I do not know my age" and "Tell me how old I am." Bishop's personified mountain seems startled by things that ought to be familiar, such as the nightly appearance of the moon: "At evening something behind me." Then comes the daily but still unsettling reappearance of the sun: "In the morning it is different. An open book confronts me, / too close to read in comfort." The rainy season's annual vapors—new to Bishop but familiar to the mountain—are no less discomfiting: "And then the valleys stuff / impenetrable mists / like cotton in my ears. / I do not know my age." At first the mountain's voice sounds like a frustrated adolescent, but by the end it has settled into the patterns of a querulous elderly relation: "I do not mean to complain. / They say it is my fault. / Nobody tells me anything. / Tell me how old I am." Finally, after seeking words for its unfulfilled yearning for understanding and connection, the mountain settles into resigned acknowledgment of isolation and uncertainty:

> I am growing deaf. The birdcalls
> dwindle. The waterfalls go unwiped.
> What is my age?
> Tell me how old I am.[52]

Bishop remained dismissive of "The Mountain," even after it was praised by friends such as Marianne Moore. She more or less begged *The New Yorker* not to publish it, instead asking that it be released and forwarded to *Poetry*, where it appeared in a special anniversary issue as what Bishop considered a mere "contribution." She included the poem in her second book, but she banished it from later collections—and it has received scarcely a word of commentary from her critics. Yet placed in its living context, "The Mountain" comes into sharper focus as an unlikely surrealistic comic gem, in which Bishop humorously relocates the deep and plaintive anxiety of such late 1940s poems as "Conversation," "Argument," and "While Someone Telephones" onto an object that she endows with sentient life. Thus, she finds a way to voice and at the same time distance her uncertainties about the comforting and discomfiting features of her newly acquired world.

Bishop's next Brazilian poem, "The Shampoo," may now be read as a veiled but poignant tribute to her new Brazilian lover. Adrienne Rich, in an appreciation published five years after Bishop's death, saw it as celebrating "a serious, tender practical rite between two women."[53] Bishop submitted the poem to *The New Yorker* on June 18, 1953, and two weeks later received Katherine White's reluctant letter of rejection. "It is perfectly horrid to have to return a poem of yours," wrote White, "especially when we are so eager to have one to publish. But though the votes were mixed on 'The Shampoo,' the noes had it in the end." For *The New Yorker*, the sticking point emerged in the last two stanzas, which give voice to a keen, if thinly veiled, expression of sensuous intimacy. In the version considered by *The New Yorker*, Lota, her unnamed and never-gendered "dear friend," is described as "demanding and too voluble, / and look what happens. For Time is / nothing if not amenable." After that hint of criticism, the poem turns gently toward the romantic, or even the erotic, with the teasing lines, "The shooting stars in your black hair / in bright formation / are flocking where, / so straight, so soon?" And the poem ends with a direct and, for the reader at least, surprising invitation: "—Come, let me wash it in this big tin basin, / battered and shiny like the moon."[54]

In explaining *The New Yorker*'s rejection of the poem, Katherine White continued, "One reason against it for us, is that this is a personal poem in which you do not quite seem to have described the occasion involved. At least it does not seem to us that you have conveyed it all; for instance, what was the dear friend too demanding and too voluble about?"[55] Of course, Bishop could hardly describe the occasion more directly without giving away the homoerotic subtext of the relationship between herself and her genderless "dear friend"—a subtext that *The New Yorker* may well have feared was already too apparent. Significantly, White did not offer Bishop the opportunity of revising the poem to make the occasion clearer. When her principal venue rejected one of her writings, Bishop sometimes lost faith in it, but she continued to believe in this one. She sent a copy to Pearl Kazin, now a *New Yorker* copy editor, with the tart comment, "Here is the little poem Mrs. White couldn't understand. I have changed three words, though, since she returned it."[56] Bishop's change had replaced the words "demanding and too voluble"—anyone who knew the outspoken Lota would readily identify her in this description—with the more alliterative and enigmatic "precipitate and pragmatical."

After "The Shampoo" had also been rejected by *Poetry*, another Bishop-friendly venue, despite this new revision, Bishop sent it on to May Swenson. Swenson responded with a lengthy meditation, stating at the outset that "it feels right, but I would have a deuce of a time saying why," and then adding quickly, "I'm dead sure it's a good poem." Using almost the same language as White, Swenson conceded that "it feels like something has been left out." However, she quickly added, "But this makes it better in a way . . . a mysteriousness, although the expression is perfectly straightforward." Grasping for more specifics, Swenson mused that "it's a kind of tribute to someone—and it's also a regret about old age."[57]

In her reply, Bishop freely explained to her fellow lesbian poet details that she could not directly unfold to an editor or reader. Beginning with her previously cited observation about Lota's "long straight black hair" with its "two silver streaks on each side, quite wide," Bishop added, "Shiny tin basins, all sizes, are very much a feature of Brazilian life. . . . [W]e used an enormous one [for our shampoo], before we got our now more-or-less-hot-running-water in the bathroom." Bishop also provided a context for the poem's opening: "The still explosions on the rocks, / the lichens, grow / by spreading, gray, concentric shocks." Bishop explained to Swenson, "I am surrounded with rocks and lichens." Her poem continues fancifully, and paradoxically, that these lichens "have arranged / to meet the rings around the moon, although / within our memories they have not changed."[58] Bishop explained to Swenson that these Samambaia lichens "have the sinister coloration of rings around the moon exactly, sometimes—and seem to be undertaking to spread to infinity, like the moon's as well."[59] What she did not add was that these still explosions on the rocks echoed the explosions within herself over her developing relationship with Macedo Soares, and that they echoed her uncertainties as well about the passing of time and the permanence of love. Swenson must have intuited some of this, however, because when she read the poem as a "regret about old age," she also saw in it "the wish that a person could change or age as slowly as a cliff—or that this person *has* that kind of foreverness—or that by washing her hair in the old basin of the moon, you could confer it on her."[60]

The American literary scholar Ashley Brown, who arrived in Brazil on a Fulbright in August 1964 and became one of Bishop's close friends, testifies that Bishop and Lota's shampoo ceremony continued long after the arrival of internal plumbing at Samambaia: "Elizabeth and Lota got along very well together, had this great ease with one another. I remember well the way Elizabeth used to wash Lota's hair. . . . Elizabeth used to make quite a thing of it. It was a ritual Elizabeth made [into] a poem."[61]

In her 1984 tribute to Bishop, Adrienne Rich acknowledged that in her early readings of Bishop, "I had not then connected the themes of outsiderhood and marginality in her work, as well as its encodings and obscurities, with a lesbian identity. I was looking for a clear female tradition; the tradition I was discovering was diffuse, elusive, often cryptic." Yet Rich was surely thinking of poems such as "The Shampoo" when she added that after further readings of this elder poet in the context of "the time and customs of the 1940s and 1950s, Bishop's work now seems to me remarkably honest and courageous."[62]

Elizabeth Bishop published "The Shampoo" at last in a July 1955 issue of *The New Republic*—two years after she had first submitted it to *The New Yorker*. A few months later, it appeared as the concluding item in her second volume of poetry, *A Cold Spring*. She would live on in Brazil for many years, observing its tattered beauty with the eye of an outsider but also with the insider perspective that her life with Lota afforded. From this unique point of vantage, in a world she could never have foreseen, Bishop found the time and inspiration to weave her body of poetry, prose, and correspondence.

CHAPTER TWELVE

SAMAMBAIA

Wouldn't you like to live on a South Sea Island—and forget calendars, and church and subways, and doctors, and Logarithms?

ELIZABETH BISHOP, 1927 LETTER TO LOUISE BRADLEY

Just four months after she had made her commitment to remain in Brazil with Lota, Bishop made a July 1952 journey to Key West and New York in the company of her "hostess" to wrap up her affairs in the United States and have her books, papers, and other possessions shipped to Brazil. By mid-August, Bishop was back at Samambaia, settling into the small corner that had so far been completed of the ultramodern house whose ongoing construction Macedo Soares continued to oversee. Bishop herself began to establish a routine that she described to various friends back home, and explained that so far the social life "up here where I am is very limited—a few friends make it up the mountain over the weekends, and arrive with their cars spouting boiling water." However, most of the time, "we go to bed to read at 9:30, surrounded by oil lamps, dogs, moths, mice, bloodsucking bats, etc." Still, she continued, "I like it so much that I keep thinking I have died and gone to heaven, completely undeservedly."[1]

When she wasn't working on a poem or story, she was often pounding out a letter on her typewriter to one of her many epistolary friends in North America. As one frequent correspondent, Pearl Kazin, observed of Bishop, "She was a marvelous letter-writer, the words flowing from her fingers with an uninhibited spontaneity so very different from the reticence and restraint of her poems and stories." Kazin noted accurately that although Bishop was "far from prolific in her published work, she poured her days into thousands of letters with unstinting vitality and ease."[2] Robert Lowell went even further, asserting that "when Elizabeth Bishop's letters are published (as they will be) she will be recognized as not only one of the best, but one of the most prolific writers of our century."[3] Bishop had been a funny, fluent, and confiding letter writer since her middle teens, but during her Brazilian years, she raised her epistolary performance to a new level.

Many of these epistolary friends have acknowledged that the receipt of a Bishop letter was marked for them as a special occasion. Kazin described her early letters from Brazil appearing in flimsy airmail envelopes and offering a "free-associating potpourri of domestic details, literary gossip and judgment, politics, landscape, lamentation, weather, and joy—the joy she felt at no longer being alone, of living in a house alive with noisy, succoring normality."[4] While Bishop was maintaining this extensive correspondence, she was also absorbing almost every page of a daunting array of American and British literary magazines. These she (and Lota) avidly perused from the moment they arrived, bringing the world of letters in all its diversity to their mountain retreat outside Petrópolis. And Lota, too—whom Bishop described as an inveterate "letter snoop"[5]—would frequently take an opportunity to devour the missives Bishop was receiving from Marianne Moore, May Swenson, and Robert Lowell. Bishop also pored over every issue of *Time*, which she described to Robert Lowell as "that awful magazine that you have to read here because it has the news first, at least."[6] Yet, for the moment at any rate, the world encapsulated in *Time* magazine seemed far removed from Samambaia. As she had experienced once before in her beloved Great Village, Bishop was rediscovering at mid-century a world without electricity or indoor plumbing, a world in which horses and oil lamps remained in active use. She acknowledged to the Barkers that it was "really funny to have *Partisan Review* arrive on horseback sometimes." And she added, "It's funny to come to Brazil to experience total recall about Nova Scotia—geography must be more mysterious than we realize, even. . . . But it is wonderful to be able to work, isn't it—I hadn't been, really for so many years."[7]

In the October following her July 1952 return to Samambaia, Bishop was able to report to her "Dear little Barkers" that her "clavichord—and my 'library'" were all "sitting on the dock in Rio right now and should get here next week." The house in which these treasures would be lodged was only "about a third finished now,"[8] but it was already being written up in architectural magazines, and Bishop was sure it would prove to be a marvel. The current absence of plumbing did not trouble her, because she could wash her hair in the waterfall and swim in the nearby rock pool. Later Bishop would write to Swenson that "Lota and I both wish you were here this morning to go for a swim right now and slide in the waterfall with us and have ripe figs and prosciutto for lunch."[9] The main inconvenience caused by the absence of electricity was that there was no source to power a record player, and "music is the one thing lacking here."[10] When, after several months, Bishop's goods finally cleared Rio's customs (always a chancy business), she was able to announce to Polly Hanson, "I have my clavichord again now . . . and it is so nice, a novelty and a social asset . . . , besides being awfully nice in the evenings here."[11] Bishop was also rediscovering her long-neglected skills on the recorder.

For the first time in ages, Bishop now had at hand her entire collection of books—or, as she said to Polly Hanson, "what was left of it after having it handed around for ten years"—as well as all of her papers, drafts, and fragments of promising yet uncompleted literary efforts. Bishop also shared access to Lota's extensive book collection. Now she could settle down with time to write and read and think. She added, of having one's own books in Brazil, "One just has to, really, since there isn't much in the way of libraries here." Then she added, by way of a characteristic qualification, "I do get books all the time, though, from the British Council. . . . I am working my way through their travel section and Lota has exhausted all the works on *compost*." Meanwhile, Macedo Soares had ascertained that "the waterfall is powerful enough for a turbine." This meant that someday, "there will be electricity, a Victrola, etc., we hope."[12] In her own curious way, in this un-expected, unanticipated place, Bishop was fulfilling a long-cherished and perhaps almost forgotten dream.

When Elizabeth Bishop was just sixteen, she had shared this dream in a letter to Louise Bradley:

> But someday—this is true—I'm going to live in Tahiti or one of those is-lands with a piano and stacks of books—and the sea and sun—and stars. So you must come with me and bring the Irish harp and we'll play together—not just music. Wouldn't you like to live on a South Sea Island—and forget calendars, and church and subways, and doctors, and Logarithms? Say yes or rather, write it to me.[13]

Louise Bradley never did say or write the word "yes" to Bishop's prop-osition. But now, in its own surprising way, Bishop's youthful dream was indeed proving true, albeit on a granite mountaintop in Brazil rather than on an island in the South Seas. Here, she had plenty of sun and stars. She was in the constant presence of flowing water, and she shared access to a Rio apartment overlooking the sea. Bishop might never join in consort with Louise Bradley at a place remote from prying eyes, but she was shar-ing an intimate life in a mountain retreat with a talented, caring, and de-voted female partner. As a lifelong asthmatic, Bishop could never hope to forget doctors. And as a working writer, she lived intimately, and some-times anxiously, with calendars. But between them, she and Lota now shared an extensive personal library. She had left church and subways and logarithms far behind. And she had begun to suspect that there might be a place for her in the world, after all.

Meanwhile, the complex landscaping and construction project that Macedo Soares was overseeing continued apace, and not without moments of lively disputation between the fiery Lota and her ever-shifting crew of construction workers. One morning during her first October at Samambaia, Bishop remarked to her cousin Kay Orr Sargent that "a wild Latin-American fight about water-pipes" was going on in the next room, and this distraction made it impossible to work on any literary project but the brief letter she was then writing. But Bishop acknowledged that while "these fights sound awful to New Englanders," they really aren't "fights at all . . . & usually end up with everybody hugging everybody else and drinking little cups of coffee"[14]—those *cafezinhos* that remain an essential feature of Brazilian life. Bishop would write boastfully to her British friends the Barkers about the excellence of the coffee while at the same time bemoaning the utter paucity of adequate tea.

Although the effort to complete the house and landscaping would continue steadily for another half decade, one project Lota did complete in fairly short order was the writer's studio that she had promised to Bishop, and that had served as such an irresistible lure. This *estudio* was ready for occupancy within a year after Bishop made her commitment to stay with Lota. The *estudio* stood (and stands) perched along the lower reaches of Lota's granite mountain peak, and it may be reached after a short uphill stroll beyond the main house. As Bishop wrote to Polly Hanson in late March 1953, "I've been settled into the studio for a month now—at least all the books are in, the furniture, etc. . . . I really have a shock of joy every morning when I unlock the door." She found this new retreat "very retired and silent—except for the sound of the waterfall, and you soon get used to that, like breathing."[15] Lota had designed the studio with the practical needs of a writer in mind. Here Bishop had solitude to think as well as space to spread out her numerous projects in verse, translation, and prose, along with a large bulletin board on which to pin up her various drafts.

The studio comprised two small but accommodating rooms. The door that Bishop unlocked each morning opened into an airy reading room, which then led to a writing room provided with "a long work-bench—15 ft or so—under a long window." Bishop explained that through this tall and narrow aperture—at first her only source of light except for oil lamps—she could "look out at an enormous long panel of mountains and trees" that revealed delicate vegetation and "strange pointed hills" with "clouds drifting through them."[16] Once Bishop had placed a manual typewriter on her *estudio*'s long table, and had surrounded it with her various writing projects, she felt set up as an author in a way that she had scarcely felt before.

The waterfall that Bishop heard "dreaming audibly" as it flowed past her *estudio* window was crucial to this household's existence in more ways than one. Not only would this waterfall one day power an electric turbine; it also provided drinking water and fed a rock pool for swimming that kept Bishop, Lota, and their friends and servants cool in summer. Bishop explained, "I wash my hair and then rinse it by holding it in the water-fall—very stimulating."[17] After their return from New York, Lota added another feature of hair-grooming to the one they shared in "The Shampoo," for Lota acquired a good pair of thinning scissors, and with these, she developed the art of cutting Bishop's hair. Bishop—troubled with her unruly locks since her Camp Chequesset days—now had a personal barber. She exclaimed to Hanson, "It's such a relief," adding that her hair now "looks better than it ever has," and claiming that although it seemed unlikely, many observers had concurred that "I have stopped getting gray and am much *less* gray than I was a year ago!"[18]

Whether or not Bishop's hair was actually altering its hue in a more youthful direction, Bishop herself was certainly feeling renewed. And she was enjoying nearly every aspect of her surprising new life. That life did, however, pose its own particular challenges. For example, as she explained to the Barkers, "My Anglo-Saxonism is *really* shocked by the mails—no one would ever dream of writing a letter within the country, and that is not exaggeration. I've tried—letters from Petrópolis to Rio just never appear."[19] Since Bishop was not only a devoted and prolific letter writer but a professional author continually sending drafts and proofs back and forth between her studio and her editors in New York or elsewhere, the exchange of mail was a matter of no small consequence. When May Swenson expressed uncertainty about the function of her distant friend's various ad-dresses, Bishop explained that Lota's country address was *"never to be used,"* since letters sent to Samambaia never arrived. Instead, she and Lota relied on a personal mail run maintained by their friend Mary Morse, Lota's for-mer lover and current business partner. Morse drove to Rio almost every week, and she kept her own small apartment near Lota's penthouse at Rua Antonio Vieira 5. Lota had rented her apartment in 1954 to the Rio's "'New York Times' man" to generate income. Still, their mail was saved for them "by the janitor and brought up [by Morse] once a week."[20] Over the years, more than a few of Bishop's letters were cut short by the remark that Morse was about to depart for Rio and this letter-in-progress must be concluded in order to take that journey with her.

Bishop's never-to-be-used address in the country with Lota was, as she explained to Swenson, "Sítio Alcobaçinha, Fazenda Samambaia, Petrópo-lis." As Bishop parsed the details out for her fellow poet, "'Petrópolis' is the resort town 50 miles from Rio." This town was in the mountains, "much higher and cooler than the city." There, "everyone, (who has any money) has a summer & week-end house, and a few daring people, like us, now live near the year round." Bishop added that, "We're about 7 or 8 miles from Petrópolis, where we go to market, etc." She explained that Lota had inher-ited her big tract of mountainous property from her mother, and added further that "'Fazenda' is 'hacienda'—'Samambaia'—a kind of fern—and giant—15 ft. or so high."[21]

As for Lota herself, Bishop told the Barkers, "She is delightful—extremely funny, energetic, and as her friends keep telling me 'the most intelligent woman in Brazil'—& from what I've seen of them it is certainly true." Bishop felt that Lota's intelligence, independence, and entrepreneur-ial spirit placed her in "an extremely hard position" given that in Brazil, at the time, "women can't even witness documents, etc.—it would make any-one into some kind of feminist in no time."[22] Bishop described Morse, an American woman of independent means, as someone "a few years younger than I am who's been living in Brazil for 10 or 12 years and is an old friend of Lota's, a very nice tall bony Boston type."[23] If Morse felt resentment over Bishop's arrival at Samambaia, she chose to keep it to herself, at least for the present. Morse would soon begin to build a house of her own on the Samambaia property. Bishop mentioned to the Barkers that at the end of one of her mail runs, Morse came up to the main house for lunch bearing "another letter from you-all" along with "cans and cans of the cement necessary to lay the floor."[24] Morse was not alone in transporting such materials up the steep and winding mountain road. When Bishop told the Barkers that Lota planned to sell her Land Rover as soon as the construction project was finished, she added that Lota could not have built the house without it. In fact, when a friend sought to locate Bishop and Lota at a Petrópolis café, the waiter said, "Oh yes, I know Dona Lotinha—she's always driving loads of cement."[25]

For the most part, it was Lota's task to build with wood, concrete, glass, and steel, while Bishop, tucked away in her *estudio*, would quietly build with words. But in July 1953, Bishop proudly described to Polly Hanson her personal role in a construction in cast iron. This took the form of a wood-burning stove for the principal room at Samambaia. Bishop explained, in a letter featuring a line drawing of the object in question, "It is winter here, and I am writing beside our new stove." Bishop added, "We had the iron-work man copy a photograph from a magazine—and my memories, and although it is just a rather ordinary little stove it is quite an innovation here and we are very pleased with it."[26] Bishop's minute study of the Little Marvel stove in the Bulmer kitchen in Great Village, along with the Magee Ideal in her aunt Maud's kitchen in Revere, would now pay off, since Bishop was able to explain to the builder in detail how the wood-stove's working parts should serve in concert. Lota's artisan declared emphatically that "it would never work," but "Lota kept telling him I was from Canada & of course knew all about stoves." Despite shouts and glares from the indignant metalworkers, Bishop's design functioned as she insisted that it would. Soon "smoke came out of the chimney and the room grew warmer and warmer."[27] Bishop would later commemorate this construction in cast iron by placing it alongside a Calder mobile in a watercolor and gouache that she inscribed to their friend Rosinha Leão.[28]

Lota's full name was Maria Carlota Costallat de Macedo Soares, and her ultramodern dwelling would go on to garner a long list of architectural awards. She was the daughter of a wealthy journalist and publisher who had spent some years in European exile. While in France, she attended Catholic convent school, where the nuns discovered her to be full of rambunctious pranks and found her more than a little difficult to manage. While there, the youthful Lota began to develop the advanced artistic tastes that would become a focal point of her later life. When she returned to Brazil, this European education, combined with her intelligence, her innate artistic sense, and her family's wealth and connections, served to project her into Rio's tightly interwoven intellectual elite. Lota's close friends in America included the sculptor Alexander Calder, and she owned more than one work by that modernist master. She also befriended Monroe Wheeler, the director of New York's Museum of Modern Art, on her visits to New York. And she developed friendships with many of the leading figures in Brazilian art and culture, including the painter Cândido Portinari, the poet Manuel Bandeira, fiction writer Clarice Lispector, landscape designer Roberto Burle Marx, and architect Sérgio Bernardes. Lota also developed a close friendship with Carlos Lacerda, who had acquired and built a house on one of Lota's parcels near Samambaia. Lacerda, the editor of *Tribuna da Imprensa*, was a talented and ambitious journalist and a rising conservative political star who had built his reputation on his outspoken criticism of the currently elected president (and former dictator) of Brazil, Getúlio Vargas. He was also a fine talker with a keen interest in the arts who displayed a genuine appreciation for both Lota's and Bishop's distinctive talents. Lacerda would feature prominently, and in later years not always happily, in the future lives of both women.

Outgoing, intuitive, funny, practical, charismatic, erudite, affectionate, and brusquely commanding, Lota de Macedo Soares knew how to get her way and how to live a focused, almost driven life while maintaining a wide circle of friends. Bishop felt that the architecturally dazzling house at Samambaia reflected more Lota's vision than that of Sérgio Bernardes, the youthful professional architect with a brilliant future whom Lota had commissioned to draw up the original plans. As Bishop told the Barkers, Bernardes was a "good friend of ours, but actually this is his only house that I think is really good and it is good because of Lota's taste and her fighting him every inch of the way."[29] Lota was quick to recognize and foster talent in others, and she had—since they met during Lota's 1942 visit to New York—become convinced of Bishop's poetic brilliance. When Bishop arrived in Rio in 1951, Lota saw clearly that this talented but emotionally troubled poet would benefit from the life that she could provide. Lota also saw that Bishop's wit, talent, and intimate companionship could enhance her life at Samambaia. She thus took steps to keep Bishop close to her. She could show Bishop love, encouragement, and security in a setting that the poet found entrancing, and she could perhaps, also, exercise a measure of authority or control. Lota offered Bishop a passport into Brazilian culture that, combined with Bishop's unique talent for observation, would prove of great benefit to her as a poet. Yet Lota's own often-painful family history, and in particular her ongoing differences with and silent distance from her powerful father, along with frequent quarrels with a jealous and disapproving younger sister, had left her with latent vulnerabilities that would have an unpredictable impact on their futures.

In earlier days, Bishop had traveled either alone or with a single friend or intimate companion. Lota, by contrast, functioned as the center of an entourage. This entourage included not only the Brazilian cultural leaders already mentioned, but also, during Samambaia's construction phase, a team of workers whose labors, from dynamiting rock formations to laying stone floors over a foundation of cement, were vigorously overseen by Lota, who referred to her construction crews, in her fluent and confident but not always accurate English, as her "mens."[30]

Writing to her English friends the Barkers, Bishop described the United States as "almost servant-less." Macedo Soares, on the other hand, depended on a shifting assemblage of domestics, while also gathering around her a varied array of adoptees and hangers-on who amounted almost to surrogate family. Most official of these was a young man named Kylso, whom Lota had formally adopted some years before Bishop's arrival. When Kylso eventually married, he and his wife began to produce children at a prolific rate, starting with, as Bishop told it, "three in three years (in spite of all Lota's heart-to-heart scientific talks with them)." Kylso, his wife, and his growing brood of children were frequent visitors to Samambaia, and according to Bishop, Lota sparked "a small scandal" in Petrópolis when she began referring to Kylso's offspring as her grandchildren. Bishop told the Barkers that she would watch as the minds of Lota's hearers started "to click away about when Lota had a child—when she was at that convent in France?" Bishop added with amused satisfaction, "I am called 'aunty.'"[31] Given the bleak isolation of her early years in Revere, Bishop took evident pleasure in the lively and idiosyncratic family circle she enjoyed at Samambaia.

Although Macedo Soares's father was a well-known journalist, she and her father had quarreled, in part over her sexuality, so as Bishop explained, "Unfortunately she hasn't spoken to him for years." She added of the sharply stratified world in which she now moved, with its curious intermingling of servants, hangers-on, and aristocrats, "But it is very strange to me to live in a country where the ruling class and the intellectual class are so very small and all know each other and are all usually related. It's certainly bad for the 'arts' too—it's entirely too easy to get a reputation and never do anything else, and never have to compete. Well, it's all because of NO MIDDLE CLASS."[32]

Lota de Macedo Soares's passions may have been for architecture, literature, music, and the visual arts, but her business was real estate. She was developing properties on the estate she had inherited from her mother for sale to well-to-do buyers who wished to enjoy the cooler weather in the mountains west of Rio. As Bishop spelled it out to Swenson, "The 'real estate development' is a mile or so below us, near the highway—L has kept a good big tract of Alcobaçinha to protect us from neighbors all around."[33] Another form of protection was the fact that one side of the property was a sheer rock mountain. Bishop enclosed with her explanation an advertising brochure for Fazenda Samambaia whose banner headline in Portuguese was rendered by Bishop with evident amusement as, "The ideal retreat . . . where you can build your country home: the *aristocratic* real-estate development (!)." Bishop also underlined a bullet point boasting of a projected Samambaia Country Club, adding in the margin, "Save us!"[34]

She described her social world to Lowell as a "strange tri- or quadrilingual hodgepodge that I like very much," adding, "After a couple of weeks of rain (which, by some racial illusion, I think, is called the 'summer') the cook left, and for about a month I did the cooking. I like to cook, etc., but I'm not used to being confronted with the raw materials, all un-shelled, unblanched, un-skinned, or un-dead. Well, I can cook goat now—with wine sauce."[35] A new cook named Maria was soon hired, who would stay, despite a series of firings, resignations, and rehirings, for more than a decade. Still, Bishop continued to spend much time in the kitchen, a fact that surprised Lota, since women of her aristocratic station in Brazil rarely knew their way around a stovetop or an oven. Bishop would claim to the Barkers that she was earning a "firm reputation as a marvellous cook because I make things when we have company."[36] She spoke proudly, for example, of a birthday cake she had created for Mary Morse: "My dears, it was a triumph—four layers, chocolate, full of chocolate cream, with pink peppermint icing and her name in silver *dragées*." Bishop added, with a note of competitive triumph, "Then Maria, the cook, decided to make a surprise and produced another cake in three tiers, slightly crooked, rather like a romantic false ruin." Worse (or better) still, the cook's cake was "*Heavy*— you could almost hear it thud in your stomach—and for days we gave pieces to the dogs on the sly."[37] Indeed, Bishop's forte in the realm of cuisine would prove to be baking and sweets. She was soon proffering brownies (which she claimed to have "introduced to Brazil"[38]) to Lota's guests along with homemade preserves, and her aunt Grace would sometimes send a gallon of maple syrup from Nova Scotia. Lota soon bestowed on Bishop the affectionate nickname "Cookie."

Robert Lowell and his new wife, Elizabeth Hardwick, had been traveling extensively in Europe as Bishop settled into her new life. This state of transit had temporarily slowed their rate of correspondence. But when Bishop received a 1953 letter from Lowell from the University of Iowa, explaining that he was now teaching at the famous Iowa Writers' Workshop, she declared with satisfaction that "now I have an address and you have an address, and I guess I'll just plunge in." With that, their ongoing correspondence resumed with that familiar "backward and forward flow" that Lowell claimed "always seems to open me up and bring color and peace."[39] In her own early letters from Brazil, Bishop took pains to make Lowell understand that she was keeping up with the world of letters by enumerating the magazines to which she subscribed: "I get *PR*, *Hudson*, & *Kenyon*, *Botteghe Oscure*, *Poetry*—well, quite a lot of things, down to the *Farmer's Digest*, and Lota gets the plastic arts, and down to *Ellery Queen's Monthly*—but I do miss 'little' magazines sometimes, probably." Bishop continued, "I don't feel 'out of touch' or 'expatriated' or anything like that, or suffer from lack of intellectual life, etc. I was always too shy to have much 'intercommunication' in New York, anyway, and I was miserably lonely there most of the time." Now, in her mountain retreat, she had experienced a dramatic change—fulfilling, in an unexpected way, a lifelong dream. She confessed, "Here I am extremely happy, for the first time in my life. I live in a spectacularly beautiful place; we have between us about 3,000 books now; I know, through Lota, most of the Brazilian 'intellectuals' already." Having lived among the tight-lipped Puritans of her Bishop and Bulmer families, Bishop found her Brazilian neighbors "frank, startlingly so, until you get used to Portuguese vocabularies." She added that they were also "extremely affectionate, an atmosphere that I just lap up—no I guess I mean loll in—after that dismal year in Washington and that dismaler winter at Yaddo when I thought my days were numbered and there was nothing to be done about it."[40] What Bishop did not fully realize until much later was that many of Macedo Soares's closest friends felt intensely jealous over Bishop's presence. This shy American, who was very slow to learn to speak their language, had stolen in among them and drawn away much of the brilliant Lota's attention. Yet at least for the time, these envious or resentful friends of Lota kept their own counsel as to their misgivings. After all, Bishop was clearly making their Lota very happy, and both she and Carlos Lacerda, among others, made clear their strong conviction that she was a gifted poet.

Bishop told Lowell, "You would be really fascinated by the family histories. Rio society is beyond belief. Proust in the tropics with a samba instead of Vinteuil's little phrase."[41] She took delight in the usages of her new language, Portuguese, explaining that here she was known as Dona Elizabetchy. Bishop had waited years for her mentor, Miss Moore, to invite her to use her given name, but here it was "always first names. You'd be 'Seu Roberto.' No, I guess having a degree, you'd be 'Doutor Roberto.'" Then, alluding to Lowell's nickname, Cal, and its disquieting progenitor, Bishop added, "'Caligula' would surprise no one,—I know a Tacito, an Aristides, a Theophilis, a Praxiteles." She added that "the nicknames are marvelous—Magu is the cutest—a friend named Maria Augusta."[42] In reply, Lowell mused, "I think about you continually—you and your studio and your Brazilian world. I'm sure you are as happy as you sound." Then he added, with more than a note of self-mockery, "But I don't approve at all. Like a rheumatic old aunt, I would gladly spoil all your fun just to have you back."[43] As the years unfolded, Lowell kept Bishop up to date with an amusing stream of local literary gossip, devoting special attention to the disparate trio of Marianne Moore, Randall Jarrell, and Mary McCarthy. Lowell reported that Moore said of her protégé at one literary gathering, "Poor Elizabeth, she does her best to bear up and rejoice." He added that at this event, Moore got off a steady stream of her obliquely incisive one-liners while being "always small, gracious, mobile, and beautiful. I feel utterly in love with her."[44]

In November 1953, Bishop spotted a brief and cryptic notice in *Time* recording the death in Manhattan of the heavy-drinking Dylan Thomas. The cause of his death would prove to be a cerebral hemorrhage, brought on by alcohol abuse combined with an untreated case of pneumonia. Bishop quickly wrote to Pearl Kazin, Thomas's former lover, to express her dismay over the Welsh poet's death at the age of thirty-nine. Bishop had known Thomas only briefly, when he made a famous series of recordings for her at the Library of Congress in 1950, but she told Kazin that she found him "tremendously sympathetic," adding, too, that she had "felt frightened for him" because he seemed to be moving on an extremely self-destructive course. As poets, they were very different. Lowell had acknowledged in a 1947 review of books by each of them that "nothing could be more unlike" Thomas's poetry than "the unrhetorical, cool, and beautifully thought out poems of Elizabeth Bishop."[45] Bishop told Lowell after Thomas's death that "immediately, after one lunch with him, you knew perfectly well he was only good for two or three years more."[46] Bishop's poetry reads like the work of a threatened but determined, self-protective survivor. Bishop saw in Thomas's poetry a "desperate win-or-lose-all quality," but this did not prevent her from asking Pearl Kazin, "Why oh why did he have to go & die now?" She begged Kazin at the close of her letter to tell all she could about Thomas's death, adding, "I have met few people in my life I felt such an instantaneous sympathy and pity for." She added with vehemence that "Dylan made most of our contemporaries seem small and disgustingly self-seeking and cautious and hypocritical and cold." Perhaps Bishop recognized in Dylan Thomas an inverted topos of her own personality. Certainly she felt that "in my own minor way I know enough about drink and destruction."[47] In the years to come, Bishop would experience many more such shocks of loss, as one by one a long line of poets of her own generation and the next one would face all-too-early deaths. Bishop survived to write the elegy for Robert Lowell and to quietly mourn the passing of more than a few other members of her poetic generation.

Bishop continued to struggle with asthma in her new setting, and as early as September 1952, while she was writing with such relish to her friends about her Brazilian adventure, she had begun to find breathing so difficult that she had no option but to try a new and powerful anti-inflammatory drug: cortisone. She began taking this medication both by injection and by mouth, and at first found the results to be extraordinary. All at once, she could breathe easily, and she wrote an exultant letter to her Key West friend and fellow asthmatic Martha Sauer describing the miraculous results and exclaiming, "At last, I can have a cat!"[48] But she soon found that cortisone, while it did help her breathing, was accompanied by powerful side effects, not all of them welcome. She described the experience to Robert Lowell while entering her "third ride" with cortisone in 1953: "To begin with it is absolutely marvelous. You can sit up typing all night long and feel wonderful the next day. I wrote two stories in a week. The letdown isn't bad if you do all the proper things, but once I didn't and found myself shedding tears all day long for no reason at all."[49] The following October she told the Barkers that she had spent most of the past month in bed with asthma. She added, "Finally in despair about two weeks ago I started taking cortisone again, against my wishes."[50] Bishop experienced almost immediate relief from asthma symptoms—she could breathe again!—but this was soon linked to yet another onset of cortisone-imposed elevation, leading some months later to a crash that left her able to do little else but sleep. She called this powerful but hard-to-manage medication "fearful and wonderful stuff," and hoped that someday she might "just learn how to use it." She added that "cortisone withdrawal does make one very blue . . . although I keep telling myself it's nothing but medicine and not real at all."[51] Two further side effects of cortisone that were decidedly real were an average weight gain of thirty pounds and puffiness in facial features. A glance at Bishop's face in photographs taken during her years in Brazil will generally suffice to show whether Bishop was on cortisone at that particular moment. In a 1956 letter, Bishop asked noted photographer Rollie McKenna not to publish photographs of her taken at Samambaia two years before. Bishop felt that these photographs, while in most respects "awfully good," made her unhappy because they showed her face "swollen from cortisone."[52] When several of these photos were finally published, they revealed a relaxed and smiling, albeit somewhat puffy-faced, Bishop, clad in blue jeans and a man's white shirt while lounging comfortably in a patio chair—and they quickly became among the most recognizable and popular images of the poet.

Bishop's struggles with asthma and her sequence of rides on the cortisone roller coaster no doubt contributed to a recurrence of her alcohol abuse in mid-1954. In June of that year, after a bout of heavy drinking, and at the urging of Lota, Bishop agreed to be admitted to the Hospital Estrangeiros in Rio for a rest cure. There she began a program of alcohol aversion therapy based on Antabuse (generic name: disulfiram), a powerful drug then only recently on the market. Antabuse works by removing enzymes from the patient's system that the body requires to metabolize alcohol. This unmetabolized alcohol causes painful and toxic hangover-like effects as soon as the alcohol is consumed. The intended goal is to make drinking so unpleasant that the patient becomes averse to alcohol consumption. For several years after beginning Antabuse therapy, Bishop was able, with only occasional lapses, to avoid the pattern of destructive drinking that had haunted her for so long. While she remained at Samambaia with Lota—and before she began living chiefly in Rio in the early 1960s and spending long periods by herself—Bishop found that she was able either to drink moderately or else to abstain from alcohol altogether.

The pair of stories Bishop drafted in just a week during her first euphoric experience with cortisone in October 1952 were those probing narratives of her Nova Scotian childhood, "Gwendolyn" and "In the Village." "Gwendolyn," the first of these to be completed, tells the story of the death from insulin shock of her childhood friend Gwendolyn Patriquin (in the story Gwendolyn Appletree). In actual fact, Bishop's friend Gwendolyn died on September 1, 1922, when Bishop was eleven, during one of her summer visits to her Bulmer grandparents, and for the most part, the story squares with known historical fact, though with some minor variations in detail.

"Gwendolyn" begins with what Bishop calls a "preliminary." This opening focuses on a special doll belonging to her youngest aunt, the eighteen-year-old Mary, who was now, like her sisters before her, training to be a nurse in Boston. Bishop was dazzled by her aunt Mary's special doll, which had been carefully tucked away for safekeeping and which she was allowed to play with only because she was suffering from a bad case of bronchitis. This doll, whose name her grandmother could not remember, had an array of "wonderful garments, beautifully sewn." This special creature made "the family dolls I usually played with seem rugged and childish."[53]

Bishop's story presents Gwendolyn as if she, too, were almost a doll. They were friends, and "to me she stood for everything that the slightly repellant but fascinating words 'little girl' should mean." Along with the beauty of her name ("its dactyl trisyllables could have gone on forever as far as I was concerned"), there was the fact that she was "blond, and pink and white, exactly like a blossoming apple tree. And," Bishop added, "she was 'delicate,' which, in spite of the bronchitis, I was not."[54] Part of what made Gwendolyn delicate was that she had diabetes. "I had been told this much and had some vague idea that it was because of 'too much sugar,' and that in itself made Gwendolyn even more attractive, as if she would prove to be solid candy if you bit her." Bishop recalled that her grandparents spoke disapprovingly of how much sugar Gwendolyn's family was feeding her, and she alludes to their saying that "her parents would not obey the doctor's orders and gave her whatever she wanted to eat." But long after Gwendolyn's death, one of her surviving brothers, who had read Bishop's story, insisted his parents had no idea that sugar was a danger to individuals with diabetes. This seems quite probable, since the risks of sugar for diabetics was only just becoming known in the early 1920s, and the pioneering research on these risks was taking place at Massachusetts General Hospital, where Bishop's mother and aunts had trained as nurses. It seems most likely that Bishop overheard concerned or disapproving comments from her aunts and grandparents, who were reticent to impose their views on others, even as Gwendolyn's parents remained ignorant of the risks their child was running.

One night, Gwendolyn slept over at Bishop's house, sharing Bishop's small bedroom, and that night, according to the story, she told Bishop matter-of-factly, "I am going to die." And indeed, "Two days after this visit, Gwendolyn did die." Gwendolyn's funeral took place in the Presbyterian church, directly across the Great Village green from the Bulmer house, but as Bishop tells the story, she was not allowed to attend. For some reason, Bishop wrote, "I wasn't even supposed to know" that the funeral was taking place, even though she could see the mourners gathering in plain sight outside the church a short distance away. Her grandmother stayed home with her and sat by herself in the kitchen watching through a window. Bishop could tell that "she was crying and crying between her own peeks at the mourners." Her grandmother's handkerchief was "already very wet," and "she was rocking gently." Bishop described herself sneaking into the parlor to gain her own private vantage point on the proceedings, and she dramatized her shock when she noticed that Gwendolyn's white coffin had been left alone outside the church door by two men in black, leaning upright at a slight angle against the wall of the church. What struck her as she looked through the parlor's lace curtains was the knowledge that Gwendolyn's body was "shut invisibly inside" the coffin "forever, there, completely alone on the grass by the church door." This shock sent her "howling to the back door, out among the startled white hens, with my grandmother, still weeping, after me."[55]

The story closes with a final scene in which Elizabeth is playing alone with her cousin Billy, the son of her uncle Arthur (and therefore the brother of the child whose death, which "made him white forever," is memorialized in "First Death in Nova Scotia," a poem completed three years later). Since neither Elizabeth nor Billy had been permitted to take part in the funeral, their experience of mourning remained incomplete. Soon Elizabeth remembered her Mary's special doll, which she had been forbidden to touch again, and she and her cousin improvised a funeral service of their own. Then, according to Bishop, "I don't know which of us said it first, but one of us did, with wild joy—that it was Gwendolyn's funeral, and that the doll's real name, all this time, was Gwendolyn." The wild joy surely arose from the emotional relief attached to the fact that they might finally complete the process of interrupted grieving that had been forestalled by the young pair's exclusion from the village's ritual of mourning. "But then," the story continues, "my grandparents drove into the yard and found us, and my grandmother was furious that I had dared to touch Aunt Mary's doll. Billy was sent straight home and I don't remember now what awful thing happened to me."[56]

Not long after Bishop submitted "Gwendolyn" to *The New Yorker*, where it was promptly accepted, she followed it with "In the Village," which Bishop claimed had been rushed to completion during that first encounter with cortisone, though she had drafted, as far back as 1936, an initial treatment of its events in her "Reminiscences of Great Village." This submission involved a far more extended negotiation with *The New Yorker*, whose editors felt that the story's oblique handling of time and point of view might make it difficult for their readers to follow. Bishop was frequently diffident in the face of her editors' critiques, but in this case she felt convinced of the story's merits and importance. After Bishop threatened to send it to another journal, *The New Yorker* at last agreed to publish it without significant changes. As explored in Chapter 2, Bishop's account of the climactic breakdown her mother, Gertrude, experienced when the poet was five years old, opens with the echo of her mother's scream. The story closes with an altogether different sound, the sound of the hammer of the blacksmith, Nate, in lines that lay out on the page like poetry: "Clang / *Clang.* / Nate is shaping a horseshoe." The blacksmith's clang evokes an instant, almost ecstatic reaction: "Oh, beautiful pure sound! / It turns everything else into silence." Yet again, the hammer strikes: "*Clang.* / And everything except the river holds its breath." Can the power of Nate's hammer heal her loss? At least for a time, that sound seems to silence the haunting echo of her mother's outcry, for "now there is no scream. Once there was one and it settled slowly down to earth one hot summer afternoon; or did it float up, into that dark, too dark, blue sky? But surely it has gone away, forever." The power of Nate's hammer would appear to align with the power of art. It cannot truly make her (or we, the readers) forget the scream—at least, not forever. But the blow of the hammer can speak in its own voice, and through that speaking it makes its own inalienable claims. "*Clang.* / It sounds like a bell buoy out at sea. / It is the elements speaking: earth, air, fire, water." Tied though it may be to the most fundamental things on earth, the clang of the blacksmith's hammer cannot erase the loss of "all those other things—clothes, crumbling postcards, broken china; things damaged and lost, sickened or destroyed," and it cannot really erase the sound of "the frail almost-lost scream." But the power of the blacksmith's art offers its own compensations, and the story ends with the cry,

Nate!
Oh, beautiful sound, strike again![57]

When he read "In the Village" in *The New Yorker*, Robert Lowell was deeply impressed. Remembering his own recent time in Holland, he described the story as having "a great ruminating Dutch landscape feel of goneness" and added, thinking of Nelly, the large bovine companion who the five-year-old child Elizabeth guides to her distant pasture, "I could weep for the cow." Speaking of both this story and "Gwendolyn," Lowell added, "I feel they are perhaps parts of a Nova Scotia growing-up novel—though of course they are rounded short stories." Bishop would continue to regard this story as one of her greatest achievements. She would read it to friends at Harvard, tears streaming down her face, when she wanted them to understand the basis of her early experience. And the story almost certainly owes its existence to her life at Samambaia.

Bishop's fascination with rural childhood continued through her discovery of *Minha Vida de Menina*, or "My Life as a Young Girl," a book recommended to her by a series of friends not long after her arrival in Brazil. Bishop described it as "a diary, the diary actually kept by a girl between the ages of twelve and fifteen in the far-off town of Diamantina, in 1893-1895."

The book was published in a small press run in 1942, under the authorial pseudonym Helena Morley, "chiefly with the idea of amusing the author's family and friends." It had achieved a surprising success, finding a wide public in Brazil and attaining the status of a minor classic. Bishop felt instantly drawn to this small volume, rich with incidents that Bishop found "odd, remote, and long ago, yet fresh, and funny and eternally true." The small provincial town reminded her of her own Great Village, yet with a difference, since the longer she stayed in Brazil, "the more Brazilian the book seemed."[58] When Bishop became interested in translating *Minha Vida de Menina*, she learned that the author was now living with her husband in posh circumstances in Rio. This author, Dona Alice Brandt, who was of humble origins, married a cousin who had risen to become a leading figure in the Brazilian financial system. Seu Augusto Mário Caldeira Brant was in his late seventies, and serving a second term as president of the Bank of Brazil. Bishop met Dona Alice after one of Brazil's leading poets, Manuel Bandeira, arranged an introduction, and she received encouragement to proceed with her translation, which would help her hone her skills with Portuguese and draw her more deeply into the fabric of Brazilian cultural and political history. Bishop began work on the translation in 1953, consulting with Lota as she went, and achieved steady progress. In August 1954 she told the Barkers, "I have got my translation about ready to mail off to the publisher—or fifty pages as a sample; and I'm having photographs reproduced to go with it—I'll try Houghton Mifflin first, at least. I am sure it is a 'find,' but I don't know whether I'll be able to convince a publisher."[59] Yet while Bishop developed into an outstanding translator of Brazilian poetry and prose, she was always diffident, even after many years in Brazil, about speaking the language, even though her understanding of spoken Portuguese became nearly perfect. Many native English speakers, even those who have mastered Spanish or French, find Portuguese difficult to pronounce, and in Bishop's case this sense of difficulty was intensified by the keen performance anxiety that had brought an early close to any dreams she had once harbored of a career as a concert pianist.

Bishop would soon strike comic gold while exploring this theme in the light verse poem "To Manuel Bandeira, with Jam and Jelly," which highlights the irony that although both she and he are "translators of each other's tongue," each was so shy about pronouncing the other's language: "how can I possibly forget / that we have scarcely spoken yet?" Thus, as Bishop phrased it with mock-heroic grandiloquence, they faced the conundrum of "two mighty poets at a loss, / unable to exchange a word, / —to quote [Senator Joe] McCarthy, 'It's the most / unheard-of thing I've ever heard.'" Bishop was reduced to making an offering of preserves to show her appreciation, although she begged Bandeira to "please believe I've never thought / 'Your book is fine, I like it lots' / is best expressed by apricots," or that "'You put all rivals in the shade' / is well-implied in marmalade." Therefore, she hoped, if she might be allowed the expression, that "this silent jelly" would "speak sweetly to your poet's belly."[60] Bandeira responded in kind with his only known verse statement in English, a couplet announcing, "I wish I had two bellies / because of your good jellies."

Bishop endeavored to translate *Minha Vida de Menina* in order to share with English-speaking readers the pleasure of her discovery of this singular classic, but she also hoped to earn a meaningful sum of money from its publication, which she found always easier to accomplish when working in prose than in verse. For within a short time, Bishop's and Lota's finances had become increasingly interwoven. In general, Bishop took care of her daily expenses while Lota provided the salubrious setting of Samambaia. But Lota's costs were significant. She relied on an extensive staff of domestics. She had numerous adopted children and hangers-on. She liked well-engineered European sports cars and finely finished American domestic goods. And when Lota was possessed by an artistic vision—as she was by the construction of her house—she was determined to carry this vision through to the end, without compromise and at whatever cost. She was also an avid collector of contemporary art. Even on a basis of friendship, Calders and Portinaris didn't come cheap. What's more, when the two traveled together, Lota insisted on going first-class. All this required money, and Lota was frequently living on the edge of her considerable income. After the first of a long series of severe inflations that Bishop would experience in Brazil hit in 1954, the value of the cruzeiro plunged on world markets, and prices for Lota in Europe effectively doubled overnight, causing the couple to cancel a planned trip to Paris. The effects on the common people of Brazil were far worse, of course, with Bishop noting that in Brazil "food prices are incredible and I just don't know how the poor poor people are keeping alive."[61] Lota's income retained much of its effective value within Brazil, as did Bishop's, but for foreign travel the pair came to rely increasingly on the income in hard American dollars that Bishop could earn from writing or grants. Bishop came to feel consistent pressure, both within herself and from Lota, to finish this poem or place that story or translation so that the two could carry out a projected plan for foreign travel.

While Bishop was working on her translation of the book that became *The Diary of "Helena Morley,"* she was also seeking to publish her second book of poems, and was frustrated by a long series of delays with Houghton Mifflin. Her publisher was concerned by the comparative brevity of the book, and therefore hoped that Bishop could give them additional poems. Bishop had some in progress, but none of them had gelled into completed form. For much of her time in Brazil so far, she had been focusing on prose or on translation. At last a resolution was reached. Houghton Mifflin proposed publishing Bishop's second book, *A Cold Spring*, in the same volume with her first book, *North & South*, which was now out of print. This would make, in effect, her "Collected Poems." Bishop resisted at first, but soon came around to accepting this extremely sensible idea. Bishop suggested the simple overall title *Poems*. The volume was published in 1955 under the full title *Poems: North & South—A Cold Spring*. Brazil is comparatively absent from this book, a sign that she had not yet sufficiently digested her Brazil experience to render it into poetry. Only "Arrival at Santos," "The Shampoo," and "The Mountain," all written shortly after her arrival in Brazil and conveying the shock of first impressions, appear near the end of *A Cold Spring*.

Poems is dedicated to Dr. Anny Baumann, Bishop's recognition of Baumann's importance to her through what had been the hardest period of her adult life so far. Robert Lowell added a glowing blurb that begins with a comment on his friend as a person: "Miss Bishop has a good heart and a good eye." He then delineates "three virtues, each in itself enough to make a poet. (1) She knows her own tongue. Her tone can be Venetian gorgeous or Quaker simple; she never falls into cant or miserliness." To this Lowell added, "(2) Her abundance of description reminds one, not of poets, poor symbolic, abstract creatures—but of the Russian novelists." Finally, he raised the matter of her craft. Lowell—himself a consummate craftsman—was in a position to appreciate the fact that "in all matters of form: meter, rhythm, diction, timing, shaping, etc., she is a master."

The most compelling notice of *Poems*, however, was written by Randall Jarrell. In a 1955 review of "The Year in Poetry" for *Harper's*, Jarrell composed a notice of Elizabeth Bishop's latest book that would prove prophetic in more ways than one. He began, "Sometimes when I can't go to sleep at night I see the family of the future. Dressed in three-toned shorts-and-shirt sets of disposable Papersilk, they sit before the television wall of their apartment, only their eyes moving." Except for the Papersilk, Jarrell's prediction was accurate so far. He continued, "After I've looked a while I always see—otherwise I'd die—a pigheaded soul over in the corner with a book; only his eyes are moving, but in them there is a different look. Usually it's Homer he's holding—this week it's Elizabeth Bishop." Jarrell, who was noted for his prescience as a critic, declared of Bishop's new collection, "Her *Poems* seems to me one of the best books an American poet has ever written: the people of the future (the ones in the corner) will read her just as they will read Dickinson or Whitman or Stevens, or the other classical American poets still alive among us." Acknowledging that "I don't know of any poet with so high a proportion of good poems," Jarrell listed thirty-one titles in the collected volume as among his personal favorites.

He admitted, "This is a ridiculously long list, but if I went back over it I'd make it longer." Musing on whether he could find any faults in the volume, Jarrell acknowledged that "some of the later poems are too exclusively descriptive—and there are fifty-four poems in the book, not several hundred." Yet for Jarrell, what mattered is that her poems "are honest, modest, minutely observant, masterly; even their most complicated or troubled or imaginative effects seem, always, personal and natural, and as unmistakable as the first few notes of a Mahler song, the first few patches of a Vuillard interior. (The poems are like Vuillard or even, sometimes, Vermeer.)"[62]

Bishop was overwhelmed by Jarrell's review, and in particular by his pairing of her work, at its best, with the great seventeenth-century Flemish painter Johannes Vermeer. In her letter of thanks to Jarrell, she exclaimed, "I couldn't believe it at first, honestly—had a ridiculous fancy that it must be a misprint. . . . I still, from the bottom of my heart, honestly think I do NOT deserve it," but, she acknowledged, "It has always been one of my dreams that someday someone would think of Vermeer, without my saying it first." Then, she added jauntily, "So now I think I can die in a fairly peaceful frame of mind any old time, having struck the best critic going that way."[63] Bishop's poetry submissions to *The New Yorker* were laden with modest, or even self-disparaging, disclaimers. She offered such a masterpiece as "At the Fishhouses" to Katherine White with the words that she was presenting, "I'm afraid, another unusable poem."[64] And she submitted "Cape Breton" with the discouraging words, "I don't know whether you could possibly be interested in another piece of plain description from me or not."[65] White brushed such doubts aside with a prompt acceptance, describing "At the Fishhouses," accurately, as "beautiful and magical."[66] Yet Bishop's own dream that someone might one day compare her work to the luminous Vermeer, and her awed delight when the most discerning critic of her age actually said so, suggests that underneath that self-protective armor of modesty, Elizabeth Bishop understood all along just how good a poet she actually was.

CHAPTER THIRTEEN

"O PRÊMIO PULITZER!"

While researching her translation of *Minha Vida de Menina*, Elizabeth Bishop made a journey in April 1956 to Diamantina, Dona Alice Brandt's childhood village. Once noted for its diamond production, Diamantina is at the center of the state of Minas Gerais (General Mines), four hundred miles to the north of Samambaia, and two hundred miles north of Belo Horizonte, the nearest large city and the capital of Minas Gerais, a state that Bishop described as "bigger than Texas."[1]

Lota de Macedo Soares refused to travel in Brazil, so Bishop undertook what would be the first of many such journeys into the Brazilian interior without her partner. Due to an absence of roads, Bishop flew to the small, mile-high town in the company of a friend who was soon required to return. Bishop might have felt isolated during the balance of her stay, except that she soon became an object of great local curiosity and solicitude. As she told the Barkers, the "tiny town took such an interest in my every move" that shopkeepers emerged from their doors to walk with her wherever she went, and she was graciously invited by several villagers into their homes.[2]

Solitary lunches in the airy and spacious dining room of the ultramodern Hotel de Turismo, designed by Oscar Niemeyer[3]—she was frequently the only guest—became public happenings as small girls on their way to convent school lined up to examine her at each repast with noses pressed against the dining room's floor-to-ceiling plate glass windows.[4] Many citizens of Diamantina, in response to Bishop's detailed inquiries, helpfully explained and repeated the names of locally significant objects. One morning Bishop found herself unexpectedly summoned by an American diamond mine owner and his wife to their hydraulic mining operation forty miles distant, evidently because she offered this couple an opportunity to speak a bit of English. Bishop found hydraulic mining "interesting but horrible." She confessed to Swenson, "I even manned the hydraulic cannon or whatever it is and brought down a few tons of landscape myself"—a mining practice, Bishop added with relief, that is "outlawed in almost every other country."[5]

Bishop found the village culture altogether worthy of her attention. "It's a tiny place, the highest town in the country," filled with "wild, marvellous rocky scenery, seas of rocks," and "desolate, and surprising waterfalls." She was fascinated by this setting's parallel obsessions with "religion and gambling." She found elaborately appointed crucifixes on every peak, as well as sixteen churches crowned by an "ugly Cathedral from which they broadcast terce every evening at sundown, so that the whole place vibrates with Hail Marys." As for gambling, she spotted men "panning for gold and for diamonds in every stream."[6] As Bishop absorbed the particularities of this distinctive locale, many of which would soon appear in the detailed introduction to *The Diary of "Helena Morley,"* an event was unfolding a hemisphere away that would have significant impact on her life in the weeks and years to come. Bishop had been awarded the Pulitzer Prize for *Poems: North & South—A Cold Spring*. She did not learn of the award for this book, published with such evident diffidence, until after her return to Samambaia in early May.

Bishop's post-Pulitzer letters to friends characteristically postpone all reference to the prize until several paragraphs in, after which she dwells on the award in detail with her familiar blend of apology, close observation, and bemusement. Writing to Lowell about "this Pulitzer business," she acknowledged, "It was very funny here—a reporter from *O Globo* shouting at me over the telephone, and I kept replying in a cool New Englandy way, 'Thank you very much,' and he shouted again, 'But Dona Elizabetchy, don't you understand? O Prémio Pulitzer!'"[7] Bishop added in a letter to Swenson that when the call from *O Globo* came in, she was alone at Samambaia except for Maria the cook, and "I'm afraid she was not sufficiently impressed."[8] But soon enough, the prize became a very public happening and even a source of fun, although it "disrupted our lives and work for about three weeks completely." The property was thronged with "reporters, radio-men, television-men, god knows what all," who were "tracking mud over our white stone floors, with Lota trying to protect and interpret and please all at the same time."[9] Bishop accurately linked the journalistic fascination with the Pulitzer to the fact that it is "really a newspaper thing," and she explained to James Merrill that one reason for the attention was that "the Poet and Literature are still much more news, and elevated, than they are at home."[10] The cash prize of five hundred dollars struck Bishop as surprisingly small in relation to all the commotion, especially in light of the fact that Lota had just ordered twenty-seven thousand bricks for their terrace. Bishop had recently won a *Partisan Review* Fellowship whose cash value exceeded the Pulitzer's more than fivefold, yet that sotto voce award had excited no fanfare at all.

Bishop, Lota, and even the cat Tobias, "a big blur," soon appeared in local newsreels, "vying with Grace Kelly."[11] Bishop added dryly to Pearl Kazin that word of her newfound notoriety had even reached her native Worcester, where her aunt Florence Bishop granted an interview to the local papers. There she displayed what Bishop termed "true family ambivalence" when she observed that her niece might have made a better pianist than poet. Florence added, for good measure, that "lots and lots of people don't like her poetry, of course."[12]

Newsmen reported that Bishop and Lota led "an austere life, without a radio," and Bishop acknowledged to Lowell that she did plan to fulfill a long-cherished dream by funneling much of her Pulitzer cash into a "high-fidelity victrola."[13] This was, however, dependent on whether the player could be adjusted to "our rather erratic electric current."[14] *O Globo*'s own interview with Bishop noted that despite her graying hair, this forty-five-year-old poetess had a youthful face. It described her as a "confirmed spinster" who had perhaps remained unmarried because "to no one man could she dedicate her immense affective potential." Yet the article also described, with approval, Bishop's "emotional affinity" with the woman with whom she shared a home, "the vivacious and intelligent 'Dona Lotinha,'" whose presence, readers were told, furnished "the final argument" in Bishop's decision to remain in the "charming highland" of Samambaia, a setting where this poetess was surrounded by cats, flowers, and even a striking toucan. Perhaps more than a few of *O Globo*'s more astute subscribers managed to read between the lines and deduce the true nature of the bond connecting the youthful Dona Elizabetchy with the vivacious Dona Lotinha.

The *O Globo* piece concludes with Bishop taking her leave of her interviewer and wending her way up the footpath toward her quiet *estudio*. In those quiet rooms, the interviewer mused, Bishop would find herself surrounded by Samambaia's semitropical flora, and she could again "breathe in the atmosphere of dream and rest that she writes about in her poems."[15] *O Globo*'s florid account of their lives surely provided no little amusement for Dona Lotinha and Dona Elizabetchy. But as Bishop explained to Anny Baumann, although she felt the honor of the Pulitzer "undeserved," the award was particularly helpful in Brazil, because "now Lota doesn't have to prove to her friends personally that I do write poetry."[16] In fact, even the produce man at the local market was impressed. When Lota confirmed that Dona Elizabetchy was indeed the figure in the photo he had spotted in the papers, this purveyor of vegetables exclaimed over the extraordinary good luck of his customers. Why, just last week, another frequent shopper had bought a lottery ticket and won a bicycle![17]

Something of the dreaminess alluded to in *O Globo*'s report inhabits the opening lines of Bishop's "Questions of Travel," a poem published in *The New Yorker* in January 1956 that draws on the lofty view from her Samambaia *estudio*. As she wrote to Lowell at the time of the poem's composition, "I get up in the freezing dawns here and begin with all the confidence in the world. The mountains look exactly as if floating in *vin rose* then, with a white bowl of milk down below us."[18] In its opening, "Questions of Travel" dwells on her view from the mountains, highlighting a phenomenon that seldom, if ever, troubles a New Englander or Nova Scotian, and that would be flat-out impossible in Key West; for she finds that there are "too many waterfalls here." These waterfalls, formerly isolated objects of wonder for Bishop in her native lands, now seemed in Brazil, among the ridges and gullies of the Serra dos Órgãos during rainy season, to be overwhelming in their plenitude. Forming "mile-long, shiny, tearstains," she watched as they hurried "too rapidly down to the sea." Such multitudinous waterfalls and the crowded streams that quickened them seem forced into being in the poem by "the pressure of so many clouds on the mountaintops," making them "spill over the sides in soft slow-motion," so that, by means of a magical metamorphosis, they seem to be "turning to waterfalls under our very eyes." Bishop had moved beyond the tourist phase of observation highlighted in "Arrival at Santos," and now wrote from the standpoint of the long familiarity of a trained observer, but she had not yet lost (and never would) her capacity for spontaneity nor her capacity to convey details through the eye of the outsider, as a person who is in but not quite of the place she writes about with such attention and authority.

Bishop then turned from this intense, dreamlike lyricism toward the series of questions of travel promised in her title, questions numbering finally thirteen in all. The first of these arises directly from her own recent travels: "Should we have stayed at home and thought of here?"—and if so, "Where should we be today?" Where indeed would Bishop have been if she had not chosen to journey to Brazil and then to remain there with the vivacious Dona Lotinha? Bishop's mind then turns toward the ethical, and raises a question that frequently struck her during the moment of observation: "Is it right to be watching strangers in a play / in this strangest of theatres?" Then, too, is it merely "childishness" that makes one want to be in a new hemisphere of the globe, "to see the sun the other way around?" But then, she asks, what if one had missed the "tiniest green hummingbird in the world?" At last, the poem finds its way toward its core question: "Oh, must we dream our dreams / and have them too?" Certainly this was what Bishop was endeavoring to achieve at Samambaia. Could she still dream the dreams of romantic escape to far-off lands that she had shared with Louise Bradley so many years before—and could she have these dreams, too, among the clouds and waterfalls and hummingbirds of Samambaia?

Having articulated her core questions, Bishop turns to claims in favor of her choice of travel, for "surely it would have been a pity, / not to have seen the trees along this road, / really exaggerated in their beauty, / not to have seen them gesturing / like noble pantomimists, robed in pink." Wouldn't it have been a pity not to have heard the "sad, two-noted, wooden tune" of hand-fashioned, asymmetrical clogs "carelessly clacking over / a grease-stained filling-station floor"? Wouldn't it have been a pity to have missed the music of a "fat brown bird," singing in a bamboo cage shaped like a church of "Jesuit baroque"—just such a cage, and such a bird, as Bishop had found hanging over a filling station's broken gasoline pump? Such tattered beauty would always prove irresistible to Elizabeth Bishop. Still, with italic emphasis, her meditation on travel confronts a question raised in all the great romantic nature lyrics: "*Is it lack of imagination that makes us come / to imagined places, not just stay at home?*" All her life, Bishop had been taking the risk of traveling to imagined places and had woven her actual experiences of those places into her poetry. Now, in the past half decade, she was still facing a new "*continent, city, country, society,*" and this pushed her toward one final question of travel. Bishop's choices may have been "*never wide and never free,*" but despite moments of uncertainty or indecision, she had dared to make them. As her poem appeared in *The New Yorker*, she was entering her fifth year in Brazil, and there would be more to come. In life, one must be either "*here, or there*," and hence, she felt forced to query, "*No. Should we have stayed at home, wherever that may be?*"

"Questions of Travel," her first major poem on Brazil since "The Shampoo," appeared in the January 21, 1956, issue of *The New Yorker*. Carlos Lacerda, who was then enduring temporary exile in New York, spotted the poem while waiting in a dentist's office. Bishop told the Barkers that Lacerda had immediately dashed off a translation of lines from the poem into Portuguese and sent this off, with some comments, to his newspaper in Rio. Bishop was surprised to read the poem in Lacerda's translation long before her own copy of *The New Yorker* arrived at Samambaia.[19] With such unanticipated comings and goings between her own various continents, cities, countries, and societies, Bishop's sense of home must have seemed particularly fluid at this moment. Bishop had surely entered into a singular domestic space, one she could never have imagined during her earlier life in Worcester, Great Village, or Revere.

Bishop's chosen domesticity meant that even a Pulitzer Prize might have to compete for surprise of the year. In a letter to May Swenson, Bishop described a lively luncheon with friends that was interrupted by a shriek when someone spotted a five-foot-long snake dragging a baby *João do Barro* bird out of its "big clay oven-like" nest. The baby bird's legs were "still feebly waving" out of the reptile's jaws as it slithered quickly down the tree. Lota dashed for her .22 carbine and "*said* she got the snake with her first shot—probably she did; she's pretty good."[20] Sadly, the baby bird was dead, but the others in the nest had been saved. After this encounter, the group returned to lunch and continued their lively conversation.

Liberated from the pressure of providing new material for her second book, *A Cold Spring*, Bishop began to publish a steady stream of poems in *The New Yorker* and elsewhere, including the Great Village–based "Manners" and "Sestina," and such Brazil-centered poems as "Filling Station" and "Squatter's Children." Four months after Lacerda spotted "Questions of Travel" in a Manhattan dentist's waiting room, Bishop's "Manuelzinho" appeared in *The New Yorker*'s pages in a May issue. This poem, purportedly spoken by "a friend of the writer" (i.e., Lota), offers, in fact, the poet's and her friend's quite distinguishable voices moving in alternation. The poem brings to life, by his actual name, the character of one of Lota's longtime gardeners, an individual Bishop saw and interacted with almost every day. Its opening lines succinctly characterize his position as "half squatter, half tenant (no rent)— / a sort of inheritance." Manuelzinho is "white, / in your thirties now, and supposed / to supply me with vegetables." Then Lota's inflection emerges decidedly with the words, "But you don't; or you won't; or you can't / get the idea through your brain— / the world's worst gardener since Cain." The poem then shifts to Bishop's lyrical voice with the rumination, "Tilted above me, your gardens / ravish my eyes. You edge / the beds of silver cabbages / with red carnations, and lettuces / mix with alyssum." Then umbrella ants and a weeklong rain destroy these artistically arranged gardens, and Lota's tone of exasperation returns. Through the ongoing alternation of viewpoints, almost like a lively but sotto voce conversation between Bishop and Lota, the poem builds, with empathy and humor, toward a complex understanding of this poor, proud, and individualistic man. Bishop also brings forth a critique of certain characteristics of the Brazilian gentry—in particular, its paternalism and its condescending puzzlement over their tenant's curious ways. Yet Bishop also makes clear her understanding of her own complicity in the situation. She might feel sympathetic as Manuelzinho trots lightly over Lota's property in the constant drizzle of rainy season with his head and back covered only by "a sodden burlap bag"—but then she settles herself again beside the stove and goes on "reading a book." Lota's voice enters next, her notes of affection colored by anger as she asserts that her tenant-gardener might be stealing her telephone wires, along with further seriocomic offenses. When he paints his hat green, his mistress labels him "Klorophyll Kid," to the amusement of her distinguished visitors. Still, Bishop refuses to swath Manuelzinho in a plaster cast of false dignity. We see him warts and all, clinging to what shreds of individuality and pride he can muster.

Bishop ends her poem with words of direct address:

You helpless, foolish man,
I love you all I can,
I think. Or do I?

Then she offers a personal gesture:

I take off my hat, unpainted
and figurative, to you.
Again I promise to try.

Underlying "Manuelzinho" is Bishop's recollection of Christianity's radical imperative to "love thy neighbor"—which the poem counterpoints with the fact that although one might try to love one's neighbor, it isn't always easy. *The New Yorker* eagerly paid for the poem's 150 lines, and Bishop would later acknowledge to the Barkers, "I've earned so much money off the poor little man now I feel guilty every time he comes to the kitchen door with a bunch of monster radishes."[21]

She was entering her mid-forties when she told the Barkers, "Oh dear. Everyone, and now you, seems to write to me about age these days. . . . One friend typed me several panicky pages because her oculist had suggested bifocals!" Bishop's response was to say, "I don't know why, but I just don't give a damn. I think I actually look younger than when you saw me."[22] In fact, in mid-1956, Bishop was in excellent form both emotionally and physically. She had recently won the Pulitzer, and she had completed and published a series of strong poems, with more on the way. She was close to completing her translation of *Minha Vida de Menina*. And she was enjoying a spell of remarkably good health. She explained that she had found a good asthma doctor in Rio who refused even to charge her for his services, and that she had remained almost asthma-free the past several months. Freed from the shackles of cortisone, she could write to her aunt Grace in July 1956 that she had achieved the sylphlike weight of 118 pounds, adding that she was having a suit and two dresses made because she "hadn't any new clothes for four years! So I have to stay at 118. If I gain an ounce, I won't be able to get into them."[23] Bishop claimed again to the Barkers, "My hair has stopped getting white, really (no alcohol, probably) and L and I both hope to reach 115."[24]

The exterior walls at Samambaia feature extensive runs of plate glass, with roofs made of rippled aluminum. Lota's original plan had been to cover the aluminum with a layer of thatch,[25] but this idea had to be abandoned because of the danger from fire balloons, which were powered by jellied petroleum and were released to fly in the sky. Bishop was fascinated by them even back in Walnut Hill, as we learn from her story "A Flight of Fancy." Bishop's experience at Samambaia was woven into the fabric of her poem "The Armadillo," a poem that begins by describing with singular delicacy a Brazilian scene witnessed from her mountaintop at Samambaia. Here she watches those "frail, illegal fire balloons . . . / climbing the mountain's height." They are illegal because of the danger they represent to the forest and houses below as a result of the flaming jellied gasoline that fuels them, but they steal one's heart because of their beauty as they steer gracefully "between / the kite sticks of the Southern Cross // receding, dwindling, solemnly / and steadily forsaking us." Such beauty and delicacy persist until "the downdraft from a peak" sucks one of the fire balloons forcefully downward against the granite cliff that towers over their house. This errant fire balloon, whose flaming fuel acts very much like napalm, splatters "like an egg of fire / against the cliff behind the house." When "The flames ran down," the jellied petroleum clings to the trees and sets off a massive conflagration in the forest below. A pair of familiar nesting owls "shriek up out of sight,"[26] confronting the viewer and the reader with a definite tone of violence. In the poem's penultimate stanza, Bishop moves with extraordinary deftness, even within a single line, from a tone of extraordinary gentleness to a tone of shocked horror, and almost of rage, as suddenly a "baby rabbit jump[s] out" of the burning forest:

> short-*eared, to our surprise.*
> *So soft!—a handful of intangible ash*
> *with fixed, ignited eyes.*

Are the rabbit's ears short because they have been burned off? And does the rabbit appear like "a handful of intangible ash" because of its plush fur, or is its entire body literally turning to ash after being consumed by the flames? The rabbit's "fixed, ignited eyes"—these, at least, are so far intact—seem themselves to be on fire as they reflect (like a deer in the headlights) the man-made fire that obliterates their world. The poem ends on a note of direct protest unusual in Bishop's work when it directly accuses the fire balloons, and by extension the people who have launched them, of the heedless destruction they have caused:

> Too pretty, dreamlike mimicry!
> O falling fire and piercing cry
> and panic, and a weak mailed fist
> clenched ignorant against the sky![27]

This closing has been subtly and effectively prepared as the poem builds gradually from delicacy toward a surprising violence.

Robert Lowell was deeply impressed when he read "The Armadillo" in typescript, describing it to Bishop in a June 10, 1957, letter as "surely one of your three or four very best."[28] Three years later he confessed "I carry 'The Armadillo' in my billfold and occasionally amaze people with it."[29] He was so taken with the poem that Bishop dedicated it to him when it was later collected in her 1965 volume *Questions of Travel*. Lowell's earlier style is noted for its sustained—and sometimes almost overwhelming—violence of tone, which Bishop termed in her *Life Studies* blurb as his "now-familiar trumpet-notes."[30] Lowell found a more subtle and modulated way to incorporate elements of violence into his work in Bishop's "Armadillo," which he acknowledged to be the model for his own most popular poem, "Skunk Hour," a poem he dedicated to her. Bishop's "Armadillo" revealed to Lowell a technique of modulation, a means of shifting gears with an almost seamless alternation between an understated lyric or prosy evenness and something more violent, sudden, and aggressive. In Kay Jamison's important new study of Lowell, she characterizes Lowell in her title as *Setting the River on Fire*. But it was Bishop's "Armadillo" that added to Lowell's bag of tricks as he observed her quite literally *setting the forest on fire*.

Bishop won a two-thousand-dollar Amy Lowell Poetry Travelling Scholarship, as she told the Barkers in January 1957.[31] And this meant, as she told May Swenson a few weeks later, "we're really coming to New York. Around April 1st, and staying probably about six months." Bishop mentioned that she was boarding her toucan with the animal-dealing neighbor from whom she had received him, "banding his leg so I'll get the same dear Sammy when I get back."[32] She added that Farrar Straus had taken her translation of *The Diary of "Helena Morley."* Robert Giroux, who was to be her admiring publisher for the rest of her life, and after, admitted later that although the *Diary* was a "fine and charming book," his publishing house had only taken it because they wanted to become the publisher of her next book of poems. He added, "We had to wait eight years for Elizabeth's new poems, *Questions of Travel*, but it was worth it."[33] Bishop wrote to Howard Moss in January about her plan to come to New York with Lota in early April.[34] This would be Bishop's first excursion to the United States since she and Lota had returned to Key West and New York to collect her belongings and arrange for their shipment to Brazil.

She arrived with Lota in New York on March 31, with plans to stay half a year. They sublet an apartment at 115 East Sixty-Seventh Street, on Manhattan's East Side, between Park and Lexington Avenues. This was a far tonier address than the one Bishop had maintained on King Street in the 1940s, just on the edge of a factory district in Lower Manhattan. Bishop and Lota's trip to the United States was an expedition with multiple purposes. Bishop planned to settle the terms of publication for *The Diary of "Helena Morley"* with Farrar, Straus & Giroux, and establish a relationship with a new literary agent. Lota planned to purchase crate-loads of American manufactured goods to ship back to Samambaia. One reason they planned to stay for six months in the United States was that it would allow them to buy an American car and ship it to Brazil without paying duty. They could then sell it for a considerable profit in Brazil, where the prices for American cars (and other goods) were often double the US price. Such an automobile sale would help offset much of the cost of the trip.

They settled into their small East Side apartment in April 1957, and from the start their social lives were extremely active. Many friends who knew Bishop from her heavy-drinking days at Yaddo and in New York, including Pauline Hanson and May Swenson, were delighted and relieved to see how much Bishop had improved in health, mood, and appearance during her time in Brazil. At one party where others were imbibing, Bishop was noticed not to be drinking and she remarked that she now simply had no interest in alcohol.

In an apology to the Barkers for not writing until they had been in the city three months, she said, "We've been having a wonderful time, on the whole. It is fun to come back, and 5 years, I decided, is just about right—all is forgiven, all passion spent, and yet no one, as yet, looks too much aged, etc.—and everyone seems so improved. (Or is it just me?—that's what worries me from time to time.)" They were also enjoying "week-ends in Connecticut at modern homes with Calders in the living room, tarragon in the dining room, and neuroses in the bedrooms." Bishop picks up her letter to the Barkers three days later:

> *Lota arrived with an old school or convent friend, Brazilian, and then about six more Brazilian gentlemen appeared—they had just arrived at the airport 2 hours before, parked their wives at the Waldorf Astoria, and rushed*

immediately to see Lota—without whose advice on matters of taste, art,
restaurants, etc., they can't manage to exist![35]

Yet while Bishop's business in New York was to meet with her publisher about her translation of *The Diary of "Helena Morley,"* Lota's reasons for being in the city were also by no means merely social, since she was there to acquire tools and furnishings that she considered necessary to the completion of Samambaia. Bishop complained to Lowell about a walk down New York's Third Avenue with Lota: "There are a few too many hardware stores along it for us to make much headway."[36]

Bishop was not only an observer of the greater New York area of late 1957; she and Lota made, in their own way, a singular pair, and they were being observed in turn by American friends, and in particular by the hawkeyed novelist and social commentator Mary McCarthy, who recalled speaking frequently with Bishop during 1957. McCarthy's character "Lakey," Elinor Eastlake, from her 1963 bestseller *The Group*, is surely a composite, like most fictional characters drawn from life. But Eastlake, whose nickname echoes Bishop's early nickname "Bishie," is almost certainly modeled in many of her most important characteristics on Elizabeth Bishop herself, just as Lakey's lesbian lover, "the Baroness," is surely modeled on the worldly and aristocratic Lota de Macedo Soares. This 1957 visit to New York gave McCarthy the opportunity to take the measure of Bishop and Lota as real-life individuals and to use them as models for notable characters in her smash bestseller. In the 1966 film version of *The Group*, Lakey was played by a young Candice Bergen in her first major role. This fictional characterization as Lakey may have been Bishop's first appearance as a significant figure, real or imagined, in fiction, film, or theater—but it would certainly not be her last.

Bishop and Lota arrived in Bangor, Maine, by plane on August 2 to begin what they expected to be an extended stay with Robert Lowell, his wife, Elizabeth Hardwick, and their baby daughter, Harriet, at their home in Castine. However, their arrival coincided with the early stages of a manic episode of Lowell's. Lowell, who had also been drinking, began to make amorous advances toward Bishop, suggesting as well that he might visit Bishop in Brazil without his family. Bishop reported Lowell's statements to Elizabeth Hardwick, and Bishop and Lota left Castine far sooner than they had planned. On August 9, Lowell wrote a letter of apology to Bishop in New York, saying, "Thanks for speaking to Lizzie about your misgivings." Lowell apologized for his "abysmal myopia" and said that he sometimes had a "headless heart." Bishop wrote Lowell from New York, on August 11, in a letter that crossed with his. Bishop began on a cheerful, newsy note, as if nothing had happened. After her initial paragraphs she cited George Herbert's translation of an Italian "Treatise on Temperance and Sobriety," and echoing the language of Herbert's treatise, she closed by urging, "Dear Cal, do please please take care of yourself and be an ornament to the world (you're already that) and a comfort to your friends." No doubt she intended this counsel partly for herself, as she certainly did with the comments that followed: "There *are* many hopeful things, too, you know. Sobriety & gayety & patience & toughness will do the trick. Or so I hope for myself and hope & pray for you, too."[37]

Lowell thanked Bishop for this letter, saying that along with its "cheerful tempering of the spirit," it had also "brought me terrific relief. I feared I was forever in exile." In his letter about the incident, Lowell spent numerous typescript pages describing in comic terms a long sailing expedition on the Maine coast with Richard Eberhart, all of which was working up to a statement about his recent advances on Bishop. Lowell closed with a retrospective passage about their past that has since become famous. He confessed that "asking you is *the* might have been for me, the one towering change, the other life that might have been had." Lowell added that, for him, it had been "that way for these nine years or so that intervened. It was deeply buried, and this spring and summer (really before your arrival) it boiled to the surface. Now it won't happen again, though of course I always feel a great blytheness and easiness with you. It won't happen, I'm really underneath utterly *in* love and sold on my Elizabeth, and it's a great solace to me that you are with Lota, and I am sure it is the will of the heavens that all is as it is."

Lowell managed to avert the worst in this manic episode, at least temporarily, and thereafter wrote the poems that would form the core of his breakthrough book *Life Studies*. He modeled what would come to be his most famous poem, "Skunk Hour," on Bishop's deeply Brazilian "The Armadillo," which he had read in typescript. Both are poems about a locality that involve what Lowell called "drifting description" as they move toward a powerful and dramatic ending. Bishop wrote an extraordinary tribute to Lowell's poetic achievement in "Skunk Hour" and *Life Studies*, first in a letter to him and, later, in her blurb for *Life Studies*.

Bishop visited Marjorie Stevens in Key West, saying to the Barkers, "I made a flying trip to Key West to visit an old friend for a week, too—hot as hell, but very beautiful and deserted pretty much at that season, so I was glad I'd gone—she took some days off (she works for the Navy there) and we bicycled. Swam, made calls, and talked, mostly." This was the last time Bishop saw Stevens, who died not long after.

A week before they left, Bishop and Lota gave "a PARTY—A HUGE ONE."[38] As she told Lowell on September 29, "This is to be our last fling and I wish you were to be here—."[39] Since their apartment was too small, they were hosted by their friends Fizdale and Gold, the noted piano duo, in their large apartment on Central Park West. Bishop wrote:

> It was the nicest party I've ever given—mostly thanks to the "boys"—one of them cooked meatloaf, made a wonderful supper, etc. Every time I called up and added people to our list, he ordered another pound of beef—finally used 8 pounds. There were about 40 guests and 20 stayed to supper, and I realized when we finally got home, I'd been on my feet from 5:30 until 1:30. Nobody got tight except Alexy Hiaff and one old friend of mine and they were nice about it—Tom [Wanning], my friend, got to hugging, and Alexy to hand-kissing, that was all. Others you'd know were Eleanor Clark (the boys know her) and her husband, Rob. Penn Warren, whom I've always liked

very much although I don't know him at all; Marianne Moore, Louise Bogan,
Dwight MacDonald, Monroe Wheeler & Glenway Westcott, Cummings's
wife (c. is in the hospital), Loren of course, & her husband, my editor, Gi-
roux (do you know him?), Zabel, who had just arrived from Yaddo and en-
joyed himself more than anyone, I think—my darling German doctor who
arrived about 10 all dressed up—I'd asked Katherine Anne, but she couldn't
get to N.Y.—well, lots more, and it did seem to go off very well and everyone
seemed to be looking very pretty! I do wish you could have both been there.[40]

Bishop and Lota's freighter departed from New York on October 11,
after a stay in New York of nearly seven months. They traveled on the SS
Mormacstar on what Lota called "The Long Voyage Home," a journey of
more than two weeks. As the freighter sailed south along the Atlantic coast,
Bishop sent witty postcards to Lowell from US ports of call, beginning with
Charleston, South Carolina, and then Savannah, Georgia, the latter signed
"Recessively yours— / E.B." accompanied by the postscript "—next stop
Curoção—." Lowell's next letter from Boston was addressed to "My Darling receding Elizabeth." Upon their arrival in Rio, Lota and Elizabeth
slowly extracted from Brazilian customs, over a matter of weeks, the mountains of manufactured goods that Lota had purchased in the United States.
In the two years that followed, Bishop and Lota entered what was perhaps
one of the most settled periods of Bishop's life. The house was now virtually complete. She was in more or less consistently good health. The political climate of Brazil was relatively stable. Her big prose projects were
behind her. And she was entering one of her most satisfactory periods of
poetic productivity.

The record hot summer of 1958 meant many visitors. The blowup in
Castine was for the moment behind her, and she and Lowell had settled into
what was, for most of the next decade at least, a more calm and stable relationship. The fact that she loved *Life Studies*, a book whose form and style
she had partly inspired, no doubt helped with this. Bishop embarked, without Lota, on a trip to Brasília and the Brazilian interior in the company of

Aldous Huxley and his second wife, Laura Archera Huxley. They visited an Indian tribe in the Brazilian rainforest, which Bishop described to Lowell as a "wonderful cheerful time," although she acknowledged that it was "depressing to think about their future." She described her indigenous hosts thus: "They are quite naked, just a few beads; handsome, plump, behaving just like gentle children a little spoiled. They were very curious about Huxley and one who spoke a little Portuguese said he was 'homely . . . homely.'" Bishop, however, must have made a more favorable impression, since a widower in the tribe "asked me to stay and marry him—this was a slightly dubious compliment. Nevertheless the other ladies along were quite jealous."[41] Sometime later, they received a visit from the ever-cheerful Alexander Calder and his wife, Louisa (a niece of Henry James). Bishop wrote to Howard Moss that "Calder went samba-ing all over the terrace, wearing a bright orange shirt, just like a calendula swaying in the breeze."[42]

CHAPTER FOURTEEN

APARTMENT IN LEME

After eight years in Brazil, Elizabeth Bishop had come to know various aspects of Brazilian culture on a personal level, though she was acutely conscious that she was always viewing these features as an outsider. In mid-October 1959, Bishop submitted two new poems to *The New Yorker*, the more important of which, "Brazil, January 1, 1502," captured an earlier and more historically important moment of entry into Brazil by seaborne outsiders than the one she shared with Mary Breen in November 1951. In 1502, these intruders from another world encountered no customs officials who might seize their bourbon and cigarettes. No poorly adhering postage stamps existed yet to peel off their letters home. For this was the moment when the armored invaders from Portugal arrived and encountered a land they found startlingly different and yet "not unfamiliar." And as the poem pictures it, these Christians in "creaking armor," who were "hard as nails / tiny as nails / and glinting,"[1] encountered a vast half continent and immediately launched on the project of seizing control of it, and the native women if they could catch them, from its unsuspecting indigenous peoples. And as they set out "directly after Mass" on this agenda, "humming perhaps / *L'Homme armé* or some such tune," they began without pause the task of ripping into the "hanging fabric" of the landscape, "each out to catch an Indian for himself,"[2] while seeing no apparent contradiction between, on the one hand, their religious rites and values, their elevated concept of courtly love, their appreciation of fine music, and, on the other, a fresh opportunity for sexual and economic exploitation.

When Robert Lowell encountered Bishop's "Brazil, January 1, 1502" in *The New Yorker*, he wrote to her immediately, saying in a January 4, 1960, letter, "Your poem is one of your most beautiful, I think—wonderful description, the jungle turning into a picture, then into history and the jungle again, with a practical, absurd, sad, amused and frightened tone for the Christians."[3] Lowell had immediately recognized the subtlety with which Bishop had blended observation on nature, culture, the arts, and politics into a single deftly interwoven narrative.

Bishop, through her connection with Lota, would soon find her own life increasingly interwoven with the exigencies of Brazilian politics. The scene of her life would now shift decisively from the natural surroundings of Samambaia to the more confining quarters of Lota's apartment in the Leme district of Rio de Janeiro. In October 1960, the election for the Brazilian presidency was won by Jânio Quadros, who was running independently on a platform that promised to clean up political corruption (a new broom was his campaign symbol). Quadros had the backing of the largest conservative party, the National Democratic Union, but he also succeeded in positioning himself as the candidate of the common people, opposing the graft considered to be endemic within the still-powerful Vargas organization. Under Brazil's constitution, the vice president could be from a separate party, and João Goulart, a left-leaning man of ideas with previous ties to the departed "moderate dictator," Getúlio Vargas—and a political enemy of Quadros—won the vice presidency. Thus, the two highest executive positions in Brazil were divided by party. At the same time, Lota's close friend Carlos Lacerda was elected governor of the state of Guanabara (a new state formed out of the city of Rio and its environs when the capital of Brazil moved to Brasília). These political crosscurrents would have significant consequences for Bishop and Lota in the coming years.

Macedo Soares was soon invited by Lacerda to name her job within his government. Lota decided to focus on the task of converting a recently created three-mile-long landfill on Rio's Guanabara Bay into a large city park, the Parque do Flamengo.[4] Lota's aim was to turn this stretch of dirt and rubble into Rio's equivalent to New York's Central Park. Bishop, of course, was pleased. At last, Lota would have a task worthy of her drive and talents. While the park was under construction, it was frequently referred to as the Aterro ("landfill"), after the foundation on which the park was built. As Bishop explained to James Merrill, "Lota is 'Chief-Coordinatress' of a big new park-highway-playgrounds-yacht-basins-restaurants, etc, etc, project on the water-front, and so far very good, I think." But while this was an important and responsible task, there were complications. "It means," she told Merrill, "a rather unsettling life—back and forth from and to Rio every week, neglecting the place where we really like living, up in the mountains. We are gradually getting it organized so we have two sets of everything necessary and mostly lug books, and meat and drinking water and eggs in ice-buckets, to Rio—and laundry back."[5] Bishop soon found, not at all happily, that she was spending most of her days in Rio, and one March 1962 letter is querulously addressed to Lowell from "Samambaia, for a change."[6]

Lota soon discovered that many of those she worked with entertained doubts regarding her qualifications or authority to perform her appointed role. She might have a clear vision for the Parque do Flamengo, but she lacked a degree or professional certification in landscaping or architecture. She was a woman in a man's world. And she was a political appointee whose authority rested on a governor who might not remain in power forever. So Lota often found it difficult to secure the full cooperation of the male professionals and lifetime bureaucrats over whom she had been placed or with whom she was required to work in collaboration. She had to rely on her forceful personality and her close connection to Carlos Lacerda, with whom she did not always agree in matters of detail, to make steady progress on the park. It soon became clear that Lota was in for long days of work that would often prove harrowing.

In contrast to the stress of Lota's day job, a new source of domestic happiness appeared. Mary Morse, working around various Brazilian rules forbidding adoptions made by foreign nationals, succeeded in adopting in the winter of 1961 the first in a series of children, a three-month-old girl named Monica. Bishop described this good-natured child as "such a good, gay, healthy baby—and her disposition puts us all to shame,"[7] and her letters are filled with accounts of Monica's charming character and behavior. Monica Morse herself now claims that she grew up with three strong mothers, Mary Morse, Lota de Macedo Soares, and Elizabeth Bishop, and she remembers many happy hours, especially during a lengthy trip she took to the United States, spent playing on the floor in Bishop's *estudio* while the poet was leaning over her desk, at work on her writing.

On August 25, 1961, Jânio Quadros, the recently elected president of Brazil, resigned from office abruptly after just seven months in power, alleging that "terrible forces" were aligned against him. This prompted a political crisis since Brazil's vice president, João Goulart, was of the opposition party and many military leaders and political conservatives felt that the vice president was too radical to assume the role of the presidency. Goulart was abroad on a trip to China, and for the moment Brazil's political future remained uncertain. Quadros's supporters, the conservative National Democratic Union party, were reluctant to allow their political opponent to assume the reins of the Brazilian government. After a tense period of uncertainty, an awkward compromise, involving a temporary shift to a parliamentary government ruled by a prime minister, ultimately allowed Goulart to assume the presidency as figurehead pending a national plebiscite. Yet the political situation in Rio and Brazil remained unstable.

As these political developments unfolded, Bishop herself was hard at work on her volume *Brazil*, for Life World Library. In December 1961 she traveled to New York with Lota to finalize the text of *Brazil* with her editors, and she was by no means happy with the result, which she felt altered the focus of her book in fundamental ways. Despite her intensive editorial work, she did manage to attend a dinner party at the Lowells' apartment that featured as guests T. S. Eliot and his wife, Valerie. Bishop also consulted with Lowell and Elizabeth Hardwick as they began to plan a trip to Brazil sponsored by the Congress for Cultural Freedom.

Shepherded by Keith Botsford, agent for the Congress for Cultural Freedom, Lowell arrived in Rio with his wife, Elizabeth, and daughter, Harriet, on June 25, 1962. The Lowell family took an apartment in Rio, and when he was not lecturing or giving readings, Lowell spent much of his spare time with Bishop. The trip was originally intended for six weeks, but the visit had gone so pleasantly that Lowell and his family extended their stay for an extra two weeks.

Lowell was especially impressed by a visit to Bishop's *estudio* at Samambaia, where he witnessed many Bishop poems-in-progress, some of them years in the making, fastened to a bulletin board above her long desk. More than a decade later, in his volume *History*, Lowell dedicated a poem to Bishop in which he asked, "Do / you still hang your words in the air, ten years / unfinished . . . ?" These words seemed suspended in both place and time, "glued to your notice board with gaps / or empties for the unimaginable phrase." It was this working method, this willingness to wait for words with a patience few poets seem ever to have possessed, that allowed her to become Lowell's "unerring Muse who makes the casual perfect."[8]

Unfortunately, in his final weeks in Rio, Lowell began drinking too much and showing signs of veering into one of his manic episodes. Bishop later reconstructed this series of events in a typed diary that created a chronology of her observations of Lowell's escalating behavior, with entries reaching back to August 20. On September 1, Elizabeth Hardwick and Harriet sailed back to New York as planned. Two days later, on Lowell's insistence, and over Bishop's objections, Lowell and Botsford flew from

Rio to Buenos Aires, where Lowell was scheduled to give further lectures and readings. In Buenos Aires, he continued to drink excessively and now demonstrated signs of a full-blown manic attack. Botsford, exhausted, discomfited, and under the assumption that Lowell's behavior was solely the product of too much alcohol, returned to Rio on September 8. He did not report Lowell's condition to Bishop, who only learned of the situation accidentally two days later. Lowell was now on his own in Buenos Aires and potentially in grave danger because he was behaving erratically and making wild political statements in a country then ruled by a military dictatorship. Bishop was concerned that Lowell might be beaten up or imprisoned. On the evening of September 11, Bishop received an alarming telegram sent by Lowell from Buenos Aires:

> DEAREST ELIZABETH COME HERE AND JOIN
> ME ITS PARADISE! ALL MY LOVE
> CAL[9]

Deeply concerned, Bishop tracked down Botsford and convinced him, with confirmation by telephone from Lowell's New York doctor, that Lowell's behavior was not merely drunkenness but mania. Lowell's doctor agreed with Bishop that Lowell should be found in Buenos Aires and returned to New York as soon as possible. On September 11, the day Bishop received Lowell's telegram, Botsford left for Buenos Aires to retrieve Lowell. The following day, Botsford reported that Lowell was already in a Buenos Aires hospital, the Clinica Bethlehem, and "much calmer." Bishop noted in her reconstructed diary that she sent a telegram to Lowell's hospital, on September 13, with the text, "We are thinking of you. Get better quick. Love always. Elizabeth."[10] Four days later, Bishop learned that Lowell had to remain hospitalized in Buenos Aires for two more weeks before he could return to New York. Ultimately, Lowell's friend Blair Clark arrived in Buenos Aires and flew back with him to New York, where he was met by Elizabeth Hardwick and moved to the Institute for Living in Hartford, Connecticut, to begin his recovery. Bishop would write following Lowell's return to America, "I do hope you are well, Cal, and only remembering the best things we did and saw here."[11]

M eanwhile, the conflict continued to intensify between the left-leaning forces supporting the new president, Goulart, and conservative figures such as Governor Lacerda, who alleged that Goulart had pro-communist leanings and asserted that in their opposition to him they were supporting democratic institutions. Macedo Soares sided with her patron Lacerda, and for the moment at least, Bishop also saw the situation from Lota's point of view. In January 1963, Goulart won a convincing victory in a plebiscite that restored his presidential authority, and by this time, Bishop was beginning to experience doubts about Lacerda as a political leader. She told Lowell she was turning "utterly sick of public Brazil, political Brazil." Yet American politics was also passing through a deeply troubling phase, one that could at times inspire Brazilian sympathy. Following president John F. Kennedy's assassination on November 22, 1963, Bishop wrote to James Merrill in December 1963, "Brazil was overwhelmed by Kennedy's death.—I am still getting formal speeches of 'condolence' from taxi-drivers and anyone who spots me as an American—still very easy after ten years here—."[12] Bishop was worried both by the often-violent left-wing rhetoric issuing from President Goulart and by the anti-communist rhetoric of Lacerda, which Bishop felt verged on "McCarthy-ism."[13] Yet even as she steadily wearied of politics, she declared that what she called "the other-under-side" of Brazil, such as the humor of the people and their indigenous culture, "I like more & more."[14] As Lota worked all-out on Flamengo Park with her fatigue level continuing to mount, Bishop was turning her attention to other pursuits and writing letter after letter from the apartment in Leme to her friends at home. In addition, she was taking a growing interest in Lota's nephew Flávio Soares Regis, who was showing a distinct interest in and talent for poetry and the other arts.

The political situation in Brazil in spring 1964 passed through a crisis. The causes and implications would only slowly become clear. Inflation was rampant, currency having only one-tenth the value it had had two years before, and political rhetoric on both the right and the left was escalating rapidly. On March 13 President Goulart made a speech at a large rally in Rio in which he promised to implement sweeping measures, including land confiscation and nationalization of private companies. He suggested that these measures would be carried through even if opposed by the National Congress. In turn, his opponents accused him of pro-communist leanings and of trying to overthrow the constitution and establish himself as a populist dictator. The populist forces under Goulart appeared at first to be ascendant—only to be suddenly overturned by resistance from the regular army, acting, or so it claimed, in defense of the constitution. When Brazilian marines (naval fusiliers) mutinied against their officers, threatening military discipline and authority, Goulart supported them. Meanwhile, top military leaders had privately concluded that he would have to be removed via a coup, and Rio became the scene of this carefully orchestrated military operation on March 31 and April 1, 1964.

At first, both Lota and Bishop sided with the military intervention. Like many other members of the Brazilian upper and middle classes, Lota was alarmed by Goulart's inflammatory rhetoric. And the coup appeared to many Brazilians to be a spontaneous uprising on the part of the military to protect local administrative structures and defend the Brazilian constitution. The military leaders, under chief of staff general Humberto Castelo Branco, presented themselves as temporary guardians of democratic institutions who would relinquish power and hold scheduled national elections as soon as order was restored. Carlos Lacerda energetically supported the military takeover. He was planning to run for president of Brazil in 1965, when the deposed President Goulart's term expired and a new election, presumably, would be held. He assumed that as a strong opponent of Goulart and the most prominent conservative politician in Brazil, he would have the generals' support when this election was held. But all of this depended on the willingness of the "temporary" military government to actually relinquish power.

Following this political uprising, Bishop managed to convince Lota to go with her on a vacation to England, which would take her away, at least temporarily, from the tumult, anxiety, and unrest of their life in Rio. The plan was for Bishop and Lota to arrive in Milan in mid-May 1964, and spend a month making "a triangular tour through northern Italy,"[15] including stays in Tuscany and Venice and then a journey back to Milan. Bishop would then carry on to England alone, where she would see her friends Kit and Ilse Barker, while Lota flew back to Rio. Bishop planned to return to Rio by boat, leaving from England in July. As the time for their departure approached, Bishop exclaimed to the Barkers from Rio, "Heavens—it can't be true. Lota was up playing a samba record in the gramophone, and *dancing* the *samba*, at 6:30 this morning—when usually she's anti-music until tea-time—so I see she's happy to have a trip, too."[16] They arrived in Milan on May 14, 1964, and at the end of her time with Lota in Italy, Bishop wrote Lowell from Milan, "We had a wonderful four weeks and they very obligingly seemed much longer than that."[17]

After Lota departed for Rio as planned, Bishop used her time in England to tour London and visit her friends the Barkers at their charming home: the Old Cottage, in Petworth, Sussex. By then, she had written them more than one hundred letters from Brazil, but had not seen either of her dear friends in fourteen years. Ilse Barker recalled Bishop's stay with them in Sussex as "a very happy one. She was in very good form. She didn't drink. She had been really at the bottom of the world in Yaddo in 1950 to 1951." But on this visit, she was "relaxed and enjoying herself." Barker even appeared to endorse Bishop's claim that she had grown more youthful in Brazil, for she observed that Bishop "seemed younger than when we met at Yaddo and was very talkative." Barker also noted Bishop's interest in their son, Thomas, who was not yet two. Barker claimed that Bishop had "this wonderful feeling for babies and small children. Everything to do with them fascinated her, and she was undemonstratively good with them."[18]

Bishop set off for Rio from Lisbon on the SS *Brazil Star* in late July and arrived in Brazil in early August, greatly cheered by her excursion. But when Lowell queried her about the state of politics in Brazil, she confessed, "I'd rather not think about it."[19] On July 22, 1964, while Bishop's ship was still sailing to Lisbon, the military government, led by president Castelo Branco, announced its decision to postpone presidential elections for three years, news that made Bishop confess to Lowell, "I wish I weren't going back, almost."[20] One specific consequence of the deferred elections was that Lacerda would have to delay his plans to run for president of Brazil. What neither Lacerda, Lota, nor Bishop anticipated was that the generals would subsequently rewrite the Brazilian constitution to ensure that only the designated military candidate would have a chance to win future elections. Repressive measures grew in severity following Castelo Branco's death in 1967, and the military government retained its repressive rule over Brazil until 1985.

Unhappy with these political developments and with spending so much time alone in the Rio apartment, Bishop turned her attention to the beautiful baroque city of Ouro Preto (Black Gold). The Lowells had accompanied her to Ouro Preto in 1962, and she had also toured the city with Anny Baumann, when Baumann at last had paid her a visit in 1964. A small colonial city in the state of Minas Gerais, Ouro Preto was the focal point for a major Brazilian gold rush of the eighteenth century. It was then neglected after the gold ran out and remained substantially unchanged well into the twentieth century. Its most notable feature was a sequence of splendid baroque churches, built with riches from the gold rush, that stand atop each of the city's steep hills, crowned by the extraordinary church of São Francisco de Assis. Bishop had always felt a deep affinity for the baroque, and for architecture as well. And here was a concentration of baroque art and architecture impossible to match in the New World and hard to surpass even in the Old. As Lota became ever more preoccupied with her work on Flamengo Park, Ouro Preto—with its mountainous setting and roots in Brazil's colonial past—became an increasingly important place of refuge for Bishop.

There she developed an intense friendship with Lilli Correia de Araújo, the proprietor of a charming inn that she had named Chico Rei, after a legendary figure in Brazilian history and mythology who had found a means to fight the slave trade. First he bought his own freedom and then the freedom of his family members. At last he acquired one of the Ouro Preto gold mines and used the profits to buy the freedom of other slaves. On a 1960 visit to Lilli Correia de Araújo's establishment, Bishop left behind in the guest book a brief poem of tribute, "Let Shakespeare & Milton / Stay at the Hilton— / I shall stay / At Chico Rei."[21] Although the scale of Chico Rei is modest, Bishop claimed to the Barkers that Ashley Brown had described it to her as "*one* of the few great hotels left in the world." With the passage of time, Bishop's friendship with Lilli developed into a passionate, if brief, affair. Following the death of her husband, Lilli had decided to have sexual relationships only with women, in honor of his memory. As a tribute to Lilli, Bishop composed, with illustrations in two distinct versions, a poem that begins, "Dear, my compass / still points north / to wooden houses and blue eyes, // fairy tales where / flaxen-headed younger sons / bring home the goose, / love in hay-lofts, / Protestants, and / heavy drinkers." In such a place, the "swans can paddle / icy water, / so hot the blood / in those webbed feet."[22]

After many visits to Ouro Preto, Bishop decided in fall 1965 to buy a lovely house in that city. As she told the Barkers, "I don't need another house at all . . . but I couldn't resist it." Bishop claimed to her friends that when Lota saw the house "she was equally besotted."[23] This house, dating as Bishop said from 1720 to 1740, stands along the road leading out of Ouro Preto on the way to the nearby village of Mariana. From its rear windows and balcony, it features a spectacular view of the hills and churches of the city. This house, which Bishop would name Casa Mariana in honor of Marianne Moore and the village down the way, would require extensive renovation. Taking on such an effort would place Bishop in a position previously held by her grandfather, her father, and most recently Lota herself: that of a general contractor overseeing a major construction project. Alas, Bishop would turn out to be less ideally suited to this task than were her predecessors.

One Rio poem that Bishop began in the early 1960s but was unable to finish until near the end of her life is "Pink Dog" (1979), which melds together the intensity and the complexity of her response to Rio in the early 1960s. As a way of reflecting the appalling urban poverty of Rio, Bishop shrewdly exploits the "awful." And yet the poem also contains a bracing admixture of the "cheerful." The poem's triple rhymes—quite exact through the poem's first three stanzas—offer a discomfiting echo of her Key West "Roosters." The perfectly rhymed "rabies / scabies / babies" is surely one triplet that has never before appeared in the history of the language; the discomfort it causes is essential to its effect. Bishop plays with both one's sympathies and one's instinctive squeamishness. She knows that she can get a reader to accept a poem in which she speaks directly to a suffering and homeless dog more easily than one addressed to a similarly bereft human. Bishop is, of course, suggesting that the sick and homeless can't help looking indelicate, and she gradually leads readers through the initial shock toward something like empathy. This is a female dog, "a nursing mother by those hanging teats," and many phrases hint at a human subtext, in which a violated domesticity is examined with grisly humor. As the poem brings this human subtext to the surface, the rhymes relax at times into the inexact; paradoxically, this makes the poem more comfortable on the ear just as the human dimension becomes most unsettling.

> *Didn't you know? It's been in all the papers,*
> *to solve this problem, how they deal with beggars?*
> *They take and throw them in the tidal rivers.*[24]

Such had become the practice of a group of right-wing vigilantes, and many of Lacerda's fiercest critics claimed that he supported them, although he always strenuously denied it. In any case, Bishop's decision to write a poem on this theme, a scene where "idiots, paralytics, parasites" are shown to be "bobbing in the ebbing sewage, nights / out in the suburbs, where there are no lights," may be taken as a sign of her increasingly critical attitude toward Lacerda. Bishop's speaker continues to address the homeless pink dog, counseling sympathetically:

> *If they do this to anyone who begs,*
> *drugged, drunk, or sober, with or without legs,*
> *what would they do to sick, four-leggèd dogs?*

Echoing the samba beat she savored in the political protest songs circulating in Rio, Bishop sets her own slashing ironies against a light verse rhythm that becomes, in context, curiously unnerving. The poem's tough, satiric edge, its clear-eyed, anguished comedy, recalls the Aristophanes of *Lysistrata*:

> *In the cafés and on the sidewalk corners*
> *the joke is going round that all the beggars*
> *who can afford them now wear life preservers.*

This is a bleak joke indeed. More painful irony emerges in the speaker's concluding advice that the dog hide its nakedness in a *fantasía*, one of the elaborate costumes created and worn by Rio's poor during each annual Carnival celebration: "A depilated dog would not look well. / Dress up! Dress up and dance at Carnival!"[25] Carnival's gaiety emerges here as a desperate deferral strategy, an attempt to deny, postpone, or dance away life's most unsettling problems. Yet one feels that Bishop really means it when she says in the previous line, "Carnival is always wonderful!" The simultaneous and parallel existence of loveliness and squalor, of gaiety and tragedy, of acceptance and irony, is something Bishop's poem attempts neither to justify nor deny.

On October 29, 1964, a different form of celebration occurred when Elizabeth Bishop was honored with a major award from the Academy of American Poets at a ceremony held at New York's Guggenheim Museum. Since Bishop, far away in Brazil, was unable to attend, Lowell and Randall Jarrell stood in for her, with Lowell introducing Jarrell, and Jarrell reading a selection of Bishop's poems. Lowell opened by saying that "this is a very dear evening to me," before adding, "Elizabeth Bishop is the contemporary poet that both I and Randall Jarrell admire the most." Before turning the podium over to Jarrell, Lowell paused to observe of Bishop that "her poems come slowly. You feel she never wrote a poem just to fill a page. If the poem stops coming, she'll often put it away several years—or forever if it doesn't come. I think she's hardly ever written a poem that wasn't a real poem." He also praised the "beautiful formal completeness to all of Elizabeth's poetry." Lowell concluded his brief remarks by observing, "I don't think anyone alive has a better eye than she has, the eye that sees things and the mind behind the eye that remembers." He added that "the person that remembers would be very hard to characterize, but it's a person with a good deal of tolerance and humor. Really, it defeats me to sum up the personality, but that's far more important than the description, even."[26]

One new friend Bishop made in 1964 was Ashley Brown, a professor of literature at the University of South Carolina and a close friend of Flannery O'Connor's. After he had arrived in Rio on a Fulbright lectureship, Bishop and Brown became close friends, and spent much time together in Rio talking about literature, politics, and life. Bishop told Swenson that "we sit and chat like two old ladies on a porch in the south . . . and strange to say he manages to convey all his soft southern gossip without ever being mean at all."[27] They also made frequent excursions together to Ouro Preto. Brown joined Bishop and Lota to witness a spectacular edition of Carnival in 1965, celebrating Rio's four-hundredth anniversary. Brown noted that Lota "was very much involved with the park during the time I was there" and also that as work on it had matured, the park had become "an incredibly popular thing." He also added that Lota was interested "in every last phase of the park. . . . She was a perfectionist." Brown became aware through Lota and others of Bishop's issues with drinking, and he noticed that when he visited Lota's apartment, "there was bourbon for me" but "most of the time Elizabeth didn't drink anything at all." He recalled one occasion when he had been invited to dinner and found that "Elizabeth was pretty well out." He was told by Lota that there would be no dinner and concluded that "Elizabeth had simply been on a little bout that day."[28]

Bishop continued to find poetry in her immediate surroundings, although now she was returning to urban settings rather than the landscapes and intimate portraits that had dominated her work of the Samambaia years. One poem that remained in draft until her death is "Apartment in Leme," in which, as in "Pink Dog," Bishop articulates an explicitly political reflection on her long sojourn in Brazil. The apartment Bishop shared with Lota was on the edge of Rio's Leme district. And as the day dawns in "Apartment in Leme," the poet finds

> It's growing lighter. On the beach two men
> get up from shallow, newspaper-lined graves.
> A third sleeps on. His coverlet
>
> is corrugated paper, a flattened box.
> One running dog, two early bathers, stop
> dead in their tracks; detour.[29]

While in "Pink Dog" a "depilated" female dog suffering from scabies emblematizes the otherness of the urban poor, here both human bathers and a "running dog" veer off to avoid the figure of a sleeping homeless man. Yet "Apartment in Leme" also celebrates the power of the sea as a feminine presence that borders on and defines the geographical outline and emotional atmosphere of Copacabana: "Because we live in your open mouth, oh Sea, / with your cold breath blowing warm, your warm breath cold."[30] Although the poem, which exists in more than thirty pages of drafts, was unfinished at her death, some lines are luminous, and it's hard to avoid the feeling that one is in the presence of a major poem in the making. Indeed, the fact that Bishop contemplated dedicating this poem to her close friend Robert Lowell, as she indicates in an August 2, 1965, letter, shows that Bishop herself thought highly of its possibilities. So does the fact that she regarded it as potentially "a bit better than 'The Armadillo,'"[31] the Brazil poem she did dedicate to Lowell and which he held in particularly high esteem.

Another poem of her Brazilian neighborhood that she completed far more quickly is the extraordinary ballad "The Burglar of Babylon," which wove into a compelling narrative an event that took place before her eyes. This was the widely publicized manhunt for an escaped convict known as Micuçú, who was raised in the nearby favela (or hillside slum) of Babilônia in the Leme district of Rio. Micuçú was pursued in the hills surrounding Lota's Leme apartment by soldiers and army helicopters, and the hunt could be followed through binoculars from Lota's balcony. This pursuit finally resulted in Micuçú's death. Marianne Moore told Lowell that she considered "The Burglar of Babylon" to be Bishop's finest poem. Lowell added for his own part that it was "surely one of the greatest ballads in the language" and that it "oddly enough gives more of Brazil than your whole Life book." He added mordantly, "I wonder what Carlos [Lacerda] would make of it."[32] A Brazilian interviewer described Bishop's poem as "majestic" and found in it "an indescribable melancholy." Bishop's "Burglar of Babylon" begins by somberly noting that "on the fair green hills of

Rio / There grows a fearful stain: / The poor who come to Rio / And can't go home again." These migrants from rural poverty now find themselves trapped in urban poverty. Like the confused migration of "a million sparrows," they have "had to light and rest" on these fair green hills in the favelas of Rio, often finding shelter in dwellings constructed of corrugated boxes or other discarded materials.

When the poem shifts its attention to the escaped convict, Micuçú, it sees him as intensely human. He refuses to live any longer through his fated existence of imprisonment. "Ninety years they gave me," he tells the auntie who raised him as a son. "Who wants to live that long? / I'll settle for ninety hours, / On the hill of Babylon."[33] Most of the remaining poem is told from Micuçú's point of view: what he sees, what he hears, how he feels. After long days of running, and with the soldiers inexorably closing in, he spends an anxious night in a tree, only to awaken "soaked with dew and hungry."

Micuçú looks down from his hilltop across the familiar expanse of Copacabana Beach. He sees the accustomed beach umbrellas and the outspread towels on the sand. To him, the "heads of those in swimming" were like "floating coconuts." He can hear the peanut vendors' whistles coming up from the beach, and almost hear the gossip of the women with their market baskets. But his own life is now inexorably cordoned off from these familiar sights and sounds. Soon, a soldier approaches, and when Micuçú tries to dash for shelter, the soldier fires his weapon and Micuçú "got it, behind the ear." Then, in an extraordinary moment, we enter Micuçú's mind and witness his final thoughts: "He heard the babies crying / Far, far away in his head, / And the mongrels barking and barking. / Then Micuçú was dead."[34] The poem closes as it began, with the incantatory naming of the hills of Kerosene, Skeleton, Astonishment, and Babylon. Bishop told her friend Ashley Brown that most of the poem "was written in a single day. It naturally presented itself as a ballad." Bishop's haunting tale suggests that as long as the favelas stand in their present form, the cycle of poverty, crime, and death will continue without end. Yet although the poem was written quickly, it is freighted with the full substance of her experience in Brazil, accumulated since her arrival at Santos so many years before.

Even as she was writing powerful narratives such as "The Burglar of Babylon," Bishop's relationship with Lota was showing increasing signs of strain. The easy, mutually supportive camaraderie of their earlier years had been eroded by Lota's continuing preoccupation with Flamengo Park. Frustrated by the difficulties of a job made even harder by her status as a woman, and as a talented amateur without a formal degree, she grew increasingly irritable, distracted, and fatigued, even as the park neared completion and began to show the signs of success noted by Brown. Bishop, who much preferred being home at Samambaia, was growing ever more weary of life in Lota's Rio apartment—facing shortages and rationing and political turmoil, and with Lota mostly away at work and exhausted and critical when at home. Bishop, always subject to the risks of binge drinking, now turned increasingly to alcohol.

Bishop alluded only indirectly to this increasingly untenable situation when she mentioned to Lowell in December 1964, "I've tentatively accepted going to teach at Roethke's old job" at the University of Washington, Seattle, "but not till Jan. 1966." She was considering trying it out "for one term or two. I want to see that part of the world, and I only hope I can persuade Lota to come along for part of my stay, too."[35] In a March 1965 letter to Lowell, Bishop's acceptance of the Seattle job remained tentative, because, for one thing, "Lota is against it."[36] Bishop was still hoping that Lota would join her for at least part of her term in Seattle. Meanwhile, Lota continually reminded Bishop that she had never taught before, asserting that Bishop was not cut out to be a teacher. Bishop would defer her decision about whether to accept the Seattle position until the last possible moment, but she finally accepted it, desperate for an escape and feeling she had no alternative.

The park celebrated its formal opening on April 3, 1965, and Lota was now receiving many tokens of public affection and esteem for the part she had played in turning what just a few years before had been a three-mile-long landfill of dirt and rubble into a beautifully designed modern park. But she had no official position within the Guanabara bureaucracy, and she had depended on the governor, Carlos Lacerda, for support. Lota's relationship with Lacerda had by now frayed almost to the breaking point, and in any case, Lacerda's single five-year term was approaching its close. Still, even with Lota's authority slipping away, Bishop told Swenson that Lota "works about 18 hours a day, has lost her voice, is being violently attacked by some politicians, and this morning started off with a toothache and gumboils, *coitada*."[37] These attacks included one from her former close friend and associate, the distinguished landscape architect Roberto Burle Marx, who later explained regretfully that in the heat of the moment, he had written a "very strong article against" Lota, who at the time had become "a little authoritarian" and was imposing decisions that he thought were ill-considered.[38] Bishop claimed that she only saw Lota for the ten minutes her partner required to eat dinner, and this is one reason she was spending increasingly long stretches of time in Ouro Preto. After one particularly long stay, Lota, making the nine-hour drive over difficult roads, "finally came and *got* me."[39]

The time might have seemed ripe for Lota to bow out gracefully, with the park now officially opened and its "Coordinatress" covered with well-earned laurels. After this Lota might have returned with Bishop to the quiet of Samambaia and there recovered her health and good spirits. But bowing out gracefully would have meant relinquishing control of *her* park to the state of Guanabara. Bishop would surely have been delighted by such an outcome, but a surrender of control of this order was not in Lota's nature, even with her political patron out of power and her party out of favor. And so Lota's battle for control over the park would go on in the years to come, even as the odds of maintaining that control steadily dwindled toward zero.

Meanwhile, Bishop's own career was moving forward. In October 1965, Farrar, Straus & Giroux published her third book of poems, *Questions of Travel*. It bears a dedication in Portuguese to Lota for which Bishop chose the last two lines of a sonnet, by the celebrated sixteenth-century poet Luís de Camões, whose final lines read:

> *Because it is such bliss*
> *Giving you what I have and what I can,*
> *The more I give you, the more I owe you.*[40]

What the speaker gives is "my life, my soul, my hope, all / that I have." Yet for Camões's ardent lover, "the profit taken is mine alone."[41] Following this passionate dedication—conveniently indecipherable to English-language readers not familiar with Portuguese—the volume begins with a section titled "Brazil." Its twelve poems are arranged in a sequence, worked out in consultation with Ashley Brown, that opens with a poem from her previous book, "Arrival at Santos." This is followed by a very different poem of arrival, "Brazil, January 1, 1502," and then by the title poem, "Questions of Travel." The sequence then turns toward Samambaia, with poems such as "Squatter's Children," "Manuelzinho," "Electrical Storm," "Song for the Rainy Season," and "The Armadillo." The Brazil section closes strongly with her poem of the Amazon, "The Riverman," her poem of Cabo Frio, "Twelfth Morning," and her poem of Rio, "The Burglar of Babylon."[42] The volume's second section is titled "Elsewhere," and it begins with her auto-biographical story "In the Village." This story is followed by her crucial Nova Scotian poems "Manners," "Sestina," and "First Death in Nova Scotia," accompanied by many other fine poems, including "Filling Station," "Sunday, 4 A.M.," "Sandpiper," and "Visits to St. Elizabeths." Lowell's book jacket blurb asserted that "what cuts so deep" in Bishop's work is that "each poem is inspired by her own tone, a tone of large, grave tenderness and sorrowing amusement." Lowell noted what he termed her "humorous, commanding genius for picking up the unnoticed, now making something sprightly and right, now a great monument." He added that at one time her poems, "each shining, were too few. Now there are many."[43] In a letter to Bishop, he named nearly all the poems in the book, one by one, as individual favorites, citing the special qualities of each, referring to "Filling Station," for example, as "one of your best 'awful but cheerful' poems," and finding "The Riverman" to be "a very powerful initiation poem that somehow echoes your entrance in Santos."[44]

On October 27, military leader Castelo Branco—representing the military government that had overthrown Goulart and taken power in April 1964—issued a proclamation banning all existing political parties and imposing legal guidelines for new parties. In effect, only a single opposition party, approved by the military government, would be allowed to exist. In a November 18, 1965, letter to Lowell, Bishop, out of loyalty to Lota's point of view, still attempted to argue circuitously that "it is NOT a 'dictatorship' here."[45] Lowell responded in a mildly chiding tone: "You are very subtle about dictatorships."[46]

Still, Bishop made it clear that she was completely disenchanted with the rising military government. By November 1965, Bishop found herself in a genuine quandary regarding her life in Brazil. She still loved Lota, but their life together had become increasingly difficult, and with the publication of *Questions of Travel*, her reputation in America continued to grow. She had continued to win grants and awards while in Brazil, but aside from these she had received little direct benefit in Brazil itself from her artistic achievement and was still seen by certain of Lota's friends as her troublesome appendage. It had become very difficult to resist the teaching offers arriving from the United States. As of November 10, Bishop explained to Swenson that she remained undecided about actually going to Seattle and was inclined to back out. But ultimately, her purchase of the house in Ouro

Preto helped make the decision for her. Bishop needed the substantial income she was being offered by the University of Washington in Seattle to help pay for the restoration work. At last, in a November 19 letter to Lowell, she announced her determination to accept the job, and just a few days after Christmas, she boarded a plane to Seattle to begin a new career as a visiting professor of literature and creative writing.

CHAPTER FIFTEEN

NO COFFEE CAN WAKE YOU

Four months after she arrived at Seattle's University of Washington in January 1966 to launch her college teaching career at the age of fifty-four, Elizabeth Bishop was interviewed by the young Tom Robbins, who five years later would publish his bestselling first novel, *Another Roadside Attraction*. Robbins declared in the April 1966 issue of *Seattle* magazine that "the most exciting thing to happen in poetry in Seattle this year was the arrival here of a poet who is . . . female, middle-aged, shy, soft of voice, and pale as a winter moon. Her name is Elizabeth Bishop."[1] Robbins attributed to Bishop a bearing that "seems more like that of a librarian than a conjurer of exotic images." Yet he discerned that there was more to this pale, soft-voiced woman than met the eye. Robbins cited as evidence "a young peyote-eating bohemian" encountered on a University District corner "avidly reading Miss Bishop's latest volume of verse and saying, 'Man, there are some groovy trips in here.'"[2] Robbins added that the recently published *Questions of Travel*, whose Brazil-based poems he felt bore comparison to the paintings of Paul Gauguin, "is enjoying a brisk sale in Seattle bookshops."[3] Robbins himself found Bishop's poems "filled with an atmosphere of timeless calm and impregnated with a magical view of reality."[4]

Robbins noted that upon her arrival, Bishop not only "left behind the kaleidoscopic charms of vast Brazil" but also broke an "impressively long boycott of academia" for such a "luminary in her profession." Bishop agreed she was perhaps the only American poet of her generation who had not earned her living as a teacher, adding, "This is the first time that I have ever taught, and I hate, in a way, to have spoiled the record."[5] An earlier generation of poets had followed more varied careers, and Robbins speculated that Bishop's absence from "the campus, the clique, and the cocktail circuit" might be "partly responsible for the freshness and originality of her work."[6] The creative writing curriculum had grown steadily during Bishop's absence in Brazil, and university teaching was now functioning as the nation's most consistent source of funding for poets and writers, artists and composers. Bishop had refused prior teaching offers from major American English departments, as noted by Robert Heilman, the chair of Seattle's English department, and he was unsure of his prospects of securing Bishop's services for the winter and spring of 1966,[7] but the time had arrived for Bishop to try her hand at teaching. Bishop told Robbins that she accepted the job because she needed the money for a new roof on her house in Ouro Preto. But she also needed to put some temporary distance between herself and her increasingly troubled and censorious partner, Lota de Macedo Soares. Despite the anxiety she felt about encountering a sea of expectant student faces after decades outside of academia, this stint as a teacher would allow her to reap the reward of income and professional recognition she had earned over years of distinguished artistic achievement.

When Bishop entered the classroom as an instructor for the first time, she was taking a post long held at the University of Washington by the noted poet-teacher Theodore Roethke, who had died suddenly of a heart attack in 1963. Years earlier, as Bishop once reported to Lowell, Roethke had described her as a "quick kid in a caper" after Bishop visited him in his disorderly hotel room and helped him swiftly pack his bags to catch a departing train at New York's Grand Central Terminal.[8] The English department had decided that instead of hiring a longtime replacement for Roethke, they would engage a succession of poet-instructors on an annual basis, each of whom would teach for two terms of the regular trimester in a given academic year. Bishop was the second poet to fill this post, the first being Henry Reed, a witty English poet best known for his droll "The Naming of Parts" and for "Chard Whitlow," his spot-on parody of Eliot's *Four Quartets*. The diverting and bibulous Reed, who had returned to the university as a regular teacher, would become one of Bishop's favored companions.

Following a month at the university spent feverishly prepping her first-ever college classes, Bishop at last set out to compose, on her fifty-fifth birthday, February 8, 1966, a letter of reflection to two of her favorite correspondents, Kit and Ilse Barker. Fourteen years before, on February 8, 1952, Bishop had interrupted her birthday to write a letter to the Barkers from Samambaia triumphantly announcing Sammy, the blue-eyed, gold-bibbed birthday toucan, who influenced her decision to remain in Brazil. Now, alone that evening in a Seattle apartment on Brooklyn Avenue, Bishop wrote again to the Barkers, begging forgiveness for the long delay since her last letter: "I haven't written anyone except a wave of homesick letters to Lota after I first got here—before the real work began, that is." Then, acknowledging a culture shock far more unsettling than the one she had experienced on her arrival at Santos in November 1951, she added, "I think as far as I'm concerned, everything strikes me as so totally foreign." This experience as a stranger in the land of her birth was multilayered: "First, the USA strikes me that way now—every 3 years is not enough to keep up with our progress towards death & damnation—and then I've never been west before at all, and then, above all, I've never *taught*, nor seen a gigantic university before." Yet with the passing weeks, Bishop began to adjust to a setting that at first had seemed altogether disconcerting, leading her to tell the Barkers, "If I didn't have to WORK I think I'd be having a wonderful time!"[9] She added to Anny Baumann that "everyone is so nice and *polite* to me, compared to my darling Lota, I can't get used to it." She also feared that Lota was becoming more and more like Carlos Lacerda: "This is the universal complaint about both of them—not just mine—*no one can talk to them.*"[10]

Her duties at the university included teaching a writing workshop attended by twenty students and a class of eighteen in literature. Like innumerable first-time college instructors before and since, Bishop expressed astonishment at the scanty preparation of her students. A Vassar classmate claimed Bishop was "the most erudite freshman since John Stuart Mill," and in the years since college her circle had included members of the intellectual and artistic elite on three continents. So the expectations she placed on her Seattle students could not have been entirely realistic. Even so, she confessed, "I do like them, almost every one of them—only one young Jungian I can't stand."

Bishop's first lodgings had comprised a single room in a cramped and noisy hotel. She had regretfully refused an offer of lodging in Roethke's widow Beatrice's home, because of its distance from the campus (she still couldn't drive) and because of her allergy to dogs, of which Beatrice had many. After a brief stay in her unsatisfactory hotel, Bishop shifted to a motel that proved equally unsuitable. Then, as she noted to the Barkers with astonishment, her students took it upon themselves to transfer Bishop and her few possessions—lock, stock, and barrel—to her present, more comfortable Brooklyn Avenue apartment. They had also provided an assortment of scrounged furniture. She told the Barkers, "I am standing up writing this on the kitchen sink—since I have one rocking chair, one large brass bed and one book-case so far—& a sofa—but 2 rooms, at least." Most remarkably, "the students *did* it—found the place, rounded up the furniture, and *moved* me—while I spent the day 'down-town.'" She was surprised to find "every brassiere and toothbrush in place when I got back. The motel-lady—my last home . . . said 'those boys & one girl too certainly had fun moving you.'"[11] Among the coorganizers of this endeavor were two young admirers who would figure significantly in her life, an auditor in her poetry class, Wesley Wehr, and that "one girl," Roxanne Cumming.

Along with these efficacious devotees, Bishop quickly discovered another helpful presence who would become a lifelong friend, Dorothee Bowie, who would serve for twenty years as the smart and capable assistant to the chair of the English department at the University of Washington. Bowie understood the many unwritten rules, taboos, and rivalries that permeate academia. As Bishop explained it, Bowie had "saved my life a good many times already." The department's current chair, Robert Heilman, a prolific scholar and a friend to poets, also made Bishop's new life easier, but her new friend Dorothee shared Bishop's love of gossip and her dry sense of humor. Bowie quickly recognized in Bishop a needy person with a serious problem with alcohol, but she also declared, "I thought she was worth whatever help I could give her." Bowie felt that these emotional difficulties stood apart from Bishop's strengths. These challenges "had nothing to do with this rather marvelous human being that I knew. In her good times she was just really one of the wittiest, funniest, most marvelous people I have ever known."[12]

Bishop mentioned in her birthday letter to the Barkers that in her first flush of panic over facing a college classroom alone, she confided to Bowie, "If ever I really want to leave I thought I could stand up and shriek I HATE ROETHKE, and that would do it." However, Bowie remarked dryly, "That wouldn't work, dear. Too many people would agree with you."[13] Roethke, three years Bishop's elder, was a brilliant poet who was in several ways Bishop's obverse. Both were exceptionally keen and exact observers of nature, and both were heavy drinkers. But Roethke's favored form, especially in his later years, was the long and sweeping poetic sequence. His flair for natural observation was linked to a more romantic style of heart-on-sleeve emotion. Roethke's first book, published in 1941, was titled *Open House*—hardly a title the author of *A Cold Spring* might have chosen. Bishop acknowledged to Robert Lowell that she didn't really hate Roethke, but "one hates feeling like his ghost—and I think some of his influence has been very bad—although," as she acknowledged with characteristic balance, "at the same time I think he attracted a lot of good potential poets here—and I am still getting some of those."[14] Lowell had earlier encouraged Bishop to accept the Seattle job, observing that after his own visit to the university for the 1965 Roethke Memorial Reading, "Everyone seems terribly excited and eager for your arrival. Where you are known—it's now very wide—you have about the most convinced and authentic fans of anyone writing."[15]

Wesley Wehr, who had previously studied with Roethke and was now auditing Bishop's poetry workshop, stood out for Bishop from his fellow students in several ways. He was a talented painter, who, in Bishop's words, could create, in a manner not unlike herself, "so much space, so much air, such distances and loneliness" in his small, brightly colored works of art, which he would fan out before him "like a set of magic playing cards."[16] Wehr was also an obsessive collector of curious objects as an amateur but talented paleobotanist. Roxanne Cumming would recall many years later an occasion when Wehr, as a passenger, asked that a car be stopped because he had noticed a segment of fossilized pig bone in a ditch along the highway. Once the car screeched to a sudden halt, Wehr scrambled toward the ditch and extracted the ancient porcine specimen for his paleontological collection. At thirty-seven, Wehr was far closer to Bishop's own age than most students in her workshop. The two spent much time together outside of class, and Wehr took notes on all he heard from his new mentor both inside and outside the classroom. Two years after her death, Wehr published his concisely Boswellian memoir, *Elizabeth Bishop: Conversations and Class Notes*.

Wehr's class notes suggest that despite her initial lack of classroom polish, Bishop's greatest strength as a teacher was her determination to guide her students toward seeing and thinking in fresh ways. Extracts from Wehr's class notes cite Bishop urging her fledging authors to "use more objects in your poems—those things you use every day." To encourage her students to write about "the things around you," she assigned a thirty-line poem about Seattle, offering a list of local objects they might include. Drawing on her own precocious mastery of traditional forms, Bishop set out to

drill her students on rhyme, form, and meter, adding that, as budding poets, "You should have your head filled with poems all the time, until they
almost get in your way." And she urged that if they wanted to grow as writers,
"I would suggest that you read one poet—all of his poems, his letters, his
biographies, everything *but* the criticisms on him."[17] As a young poet Bishop
had herself devoured Shelley, Herbert, Hopkins, Moore, and many others
along similar lines, with the added twist—in Moore's case—of being the
recipient of her mentor's letters and a firsthand observer of her life.

Wehr recalled in vivid detail a more private moment. As Bishop prepared lunch for the two of them in the kitchen of her new apartment, Wehr
called out to her, "Elizabeth, I need to ask you for some advice about love."
At this, Bishop stood in the kitchen doorway, stared at him pointedly, and
proclaimed, "You want to ask me a question about W-h-a-t? Did you say it
was about *love?* What would *ever possibly* give you the idea that *I* of *all*
people would know *anything* about a thing like *that?*" Bishop continued,
saying that if Wehr ever knew "much about my personal life, you certainly
wouldn't want to come to *me* for any sagely advice about a thing like love."
She added, sadly, "I've usually been as confused about it as just about anyone else I've known." She pointed Wehr instead to the work of W. H.
Auden: "If *he* doesn't know something about love, I just don't know who
else does." Yet later that afternoon, she apologized for her outburst and
ventured a piece of advice: "Since you did ask me . . . I will say this much:
if any happiness ever comes your way: GRAB IT!"[18]

Certainly, Bishop's love life at that moment *had* reached a significant
level of confusion. Back in Rio was Lota, with whom her life had become
so difficult. Bishop had also recently experienced a brief but passionate love
affair in Ouro Preto with Lilli Correia. And even as she spoke, Bishop was
in the process of beginning a new affair with Roxanne Cumming. Cumming recalled in an interview more than fifty years later that Wehr had
suggested, "Let's go hear Elizabeth Bishop" (give a reading of her poetry).[19]
Roxanne Cumming (known in earlier biographical accounts under the pseudonym Suzanne Bowen) was then twenty-four years old. She had been married

for four years to the painter William Cumming, a leading figure in the Northwest School of painting. Bill Cumming was twenty-five years her senior, she was the fifth of his seven wives, and she was pregnant by him with her first child. In later years, Bill Cumming would characterize their relationship as tempestuous.[20]

Soon after, Roxanne and husband attended a dinner in Bishop's honor at a Japanese restaurant, seated around a low table along with the poet Carolyn Kizer, Northwest School painters Leo Kenny and Richard Gilkey, and writer Tom Robbins. The next day, Bishop invited Roxanne Cumming to visit her at her unsatisfactory motel, and it was then that Cumming determined that such accommodations would not do. With Wehr's support in recruiting his fellow classmates, they chose a new apartment for Bishop and coordinated the move of her belongings and the scrounging of her furniture. As Cumming later recalled, it was she who supplied the large brass bed Bishop referred to in a letter to the Barkers, an article of used furniture (of a type much coveted in the 1960s) that she had recently bartered for with Wesley Wehr in return for two homemade pot roast suppers. Cumming noted that in Bishop's interchanges with others, she would quietly observe her interlocutors, while asking herself the question, "Can this person be trusted?" and then the question, "Can this person help me?"[21] Within a month of her arrival in Seattle, Bishop had certainly found such helpers in Bowie, Wehr, and Cumming. And in Cumming, Bishop had also found a lover. Cumming recalled that she was drawn to the "snarky humor, the whimsey" she found in Bishop, characteristics that contributed to "the deep, odd bond"[22] they shared.

Although Bishop had resisted coming to Seattle and had almost fled in panic, when the end of her second term approached, she began to show signs of a serious reluctance to leave, partially due to her anxiety about the state of Brazilian politics and also about the physical and emotional state in which she might find Lota when she arrived. For a time she contemplated a long voyage home via the Panama Canal, so that she could collect her thoughts and return to working on her own poetry after a lengthy hiatus. Despite her uncertainties about teaching and her sometimes unorthodox methods, her efforts in the classroom might serve as a useful credential for future employment. Her six months in the United States had demonstrated that she could make a life for herself in America if she chose. Now Bishop was returning to Brazil and her earlier life with Lota, without knowing for certain what she might find when she arrived.

Bishop found on her return that, as she told Moore on June 23, "Lota is in a bad state from overwork on her park." And since Guanabara had a new governor, from a rival political party, Lota was losing any control she had once had over the project that had consumed her for so long. As outgoing governor, Carlos Lacerda had tried to protect Lota's authority by creating a foundation for the park with Lota at its head, but courts refused to accept the foundation's authority. Others might have recognized that under her guidance, Flamengo Park had become an essential part of the fabric of Rio, and that with her patron out of power and the park virtually complete, this might be the time to let go. But Lota was utterly unable to relinquish ownership of the things she valued most.

On July 31, Cumming sent Bishop a cable announcing the birth of a baby boy named Hugh. In mid-August she told Bowie, "It's enough to say that Lota is really sick, almost had a heart attack, and finally was forced to stop working for a while—we have all been telling her this for five years, but it did no good."[23] She admitted to Dr. Baumann that *"I have cheated,"* but she also expressed frustration over what she described as Lota's repeated claims that she had "'spent 6 months drinking' in the US."[24] She was also frustrated by Lota's continuing anger over her having taken the position in Seattle and by Lota's refusal to even mention the university or speak about her work there. Bishop made clear to her friends that she had received other job offers and that the alternative of remaining in the United States and working at a good salary was open to her. Bishop had even been offered the surprising figure of twelve thousand dollars for a six-week reading tour. She had found, as well, a younger lover in Roxanne Cumming. Bishop had renounced all of this because she wished to return to Brazil and rebuild her relationship with Lota.

While she acknowledged to Baumann that many of her problems with Lota had been her own fault—especially her drinking—she told Baumann that after her return, Lota refused to recognize that "I have perhaps grown up a lot (!—about time) in the past fifteen years, and can really manage pretty well on my own."[25] Much of that growth, particularly in the 1950s, she surely owed to the liberating and supportive environment Lota created. But much of the growth in the years that followed she had achieved on her own, during a time when she had been forced to work toward her own independence. Over the past years, Bishop had demonstrated her independent earning power and literary standing in the United States, things she had achieved through her own efforts as a professional writer. Lota had once encouraged these developments enthusiastically, but she now found them threatening. Bishop was dismayed, upon her return, to find herself continuously scolded and infantilized by a once deeply supportive lover who had now been captured by twin obsessions: retaining control of her park and over Bishop herself.

Perhaps the solution might be for she and Lota to take a long vacation together in Europe, where they could spend time with each other far away from the competitive pressures of Rio. Setting out in the late fall of 1966, the two traveled to England and the Netherlands. But after a promising start to the trip, Lota grew impatient to leave in order to resume her struggles in Rio. When Lota arrived back home, she had to be hospitalized immediately.

Lota also felt threatened by the possibility of infidelity on Bishop's part. Bishop had humorously described her as a "letter snoop" many years before. Now Lota discovered letters that Cumming had written to her. Understandably, she felt betrayed, and this caused a serious rift between them. Lota was suffering from arteriosclerosis and high blood pressure, and the stress of working on the park had taken a toll on her, and also on Bishop herself. In January 1967, Bishop wrote to the Barkers and Dorothee Bowie from Casa de Repouso São Vicente, where she was recovering from stress and alcohol abuse. Later, Bishop spent two weeks in the Clinica Botafoga for asthma and drinking. She explained to her friends that while she was in these rest homes, Lota was undergoing psychoanalysis with Decio Soares de Souza. Bishop still professed to feel a strong bond with and commitment to Lota, but living in her company was becoming increasingly difficult. In July 1967, Lota's therapist recommended a separation. He suggested that Bishop and Lota remain apart for several months, fearing that any earlier meeting might be dangerous to Lota's health.

A temporary separation, lasting until December 1967, when Lota would presumably be in better health, was called for. Following de Souza's orders, Bishop flew to New York on July 3, where she stayed in the vacant apartment at 61 Perry Street owned by Loren MacIver and Lloyd Frankenberg, who were traveling in Europe. Lota wrote a series of long letters from Brazil to Bishop in New York. The primary object of these letters was to seek reconciliation with Bishop and a continuance of their relationship. During the course of this prolific series of letters, Lota's tone alternated between affection and accusation. Bishop responded to these letters in ways for which Lota generally expressed warm gratitude. Unfortunately, Bishop's letters to Lota were destroyed by Mary Morse, according to her daughter, Monica.[26] Throughout her letters to Bishop, Lota expressed what amounted to an obsession over the mutual disclosure of their wills. Bishop resisted sharing her will's contents with Lota, and the latter appears to have suspected that Cumming might be a beneficiary of Bishop's will, a suspicion that later turned out to be well founded.

Bishop told her Brazilian friends, the sisters Rosinha and Magú Leão, on August 27, "Lota has been absolutely wonderful about writing letters but I worry about her dreadfully—do tell me how she seems to you. Decio now thinks she shouldn't try to come here before December, and it seems like a long way off, but I suppose I can stand it."[27] But Lota could not stand such a delay in seeing Bishop, and her letters began to insist that she must depart for New York very soon. Monica Morse recalls being told some years later by Mary Morse that Lota tried to make one unauthorized trip to New York in early September. Lota's maid, Joanna Dos Santos da Costa, alerted Mary Morse about Lota's attempt at departure, and Morse followed Lota to the airport and pulled her off the plane. This account appears consistent with a hurried telegram Lota sent Bishop on September 7, 1967, reading, "PLEASE DON'T WORRY TRUST ME TERRIBLY HAPPY SEE YOU SOON."[28] Still, having been thwarted in one attempt to travel to New York well before the departure date approved by her medical adviser, Lota then worked on Doctor de Souza and Mary Morse and finally won their extremely reluctant assent to her departure. Decio de Souza later wrote to Bishop that Lota stated more than once, "I know I should not go, but I must." He added that he understood Lota's "must" to mean "Ananke," a term from Greek tragedy where, as Decio explained, "man is pictured as a slave unconscious of Fate's hidden maneuverings."[29]

On September 16, Lota's telegram announced that she was "ARRIVING SUNDAY 17."[30] Bishop later told her friend Rosinha Leão that when she met Lota at the airport, "the minute I saw her I realized she was very sick indeed and that Decio had been a damned fool to let her come."[31] She added that Lota "clutched me as if I were her last hope in the world." Since it was a pleasant day, they made their way on foot through Greenwich Village, then went out to dinner, returning to the Perry Street apartment at eight p.m. Each drank, as she recalled to Rosinha, "one small glass of Dutch beer," and each took "*one* Nembutal" to induce sleep. Lota protested that nine thirty was too early to go to sleep on one's first night in New York, then fell asleep in mid-sentence. Bishop also closed her eyes, adding later, "How I hate myself for having eve[r] fallen asleep." Early the next morning Bishop was awakened by noises in the upstairs kitchen and, rushing in that direction, found Lota "staggering down those steps with a little bottle of Nembutal in her hand." When Bishop repeatedly asked how many Nembutal, a powerful barbiturate, Lota had taken, she replied, "Ten or twelve." Bishop added mournfully that "those were the last words I heard her say."

After a call to Dr. Anny Baumann, Bishop fetched her friends Harold Leeds and Wheaton Galentine, who lived on the opposite side of Perry Street. Together they hurried Lota into a taxi and took her to St. Vincent's Hospital, two blocks away, where she was admitted to the intensive care unit, and where she remained in a coma, as Bishop wrote in her September 23 letter to Rosinha. Bishop insisted to her friend that "we did *not fight*," adding that she felt that Lota was simply in a state of extreme depression. She also added, hopefully, that the doctors "are *pretty* sure she will live now . . . it all depends on her heart." But sadly, Lota died two days later, on September 25. She had never regained consciousness during the eight days she spent in St. Vincent's Hospital. Since Dr. Baumann had insisted that Lota receive no visitors, Bishop did not see her lover of fifteen years again alive after Lota entered the hospital doors, even though, as she told Rosinha, she would be there "every minute, if they'd let me."[32] Bishop was now compelled to send Rosinha a desolate telegram announcing that Lota had "DIED TODAY TRYING TO TELEPHONE YOU = ELIZABETH."[33]

Bishop suffered acutely from grief and guilt during this period and in the months that followed. She wrote a long series of letters to mutual friends in Brazil, describing Lota's death and her own experience. Anny Baumann patiently answered Bishop's repeated questions about the medical circumstances of Lota's death. Dr. Baumann stressed in response to repeated questionings by Bishop that the only drug found in Lota's bloodstream was Valium.

The death of Lota de Macedo Soares raises far more questions than it answers, questions that Bishop would wrestle with for many years. Why did Lota fly to New York in a state of severely impaired health on September 17, against the wishes and advice of both her doctor, Decio de Souza, and her partner, Elizabeth Bishop? Why did Lota cable the words "PLEASE DON'T WORRY TRUST ME"[34] to Bishop several days before she departed for New York, after Bishop expressed anxiety about the wisdom of her coming? Why did Lota bring with her—as Bishop noted to the Barkers after her death—twelve pounds of coffee, along with "so many presents, and all her good clothes, and lists of errands to do for other people"?[35] Why did she take a heavy dose of Valium on the night of her arrival, after what Bishop consistently described as a very affectionate evening? Was Lota aware that even massive doses of Valium are rarely fatal, and that Valium is therefore rarely a successful suicide drug? If Lota knew this, and hoped to survive after giving Bishop a powerful shock, had Lota overlooked the fact that her impaired health, combined with the effects of an intercontinental flight on a person with extremely high blood pressure, might lead to an unexpected coma and even death?

Why, as Bishop would long wonder, did Lota insert into her will, amid pages of legalistic Portuguese, the French phrase "*Si le bon Dieu existe il me pardonnera, c'est son métier*" ("If a good God exists he will pardon me; it is his job")? Bishop speculated to the Barkers, "That looks a bit like premeditation, I'm afraid—and of course there had been an awful suicidal stretch some months ago."[36] Given Lota's obsessive concern with her will, why did she cause her own death in such a way as to furnish her sister, Marietta Nascimento, with a pretext to contest that will on grounds of insanity? Had Lota anticipated the legal battles she would impose on her coheirs, Bishop and Mary Morse? Most of Morse's own money was tied up in the Samambaia estate, which is why Lota had left the estate to her. According to her daughter Monica, Mary Morse and her many adopted children found themselves almost destitute until Mary, with the help of her brother, at last overcame Marietta's challenges to the will.[37]

At the core of all of these questions lies a final series of uncertainties. Did Lota arrive in New York with the definite intention of ending her own life? If she did have that intention, then traveling thousands of miles to kill herself under the roof she was sharing with Bishop might be viewed as an act of vengeance or aggression. Bishop later told friends, "I'll never really know whether it was deliberate or a mistake or what."[38] She would live with that uncertainty for the rest of her days, and she added, in the immediate shock of her loss, "I have no idea what to do with my life anymore."[39] Years later, reflecting painfully on all that coffee Lota had carried with her, Bishop would open the draft of her unfinished "Aubade and Elegy" with the single unpunctuated line, "No coffee can wake you no coffee can wake you no coffee."[40]

Bishop received numerous letters of condolence from Brazilian friends, many of them saying in effect, "Don't blame yourself," but Bishop found this difficult. Lota's doctor, Decio de Souza, wrote to Bishop on October 18, saying he understood that Bishop might blame him for letting Lota go to New York in a state of such ill health. But he was forced to admit that in the face of insistence by a personality like Lota's, "I am not omnipotent." He added, in a statement that seems to apply in many ways to the situation over which both he and Bishop ardently strove for a different outcome, "We are not gods."[41]

Bishop had sent Lota's body back to Brazil, where it was given a state funeral. Her death was covered in the newspapers and became the subject of public lamentation. Bishop was advised by Dr. Baumann that she was in no condition to return to Brazil herself until she had taken the opportunity to recover emotionally. Then Bishop fell and broke her left shoulder and arm, and she spent some weeks recovering, living for a time in the Lowells' vacant Manhattan apartment. Even the day before her departure for Brazil, she was typing her letters in all capitals because, with her arm in a cast, she could not work her typewriter's shift key.[42]

When Bishop finally flew to Rio on November 15, seven weeks after Lota's death, she discovered that with a few exceptions, including Magú Leão and Stella Pereira, nearly every one of Lota's friends had turned against her, including Mary Morse, who, as Bishop then reported and Monica Morse later confirmed,[43] burned Bishop's letters to Lota. According to the terms of Lota's will, Morse was to inherit Samambaia and Bishop was to inherit the Rio apartment and several rental offices there, with the expectation that Bishop could readily sell these and convert them into cash. With Lota's sister, Marietta, contesting the will, both Morse and Bishop would face ongoing legal wrangles before the estate was finally settled in their favor. Bishop had anticipated that she and Morse would work together to defeat Lota's sister's contesting of the will, but with the unexpected rupture Bishop experienced between herself and Mary, each was forced to go it alone in the face of Lota's sister's challenge. Marietta's son, Flávio, did remain a loyal friend of Bishop's, and in a letter Bishop typed in all caps to Bowie because of her broken arm and shoulder just before her departure for Rio, she said that Flávio was "TERRIBLY EMBARRASSED BY HIS MA'S BEHAVIOR."[44]

In January 1968, Bishop wrote a long letter to Maria ("Maya") Osser, a Brazilian friend, expressing her frustration with the situation she had experienced in Rio and at Samambaia. She described her six weeks in Brazil as "the very worst stretch I remember ever having gone through." She noted that she had received nice letters in America from many Brazilian friends, but when she arrived in Rio she encountered "an undercurrent of real hostility among most of the people I had thought my best friends there." Speaking of her difficult time at Samambaia, where many of the furnishings Bishop considered hers, either through purchase or as gifts, had been bequeathed in Lota's testament to others. These items had been carried off from Samambaia during Bishop's absence. She asked Maya Osser, "Can you imagine arriving at the only home (forgive me for being corny, but it's true) I have ever really had in the world and finding it not only not mine— I had agreed to all that—but almost stripped bare?" According to the terms of the will, while Morse would inherit Samambaia itself, Bishop's personal property would, of course, remain her own. Yet as Bishop told Osser, following Lota's death, "Friends had gone up from Rio—how soon after the funeral I don't know—and taken everything. Mary left me the linen on my bed, 2 towels, 2 plates, forks, knives, etc. This was my HOME, Maya. Do people think I have no feelings?"[45] Bishop told Lowell that she felt she was being "used as a sort of scapegoat" because "Lota's death left everyone feeling somewhat guilty and then I appeared and was unconsciously used in that way."[46]

Monica Morse reports that following Bishop's return to Rio after Lota's death, her adoptive mother, Mary, forbade all future meetings between the two. However, she added that "Elizabeth never forgot me." Bishop continued to send her favorite of Morse's adopted children birthday cards and presents for as long as she lived. Morse further recalls that because the military government soon placed a ban on any historical recognition of Lota for her work on Flamengo Park and because Mary had little to say about Bishop, she only learned that the other two of her "three strong mothers" were famous and historically important figures when she went to study in England in the early 1980s. Monica added that she wished to study in America during the 1970s, but that Mary had forbidden it, likely, in Monica's eyes, because Monica might track down Bishop in America and perhaps never return to Brazil.[47]

Bishop was writing to Osser from San Francisco because she and Roxanne Cumming had agreed to reunite, upon the urging of Anny Baumann, who feared that Bishop would otherwise find herself bereft. They had settled on San Francisco after considering such options as New York and Puerto Rico, in part because then Bill Cumming would be near enough, in Seattle, to visit with his two-year-old son, Hugh. Bishop was writing from a hotel just before she moved into the San Francisco apartment she would share with Cumming. On January 4, 1968, she wrote to Frani Blough Muser, explaining, "I just couldn't seem to start living alone right away—and I couldn't bear New York right now."[48] Bishop acknowledged to Osser, "I left Brazil with a very heavy heart," and added, "I feel now as if I'd been living in a completely false world all the time." She also added that nearly all of Lota's friends "totally misunderstood the strength of the bonds between Lota and me—or, now that she's dead, they *want* to misunderstand them." Bishop insisted, "I'd give everything in this world—a foolish expression but I can't think what I'd give, but 'everything,' certainly—to have Lota back and *well*." And in an effort to keep her relationship with Maya alive after these frank declarations, Bishop added, "I am very fond of you and don't want us to stop being friends," but she acknowledged, "I am brokenhearted—those last years were so awful, so exhausting." She admitted, "I didn't behave the way I wish I could have, often, but you must believe me when I say we loved each other. Other people do not have the right to judge that."[49]

Bishop told Frani that she had spent six difficult weeks in Brazil, during which she shuttled back and forth between "Rio—Petrópolis—Rio—Ouro Preto—Rio." She collected her papers and books from Samambaia, and spent six weeks packing the papers from the Rio apartment, which she shipped "hither and yon," and she would sell the Rio apartment she had shared with Lota in happier days "as soon as I can."[50] She spoke to Frani of spending long, rainy afternoons with Lilli and the poet Vinicius de Moraes during her stays at Chico Rei. Bishop said of Vinicius, "I'd known him before but this time we were practically living together and got very friendly and he is very sweet and generous." The phrase "and got very friendly" is added as a handwritten insertion.[51] Bishop later told her friend Lloyd Schwartz that on some nights, after several drinks, she and her friend Vinicius would find themselves in bed together in one of their rooms at Chico Rey.

Roxanne Cumming would later recall of Bishop and Moraes that "they really loved each other,"[52] but whatever relationship Bishop formed with the oft-married Vinicius was nonexclusive. Moraes encouraged Bishop to resettle in San Francisco, terming it America's most attractive city. Bishop's letters from January 4, 1968, to Frani Blough Muser and to Maya Osser about her recent trip to Brazil represent opposing sides of the same coin about her ongoing feelings about the country that had long been her home. Given the length and depth of introspection in these two letters, Bishop must have spent the entire day feverishly typing. Although Bishop would continue to return to Brazil for many years, from this moment on, her life there would shift entirely in the direction of Casa Mariana and the circle of friends she had made for herself in Ouro Preto.

Five days after she completed her January 4 letters to Maya Osser and Frani Blough Muser, Bishop and Cumming moved into their apartment at 1559 Pacific Avenue. Bishop was also preparing her *Complete Poems* for publication by Farrar, Straus & Giroux then.

In San Francisco, Bishop became acquainted with the poetry scene after Cumming adopted the simple expedient of inviting all the notable poets in San Francisco to a party at their Pacific Avenue apartment, including Robert Duncan, Denise Levertov, Kenneth Rexroth, Thom Gunn, and others. Many inhabitants of San Francisco's poetry scene viewed Bishop as an old-fashioned easterner who sometimes employed such dated conventions as meter and rhyme, but on the whole Bishop enjoyed her more or less pressure-free literary relationships, and she befriended the expatriate English poet Thom Gunn, among others. Bishop wrote to the Barkers in March 1969 about one party that included such fellow writers as Robert Duncan: "Everyone got rather tight (except me—I haven't drunk for months now)—and very gossipy."[53] By then, Bishop, even when cold sober, could enjoy an evening of dishing over the local literary scene. Bishop confessed that when she participated in a poetry reading as one of twelve "mostly wild" poets for the benefit of striking San Francisco State teachers, she refused the "jugs of awful cheap wine" being passed around backstage, but she "did accept some drags of 'pot'—the cigarette was wrapped in bright-red cherry-flavored cigarette paper." When Denise Levertov learned that Cumming was serving as Bishop's secretary, she decided that she needed a secretary as well, and employed Cumming one day a week in that capacity. Cumming recalled that Bishop was reluctant to be separated from her, and would read in a nearby armchair while her young partner worked on Levertov's papers.[54]

In April 1969 Bishop, accompanied by Cumming, gave readings on the East Coast, including one at Harvard University, where she was introduced by Robert Lowell and met the poet Frank Bidart, who would become her protégé, for the first time. The plan was then to put the money from these readings "in our money belts and take off for Brazil, on May 15." In May 1969 they arrived in Ouro Preto, where they settled into Bishop's home. Bishop was visited in Ouro Preto by her friends, the piano duo of Robert Fizdale and Arthur Gold. In August 1969 Bishop wrote to the Barkers from Ouro Preto, hinting at the fact that Cumming was showing signs of psychological instability with the words, "The summer (winter) has been just too awful to be written about, so I'll skip the whole thing and concentrate on the present." With the reconstruction of Casa Mariana still in progress, she and Cumming were "NOT in my house but in Lilli's house across the street, a tumbling-down, magnificent ark that always gives me asthma because it is so cold, damp, and mostly, mildewed. . . . MY house is a dream of beauty, really, and someday perhaps you'll visit it." But in an effort to get the reconstruction completed, she was spending most of her time "fighting with workmen, neighbors, lawyers."[55] She acknowledged that she was tempted to call the house Bishop's Folly, but settled instead on Casa Mariana, "primarily in honor of Marianne Moore, and also because it is on *the road to Mariana*, a little town full of ecclesiastical remains,"[56] including impressive baroque churches. She explained that, "since it wasn't yet habitable, Roxanne & I have had a rather uncomfortable and miserable summer. . . . Things gradually seem to be improving now, however, and I really hope to move over in a few days, at least to camp in the place, start arranging books, and at last, at last, get to work again."[57]

In October 1969, Bishop explained to the Barkers, "We moved into the house long before it was ready but what a relief even so—it is beautiful even with many things and thousands of books still just in PILES." She added that, "we were lucky enough to get a wonderful maid—named Aurea— one of an especially bright, large black local family—cousin to the local young 'restorer,' whom I have always seen here and who got scholarships to study in France Belgium Harvard etc—a darling modest man who came back here to marry and is the official 'Patrimonio' (like the National Trust) man for this state."[58] While Bishop was experiencing these challenges and adventures in Brazil, her *Complete Poems* was published in New York. Bishop later told Mildred Nash that the title was based on a misunderstanding between herself and her publisher. *Collected Poems* would have been a more accurate title. *Complete Poems* brought together the three volumes *North & South*, *A Cold Spring*, and *Questions of Travel*, as well as a significant body of new or previously uncollected work.

Cumming returned temporarily to San Francisco, leaving Bishop alone. In December 1969 Bishop wrote to Lowell expressing the crisis she now found herself in. Lowell told Bishop that among her fellow poets in America "every one loves and reveres you so," but such was by no means the case in Brazil.[59] She told Lowell: "It has been a totally wasted stretch—and had been for a long time before that, too. Oh, maybe some of it will seem comic, sometime, but if I had stayed in NY or SF, I think I might have worked on the Brazil book & even managed to say some nice things . . . now I've forgotten what they were! I suppose I had Lota for so long to intervene for me, in Petrópolis, at least—and I really was happy there for many years. Now I feel her country really killed her—and is capable of killing anyone who is honest and has high standards and wants to do something good . . . and my one desire is to get out. But how to LIVE?"[60] Bishop had written to the Barkers a few days earlier about Casa Mariana, "It is the most beautiful house in its ancient way in the city—or in the world—and now *I want to sell it.*"[61]

Bishop wrote the Barkers with genuine anger as 1970 began, expressing frustration with the slow reconstruction process, now in its fifth year: "AND the bloody lawsuits going on in Rio." Under the circumstances, she added, "All I can think of is getting out alive. In fact, I'm quite amazed I *am* still alive, every morning." Expressing frustration with what she considered to be the betrayals of people she thought were her friends, she added, "I see now I have been very stupid or naïve all my life: I truly didn't realize how cruel and vicious people one actually knows could be, until I was 58 years old."[62]

Cumming returned to Ouro Preto but in Bishop's view began to show increasing signs of mental instability. At the same time, Bishop was involved in ongoing legal battles involving Lota's estate. In March 1970, she told the Barkers, "I was feeling just too wretched to write anything except to people I didn't know, publishers and so on, for a long time—now things seem a bit better, even if all the problems are still unsolved—or maybe I am just feeling better—physically, and have made up my mind what to do about them, and that gives one a slightly above-it-all feeling . . . or is that the often referred to 'remoteness' of old age?"[63]

Bishop learned about the National Book Award for her *Complete Poems* when she was at the telephone exchange at Ouro Preto and heard the sound of her publisher Robert Giroux's voice coming over the telephone line from the desk of a different operator. Bishop decided that she could not manage the trip to the United States to receive the award, which would have had to occur on very short notice, so Robert Lowell accepted the award in New York in her stead.

At last, despite previous efforts to deny it to herself, Bishop became convinced that Cumming had become, for the time, mentally unstable. She wrote to the Barkers on May 13, "I have been having a very difficult time and am not quite out of the woods," adding that "Roxanne and I should have realised that she was sick long, long ago, and did realize about three months ago—had a very bad breakdown. I won't go into the sad and really awful details, poor child—poor, *poor* child—but anyway, after ten days or so in a hospital in Belo, she finally was able to make it, with Boogie [the nickname of her son, Hugh], to the U.S. on the 11th." She added, expressing her own ongoing anxiety because she had not yet heard from Seattle any confirmation of Cumming's safe arrival, "At least, I hope she made it—a friend [José Alberto Nemer] flew with her to Rio, to get her aboard the plane there to San Francisco." Bishop continued, "Of course the person I feel sorriest of all for is Boogie—who was very upset and confused. I just hope it won't hurt him too much. It is all too much like my own early days."[64] Bishop wrote to Dorothee Bowie two weeks later that she had at first failed to recognize the signs because her partner could be "so convincing that it can get to be almost a *folie à deux*."[65]

In the context of these events, Bishop began writing a series of long letters to Bowie, who was familiar with Cumming from their overlapping artistic circles in Seattle. In a June 14 letter to Bowie, with reference both to her own situation and to difficulties her friend Dorothee was facing with her husband, Taylor, Bishop wrote that it "has taken me the hard way . . . to discover about myself—WHY I let people treat me so abominably, and keep right on, being nice and forgiving, over & over & over, like a perfect sap . . . (and after thinking it's my fault)."[66] Following this difficult epiphany, Bishop wrote to Bowie five days later, "I find I am feeling much better—like crawling out from under a wrecked automobile or something— maybe I'll soon start thinking better, too."[67] Just four days before this letter to Bowie, Bishop showed one sign of feeling better. She had completed one of her most masterful poems, "In the Waiting Room," and submitted it to *The New Yorker.* And just days after Cumming's departure, Bishop had submitted another poem of compelling mastery, the autobiographical "Crusoe in England." These poems, each having undergone a long gestation only to be completed quickly, under duress, were promptly and enthusiastically accepted by editor Howard Moss. Continuing this phase of transition, she had recently accepted the offer of a full-time teaching post at Harvard University for the fall term of 1970. Robert Lowell, with the help of his friend William Alfred and his fellow poet Robert Fitzgerald, had convinced the Harvard English department to hire Bishop in a term position, to replace him while he remained in England with his new love interest, Caroline Blackwood.

Bishop's "In the Waiting Room," which she had completed in the immediate wake of her crisis with Roxanne Cumming, explores a different kind of crisis: the crisis of identity she shows herself experiencing as a girl of almost seven years old. The poem begins matter-of-factly, a tone characteristic of many of those openings Lowell termed "Quaker-simple." The Aunt Consuelo of the poem represents in pseudonym her aunt Florence Bishop, and in its biographical context the poem parallels the ending of her story "The Country Mouse," where she is on the verge of a physical and emotional breakdown after her dislocation from the Bulmer house in Great Village to the gloomy and unwelcoming abode of her Bishop grandparents in Worcester. While waiting in this liminal state, Bishop engaged in what would prove to be a favorite pastime, traveling vicariously in the realm of books and illustrated magazines, in this case the February 1918 issue of *National Geographic*. What the child sees proves quite disorienting and involves quite a leap from the wintery Worcester context. These photographs include "the inside of a volcano, / black, and full of ashes; / then it was spilling over / in rivulets of fire." The pages of the *National Geographic* are full of startling figures, including a then-well-known married couple who were considered the quintessential American explorers, "Ossa and Martin Johnson / dressed in riding breeches, / laced boots, and pith helmets." Then comes a group of perhaps still more unsettling images, since they point to a series of intense cultural differences. "Long Pig" refers to a human carcass about to be consumed by members of a tribe who engage in cannibalism.

The child tries to pull herself into the present world, reminding herself that she is only reading a magazine in a dentist's waiting room, but even if foolish or timid, her aunt, whose groan of pain she overhears, is a member of a larger tribe than her Worcester family. Suddenly, it would seem the child is swept out of herself, and she tries to cling to familiar realities. To be "an *Elizabeth*" and at the same time "one of *them*" might just be the most unsettling thing of all. All around her, the child is faced with seemingly unanswerable questions of identity. In the overheated waiting room, these thoughts and feelings create an effect of vertigo. Then suddenly, the wave of vertigo passes, and the child finds herself back in a familiar world that perhaps has changed forever.

Since January 1966, when she arrived in Seattle, Washington, to begin teaching at the college level at the age of fifty-five, Bishop had experienced a series of overwhelming events. She had faced the mental breakdown and suicide of a woman she had loved and with whom she had shared the happiest years of her life. She had been ostracized, rightly or wrongly, by a city full of people she had thought her friends. She had faced the mental breakdown of another lover in a remote mountain town in Brazil while living in a house that was still under construction. And now she was completing a poem exploring a crisis of identity that she herself experienced while passing from the age of six to seven. In the context of these discomfiting experiences she found herself asking, what "held us all together, / or made us all just one?" This is a question that "In the Waiting Room" does not attempt to answer.

In July 1970, James Merrill arrived for a visit. Bishop found that his company offered her a tremendous experience of relief. As she wrote to Fizdale and Gold, "Jim Merrill was the perfect guest, while I was far from the perfect hostess, being in the middle of a nervous breakdown (or something), I believe." Yet it was during the course of this visit that Merrill drew the conclusion that "It was *du coté de chez* Elizabeth . . . that I saw the daily life that took my fancy . . . with its kind of random, Chekhovian surface, open to trivia and funny surprises, or even painful ones, today a fit of weeping, tomorrow a picnic." It was then that Merrill decided, "Elizabeth had more talent for life—and for poetry—than anyone else I've known, and this has served me as an ideal."[68] At one point, a Bishop friend entered the house while Bishop was tearfully recounting to Merrill her many recent tribulations, and when this friend displayed consternation, Bishop said in Portuguese, "It's all right, Jose-Alberto. I'm only crying in English." Merrill later recalled that following "a solid week of rain" in Ouro Preto, Bishop proposed a visit by taxi to a nearby town. As the taxi jounced through the countryside, it passed "all at once *under* a rainbow—like a halo on the hill's brow." After Bishop spoke a few words in Portuguese to the driver, the latter "began to shake with laughter." Bishop explained that in the north of Brazil, "they have this superstition—if you pass underneath a rainbow you change sex." Merrill added mordantly, "We were to pass under this one more than once."[69]

Certainly over the course of its first ten months, 1970 proved to be yet another difficult year. As the time for her departure to begin her teaching term at Harvard approached, Bishop wrote a note to the Barkers: "Life has been very difficult for so long now, but I think I am seeing my way ahead a bit."[70] Bishop was working to wrap up a book of translations of Brazilian poetry into English, which she was coediting with her friend Emanuel Brasil. Brasil spent several days in Ouro Preto with her, where they worked together on it intensively. This notable volume would be published in 1972 as *An Anthology of Twentieth-Century Brazilian Poetry*. It featured fourteen translations by Bishop herself, including seven poems by the much-admired Carlos Drummond de Andrade, whose work, like Bishop's, often turns on a deep exploration of memory and family. The volume also featured further translations by a range of distinctive American poets, including Paul Blackburn, Richard Eberhart, Barbara Howes, Galway Kinnell, James Merrill, W. S. Merwin, Louis Simpson, Mark Strand, Jean Valentine, and James Wright. It remains one of the most notable attempts to bring the twentieth-century poetry of Brazil into English.

Bishop acknowledged that after James Merrill's heartening visit, "I sort of gave up for two weeks or so—literally couldn't do anything at all, I was so tired and also all my troubles seemed to catch up with me." But not long after this bout of exhaustion, the time arrived to prepare for her departure to Boston, where Bishop's Harvard classes would begin on September 28, 1970. Bishop was delighted to find a responsible couple who could stay in her house while she was gone, which she dryly called "my greatest piece of luck in several years." The husband, Donald Ramos, was an "American, Portuguese descent, here on Ford grants, etc. doing research—very simple, bright, I think, and responsible." Ramos had agreed to sort through Bishop's masses of papers while she was gone. As always, now Bishop confronted the problem: "What to do with valuable letters & M.M.S . . . ???" Once she left Ouro Preto behind, Bishop anticipated "a grim, lonely week of dressmaking and seeing lawyers in Rio, before flying on to Boston."[71]

Bishop composed a letter to Dorothee Bowie from the Hotel Serrador in Rio on September 15, 1970, along similar lines, saying that "this is and will continue to be a very grim stay in this supposedly glamorous city." Because Lota's friends had by now nearly all turned against her, Bishop admitted, "I haven't any friends here I care to look up any more." Still, she had much to do in Rio, since she felt she could not arrive to teach at Harvard with a few pairs of blue jeans and otherwise only rags. "I have to get a few clothes made with the only dressmaker I like in the world, to see the two lawyers *here* [she had been consulting others in Boston and San Francisco], to pay my Brazilian taxes, if possible," and "to re-new my passport—long expired." She regaled Bowie with a tale laden with incongruity. She had chosen a "big downtown travelling salesman's hotel," as its only female patron, because it was close to her dressmaker. Bishop's plan was to appear at her poetry readings "in a black silk pant-suit with pink blouse . . . WOW." But when the dressmaker's husband brought fabric samples to Bishop's hotel room at the Serrador, "he was ignominiously ordered out of my room. This would never happen at a beach hotel, where you can be as immoral as you want." She added wryly that "poor OLD me, and poor much *Older*, and stone deaf, Mr. Lauro, must look awfully wicked."[72] Wicked or not though she might be, Bishop's plan was now to catch a flight directly to Boston on September 24—just two days before her Harvard classes were due to start. Ouro Preto and Casa Mariana still held a place in her heart, and she would return to her house in Brazil each spring for the next several years. But on her journey to Boston, she would carry with her few fond memories of the tattered beauty of Rio.

BREAKFAST SONG

As the Thanksgiving holiday approached in 1970, Alice Methfessel, the young woman who would become the romantic partner and muse of Elizabeth Bishop's last years, wrote a brief note on the letterhead of Harvard University's Kirkland House, where Bishop was then living, and where Methfessel served as house secretary. In this note she detailed the many qualities she found in Bishop that made her feel thankful. These included kindness, and affection, trust and generosity, spontaneity and thoughtful use of words, as well as, of course, Bishop's sense of humor. Methfessel signed her first name, Alice, in her large, bold, looping hand, under a closing offering lots of love.[1]

Methfessel's next missive, written three days after Christmas from her parents' home in the Pocono Mountains resort area of Buck Hill Falls, Pennsylvania, was addressed to Dearest Elizabeth. It spoke of the marvelous skiing and looked forward to a reunion soon with Bishop in Cambridge, Massachusetts. Methfessel added a postscript, mentioning of a Christmas gift she acknowledged that she had with her, a beautiful bracelet Bishop had given her. She added that she felt rather special when she wore it—because it served as a constant reminder of Bishop's affection.[2] Methfessel's young nephew Gary, who regarded Methfessel as his "cool aunt from Boston" and whom he valued highly for the sympathetic attention she always paid to him and his siblings during holidays with the family, would later recall that his aunt never once mentioned Bishop in his presence.[3] He only learned of the relationship between his aunt and the famous poet after Bishop's death. But Gary Methfessel's aunt evidently enjoyed carrying with her to family gatherings this quiet token, almost as a secret talisman of the special bond she had formed in just a few months with her new female lover.

Bishop replied to Methfessel's post-Christmas tribute from the Cosmopolitan Club in Manhattan, where she was seeing old friends. She acknowledged, "I miss that loud, cheerful voice & think I am doing awfully well to keep my spirits up without it to direct me several times a day."[4] Within a few short months, Bishop had come to depend on her twenty-seven-year-old partner's attentiveness, affection, practicality, and lively spirits. In early February 1971, when Bishop was about to make a planned flight back to Ouro Preto after completing her first fall at Harvard, Methfessel wrote a brief note wondering how lonely she might feel after Bishop's departure and admitting that her little heart was ready to burst with the affection she felt for her elder partner. Bishop spent her sixtieth birthday in flight, aboard a Varig Airlines jet transporting her from Boston to Brazil. Methfessel's next lively letter, written just after Bishop's plane took off, is dashed off in her large, open hand. Beneath a smudge mark on the page (described by Methfessel as a tear), she acknowledged she had never felt lonely or so cut adrift. Methfessel acknowledged, too, that it seemed impossible that Bishop might now be in a silver capsule hurtling away from her at an incredible speed.

Over the course of the next few weeks, Methfessel would send to Bishop's home in Ouro Preto more than twenty-five handwritten or typed letters, cards, and aerograms. Methfessel's loud, cheerful voice came through even in her correspondence, for the tenor of these numerous airmailed epistles boils down to three simple words: I LOVE YOU! In fact, these words in full caps appeared frequently in the missives flooding Bishop's mailbox at Casa Mariana. After the fraught relationships Bishop had recently experienced with Lota de Macedo Soares and Roxanne Cumming, this new and warmly affectionate bond with the young Alice Methfessel must have come not only as an overwhelming relief but as an overpowering surprise.

When Bishop arrived in Cambridge for her first semester teaching at Harvard University, she was the recent survivor of a series of personal catastrophes or near-catastrophes. Yet as a poet, Bishop was in the process of entering into her last and greatest creative phase. Three important advocates on Harvard's English faculty had helped to engineer her current appointment. Her advocate of longest standing was Robert Lowell, who had begun teaching at Harvard in 1963, and Bishop had originally expected to work alongside Lowell. But in the fall of 1970, Lowell began a long leave of absence from Harvard while he pursued a relationship in England with the aristocratic British author Caroline Blackwood, who would one day become his third wife. Closer at hand were William Alfred, the colorful Irish-American professor and playwright best known for his award-winning 1965 drama *Hogan's Goat*, and Robert Fitzgerald, a fine poet and a renowned translator of Sophocles, Homer, Euripides, and Virgil. Following the successful reading Bishop gave at Harvard in 1968, these three had worked in tandem to encourage Harvard's English department to hire Bishop to a term position, although Alfred recalled that this effort had not proved difficult, since members of the department "said they'd give their eye-teeth to have her come."[5] On her arrival, she was first lodged temporarily at Harvard's Warren House. Bishop told her friend Frani that she had spent her first evening there with Bill Alfred, and that "he was terribly kind the next day—spent the whole day getting me through the red tape."[6] Bishop's letters to others would frequently express her sense of obligation to Alfred for his help in navigating Harvard's bureaucratic intricacies and tricky department politics. For his part, Alfred recalled, "Our friendship was merry." He declared, "I felt the privilege of her notice as a great gift," adding that "Elizabeth was just endlessly energetic in her friendships," and that "she had the gift of making you feel that you were her intimate."[7]

Not long after Bishop's arrival in Cambridge, she made preparations to move from Warren House into "a suite in Kirkland House—two rooms and a real kitchen." This was a suite Alfred himself had once occupied, and it would cost Bishop a mere five hundred dollars per semester. In return, Bishop was expected to share occasional meals with the "boys" in residence. But at least one item of business from her former life remained to be settled. Amidst her frantic efforts to prepare for her upcoming university classes after her unsettling months in Ouro Preto, Bishop had to make time to fly to San Francisco to complete the depressing task of clearing out her former Pacific Avenue apartment, because the building was about to be sold. The ever-obliging Dorothee Bowie made the trip from Seattle in order to help her with this move.

On her return to Cambridge from San Francisco, Bishop wrote from Kirkland House to Loren MacIver that she felt she was doing well "for a scared elderly amateur 'professor.'"[8] Her teaching schedule would include two seminars of three hours, one on Wednesday afternoon and the next on Thursday. This would give her five days to recover and prepare for her next classes, leaving time to catch up on her correspondence and perhaps even to compose some of her own poetry. Letters to various friends from this time include brief and characteristically cagey mentions of Alice Methfessel. She told Swenson, for example, "The secretary of Kirkland House, a very friendly girl, is about to introduce me to the mysteries of the laundry, in the basement here, and I have to buy *groceries*." Her letters to Bowie are also populated with a series of brief, allusive references to Methfessel, who is soon described as lending Bishop her apartment at 16 Chauncey Street during the day as a quiet place to work. With the aid of this new comforter, Alice Methfessel at Kirkland House, and the guidance and advocacy of professors Alfred and Fitzgerald at Harvard, Bishop found herself settling into a new kind of life in Cambridge.

Yet Bishop had by no means left all of her past behind her. Even as she was beginning to feel more at home at Harvard, Bishop expressed concern to Bowie and others about her sense of risk at being publicly confronted by Roxanne Cumming, whom she knew to be in the Boston area. Then, in a November 2 letter to Bowie, Bishop wrote, "R[oxanne] has appeared on the scene. Just as I was beginning to relax a bit—and Wednesday the seminar had gone very well, and then on Thursday much better, it seemed to me." Yet as this Thursday class ended, a figure confronted her in the doorway. It was Cumming. Bishop described to Bowie that as she emerged from the gloomy classroom and entered the dark hallway, "I really thought for the first time in my life I was seeing a ghost; I just couldn't believe it. But the figure didn't go away, and sure enough it was R." Earlier that day, Cumming had appeared at Kirkland House, seeking out Bishop. "Alice and the other secretary guessed something was very wrong but didn't know what." Bishop explained to Bowie that Cumming was demanding references in support of applications to college. She also made accusations of having been mistreated by Bishop's friends and by medical personnel in Ouro Preto. Bishop apologized to Bowie for sending such "a delightful letter for you to start your week off with. . . . And I have so much work to do! God help me."[9] Employing the aid of Robert Bowditch, her lawyer in Boston, Bishop took steps to keep Cumming at a distance, explaining to Bowie, "I can't have her making a scandal here."[10] Perhaps it was on this day that Bishop told Alfred, "I'm blue," when he made a visit to her at Kirkland House. Alfred recalled that on that occasion, "she fell off the wagon (most of the time I knew her, she was on Antabuse), and I fell off the wagon. We both got blue-eyed drunk."[11] Cumming made no further appearances at Harvard, but a month later, at a poetry symposium in Chicago, Cumming appeared again. At this event Bishop managed adroitly to give her pursuer the slip, but she remained nervous about future unexpected encounters.

Cumming made clear to Bishop and her lawyer that she felt she was owed compensation for the time and effort she had devoted to Bishop in San Francisco and Ouro Preto, including her services as Bishop's personal secretary. Some months later, the two agreed on a settlement. Cumming had enrolled for the spring term at a leading Boston-area college, and Bishop explained in a February 1971 letter to Bowie that she would pay half of Cumming's tuition ($450) for that spring term and half for the term that followed—and that this arrangement would bring their once-intimate relationship to a close. In some of her guiltier later moments, Bishop would lament to friends that she had ruined Cumming's life as well as Lota's. But in fact, Cumming, who, according to Bishop had "said she was going to 'show me'"[12] that she could be successful, made good use of the tuition benefit she derived from Bishop. In a display of her own talent and resilience, Cumming garnered an undergraduate degree, studied medicine, became a physician, and practiced successfully in Massachusetts and elsewhere for many years until her retirement.

The poet Frank Bidart, who had been for several years Lowell's close friend and protégé, soon became a close and important friend of Bishop's as well. Bidart recalled that he first met Elizabeth Bishop in 1969 at one of Lowell's Tuesday morning office hours. Bidart noticed that she had a mink stole on and that "she looked like a Scarsdale matron. She did not look like a poet." Bidart felt that, "in Merrill's wonderful phrase," Bishop was "impersonating an ordinary woman." Bidart recalled the reading she gave that afternoon as wonderful, with Bishop's fine translation of Carlos Drummond de Andrade's "Traveling in the Family" standing out. With Lowell away in England in 1970 and Bishop coming to Harvard, he wrote to Bidart "that I should meet her when she came and that there was no one who was as much fun as Elizabeth Bishop." When Bishop and Bidart did meet up, Bidart said, "We just got on. The connection between us was very immediate." Asked if there was really no one more fun than Elizabeth Bishop, Bidart replied that "'fun' is a complicated word." He noted that Bishop was very engaging "and very gracious. She was not difficult and thorny. She tried very much to make social occasions alive and interesting and fun." But he added, "There was depth to the fun. It was not fun and games." Bidart also felt that with Lowell now at a distance, he became a kind of bridge between the two poets, noting that Bishop and Lowell "didn't see each other much. I had seen Lowell much more frequently. So in a way, befriending me was a way of keeping in touch with him. I think she craved that kind of intimacy with him." When asked if Lowell wanted him to look after Bishop in Cambridge, Bidart replied, "Very much so. And I wanted to look after her insofar as I could. She's someone who one wanted to help and protect."[13]

After leaving a teary-eyed Alice Methfessel behind when she flew out of Boston in February 1971, Bishop settled for the spring into her still-not-quite-completed house in Ouro Preto, in which location she received that steady stream of loving letters from her new partner. After two weeks at Casa Mariana, Bishop wrote to Dorothee Bowie, "Well, I am all right now. Just damned lonely, especially after Cambridge," and added, "I'm not sure I can take even a part-time life in this town—it's really too lonely—but maybe if I have a guest or two, I'll cheer up." Thinking partly of the military government now ruling Brazil so oppressively, she noted that at least her maid was cheerful, "and that's what I need most of all in this sad country where I'm not sure I belong any more at all."[14] In April, Bishop enjoyed hosting Frani Blough Muser at Casa Mariana before Muser set off on a trip down the Amazon. But in May, Bishop found herself in a hospital in Belo Horizonte, where she was diagnosed with typhoid fever, having neglected to keep up with her shots. Upon her release, she returned to Cambridge in early June, where she spent several nights with Methfessel while deciding that she would in fact take the fifth-floor apartment Alice had found for her at 60 Brattle Street, conveniently located a few blocks northeast of Harvard Square. But while her typhoid fever had been cured in Brazil, she was still feeling quite unwell when she arrived in America. Traveling to New York to see Anny Baumann, she received a characteristically thorough examination and, following the tests Baumann ordered, a characteristically accurate diagnosis by her trusted physician. She learned that she was suffering from a particularly "ghastly" form of amoebic dysentery, along with "three other kinds" of dysentery as well, and she acknowledged that "it was no wonder I'd been feeling poorly," confessing, "I always blame my own lack of moral fibre, of course, when I feel tired and get gloomy."[15] She returned to Cambridge, where she underwent a lengthy course of treatment. When finally cured of these debilitating ills, Bishop, with her usual resilience, returned to Ouro Preto in July. There her young artist friend José Alberto Nemer stayed for a month at Casa Mariana, "so it isn't so lonely."

During their June together in Cambridge, Bishop and Methfessel worked out a plan to meet in Quito, Ecuador, on August 1. They would then travel in company to the Galápagos Islands, ending their monthlong vacation together with a pilgrimage to Peru to scale the heights of Machu Picchu. Then they would return to Cambridge by September 2 to give Bishop time to prepare for her fall 1971 classes at Harvard. A week after her return, Bishop wrote to Anny Baumann from Methfessel's Chauncey Street apartment, as she was awaiting the final furnishing of her own new apartment on Brattle Street. She declared that her journey with Methfessel to Peru and the Galápagos Islands had been "a wonderful trip," although she suspected that several postcards she tried to send to Baumann from the islands had been perused by the young local postmaster and discarded. Bishop found the Galápagos, once studied so carefully by her beloved Darwin, to be "absolutely marvelous—sort of like one's idea of Paradise." The birds and animals there were not afraid of humans and "come right up to you and sit on you, or peck on your sneakers."[16] Mother seals would show off their babies to the island's visitors, then loll on the sand observing human swimmers. Bishop claimed in her 1947 "At the Fishhouses" that one seal inhabiting "the clear gray icy waters" off Nova Scotia was so curious about her that she and the seal had shared silent colloquies each evening. Now, in these much warmer waters, Bishop enjoyed casually sharing the beach with an entire pod of equatorial mother seals and their offspring.

Shortly after their return from the Galápagos, Bishop left a note in

Methfessel's apartment, where she had been working, dated only "4 PM," in which she declared, "I always feel safe when I am with you." Then, with reference to her young partner's motorcycling proclivities, she added, "Except possibly on a Honda." Bishop's brief, typewritten message then moved toward tribute, reflecting both the intensity of her attachment to Methfessel and the weight of anxiety that she had been carrying for so long. Speaking of Alice's apartment, where she sometimes worked alone on her writing and often spent the night, she said, "I love this place because I seem to feel safe here, too—or safer than I do at home. . . . Awful things are NOT going to happen—you can charm them away, or make me see things as they really are, not the morbid way I get to imagining them—when I start to drink."[17] In how many places during the course of her life had Bishop not felt safe?

Bishop's fall teaching schedule included, along with a standard poetry writing class, another class that had won the approval of her English department colleagues, one focusing, as she described it to a friend, on "just letters, as an art form or something."[18] The course had drawn such a large body of potential students that she was required to cut its enrollment by half. By choosing to offer such a seminar, hardly a standard genre in the literary curriculum of that era, Bishop made public her own affinity for the epistolary form. She told her fellow author Ilse Barker that she suspected that they both loved letter writing because "it is kind of like working without really doing it."[19] But in the years following her death, Bishop's letters have proved to be far more than a peripheral feature of her artistic legacy. The 1994 selection *One Art: Letters*, edited by her friend and publisher Robert Giroux, numbers more than six hundred engaging pages. The poet Tom Paulin, in an insightful review of this volume in the *Times Literary Supplement*, noted that one vivid passage in a letter to Lowell "leaps out as if she is an actor or a dancer, inspired by the intelligence and attention of her audience of one. For there is—it scarcely needs emphasizing—a keenly performative element in the epistolary art."[20] Bishop did not bring a performative approach to teaching or to public readings of her poetry, but she certainly did treat letters as a form of performance art. *Words in Air: The Complete Correspondence Between Elizabeth Bishop and Robert Lowell* (2008) was described by a *New Yorker* critic as perhaps "the only book of its precise kind ever published: the lifelong correspondence between two artists of equal genius." But in combination with *Elizabeth Bishop and* The New Yorker (2011), *Words in Air* has offered precedent for a new and distinctive literary genre: the letters between Bishop and a brilliant fellow correspondent. Volumes of Bishop's lifelong epistolary interchanges with Marianne Moore and with May Swenson are forthcoming. Playwright Sarah Ruhl saw *Words in Air*'s theatrical potential when she turned it into the drama *Dear Elizabeth*. And as far back as 1963, Swenson noted playfully to Bishop, "When I get ready to do your biography I'll have wonderful material from your letters." A reviewer of *Words in Air* cited yet another well-established literary genre when he described this epistolary exchange as "like a novel about two people in which the author is God and the 'narrative line is life itself.'"[21] The historic role Bishop's own epistolary output has played in the academic recognition of literary correspondence as an art form unto itself is suggested in the title of a recent volume of critical essays: *Letter Writing Among Poets: From William Wordsworth to Elizabeth Bishop* (2015).[22] So in teaching a course on "just letters, as an art form or something," at Harvard in 1971, Bishop was anticipating a trend.

One of Bishop's longtime friends, U. T. Summers, admitted to having learned a great deal about Bishop by reading her letters to others. In her 1994 review "Surprised by *One Art*," Summers noted that the poet's frequent talk of shyness and loneliness had led her husband, Joseph Summers, and herself to assume that "she had only a few select friends of whom we were two." But after immersing themselves in Bishop's selected correspondence, they discovered that "her letters to us were but a small fraction of a great outpouring of letters, not just to friends but to good friends." Summers added, "As an orphan she invested more in friends, and they in her, than is typical of most of us." Summers and Bishop were fellow asthma sufferers, and Summers acknowledged that, growing up, she had been made to feel that "the number of things I 'couldn't do' seemed infinite." Summers was startled to learn that Bishop, whose asthma was far more severe and persistent than her own, had engaged from her youth onward in such athletic activities as fishing and sailing, bicycling, hiking, and climbing. And she learned with surprise as well that, late in life, her friend had taken up cross-country skiing.

For Summers, it was astonishing to consider Bishop's travels to "remote and unlikely places . . . simply packing her syringe and medicinal adrenaline, fairly certain she was going to need them" as she traveled to Morocco, down the Amazon, to tiny settlements on the Rio São Francisco, and, in her early sixties, on to the Galápagos. Summers was also surprised by the artistic self-confidence she found everywhere in Bishop's letters under a veneer of self-deprecation, going back to the precocious skill, daring, and versatility Bishop had displayed as a poet, fiction writer, essayist, and editor while still a student at their shared alma mater, Vassar College.[23]

Bishop's previous year at Harvard had been comparatively free of asthma, but in fall 1971, Bishop suffered a severe and prolonged asthma attack while attending an event at Vassar. In this case, the episode was brought on by a sheepskin coat in her host's car. This outbreak landed Bishop in the hospital, first in Poughkeepsie and then back at the Harvard infirmary, and caused her to miss several classes. Still, she managed to complete her second fall of teaching with significant tokens of success. In a January 8, 1972, letter to Frani, Bishop said that one student "told Alice that my course was the hardest he'd ever taken! I was amazed—it seemed too easy to me."[24] Also, Bishop spoke of a classroom reading of her favorite Herbert poem, "Love Unknown," that she had asked her student to perform. The student didn't understand that in the old edition (a gift from Lowell) that Bishop brought to class, some of the *f*'s should be pronounced as *s*'s, resulting in an incredible garble. Bishop herself had to take over the reading, which she completed without further incident. Later that month she announced happily to Ashley Brown that she had recovered sufficiently from her asthma attack and that, in spite of her brittle bones, she was enjoying cross-country skiing with her partner, Alice. Speaking of her new home on Brattle Street, she said, "This apartment is pleasant—I wish it were higher up, but otherwise I like it—and I need more furniture. My first serious entertaining will be to have the Robert Fitzgeralds to dinner—on the ping-pong table."[25]

Two weeks after she moved in at 60 Brattle Street, Bishop's "Crusoe in England," which had been accepted almost eighteen months earlier—when Bishop was trapped alone and far away in Ouro Preto—appeared at last in *The New Yorker*'s November 6, 1971, issue. Bishop brings the world of her reinvented Robinson Crusoe ("none of the books has ever got it right") to extraordinary life. When May Swenson discovered "Crusoe in England" in *The New Yorker*, she told Bishop that she found it "wonderful, and sad, and absurd, and true." Terming it "a great and remarkable poem, on all its levels," Swenson saw Crusoe as a representative of "the one of a kind, the explorer, marooned, mateless—who chose uniqueness, invented his survival equipment and lives on his own world—only to find in the end that he is no exception to the common fate of all those others who never ventured."[26] Bishop responded with pleasure that Swenson had "beautifully got the point" of this poem, which historically, along with her "In the Waiting Room," defined a breakthrough into Bishop's late and self-exploratory style. Crusoe's tiny island—far more desperately sparse and barren than Defoe's—is populated by goats, gulls, and guano, by dead volcanoes and lava-coated beaches. The place's essential sterility is underlined by the painful fact that the "island has one kind of everything": a single variety of "violet-blue" tree snail, a single kind of tree ("a sooty, scrub affair"),[27] and one kind of berry, bright red, that Crusoe brews into an awful, fizzy alcoholic potion. When he drinks this home brew, it goes straight to his head and makes him roaring drunk, so that he plays his homemade flute, which "must have had the weirdest scale on earth," and, "dizzy," would "whoop and dance among the goats."[28] His pleasant dreams of food and love morph into nightmares. Standing alongside the volcano he'd "christened *Mont d'Espoir* or *Mount Despair*," he meditates upon his affection for "the smallest of my island industries," though acknowledging sadly that the smallest of them, and the one for which he had the least affection, was "a miserable philosophy."[29] Finally, offering a nearly miraculous release from his isolation, "Friday came . . . / Friday was nice. / Friday was nice and we were friends." Crusoe admires Friday's pretty body, musing, "If only he had been a woman."[30] He dreams of propagating his kind—a sore practical necessity on this desolate place. When Crusoe and Friday are at last and abruptly "taken off" their island, Crusoe discovers that, far from feeling joyous upon his return, he is bored, "drinking my real tea, / surrounded by uninteresting lumber." His greatest regret is that upon his return to England ("another island, / that doesn't seem like one, but who decides?"), he lost the friend who had relieved him of his solitude, for "Friday, my dear Friday, died of measles / seventeen years ago come March."[31]

Lowell thought "Crusoe in England" to be "maybe your very best poem, an analogue to your life, or an Ode to Dejection." He added that "nothing you've written has such a mix of humor and desperation" and that "it expresses what I have been feeling for the last two months. . . . It was all so close."[32] Lowell was not alone in finding a self-exploratory element in this poem. Frank Bidart recalled that when he told Bishop that he saw "Crusoe" as "a kind of autobiographical metaphor for her own life with Brazil and Lota," Bishop was "horrified" by the suggestion. Yet Bidart said Bishop remained "magnificently inconsistent" about the autobiographical element in her writing, since Bishop was at the same time "entirely straightforward" that the poem did relate directly to her own life.[33] It is worth pointing out that while it would be natural for people who knew her to assume that Friday's death was an allegorical treatment of the death of Lota, on the other hand Bishop's correspondence with *The New Yorker* makes clear that she had finished a draft of the poem, complete with the death of Friday, in 1965, two full years before Lota's suicide. Bishop toyed with the idea of submitting the poem to *The New Yorker* then, but finally decided it was not ready.[34] Still, Bishop's relationship with Lota was already deeply troubled in 1965, when she had the poem in draft, and earlier love poems such as "The Shampoo" and "Song for the Rainy Season" also contain anticipations of future loss. The timing of the composition and completion of "Crusoe" suggests the autobiographical relationship between Bishop and Crusoe, and between Lota and Friday. In a strange way, the poem became truer to Bishop's life as the years passed.

Another of Bishop's most powerful poems, "The Moose," was finally completed, performed, and published shortly thereafter, having taken even longer than "Crusoe in England" to find its final form. Indeed, it required a quarter century, and the pressure of a deadline, to move from contemplation to completion. Bishop imposed the deadline upon herself when she agreed to read the poem at the Phi Beta Kappa ceremony at Harvard on June 13, 1972.

"Crusoe" is a poem of isolation and dislocation, but "The Moose," dedicated to Grace Bulmer Bowers, is a poem of community, perhaps even of communion, that evokes four of the most reassuring presences in Bishop's life. These four figures, none of whom appear in the poem quite directly but all of whom were clearly in Bishop's mind, are the dedicatee, Bishop's aunt Grace; Bishop's two Bulmer grandparents; and her psychiatrist, Dr. Ruth Foster. The events described in the poem date back to the summer of 1946, when Bishop was visiting her aunt Grace on the farm of her husband, William Bowers, just outside Great Village. Bishop had received a summons to return to New York immediately so that she could sign papers that would close the sale on her Key West house at 624 White Street. Bishop boarded a bus journeying westward at the gateway to the Bowers farm, and the experience of that journey lingered in her imagination for a quarter century before its articulation and transfiguration in "The Moose." In the third of the self-analytic letters Bishop wrote for Ruth Foster in February

1947, six months after the initial event, Bishop describes an experience that became the core of her poem, although the figures named in Bishop's 1947 account undergo a significant transformation in the final 1972 completion. "The Moose" begins with a beautiful, unfolding description of life along the tidal basin of the Bay of Fundy: those "narrow provinces / of fish and bread and tea," a setting that is "home to the long tides / where the bay leaves the sea / twice a day and takes / the herrings long rides." In the single sentence that travels, it would seem, almost effortlessly over a series of six rhymed stanzas of six lines each, Bishop unfolds many of the splendors of her Nova Scotian world. During the course of this long sentence, "a lone traveller" (Bishop) and her "seven relatives" (Grace and her family) await the bus journeying toward them while "a collie supervises."[35]

In her letter to Foster, Bishop mentions being offered a drink of rum by her aunt Grace before she boarded the westward-journeying bus for the long ride toward Boston and New York. Then, having boarded the bus, she took a sleeping pill. When she awoke after midnight, in at best a semiconscious state, she heard the voices of two women seated far behind her, and these voices seemed to keep talking all night. One voice, a bit louder than the other, she told Dr. Foster, "had an intonation very much like my Aunt Grace's—much more Nova Scotian than hers is but that same sort of commiserating tone."[36]

Bishop was still partly asleep, and it seemed to her that the "other voice I couldn't hear so well . . . was you"—that is, Ruth Foster. Although, of course, neither of these comforting figures was actually present, Bishop felt she was overhearing "this endless conversation between you & aunt G." Without being able to catch the precise words, she "seemed to get the sense by the tone of voice, like an animal." For her this endless talking seemed "something like Joyce's washerwomen."[37] In her poem of so many years later, Bishop maintains the feature of the two voices talking on the bus at night behind her, but they are no longer the voices of Aunt Grace and Dr. Foster. Now they have become "grandparents' voices // uninterruptedly / talking in eternity." In "The Moose," the voices had become more audible, and she heard "names being mentioned, / things cleared up finally; / what he said, what she said / who got pensioned." The grandparents' talk includes a catalog of "death, deaths and sicknesses" along with more hopeful details like "the year he remarried." As many stanzas and a series of long, looping sentences unfold, we hear no proper names, only gendered nouns and pronouns.

Thus, we hear that "she died in childbirth. That was the son lost / when the schooner foundered. // He took to drink. Yes. / She went to the bad." And when we finally overhear a proper name it is to learn of a moment "when Amos began to pray / even in the store and / finally the family had / to put him away." The grandparents' voices are evoked as "talking the way they talked / in the old featherbed, / peacefully on and on." By dropping the projected voices of her aunt and her psychiatrist from this conversation, Bishop is able to link the voices instead to those of her Bulmer grandparents, and to the conversations she must have overheard as an all-but-orphaned child spending summer after summer in the family home in Great Village.

The poem reaches its climactic moment when the driver stops the bus with a jolt and turns off his lights because "a moose had come out of / the impenetrable wood / and stands there, looms, rather, / in the middle of the road." The moose, who proves to be "a she!" approaches the bus and sniffs at its hot hood, and for a long moment the moose contemplates the bus ("Taking her time / she looks the bus over") while the passengers contemplate the moose. She is "towering, antlerless, / high as a church, / homely as a house / (or safe as houses)." A man's voice reassures them—"Perfectly harmless"—while others remark "Sure are big creatures" and "It's awful plain." In the course of this colloquy the poet asks, "Why, why do we feel / (we all feel) this sweet / sensation of joy?" Finally, with a crisp roll of his *r*'s while saying the words "curious creatures," the driver puts the bus into gear, but still, for a moment, "by craning backwards / the moose may be seen / on the moonlit macadam." Then sight of the moose is lost and what remains is "a dim / smell of moose, an acrid / smell of gasoline." Over her lengthy process of gestation and concentration, Bishop had managed to compress aspects of her experience on many levels into a poem that had begun as a bus journey a quarter century before.

Bishop had promised the poem for the Phi Beta Kappa ceremony during Harvard's graduation week, and Bidart recalled that "finishing 'The Moose' was a crisis." Bishop would have to read this "long, intricate" poem to hundreds of people, and it wasn't yet ready. As Bidart recalled, "Elizabeth, Alice, and I had made plans to go to Bermuda for a weekend; both insisted we must go. Elizabeth took the poem with her." As Bidart looked at the poem on the plane, he felt that "except for a handful of connectives, a handful of phrases," the poem was already there. Bidart found that by serving as audience and having Bishop "talk out what the stanzas filled with gaps needed to accomplish within the narrative frame, she filled the gaps." Although many phrases were later changed, "when the plane reached Bermuda, she had a continuous draft of the whole."[38] Bishop's reading of "The Moose" at the Phi Beta Kappa ceremony was a success. Bishop was particularly pleased when Alice reported to her that a Kirkland House student, not knowing Alice's relationship to Bishop, had volunteered that "as poems go—it wasn't bad."[39] Bishop considered this the highest praise.

Bishop's relationship with Robert Lowell entered a troubled phase when in 1972 Lowell sent her the typescript of a book-length sequence of unrhymed sonnets titled *The Dolphin*. This extended poem explored his new life with Caroline Blackwood and the ending of his old life with his previous wife, Elizabeth Hardwick. As had become characteristic of Lowell's style, the book included poetry that reworked letters by both Blackwood and Hardwick. Bishop raised strong concerns about Lowell's use of his estranged wife Hardwick's letters. The concerns about using a woman's letters in this book echoes a concern Bishop raised in a very early June 30, 1948, letter disapproving of William Carlos Williams's use of a woman poet's letters in his *Paterson II*. She had then said, "Maybe I've felt a little too much the way the woman did at certain more hysterical moments. People who haven't experienced absolute loneliness for long stretches of time can never sympathize with it at all."⁴⁰ About Lowell's use of his ex-wife Elizabeth's letters, she said, in a letter that she claimed was "hell" for her to write, "I'm sure my point is only too plain . . . Lizzie is not dead, etc.—but there is a 'mixture of fact & fiction,' and you have *changed* her letters. That is 'infinite mischief,' I think." Bishop acknowledged, "One can use one's life as material—one does, anyway—but these letters—aren't you violating a trust? IF you were given permission—IF you hadn't changed them . . . etc. But *art just isn't worth that much.*"⁴¹ Lowell made significant modifications in *The Dolphin* in order to satisfy Bishop's concerns, but he nonetheless proceeded with the publication of the poem in 1973, and Bishop was by no means completely mollified by his changes. Bishop felt that she was trying to protect both Lowell and Hardwick from the negative outcome that might result from such a publication. *The Dolphin* won a Pulitzer Prize, but it also received a number of harsh reviews for Lowell's treatment of the letters of his former wife, including a particularly sharp one by Adrienne Rich, who up until then had been Lowell's close friend.

Alerted by a letter from Lowell that Hardwick had been made distraught by the reviews of *The Dolphin* and the attention these focused on the breakup of her marriage to Lowell, Bishop wrote to Hardwick, saying, "I just want to offer you all the sympathy I can and to say that awful as it is I am sure that anyone's, everyone's sympathy is entirely with you. You've always been notably brave and strong and so I hope those qualities will come to your rescue again—(and stupid reviews—even cruel books—*do* fade away fairly soon)." Bishop added, "As I think you may know, I did my damndest to stop Cal's writing a lot of that—in fact after my letters (that were hell to write) he did change a few things around for the better. . . . But—nothing could stop him, obviously. Please believe I really grieve for you and I do hope things will soon be better"—signed, "Faithfully, Elizabeth."⁴² Back in 1948, Bishop had tried to protect Lowell from Hardwick when she thought Hardwick had set her cap for him, telling Lowell to "*take care*." Now Bishop was protective and supportive of Hardwick. But her relationship with Lowell had undergone a strain. Lowell himself would conclude to Bishop of *The Dolphin*, "My sin (mistake?) was publishing. I couldn't bear to have my book (my life) wait hidden inside me like a dead child."[43]

Bishop's relationship with Lowell would recover, and they would continue as friends—a testimony to the strength of their bond.

In December 1972, near the end of her third fall of teaching at Harvard, and thanks in part to strenuous advocacy by Bill Alfred and Robert Fitzgerald, Bishop was granted by unanimous vote of the English faculty a permanent term appointment at the university, which would continue until she reached the retirement age of sixty-five. Bishop had received other offers, including one from the University of Virginia, which she was strenuously urged to accept by such admirers on the English faculty as J. C. Levenson, Irvin Ehrenpreis, and Lowell's close friend, the novelist Peter Taylor, and these no doubt gave her leverage in establishing a more secure position at Harvard. Virginia might have paid her more, but Bishop was influenced in her decision by the free access she had to the Harvard infirmary while she was on the school's teaching faculty, as well as by other health insurance benefits. And she was further influenced to stay at Harvard by the presence of Alice Methfessel. Bishop had also received an offer from the University of Washington to teach a trimester there again. So in March 1973, Bishop returned to Seattle, the scene of her initial teaching experience seven years before. There she renewed her acquaintance with old friends and, in particular, with her great sustainer, Dorothee Bowie. With a permanent teaching post at Harvard and visiting posts elsewhere, the "scared elderly amateur 'professor'" was turning herself into a professional.

The year 1972 had been a challenging one in terms of her physical health, but in terms of the creation of poems of the highest quality, it had been quite productive. Along with "The Moose," *The New Yorker* published two other such works by Bishop in that year, "Poem" and "Night

City." Howard Moss began his letter of instant acceptance of the former with the words, "What a beauty POEM is! I love it, and so does everyone else here who's read it. I wish I could read a poem like that every day for the rest of my life."[44] Bishop's "Poem" takes as its starting point what it calls "a minor family relic," a small painting ("About the size of an old-style dollar bill") by her Nova Scotian great-uncle George Hutchinson that had been gifted to her by a Bulmer aunt. Hutchinson's work had also been the subject of a much earlier poem, "Large Bad Picture."

The technically inept bad picture was an early work by Hutchinson. But this artistically talented great-uncle later settled in London, where he became a prolifically published professional book illustrator. Hutchinson, the brother of Bishop's Bulmer grandmother and a person Bishop never had the opportunity to meet, would sometimes make sketches of local scenes when he returned to visit his family in Great Village. After Bishop's "Poem" appeared, visitors to Bishop's apartment who described her great-uncle's miniature painting hanging on the wall began to refer to it as "Small Good Picture." Hutchinson's painting reveals an impressionist's capacity for using contrasting colors and dashing, suggestive brushstrokes to bring a scene to life in all its casual complexity. Bishop describes the painting as "useless and free" (each a key term of praise in Bishop's personal lexicon). Here is an object that makes no claims upon us, that has "never earned any money in its life" while being "handed along collaterally to owners / who looked at it sometimes, or didn't bother to." But now that Bishop does begin to look at it, what she notices are familiar traces of their shared Nova Scotian past.

Bishop, herself a watercolorist, presents the painting's dashing, painterly technique, sometimes with admiration, sometimes with amusement, all the while rapidly sketching in the picture's features, including "elm trees, low hills, a thin church steeple / —that gray-blue wisp—or is it?" In the foreground she finds "a water meadow with some tiny cows, / two brushstrokes each, but confidently cows; / two minuscule white geese in the blue water, / back-to-back, feeding." Always, we are conscious of paint applied to canvas: "Up closer, a wild iris, white and yellow, / fresh-squiggled from the tube."

Then, with a start, Bishop all at once discovers in the painting not just a work of art, but a re-creation of her own past:

Heavens, I recognize the place, I know it!
It's behind—I can almost remember the farmer's name.
His barn backed on that meadow. There it is,
titanium white, one dab. The hint of steeple,
filaments of brush-hairs, barely there,
must be the Presbyterian church.[45]

The steeple of this Presbyterian church in Great Village would be the one across the village common from her own house, the steeple that still held the echo of her mother's scream, as she re-created it in her story "In the Village." Minute examination of the painting itself shows not a single trace of that steeple, not even as the filaments of brush hairs, anywhere along the painting's skyline. At the poem's most dramatic point, Bishop interpolates a key image from her personal past and a key motif from her own writing to dramatize the connection between her great-uncle's painting and herself.

"Poem" now moves toward a state of epiphany, as she reflects of her great-uncle, "I never knew him. We both knew this place, / apparently, this literal small backwater." Each had looked at it "long enough to memorize it, / our years apart. How strange." She also discovers, of a place she thought she had forgotten, that "it's still loved, / or its memory is (it must have changed a lot)." Now Bishop finds "life and the memory of it so compressed / they've turned into each other. Which is which?" Throughout her career, Bishop had dealt with the triad of life, art, and memory. Now, in this small painting, she found "life and the memory of it cramped, / dim, on a piece of Bristol board, / dim, but how live, how touching in detail." And what does this amount to? What does this object that has never earned any money in its life represent? For Bishop it represents "the little that we get for free, / the little of our earthly trust. Not much." Not much, but perhaps enough. This small object has taken on a life of its own, and in the process it has come to seem not merely "about the size of an old-style dollar bill" but also "about the size of our abidance / along with theirs." And who are they with whom we share abidance? Just "the munching cows, / the iris, crisp and shivering, the water / still standing from spring freshets, / the yet-to-be-dismantled elms, the geese." Not many poems by Bishop close on an epiphany, but when one does, that epiphany always seems *earned*, as it does here. The possessions of memory cannot override the destructions of time, but a lost world still lives *there*, "dim, on a piece of Bristol Board."[46]

One of Bishop's most ardent young admirers during her Harvard years was the poet and critic Lloyd Schwartz, who would later edit several important volumes of Bishop's poems, prose, and correspondence. Schwartz had fallen in love with Bishop's poetry when one of his college teachers, Mary Curran, had read "The Man-Moth" to him and a group of fellow students in 1960 while they sat on the floor of her apartment just off Washington Square. Schwartz recalled that when he heard it, "the poem blew me away. And moved me to tears. It was such an original and powerful work, utterly surprising, and riveting." From then on, he had followed Bishop's work closely. He was now a graduate student at Harvard, with an unfinished PhD on W. B. Yeats, and had come to know Bishop slightly, through his close friend Frank Bidart. Finally, in December 1973, he worked up the courage to invite Bishop to lunch at a Harvard Square bistro, and she had accepted. During the meal they commiserated over the fact that each of them would be spending Christmas vacation in Cambridge alone. All of Schwartz's friends would be out of town, and Alice Methfessel would be far away, skiing in Switzerland. They made vague plans to possibly see each other over the break and exchanged telephone numbers. Then, since

Bishop knew Schwartz to be a poor graduate student, she insisted upon paying for the meal.

Early in January, Schwartz received a phone call from Bishop, who had broken her shoulder and was in the Harvard infirmary. Very apologetically, Bishop asked Schwartz if he would come to the infirmary to pick up her keys, then let himself into her Brattle Street apartment. There he was to pick up her mail, her handbag, and a steno pad she had left on the coffee table and bring them back to the infirmary. Schwartz felt it was thrilling to be able to help in any way a poet he admired so much. And in any case, his own apartment, the infirmary, and Bishop's apartment were all within a few blocks of one another, so this favor caused him really no trouble. Schwartz later concluded that Bishop's excessively apologetic tone, given his actual eagerness to help, might have been prompted by the likelihood that Bishop felt guilty that she had fallen while drinking. She had fallen down the outside stairs while descending the second floor of a Harvard Square establishment called the Casablanca (the bar was on this floor, with a restaurant below). Bishop was often at her most apologetic when she had caused another discomfiture because of her drinking. But now, in Bishop's room in the infirmary, he felt that he had the opportunity to share a privileged time with the poet. He spent that day with Bishop in her hospital room, talking about movies, records, campus and literary gossip, favorite singers, and other common interests. Before, he had found Bishop guarded, but now he found their interchange to be effortless. The only forbidden topic was any praise or discussion of Bishop's own poems. Thenceforth, throughout Bishop's stay in the infirmary, Schwartz came every day, and they spent most of the day talking.

On one occasion, Bishop was wheeled out of the room for a medical procedure, and Schwartz later confessed, "I couldn't resist peeking into the notebook. The first couple of pages had what looked like the draft of a new poem, 'Breakfast Song.'" He added, "I was moved by it—and shaken. I had never seen a poem by her in which she dealt so directly with sexual love and with her fear of death." Schwartz felt that "I had to have a copy. I wanted to read it over and over." And he also feared that Bishop would never publish the poem, and might even end up destroying it. "So I copied it and hoped it would someday come to light." Over the years, several other Bishop poems with a sexual dimension, including "It is marvellous to wake up together," have been discovered, but no other complete version of "Breakfast Song" has ever appeared, although drafts of its opening lines have been found in other notebooks. Schwartz observed, rightly, "that it would be a great loss if it didn't exist." And he added, "I still feel a little guilt about how I came to have it." "Breakfast Song" was at last published in *The New Yorker* in 2002, twenty-three years after Bishop's death and almost thirty years after Schwartz first encountered it in one of Bishop's notebooks in the Harvard infirmary.

The subject of the poem is Alice Methfessel, and in its opening she is addressed as "my love, my saving grace." A saving grace is, characteristically, the only worthwhile feature in an otherwise unworthy object, and here Bishop appears to suggest that *her* only saving grace lies not in herself but in her partner, Alice. The succeeding lines are a catalog of her partner's attributes: "your eyes are awfully blue. / I kiss your funny face, / your coffee-flavored mouth." And it proceeds lyrically enough, "Last night I slept with you." But then it takes an unexpected turn, toward a very different form of sleep: "Today I love you so / how can I bear to go / (as soon I must, I know) / to bed with ugly death / in that cold, filthy place, / to sleep there without you." There she would have to go "without the easy breath / and nightlong, limblong warmth / I've grown accustomed to?" In simple and direct language, this poem goes straight to the heart of the human existential problem.

For, as the poem proceeds:

—Nobody wants to die;
tell me it is a lie!

But no, I know it's true.
It's just the common case;
there's nothing one can do.

At last, she returns to her poem's beginnings—but with a startling twist in the last line.

My love, my saving grace,
your eyes are awfully blue
early and instant blue.

When Schwartz asked Methfessel some years later about "Breakfast Song," she said, "Oh, *that* poem." So she must have been familiar with it. "Breakfast Song" remains a poem that only Bishop could have written.

The agreement Bishop had made with Harvard to extend her teaching contract until retirement prompted her to begin thinking about finding a more permanent place of residence, and soon her attention was drawn toward Lewis Wharf, a stone warehouse building projecting into Boston Harbor that was being renovated into condominiums. Bishop looked over the property and discovered that she could secure a spacious upper-floor apartment with a panoramic view of Boston Harbor. She made a prompt decision to sign a contract to secure her preferred place at Lewis Wharf, and now it was a matter of waiting until the construction project was completed. In the spring of 1974, Bishop visited Ouro Preto, and made arrangements to have all of her property in Brazil shipped to Boston. She still hoped to sell Casa Mariana, and without that sale, buying the Lewis Wharf apartment involved a financial risk. But she had made her commitment, and her spring 1974 journey to Ouro Preto marked her final visit to Brazil, though it was a place that would linger ever in her memory and in her art.

CHAPTER SEVENTEEN

THE RAINBOW-BIRD

Elizabeth Bishop signed the deed of purchase on her fourth-floor apartment in the newly renovated granite warehouse at Boston's Lewis Wharf in March 1973.[1] But the construction process at Lewis Wharf dragged on in a succession of delays, and Bishop took possession of her condominium much later than expected. "I moved on August 8 [1974] . . . the day Nixon resigned—both unforgettable,"[2] she was able to tell Dorothee Bowie, at last.

Since her early childhood in Nova Scotia, Bishop was always drawn to live by water. What drew her to *this* particular building, just off Boston's Atlantic Avenue, was the view it offered of Boston Harbor and the Mystic River, and she took an apartment on an upper floor. As she told the Barkers, "It *is* a wonderful view, and the ships—tugs, freighters, tankers (mostly)— but also lots of sailboats—so close, is a constant pleasure—and distraction."[3] Alice Methfessel was taking over Bishop's small but conveniently located Brattle Street apartment to the north of Harvard Square, and they would share a bed some nights at either place. Alice was also taking many of Bishop's furnishings: "the ping-pong table, the kitchen table, the desk, the bookcases—the red rocking chair, etc . . . all a great help to me."[4]

Howard Moss had hoped Bishop would keep the Ping-Pong table because "one of my dreams of glory is to return to Cambridge, and beat everyone."[5] The Brattle Street address was a brief trip by car from Boston University, where she was pursuing a graduate degree in business.

Twenty-two years before, Bishop had traveled with Lota from Brazil to the United States to retrieve her belongings from storage and have them shipped to Samambaia. Now these goods, combined with the further accumulation of two decades, were slated to return to Bishop's new home in North America. Bishop had spent the first week of the previous April at Casa Mariana, industriously packing forty cases of books,[6] along with sufficient manuscripts, letters, and workbooks to one day comprise the core collection of a research library, many distinctive pieces of furniture, works by contemporary artists (most of them personal friends), a handful of family heirlooms, her own watercolors, the Dolmetsch clavichord, and a lovingly chosen selection of Brazilian folk art. As Bishop told Dorothee Bowie, she had gotten "so much done I still can't believe it."[7] As she enjoyed telling friends, she had entrusted this load of personal freight to a shipping company with the unlikely name of "FINK Transportes."[8] She was eager to start afresh in a place of her own. But she would have to wait a long time for what she called her "goods and chattels" to arrive by freighter from Brazil.

In November 1974, three months after she had first moved into her new space, Bishop told the Barkers, "*I love my apartment*—if ever I can get it fixed up." On the previous Saturday evening she had watched the *Queen Elizabeth 2* sailing out of Boston Harbor. To gain a better vantage, she and a few friends had trekked up to the laundry room at the very top of Lewis Wharf, where they found themselves sharing window space with an assortment of upper-crust Lewis Wharf denizens who likewise endeavored to see the *QE2* off on her transatlantic voyage. Bishop found it an odd scene, for then, after sunset, "surrounded by washers & dryers, . . . ladies & gentlemen—some with opera glasses," stood side by side, "all watching the gigantic rump" of the great liner turning slowly around in the darkness with the help of "three tugs—little lines of red lights—on each side." When a fire-tug chugged near and "set off all its hoses—like Versailles," Bishop concluded, "Living here does have its simple pleasures." In the same letter, Bishop noted with concern, "My goods have not come from Brazil—I am worried sick, really, and dream of everything now being sold in various antique shops."[9] Finally, in April 1975, Bishop was able to announce to the Barkers with relief that "my belongings DID finally arrive from Brazil, after 10, or almost 11 months . . . ?"[10]

It took Bishop no little time to place these objects from her past into their new home, and for months and even years to come, pockets of her living space were cluttered with unshelved cartons of books. But by 1978, when the poet Elizabeth Spires, a younger Vassar alum, arrived at Lewis Wharf to conduct an interview for the *Vassar Quarterly*, she had the pleasure of observing a spacious living room with "wide-planked polished floors, two brick walls and one wall of books, a beamed ceiling, and glass doors opening onto a balcony." Spires also noted an array of objects that seemed a virtual travelogue of Bishop's peripatetic life: "a wildly Baroque Venetian mirror, a jacaranda rocker and other old pieces from Brazil, two paintings by Loren MacIver, a giant horse conch from Key West, and a Franklin stove with firewood in a donkey pannier, also from Brazil."[11] The noted critic Helen Vendler, a frequent visitor, recalled "a *santo* in a glass case, a ship's figurehead on the wall, and a wooden birdcage, like the ones she writes about in 'Questions of Travel.'"[12] Critic David Kalstone felt that visiting Bishop's apartment was "like reading one of her poems. It was up to you to immerse yourself in the details. You were not instructed."[13] Bishop's friend Paula Dietz considered Lewis Wharf—now a chic address but not so then—"a rather gutsy place to live. It took a lot of flair to live there. . . . The interior was raw brick." For Dietz, there "was nothing dainty" in Bishop's choice of residence. "A place like that took a kind of forthright independence."[14]

As she settled into Lewis Wharf, Bishop found herself living five miles as the crow flies, or fifteen minutes by car, from the apartment at 55 Cambridge Street in Revere where she had spent so many childhood years of isolation under the eye of her aunt Maud and uncle George. An hour's drive would bring her to Hope Cemetery in Worcester, where her parents rested under their shared gravestone. Bishop had come full circle, but now she was living in a place of her own.

Just a month before Bishop took possession of her apartment at Lewis Wharf, she and Alice Methfessel, in the company of Frank Bidart, found another special place. They had rented a property named Sabine Farm, located on the island of North Haven off the coast of Maine. It was close to neighboring Deer Isle and its lobster town of Stonington, the setting of Robert Lowell's "Water," his nostalgic poem about not quite proposing to Bishop in 1948. For Bishop, this five-mile-long island, in the middle of Penobscot Bay, seemed "beautiful beyond belief—and the house is wonderful beyond belief, too." Like Lewis Wharf, Sabine Farm offered vistas over the water. But these were not of a working harbor but "a view of islands, islands, hills on the mainland, passing sails." Just as she logged the names of ships passing under her Lewis Wharf windows, here she found herself keeping track of "27 different wildflowers." On their first stay at North Haven, Bishop, Bidart, and Methfessel also enjoyed, "for Maine, incredibly good weather—bright and sunny every single day except the last 3, when the fog did arrive (but I love that, too)," and Bishop found the island, with its general store, its woods and fields, birds, and, of course, wildflowers, "very much like Nova Scotia."[15] North Haven was, in the words of her Vassar friend Hallie Tompkins, "pure Bishop terrain."[16]

Sabine Farm offered plenty of room for guests and in the future would become a regular gathering place for Bishop's friends. Bishop booked Sabine Farm for the following August, and she would return there every summer for the rest of her life. The writer, journalist, and former French Resistance fighter Célia Bertin visited Bishop on the island in 1975 and recalled, "I loved seeing Elizabeth in the kitchen in North Haven. It became a poetical place, the way she cooked, the way she talked about little things, the way she bought things," such as the catch from the local lobstermen. Of her relationships with these and the other rugged year-rounders on North Haven, Bertin added, "She loved real people." Bertin felt that although, on the surface, Bishop seemed to be simply "a little old lady with white hair," underneath "she was very special. . . . There was so much in that little body. You could feel it." And on North Haven, "It was marvelous to be with her alone because she enjoyed everything—flowers, little walks, new places."[17] Bertin's husband, Jerry Reich, added that "Elizabeth had such a talent for living in the day and making the day a celebration."[18] Bertin, familiar with members of Lota's Rio circle, recalled that "Elizabeth mentioned Lota to me almost as if Lota were still living." Bishop would never see Brazil again after her 1974 visit to pack and ship her "goods and chattels," but that country would continue to inhabit her poetry, just as the world of Sabine Farm would serve to inspire her poetry anew.

A poem Bishop completed in July 1974 appeared in *The New Yorker* the following year in seasonally appropriate fashion under the title "The End of March, Duxbury (for John Malcolm Brinnin and Bill Read)." Bishop would often drive down with Alice Methfessel to the historic seaside town of Duxbury, thirty-five miles southeast of Boston, to visit her gracious friend and fellow poet John Malcolm Brinnin and Brinnin's partner, Bill Read. They would stay in what Lloyd Schwartz has described as their "casual but elegant beach house,"[19] and not infrequently, Brinnin would invite them to stay in the house when he and Read were away. During one visit on a cold and windy day near the end of March, Bishop and Methfessel, the poem's unnamed other,[20] set off for a chilly walk along the beach, their faces numbed on one side by the "rackety, icy, offshore wind." They had hoped to reach what Bishop termed "my proto-dream-house, / my crypto-dream-house, that crooked box / set up on pilings, shingled green." The object of their chilly quest was "a sort of artichoke of a house, but greener." Bishop noted with amusement to Lowell that one motive for composing the poem was because "John B was so appalled when I said I wanted that ugly little green shack for my summer home! (He doesn't share my taste for the awful, I'm afraid.)"[21]

During her Harvard years, when she was teaching classes, evaluating student poems and papers, giving readings, attending ceremonies to receive a steady stream of honorary degrees ("I could paper my walls with them," she said), and wading dutifully through piles of unsolicited poetry manuscripts, Bishop frequently lamented that she hated being so *busy*! Bishop's "End of March" indulges in a not-altogether-fanciful yearning to settle down in this ramshackle dream house, where "there must be a stove" because "there *is* a chimney." In such a place, she would be free to "do *nothing*, / or nothing much, forever, in two bare rooms," breaking up the day by looking through binoculars (her favorite Lewis Wharf activity) and reading boring books (a yearning expressed as well by the narrator of "In Prison," composed nearly forty years before). In such a dream house, she could "talk to myself, and, foggy days / watch the droplets slipping, heavy with light." She could cap off these all-but-eventless diurnal rounds with "a *grog à l'américane*. / I'd blaze it with a kitchen match / and lovely diaphanous blue flame / would waver, doubled in the window." If only such a dream house had "a light to read by," it might prove, in the end, to be "perfect! But—impossible." And even reaching the dream house proved impossible, at least on that day, since, as she admits, "the wind was much too cold / even to get that far, / and of course the house was boarded up."[22] As she submitted "End of March" to *The New Yorker*, Bishop quipped to Howard Moss that this longish poem was her answer to Yeats's twelve-line "Lake Isle of Innisfree."[23] And Bishop's dubious house does in fact share a certain kinship with the small cabin Yeats imagines building out of clay and wattles on an uninhabited island called Innisfree, situated on a small lake in County Sligo. Harold Bloom felt that Bishop's "End of March" conjured associations on a grander scale, proclaiming it to be "another great poem of the American shoreline to go with Emerson's *Seashore*, Whitman's *Out of the Cradle* . . . and *As I Ebb'd* . . . , Stevens's *The Idea of Order at Key West*, and Crane's *Voyages I*."[24] "The End of March" holds its own amid this heady company by relying on cool understatement, self-deprecatory humor, a conversational tone, and a sense of immense power in reserve. That power, which accumulates steadily during the poem's meditative course, is finally released in the poem's closing lines in the form of a dazzling epiphany. Powerful closings are a characteristic of almost all of Bishop's work, and here, she achieves one of the most magical and transformative of them all.

The poem's two pacers along the shoreline turn away from their dream house quest, and return toward Brinnin's home in Duxbury. "On the way back our faces froze on the other side." Then, all at once, "the sun came out for just a minute," and suddenly the bleak scene is transfigured when:

> For just a minute, set in their bezels of sand,
> the drab, damp, scattered stones
> were multi-colored,
> and all those high enough threw out long shadows

Bishop emphasizes the transience of this revelation, but its fleeting nature only heightens its magical quality. The long "individual shadows" of the tallest rocks set off the brightly colored stones. The poem's closing pulls together the series of enigmas scattered throughout its opening where it suggests playfully, yet with great cumulative force, that these shadows "could have been teasing the lion sun, / except that now he was behind them." The lingering paw-prints of a large dog had earlier been jokingly imagined to be, perhaps, "lion-prints," and now the sun is seen as the lion itself:

> —a sun who'd walked the beach the last low tide,
> making those big, majestic paw-prints,
> who perhaps had batted a kite out of the sky to play with.[25]

Bishop urged *The New Yorker*, despite the magazine's policy of discouraging dedications, to allow her to dedicate this new poem to Brinnin and Read "as a thank you letter for their great hospitality to me,"[26] and the editors acceded to her wish. "The End of March," conceived in Duxbury and completed during her first summer on North Haven, coincidentally before a visit from Brinnin and Read, is a very different poem from the astringent "Crusoe in England" or "In the Waiting Room." These Bishop had finished and submitted in the wake of a desperate period of shock and isolation in Ouro Preto in June 1970. "The End of March," completed four years later, may be read, in part, as a celebration of Bishop's recovering spirits as her life began to flourish in her new Boston neighborhood surrounded by nurturing friends.

I n July 1975, Howard Moss wrote nervously to Bishop that despite his own scant prior experience, he was scheduled to teach a poetry class at Barnard College in the fall and another at Columbia the following spring, "and I'm beginning to get cold feet about both. What do you say? What do you do?" He added that "any advice would be welcomed."[27] Bishop had begun her Harvard career at fifty-nine as "a scared elderly amateur 'professor.'"[28] Now, with five years of Harvard experience under her belt, panicky fellow writers such as Moss were turning to her as they contemplated the ordeal of facing a college classroom for the first time.

Unlike her friends Jarrell and Lowell, Bishop felt no real vocation for teaching. She was quite clear, perhaps even unwisely clear at times, that she taught primarily because she needed the money. Yet she worked at the role steadily and conscientiously, emphasizing the power to turn what one sees and knows into accurate words. Bishop never developed, or strove to attain, a polished classroom persona. Brad Leithauser felt that Bishop "was not an inspired teacher. The whole thing was a chore. She was dutiful."[29] Jonathan Galassi acknowledged that she "was not a professional teacher. She was not a manager of people." Still, he felt that "she was the best teacher I ever had because there was no discontinuity between herself and her presentation of herself." Some of her students complained about being asked to memorize poetry, but Dana Gioia felt that Bishop was "onto something essential about the sensuality of poetry that I'd almost forgotten."[30] Bishop often told her students that the poems her aunts had memorized in their youth sometimes seemed the only sensible speech of which they were capable in their old age.[31]

Robert Boucheron recalled an amusing exercise Bishop set for a discussion of the sestina. Bishop asked each student to write a word on a scrap of paper and pass it to her. "She then read out the words, which were to be the final words of each line." The sestina form has six stanzas of six lines, in which the final words vary in a prescribed order, and a concluding stanza of three lines, each of which contains two of the six end-words. Boucheron recalled, "The other students picked words like 'gray' or 'stone,' while I contributed 'vessel.' After shaking her head, Bishop included it." Each student was then to construct his or her own sestina out of the same set of six randomly chosen words. Eric M. Van, who took Bishop's intermediate poetry workshop in the fall of 1975, when Lowell taught the advanced, said that by then, at least on the Harvard scene, Bishop's star as a teacher had already eclipsed Lowell's "and her class was considered the more desirable and competitive to gain entry [to]." Knowing of Bishop's penchant for students with a knowledge of traditional forms, he said, "I won my way in by, essentially a stunt: a song lyric in rhymed Alexandrine couplets." Van felt that by the time Bishop was leading his poetry workshop, she had evolved into a highly effective and engaging teacher. Van recalled that Bishop insisted her aspiring poets read two models, Hopkins and Lewis Carroll, especially the latter's "Hunting of the Snark." One repeated class exercise was to rewrite the following passage near the end of Flannery O'Connor's short story "Revelation" into a different verse form each time: "Then like a monumental statue coming to life, she bent her head slowly and gazed, as through the very heart of mystery, down into the pig parlor at the hogs." Bishop surely must have loved the way the grand and formal opening devolves down into the "parlor" with those hogs. Van was delighted when he found that Bishop preferred the rock song lyrics he himself most enjoyed working on to his more formal exercises in verse.[32]

Sometimes Bishop's discussion of her art became more personal, as when, according to Boucheron, she spoke of alcoholism as an occupational hazard of the writing trade. Bishop declared, as Boucheron recalled, that "so many poets suffered from it, and the damage to their health was enormous." Boucheron added that "she said nothing of her own drinking, but she alluded to a troubled past from which she had recovered." At the end of the seminar term, Boucheron had an hour-long conference with Bishop in her Brattle Street apartment. She dropped these semester-ending conferences after moving to Lewis Wharf, especially after learning that her fellow instructors were not holding them. Boucheron felt that Bishop presented the persona of "a Victorian lady in reduced circumstances."[33] Katha Pollitt, who admired Bishop's teaching very much, noted that "there was an aspect of the way Miss Bishop presented herself that permitted a dismissal of her as a sensual, passionate, and deeply feeling person."[34] The reality, of course, was very different. Student Dana Gioia responded to her self-presentation in his own characteristic way: "She combined the freedom of bohemian culture with the civility of certain middle-class traditions. This synthesis allowed her to feel comfortable in the world without bearing all of the weight of its conventions."[35] In her teaching as in her art, Bishop presented a multilayered persona, and it was up to the individual to interpret that persona in his or her own way. As David Kalstone might have said, in a Bishop class one was not instructed.

Anne Hussey was already well published when she sought to enter Bishop's workshop, and Bishop readily accepted her writing sample. But an administrator of the Graduate School of Arts asserted that because Hussey was a nontraditional student (she was married and had children), she would have to overcome a series of administrative hurdles before she could gain a seat in Bishop's class. This was finally settled by a personal plea to Bishop herself. When Hussey read the administrator's letter on the subject to her wished-for instructor, Bishop replied, "Oh, for God's sake!" This "endeared her to me immediately. She phoned the Graduate School of Arts and Science and that was the end of it. I was in the class." Hussey regarded her teacher with a certain awe. "I had never encountered such a big mind as Elizabeth's. It covered philosophy, literature, art, music, medicine, biology, and natural history, and more. Her memory was prodigious." Hussey recalled that Bishop could recite poem after poem from memory, and she felt that "one came away from Elizabeth's class with sixteen hours of work to do, if one wanted to pick up on what Elizabeth had said."[36] Bishop may have lacked a traditional classroom manner, but she clearly had a talent for firing the imagination of a certain kind of student with the breadth of her life and learning.

A few of Bishop's students became personal friends. One of these was Mildred Nash, also a mother with young children, who wrangled her way into Bishop's English 285: Studies in Modern Poetry during one of Bishop's last terms at Harvard. Nash was preparing to be a high school teacher and had chosen the Harvard Education School because it allowed its students to take half of their courses elsewhere. Like Hussey, Nash sometimes felt condescended to because she was enrolled in the Education School. Bishop agreed, according to Nash, that there was "an entitlement mentality at Harvard, and she didn't like that." Nash added that Bishop, as a poet and perhaps also as a woman, would never be considered for tenure, and always "felt her marginality at Harvard," a status that never varied despite her mounting fame.

Nash had two daughters and she sometimes brought her nine-year-old daughter, Becca, with her to class, which was fine with her teacher. Nash recalled that Bishop doted on children, and when she and Bishop began to socialize, Bishop "included the children in the conversation every bit as much as me." Nash specifically recalled a long conversation between Bishop and Becca on the subject of key lime pie. Nash recalled of Bishop's sense of humor that she "said funny things with a totally straight face." On their first visit to Lewis Wharf in the autumn of 1977, Nash discouraged her daughters from wearing blue jeans; they needed to dress up to meet the great poet. But when Bishop greeted them at the door she was in bare feet and wearing jeans. Nash's daughters had scored a small triumph. Nash also recalled a story Bishop told her that left her astonished. Bishop had been on an airplane on one occasion, and when the woman sitting in the next seat asked her what she did, she acknowledged that she was a poet. The seatmate then recited one of Bishop's own poems to her, forcing Bishop to admit, "I wrote that poem."[37]

In 1978, Bishop asked Nash to help her reorganize her library. Beginning in the front room, they worked through Bishop's extensive travel section, her twenty-foot row of art books, and a six-foot section of philosophy. Most of the remaining space in the living room was occupied by novels, which included not only the expected classics but also "many thick, unfamiliar volumes," although no recent bestsellers. Nash recalled that "work on any row of books invariably led to a discussion of the genre," and Nash found that she made the fastest progress when Bishop went out on an errand. Almost an entire book-wall of Bishop's study was filled with poetry. Bishop noted of the author of one book of poems, "He was the only student I ever kicked out of class, but he wouldn't stop talking—and now he even has a poem in there for me!"[38] Nash noted that after "four long but fast-passing days, the task was finished." They had agreed that her payment for this bibliophilic labor would take the form of duplicates of Bishop's books, and she came away with nine shopping bags full of such duplicates, ranging from a spare rhyming dictionary to collections of Yeats and Auden, an alpine flower book, and an autographed copy of Bishop's *Complete Poems*.[39] Later, when Nash taught a "gifted and talented" class, she would model her approach and teaching style on her experience in the classroom and the library of Elizabeth Bishop.[40]

Along with ridding herself of shopping bags full of duplicate books, Bishop was attempting to gain control of her apartment by divesting herself of other things as well. In 1975, Howard Moss expressed interest in buying Bishop's clavichord. Evidently Bishop felt that her keyboard-playing days were now behind her. She explained to Moss in a letter that this instrument was made by "THE Dolmetsch," that it had taken him months and months to finish, and that it was painted by Mrs. Dolmetsch herself. She meticulously described the painting (modeled on Ralph Kirkpatrick's), as well as the clavichord's case, which was now itself considered a work of art. She agreed to sell the clavichord at its market price (about one thousand dollars in the mid-seventies), and offered to throw in "a lot of early keyboard music."

Bishop had ordered the clavichord just after graduating from Vassar. She had taken delivery of it during her first year in Paris, and had brought it back with her to New York; then it had traveled with her to Key West, then back to New York, where it was for a time on extended loan to the great Bach exponent Rosalyn Tureck. It had gone with her to Yaddo, and then Bishop had joyfully reunited with it upon its reaching Brazil in 1953. At one point, the piano duo of Fizdale and Gold had clowned around on it next to their swimming pool. Later it had journeyed to San Francisco, where she enjoyed playing it with Roxanne Cumming and where it had undergone its last major overhaul. Bishop next had it shipped from San Francisco to Ouro Preto and finally back to Lewis Wharf, where it arrived after that eleven-month delay. Bishop explained that the clavichord was so expensive that she had paid for it in monthly installments over more than a year. Moss also bought the instrument on the installment plan, and when he sent in the final payment, he said, "Now the clavichord is all mine, and when you come over, I will play you something very easy."

In the 1960s, in Rio, Bishop had lived near the epicenter of a tumultuous era of Brazilian politics, a period that had begun with great hopes but had ended with the country in the thrall of a repressive military dictator. Bishop had responded to that environment with powerful poems such as "Brazil, January 1, 1502," "The Burglar of Babylon," and, some years later, the 1979 "Pink Dog." At Harvard in the 1970s, Bishop found herself in the midst of intricate cultural politics that placed a strong emphasis on issues of gender identity and cultural positioning, issues that for Bishop were very complex. The Mexican poet Octavio Paz, who was visiting Harvard, became one of Bishop's great friends. Paz declared, according to her fellow teacher Robert B. Shaw, that Bishop's politics "were of the 1930s. In so far as she had political or social interests, Elizabeth was concerned with social justice, that people have enough to eat."[41] If Bishop had developed these political concerns in the 1930s, they were certainly reinforced during her years in Brazil, where social justice and malnutrition were issues of daily consequence.

Poet and editor Frederick Morgan stated that what he liked about Bishop was that "she was non-ideological." Still, as Frank Bidart declared, despite her skepticism about certain aspects of the contemporary feminist movement—revealed most controversially in her refusal to appear in women-only anthologies—Bishop "was passionately feminist, and could be bitter about how the world had treated her because she was a woman."[42] According to Lloyd Schwartz, Bishop refused to be in women's anthologies because she felt it was "a form of segregation." This had been her viewpoint in the 1930s, and "why, then, should she change her position now?"[43] When Bishop felt she was being slighted *because* she was a woman, she could respond with considerable force. Even seemingly favorable reviews often contained implicit notes of condescension. Bishop bristled when Lowell and others referred to her as one of the greatest of *woman* poets. One male reviewer compared Bishop's voice to that of "a much prized, plain-spoken, pleasantly idiosyncratic maiden aunt" in a 1969 *Life* review significantly titled "Minor Poet with a Major Fund of Love,"[44] a title the reviewer evidently intended as a compliment. Bishop explained in a 1979 letter that whenever she was described as looking like anybody's grandmother or like somebody's great-aunt, her anger "brought my feminist facet uppermost."[45] She noted pointedly to Nash that "Robert Fitzgerald's older than I am and no one tells him, 'You look like anyone's grandfather.'"[46]

Bishop sometimes came under pressure from openly lesbian poets such as Adrienne Rich to be more explicit about her sexual identity. Richard Howard, who was present on one such occasion, observed that Bishop "did not regard the enterprise with favor." After Rich's visit, Bishop was showing Howard the amenities of her Lewis Wharf apartment when she exclaimed, "You know what I want, Richard? I want closets, closets, and more closets." Then she laughed.[47] Bidart felt that Bishop's resistance to making disclosures about her sexuality arose out of "her distrust of the straight world." She felt that sooner or later, she and others would be punished for being openly gay. The fact that Bishop was a generation older than Rich, Howard, or Bidart surely colored her view. Of equal, or perhaps greater, importance in understanding Bishop's reticence about her sexuality and other personal matters was the climate of silence in which she had been raised.

Four years after Bishop's death, Rich published the influential 1983 review "The Eye of the Outsider," a consideration of Bishop's *Complete Poems: 1927–1979*. She presents a reevaluation of Bishop's cultural positioning in the years just after her death. Rich draws attention to Bishop's "experience of outsiderhood, closely—though not exclusively—linked with the essential outsiderhood of a lesbian identity." She is concerned in particular "with how the outsider's eye enables Bishop to perceive other kinds of outsiders to identify, or try to identify, with them."[48] A decade later, Marilyn May Lombardi asserted that Bishop's art "expands our narrow definitions of the 'woman poet' or 'woman's poetry' and so poses a greater challenge to feminist orthodoxies than earlier readers may have been willing to admit."[49] Since then, feminist readings of Bishop have branched out in all directions, defining the significance of Bishop's legacy across a spectrum of opinion that represents the full diversity of present-day feminism. Bishop may not have been born to lead a movement, or even to be part of one, but the subtlety of her gaze and her powers of empathy and identification have often placed her at or near the cutting edge of the discourse of cultural studies in a way that might have surprised her own contemporaries at Harvard.

Bishop's life at Harvard always involved a spirited effort to keep up with her youthful and athletic partner, Alice Methfessel. By contrast, Robert Lowell, writing from the much-younger Lady Caroline Blackwood's Milgate House near Maidstone, Kent, in December 1974, revealed himself to be grappling with profound depression, expressing his weariness over the onset of old age. These worries blended in his mind with a concern that he might never bring his work to satisfactory closure: "We seem to be near our finish, so near that the final, the perfect etc., is forbidden us, not even in the game."[50] Bishop, six years Lowell's senior, responded with characteristic force, perhaps tinged with her own latent anxiety over the aging process: "I am now going to be very impertinent and aggressive. Please, please don't talk about old age so much, my dear old friend! You are giving me the creeps." She added, "The thing Lota admired so much about us North Americans was our determined youthfulness and energy, our 'never-say-die'ness—and I think she was right!" For support, she cited her own recent experience on a visit to Florida, and she described a friend who had "married again, for the 3rd time—her 2nd marriage had been at 67—and she and her husband also 76, went walking miles on the beach every day, hand in hand, happy as clams, apparently, and I loved it."[51] Yet in the year that followed Bishop's "impertinent" January 1975 response to Lowell, she fell into her own profound depression and emotional collapse. During that fondly remembered December 1974 visit to Fort Myers Beach, Bishop had stayed, along with Alice Methfessel, at Louise Crane's winter home, and quite near her old friends from her Key West days, Red and Charlotte Russell. When she returned to Fort Myers the following December, in 1975, Alice was not with her, and Bishop passed through an emotional crisis that left both her and her friends shaken. The core of the problem was an ongoing and depleting issue with her physical health that took all of Anny Baumann's diagnostic skill to resolve. She was also dealing with an acute phase in her lifelong struggle with alcohol abuse. Worst of all, she was facing the frightening prospect that she might lose her beloved partner, Alice Methfessel.

Some months before Bishop's crisis at Fort Myers Beach, Bishop had faced the daunting prospect of sorting out the freight-load of goods that had arrived at Lewis Wharf in April 1975. She was grateful for Methfessel's assistance in putting things in order, although Alice had to make time for it in the midst of her graduate courses in business at Boston University. As Bishop told the Barkers, "I am lucky to have nice cheerful Alice around (although she does get depressed about the course in 'Statistics'—but she LOVES 'Taxes' and will soon be taking care of everyone's!!!),"[52] Frank Bidart thought of Methfessel as a practical person who didn't take herself too seriously, and he also recalled that while Methfessel herself liked to drink, Bishop "drank much more than Alice," and that "Alice hated the fact that there were times when Elizabeth started drinking, and she couldn't stop." As Bidart explained it, Bishop's patterns with alcohol were entirely unpredictable. "There were times when she could drink socially and others when she would get drunk with only one drink." Bidart recalled one dinner party with David and Ann Ferry when "Elizabeth got drunk on one drink and kept repeating the same story." Bidart added, "It was tragic. As far as I could see it was never predictable when she could have a few drinks and have a good time, and when she couldn't."[53] The poet Gregory Orr recalled an episode in the mid-seventies illustrating the complexity of the situation. Orr recalled that following a "great talk" Bishop gave on a selection of her favorite poems (Herbert, Moore, Lewis Carroll, and a hymn) to a group of MFA students at the Academy of American Poets in New York, he was asked by Betty Kray, executive director of the Academy, to see Bishop safely back to her apartment. When Bishop suggested they exit their cab to

stop at a bar, they did so. Orr recalled that Bishop had two or three bour-
bons while he nursed a Coke. After these drinks, Bishop

> *relaxed a bit and began to tell hilarious stories about poets. She was relaxed,*
> *funny, wicked, delightful. I lapped it up, of course, found it fascinating and*
> *marvelous. Somehow, we got on with the rest of our trip and I came back to*
> *the Academy.*

When Orr returned, Kray was quite upset with him. Orr didn't realize
that the most important part of his assignment was to assure that Bishop did
not have anything to drink on her way home. Orr recalled that, at least on
this occasion, "it seemed to me no harm had been done and I got to know a
person and poet far different from the one who moved with great caution
and self-protective reticence around our campus." For him that time alone
with Bishop formed a "cherished part of my young days as a poet."[54]

Methfessel, on the other hand, faced, more or less full-time, the mood
swings that accompanied Bishop's drinking. She never knew which facet of
Bishop might emerge after one or two drinks: the "relaxed, funny, wicked
and delightful" one, the obliviously repetitive one, or the compulsive and
despairing one. Drinking may have helped Bishop relax from what Orr described as her "caution and self-protective reticence," and Lloyd Schwartz
recalled that it was the only time she felt able to unburden herself of the
many griefs she had endured. But Bishop's periodic inability to control her
consumption was hard on those closest to her as well as hard on her body
and spirit. According to Bidart, Bishop was always afraid that one of these
occasions, when she could not control her drinking, "would destroy her
relationship with Alice. She was living on eggshells all the time."[55]

In her early years at Harvard, Bishop taught only in the fall, but she was
teaching full-time in the spring of 1975. She was also finishing a book, the

volume of poetry that would become *Geography III*. Meanwhile, Methfessel was working hard at her business courses on taxes and statistics and growing impatient with the boxes of books piled high all over the floor of Bishop's apartment. As Bishop began to drink more heavily during the course of the late spring and early summer, Methfessel began to withdraw emotionally. She also became interested in a young man in her graduate business program, to the point that she had begun to consider marriage. Bidart recalled that before Bishop arrived at Harvard in 1970, Methfessel had a relationship with a noted English biographer who was living in Kirkland House. Bishop knew of this previous relationship, and the marriage Alice was contemplating seemed like a very real possibility. And marriage was an outcome Alice's family, who had never welcomed Bishop to their home, would almost certainly have preferred. Yet Methfessel remained indecisive, and her relationship with Bishop languished in a state of uncertainty. Penelope Laurens Fitzgerald, Robert's wife, recalled, "One day when we were at Lewis Wharf and Elizabeth was very low, Robert stayed and listened to her confidences and consoled her while Alice and I went out to buy food." She began to recognize in the course of their errand that "Alice was still very young when she met Elizabeth, and she had to worry about making a life. There was always a certain tension having to do with Alice's understandable need to remain independent and consider her future and Elizabeth's sharp dependency on Alice and her need to have her full attention and time."[56]

Methfessel's business school classes meant she was unable to spend the entire month of July with Bishop on North Haven in the summer of 1975, one reason why Bishop invited Célia Bertin and her husband, Jerry Reich, for an extended stay. It was during this stay, when Bishop must have been extremely depressed over the possibility of losing Alice, that Reich observed, "Elizabeth had such a talent for living in the day and making the day a celebration."[57]

Bishop followed her spring term of teaching at Harvard, and her July escape to North Haven, with another fall of teaching. What she did not realize until this semester was that she was suffering from a recurrence of those multiple strains of dysentery that had afflicted her in 1971, including a particularly "ghastly" amoebic variety. No doubt she had contracted such persistent and varied strains of dysentery during one of her many excursions into the Brazilian interior. In 1971, only Anny Baumann had been able to diagnose the full severity of Bishop's intestinal disorders, which doctors in Brazil and Boston had missed, and such would prove to be the case again in 1975. The combination of Bishop's distress over the risk of losing Alice, the impact of her excessive drinking, and the stubborn bout of dysentery served to sap much of Bishop's physical and emotional strength. One of the ways she responded to these pressures was through the composition of what would become perhaps her most famous poem, "One Art."

Bishop had worked on "One Art" while she was visiting her old Walnut Hill and Vassar friend Rhoda Wheeler Sheehan, whom she discovered to be teaching English at Bristol Community College, an hour's drive south of Boston. Bishop would give occasional readings at BCC and, sometimes in the company of Alice, often visited Rhoda at her family's home, Redwing Farm, near what Bishop called the "very beautiful" Elephant Rock Beach[58] in the seaside village of Westport Harbor on the Massachusetts coast. While visiting Rhoda, Bishop tended to stay at the smaller Hurricane House, which stood right on the shoreline, because she was allergic to the family's dogs in the main house. This ocean-side house had derived its name because it had washed ashore in a hurricane during the 1930s—no doubt this domicile reminded Bishop of the "crypto-dream-house" she evoked so vividly in "The End of March." Rhoda's daughters, Eileen and Marion, recalled that Bishop "tinkered" with "One Art" during one or more of her visits to Hurricane House. They also confessed that they had worried at the time that Bishop, now in her mid-sixties, might "corrupt" their mother into lesbianism during their moments alone in Hurricane House. In retrospect, these daughters now express pride at their mother's readiness—by no means

universally common in the mid-seventies—to accept Elizabeth Bishop as
the person she was.

After considerable rewriting, including the work she did at Hurricane
House,[59] Bishop's "One Art" was accepted by *The New Yorker* on November 4, 1975, midway through Bishop's fall term at Harvard. Howard
Moss, in his letter of acceptance, called it "fine—upsetting and sad, too.
But everything is handled with such skill, feeling, and just the right amount
of distance that it comes off marvellously."[60] When Bishop submitted "One
Art" to *The New Yorker*, the future of her relationship with Methfessel was
still very much in doubt, and that state of uncertainty would continue for
several months to come.

The structure of the villanelle involves a pair of repeating rhymes and a
pair of alternating refrains. The opening three-line stanza sets the pattern
that the rest of the poem follows. Bishop's "One Art" opens with a tone of
denial or bargaining over how one copes with loss:

> *The art of losing isn't hard to master;*
> *so many things seem filled with the intent*
> *to be lost that their loss is no disaster.*[61]

The conventions of the villanelle serve a psychological effect, because the
words "master" and "disaster," alternating positions at the end of each three-
line stanza, carry us willy-nilly through the entire length of the poem. Her
second stanza focuses, almost in the language of a self-help manual, on the
annoying losses suffered almost daily by such persons as a preoccupied writer:

> *Lose something every day. Accept the fluster*
> *of lost door keys, the hour badly spent.*
> *The art of losing isn't hard to master.*

Some losses, too, seem a consequence of aging, which might encroach on one's powers of recollection or understanding:

> *Then practice losing farther, losing faster:*
> *places, and names, and where it was you meant*
> *to travel. None of these will bring disaster.*

Henceforth, the poem's catalog of losses becomes more specific, and more personal. Lota had noted before her arrival in New York on that fatal trip in 1967 that the only possessions Bishop really cared about were her manuscripts and a golden pocket watch belonging to her mother. Losing the latter object must have stung. And given her lifelong search for home, Bishop's loss of her White Street house in Key West, her dispossession of that beloved residence at Samambaia, and her renunciation of the meticulously renovated Casa Mariana are losses that she could at best only struggle to dismiss:

> *I lost my mother's watch. And look! my last, or*
> *next-to-last, of three loved houses went.*
> *The art of losing isn't hard to master.*

One home still remained, in the form of her mortgaged condominium at Lewis Wharf (hence "next-to-last"). But Bishop's loss of Brazil, which she would never see again, included the loss (except in memory) of Rio de Janeiro and Ouro Preto, as well as the loss of the Amazon, the Rio São Francisco, and beyond:

> *I lost two cities, lovely ones. And, vaster,*
> *some realms I owned, two rivers, a continent.*
> *I miss them, but it wasn't a disaster.*

Her loss of one of these cities, and one of her loved houses in Brazil, was precipitated by the suicide of her lover Lota. A new partner, Alice Methfessel, had at last begun to fill the void. Alice's droll sense of amusement at life's absurdities helped to keep Bishop cheerful. Yet now Bishop might lose Alice as well, and *that* potential loss seemed truly frightening. Still, the flagging effort at self-persuasion continues even into the poem's final, four-line stanza, only breaking down in the poem's last, brilliant, heartbreaking, self-confrontational line:

> —*Even losing you (the joking voice, a gesture*
> *I love) I shan't have lied. It's evident*
> *the art of losing's not too hard to master*
> *though it may look like (*Write it!*) like disaster.*[62]

For many years, Bishop's "The Fish" had been regarded as her best and most characteristic poem; indeed, it had come to seem such a signature poem that Bishop finally declared that she would not allow it to appear again in an anthology unless it was accompanied by another of her poems. Critics cited "The Fish" as evidence that Bishop's forte, almost to the exclusion of other qualities, was precise and objective description. But almost immediately upon its publication, "One Art" replaced "The Fish" as Bishop's signature poem. And anthologists, critics, and readers now began to see Bishop's theme as loss, and found that it ran deeply through all of Bishop's poetry, including even such examples as "The Fish."

After completing "One Art," Bishop finished her difficult semester and returned to Fort Myers Beach on December 21—with Methfessel driving her to the airport in a howling snowstorm. Bishop spent time with old friends Red and Charlotte Russell, and soon after Christmas (Alice was with her family in Bucks County), Bishop's friend Rhoda Wheeler Sheehan came down for a ten-day visit. Rhoda recalled that they "had some nice times" but also, as she indicated in a later letter to Bishop, that her friend had been drinking heavily. She remembered, "When I had to go back, Elizabeth was very anxious . . . she begged me not to go [but]—I had a job and family." On top of her heavy drinking, Bishop was also taking an array of powerful medications to deal with asthma, anemia, dysentery, and depression. Shortly after Rhoda's departure, Bishop suffered from an overdose. When Rhoda heard about this, she said, "That made me feel terrible."[63]

Exactly how deliberate Bishop's actions actually were is difficult to know with certainty. She would never admit that she had consciously attempted to end her own life, and she forcefully rejected that possibility in letters to Anny Baumann, saying that she knew the consequences of suicide too well from her own experience to inflict those consequences on others. And the effects of her overdose do not appear to have been especially dangerous. A. L. Francis, who was employed by the Crane family, recounted that he was working nearby when Charlotte Russell came running over to him saying that Elizabeth had fallen on the floor and she wanted help in getting her back in bed. "So I went right over, and after a little struggle—Elizabeth was out cold, right beside the bed—she was dressed in her normal clothes for daytime." Francis continued, "Elizabeth was just left to lie there and sleep this thing out. If I'd thought she was in any danger, either Charlotte or I would have called the rescue squad. Nobody ever mentioned any suicide." Francis's opinion was that Bishop was an alcoholic who had mixed liquor with "pills to knock herself out so she could get some sleep, but she didn't make it to the bed."[64] The results of Bishop's experience, and likely her intentions, were very different from Lota's fatal adventure in 1967, but even so, the parallels remain unsettling.

Frank Bidart met Bishop at the airport upon her return in early January 1976. Her depression continued into February, and she was granted medical leave from Harvard for the spring term. After a visit with Dr. Baumann in New York, her spirits began to lift almost immediately, and there, in consultation with a tropical disease specialist, Elizabeth found a course of treatment for her multiple dysenteries that proved successful. She also learned that she had won the prestigious Neustadt International Prize for Literature, an award administered through the magazine *World Literature*

Today, which was based at the University of Oklahoma in Norman. Bishop was the first American and the first woman to win the award. Her advocates on the award committee were the French-Canadian novelist, poet, and playwright Marie-Claire Blais and the poet John Ashbery, a longtime admirer. Blais's partner was Mary Meigs, who was Bishop's old friend and, like Bishop herself, a former lover of Louise Crane's.

By the time "One Art" was published in *The New Yorker* in April 1976, Bishop and Methfessel were back together. Evidently, after a period of mutual testing and uncertainty, both Bishop and Methfessel had recognized how much they loved and needed each other. Bidart recalled that before their reconciliation, Methfessel had never made a full commitment to Elizabeth Bishop, but afterward, "I think she did commit herself."[65]

"One Art" was the last published of the poems that appeared in *Geography III*, the volume that would transform Bishop's literary reputation from that of a modest, understated master of precise description to a poet of tremendous scope and daring. Harold Bloom observed in an early review that "where the language of personal loss was once barely suggested by Bishop, it now begins to usurp the meditative voice." Bloom added in his review that "an oblique power has been displaced by a more direct one, by a controlled pathos all the more deeply moving for having been so long and so nobly 'postponed.'"[66]

Geography III proved an important critical and popular success, and following its publication, Bishop continued to produce poems of extremely high quality. The first of these to appear was "Santarém," which tells of Bishop's arrival, during her journey down the Amazon, at the place where that mighty river is joined by the Tapajós and their waters meet and only slowly blend together. In such a place, she had a sense of completion and satisfaction: "That golden evening I really wanted to go no farther; / more than anything else I wanted to stay awhile / in that conflux of two great rivers, Tapajós, Amazon, / grandly, silently flowing, flowing east." On the Amazon's waters she saw "mongrel / riverboats skittering back and forth." Here was a dream landscape—or rather, river-scape—with just enough of the awful in those mongrel riverboats to make the entire scene "bright, cheerful, casual—or so it looked."

Perhaps there was something almost paradisal for her at Santarém, but then again, not quite: "I liked the place; I liked the idea of the place." Here were "two rivers. Hadn't two rivers sprung / from the Garden of Eden? No, that was four / and they'd diverged. Here only two / and coming together." That coming together leads Bishop into one of her rare engagements with the kind of academic discourse employed by her Harvard colleagues. For her, such "literary interpretations" often tended to seem like simplistic binaries "such as: life/death, right/wrong, male/female." The gradual melding of the two rivers, of different chemical contents, so that they only very gradually conjoined, served as a metaphor for how such binary notions might, in the world as *she* saw it, "have resolved, dissolved, straight off / in that watery, dazzling dialectic." Bidart recalled Bishop struggling in "Santarém" over how to get a certain amount of "abstract, academic language" into her lines without having it "swallow up, flatten, banalize the poem."[67] Here Bishop succeeds by presenting that language through the medium of parody and then moving straightaway to her own favored imagery of the sunlit spectrum that refuses to understand the world in binary terms. It had taken Bishop nearly two decades to complete "Santarém," from the initial experience to the completed poem, which *The New Yorker* then rushed to publication for an anniversary issue. Perhaps it had required Bishop's exposure to the "academese" so prevalent at Harvard to push her writing toward completion.

I n early August 1977, Lowell had asked to visit Bishop on North Haven in the company of Mary McCarthy, Lowell's Castine, Maine, neighbor. But Bishop was still angry with McCarthy about *The Group* and did not want McCarthy's novelist eye to fall on her domestic arrangements. Bishop expressed the wish to see Lowell again soon in Cambridge or New York, but on September 12, 1977, Lowell died in a New York taxi from heart failure while he was returning to his estranged wife, Elizabeth Hardwick. Bishop's friend Ilse Barker recalled, "Elizabeth rang me the morning after Lowell died, four o'clock her time, just to talk. Cal Lowell didn't mean anything to me. It wasn't for my sake. I should imagine she spent the night emotionally disturbed, calling people."[68] Lloyd Schwartz recalled that "Elizabeth was terribly upset when Lowell died, partly because they hadn't really resolved the increasing tensions in their friendship."[69] The following summer, Barker was visiting Bishop on her favorite island just as Bishop was completing "North Haven (In Memoriam: Robert Lowell)." Barker later remembered, "We went to the library, where she wanted to look up a reference, a verse or something biblical." Clearly the stanza Barker had in mind is the poem's third, which describes one of the small coastal islands Bishop had viewed with Lowell. But the terms in which she views it are not biblical but Shakespearean:

> This month, our favorite one is full of flowers:
> Buttercups, Red Clover, Purple Vetch,
> Hawkweed still burning, Daisies pied, Eyebright,
> the Fragrant Bedstraw's incandescent stars,
> and more, returned, to paint the meadows with delight.[70]

Bishop's allusion here defines common ground between herself and the intensely learned and bookish Lowell, who tended to see nature at once in its own terms and in terms of his extensive reading. Bishop draws specifically on the well-known song that ends *Love's Labour's Lost*. In Shakespeare's song it is "daisies pied and violets blue / And lady-smocks all silver white / And cuckoo-buds of yellow hue" that serve to "paint the meadows with delight." Except for "Daisies pied," Shakespeare's flowers are mostly different from the ones Bishop carefully chronicled in her North Haven logbook. Different, too, are the sounds that populate these poems. In Shakespeare one hears the cuckoo's song: "O word of fear, / Unpleasing to a married ear." Bishop's birds are native to her coastal Maine island, and they are different but in their own ways equally lovely and disquieting:

The Goldfinches are back, or others like them,
and the White-throated Sparrow's five-note song,
pleading and pleading, brings tears to the eyes.
Nature repeats herself, or almost does:
repeat, repeat, repeat; revise, revise, revise.

Barker's memory of Bishop's efforts with her elegy underlines her lingering attachment to her dear friend, whatever their recent differences, for while they were on the island

> *she managed to finish 'North Haven,' the poem for Lowell. She read it to us*
> *and walked about with it in her hand. I found it very moving that she felt she*
> *could hardly bear to put it down, that it was part of her. She put it beside her*
> *plate at dinner. . . . You had that feeling it really was part of her and she*
> *liked to have it around with her for a while.*[71]

Lowell had been noted for his seemingly obsessive revisions of his own published work, particularly as he rewrote and rewrote the unrhymed sonnets of his various *Notebook* iterations, which turned finally into the 1973 books *History* and *For Lizzie and Harriet*. Perhaps the ultimate revision we as humans face is death itself, and it is out of this stern reality that Bishop fashioned the moving conclusion of her only published elegy:

> *You left North Haven, anchored in its rock,*
> *afloat in mystic blue . . . And now—you've left*
> *for good. You can't derange, or rearrange,*
> *your poems again. (But the Sparrows can their song.)*
> *The words won't change again. Sad friend, you cannot change.*[72]

As Bishop was completing "North Haven" on the island for which it was named, Elizabeth Hardwick was spending the summer in the Lowell house not far away on the mainland in Castine. She had received the house in the divorce settlement with Lowell, who died as he was attempting to return to her. Hardwick wrote to Bishop on August 16, 1978, that "I am looking over the harbor imagining I see North Haven, but I probably don't reach that far in the blessed bit of fog today." Hardwick explained that Frank Bidart had read Bishop's elegy for Lowell to her over the phone, and added, "I wept when I went to sit outside and think about it. Oh, the magical details of North Haven and the way you bring them with such naturalness and feeling into a human landscape, to Cal." Hardwick observed, "Your art is always able to do that—and the genuineness, the lack of strain, the truth of things." Although she had heard "North Haven" only once over the telephone, she confessed, "This poem moves me unbearably." She closed with the hope that "Frank will send me a copy soon."[73]

Elizabeth Bishop's own death came unexpectedly, not much more than a year after she received Hardwick's letter. She won a Guggenheim Fellowship, which relieved her of teaching responsibilities during the 1978–79 academic year. She went on a reading tour with Alice Methfessel in the fall of 1978, including one in November at the University of Virginia, where she shared her work with a large audience in the recently renovated Dome Room of Thomas Jefferson's rotunda. In the summer of 1979, she traveled to Nova Scotia and went on a Swan's Hellenic Cruise in Greece with Alice Methfessel. Many friends noticed that she was struggling with health problems, but none of them seemed life-threatening and Bishop rarely complained. As Anne Hussey observed, "Elizabeth was driven by curiosity and determination. She didn't like people who complained about their health or complained about anything much. She didn't want to hear about illnesses, she wanted to overcome them."[74]

In the fall of 1979, Bishop began a new teaching semester at the Massachusetts Institute of Technology. She was unable to meet her classes on September 30 and October 1, 1979, because she was hospitalized with anemia, a recurring problem, so she left assignments written out in her own hand in block capitals saying she would meet them on October 7 and 8. She was expected to attend a dinner party at Helen Vendler's along with Frank Bidart and others on October 6. She had spent most of the day with Alice Methfessel, and then returned to Lewis Wharf to dress for the occasion. According to Vendler, when Methfessel arrived at Lewis Wharf to pick Bishop up, she found her dead on the floor, not yet fully dressed for the party. Alice called Vendler, and Bidart, who had already arrived at Vendler's apartment, immediately drove to Lewis Wharf to help out. When the coroner arrived, he temporarily closed the apartment in order to certify an unattended death. The cause of death was found to be a cerebral aneurysm.

Bishop had been scheduled to give a reading with the Irish writer Mary Lavin at Sanders Theatre on October 7, the day following her death, for the benefit of the Boston magazine *Ploughshares*. Lloyd Schwartz and his fellow organizers decided that it would not be fair to Lavin to cancel the event, and that, in place of Bishop herself, five of her friends would read their favorites from among her poems. Robert Taylor noted in the *Boston Globe*, "Although the word had spread that Elizabeth Bishop . . . had died unexpectedly, an audience of 750 turned up to hear her words. They were greeted by a sign, 'Elizabeth Bishop's poetry will be read tonight by her friends in her memory.'"[75] Evidently, many in this large audience had not yet learned the news of Bishop's passing and had also either failed to see the sign or failed to understand its import. Lloyd Schwartz recalled that "there was an audible gasp of shock from a large part of the audience" when DeWitt Henry "came out at the beginning of the reading and announced that [Bishop] had died the night before." The *Globe* noted that Frank Bidart was in the audience but "too upset to read," and that Alice Methfessel, the dedicatee of *Geography III*, was also present. Schwartz later described the reading of Bishop's poems as "cathartic," and Robert Pinsky, a fellow reader, found the evening "quite moving because there was no memorial quality to it, no funerary atmosphere." Instead, Bishop's admirers "just read these incredibly beautiful and amusing poems."[76] Despite the fact that many in the audience and on the stage were "quite upset still," there was laughter along with "very wonderful poetry" delivered by a range of readers. The *Globe* cited Schwartz as saying that "Elizabeth, of course, worked fastidiously; sometimes she'd spend years thinking about a phrase or word. So there probably isn't a large body of poetry awaiting discovery."[77] Ironically, Schwartz himself would discover four previously unknown Bishop poems during a journey to Brazil, and he would publish these as part of an essay in *The New Yorker* in 1991.[78] Earlier, Lorrie Goldensohn had discovered "It is marvellous to wake up together" in Brazil. And it had been Schwartz, of course, who had made the 1974 discovery, in a Cambridge hospital, of Bishop's "Breakfast Song." Fellow scholars came across so many further intriguing finds in the Vassar archive that when *Edgar Allan Poe & the Juke-Box: Uncollected Poems, Drafts, and Fragments* appeared in 2006 under the editorial eye of Alice Quinn, it ran to more than one hundred examples of unknown poems, short and long, in varying stages of completion.

On October 21, just two weeks after the reading in Sanders Theatre, a memorial service was held in Agassiz House in Cambridge. Of the many speakers, Alice Methfessel was the first, and also the briefest. She cited E. B. White's ending to *Charlotte's Web*: "Wilbur never forgot Charlotte. Although he loved her children and grandchildren dearly, none of the new spiders ever quite took her place in his heart. She was in a class by herself. It is not often that someone comes along who is a true friend and a good writer. Charlotte was both." And she concluded that, like Charlotte, Elizabeth was both. Helen Vendler read Bishop's favorite George Herbert poem, "Love Unknown." Lloyd Schwartz closed the event by reading "Sonnet," the last poem Bishop approved for publication.

"Sonnet" had been accepted by *The New Yorker* more than a year before, on October 12, 1978, but it had not yet appeared in that magazine's pages. Schwartz recalled that although Bishop liked Howard Moss, the magazine's poetry editor, she was sufficiently annoyed to rattle off this little quatrain: "All our poems / rest on the shelf, / While Howard publishes / himself."[79]

Methfessel asked Schwartz to read "Sonnet" at the memorial, but no one in Boston could locate a copy. Finally, Moss had to read the poem over the phone to Schwartz, and it was this telephonic transcription that Schwartz shared. May Swenson's elegy for her departed friend, "In the Bodies of Words," asserted that "vision lives, Elizabeth. Your vision multiplies, / is magnified in the bodies of words. Not vanished, your vision lives from eye to eye, / your words from lip to lip perpetuated."[80] "Sonnet" had indeed been passed "from lip to lip." It appeared at last in the pages of *The New Yorker* eight days later, in the October 29 issue.

Bishop's beautiful and amusing "Sonnet" treats several of her recurring themes in fresh ways, and among its many surprises is the way it handles the sonnet form. For one thing, it doesn't look or sound like a sonnet:

Caught—the bubble
in the spirit-level,
a creature divided;
and the compass needle
wobbling and wavering,
undecided.
Freed—the broken
thermometer's mercury
running away;
and the rainbow-bird
from the narrow bevel
of the empty mirror,
flying wherever
it feels like, gay!

Traditional sonnets unfold in a stately flow of fourteen iambic pentameter lines, each line having ten metered syllables. But Bishop's lines are short and jagged, with the sixth line comprising the single word "undecided." The rhyme scheme, if there is one, is completely irregular, and the rhymes are so slant that one often isn't quite sure which words can be said to rhyme with which. Does "bubble" rhyme with "level," "needle," "bevel"—or with none of these or all three? Bishop also turns the traditional Petrarchan sonnet's octave and the sestet upside down, starting with a six-line section and closing with a section of eight lines. The opening of the sestet and the octave are marked by two key terms in the Bishop lexicon: "caught" and "freed." Caught in the carpenter's spirit-level, a mere bubble of air becomes a symbol for the human condition or even, perhaps, a metaphor for Bishop herself: "a creature divided." The compass needle takes on equally human characteristics: "wobbling and wavering, / undecided." The first "freed" figure depicts a seemingly random escape from confinement: "the broken / thermometer's mercury / running away." The poem's final image is its most complex, occupying "pure Bishop terrain." The bevel of a mirror is the slanting edge that tucks inside a mirror's frame. If the sunlight hits this slanting glass just right, the glass becomes a prism, and the refracted light might be said to emerge like a "rainbow-bird / from the narrow bevel / of the empty mirror, / flying wherever / it feels like, gay!" Schwartz recalled that Bishop declared to him that here she was attempting to reclaim the word "gay" for its more traditional usage. But such a word, in this context, seems alive and rainbow-edged. Bishop often claimed that "poetry should be as unconscious as possible." Was it impossible, then, that in composing her final line, Bishop was unconsciously linking her words "freed," "rainbow," and "gay" with the rainbow flag Gilbert Baker famously unfurled at San Francisco's Gay Freedom Day Parade in the summer of 1978, not long before Bishop submitted her "Sonnet" to *The New Yorker*?

Elizabeth Bishop was a member of a generation of writers—including Theodore Roethke, John Berryman, Randall Jarrell, Robert Lowell, and Delmore Schwartz—working at a time that must have been hazardous to poets. None of these friends and peers lived beyond the age of sixty, and only Lowell had made it that far. Bishop had lived on until the age of sixty-eight, and when she died, she was at the height of her poetic powers. As a fifteen-year-old, Bishop had declared to her first great epistolary friend, Louise Bradley, "We live but once *and I'm going to live!*" Over the course of the fifty-three years that followed, she had kept that promise.

Bishop had passed through a childhood and adolescence plagued by illness, isolation, and emotional distress. At least partly as a consequence of such early suffering and trauma, Bishop struggled throughout her adult life with autoimmune disorders, depression, and periodic alcohol abuse. Merely in order to breathe in the face of her chronic asthma, Bishop at first received and later administered to herself countless shots of adrenaline. Since the 1950s, she had also undergone many courses of powerful, mood-altering anti-inflammatory medications such as cortisone and prednisone. Over the decades, such medications had surely taken a steady toll on a body she had once described as "made of pig-iron."

In "Questions of Travel," Bishop meditates on "continent, city, country, society," concluding that "the choice is never wide and never free." But throughout her life, in search of as much freedom as she could achieve amid the choices she found open, Bishop always willingly accepted risk. No doubt, at many moments in her life, she felt like the bubble in the spirit-level or like the wavering compass needle. But through her art, and in the body of her words, she had finally become the rainbow-bird—freed.

ALL THE UNTIDY
ACTIVITY CONTINUES

A t the time of her death, Elizabeth Bishop was a respected poet who enjoyed a small but passionate core of devotees. Perhaps only this ardent core regarded her as a major poet. But throughout the 1980s Bishop's reputation steadily grew, and by the early 1990s book-length studies of Elizabeth Bishop were appearing thick and fast—each with its own distinctive story to tell, and each showing compelling new ways to read a poet many had once considered too elusive. A consensus formed among readers of poetry by the mid-1990s that Bishop was not merely an important poet, but a poet of real scope and magnificence. Meanwhile, one locale after another strove to prove its strong association with Bishop's life, and establish its valid claim as one of Bishop's important worlds, by hosting a symposium or conference.

In January 1993, leading off this sequence of retrospectives, the eleventh annual Key West Literary Seminar was devoted exclusively to Bishop. This event featured a glittering array of Bishop's friends, colleagues, and protégés, including Octavio Paz, James Merrill, Frank Bidart, Lloyd Schwartz, Richard Wilbur, Anthony Hecht, Elizabeth Hardwick, and Alice Methfessel. In his introductory remarks, Bishop's friend, fellow poet, and frequent host John Malcolm Brinnin observed that after the "death of most poets their reputation descends for a time into a trough of indifference. But, in the case of Elizabeth Bishop we have seen just the obverse of that phenomenon. From the moment of her death, it seems that her reputation has continually ascended."[1] Six weeks after this Key West seminar, Brett Millier's *Elizabeth Bishop: Life and the Memory of It*, the first full-scale biography, made its appearance. Millier's biography closes with the observation that,

> like most other poets, [Bishop] told the story of her life in her work. She told it with sorrow, humor, and almost perfect understanding of her own strengths and failures. "Awful, but cheerful," she asked Alice Methfessel to inscribe on her tombstone in the Bishop family plot in Worcester.[2]

Your biographer found these final words of Millier's particularly gratifying, since as the editor of *The Elizabeth Bishop Bulletin*, the newsletter of the newly founded Elizabeth Bishop Society, I had picked as its journalistic motto the words "All the untidy activity continues." This motto seemed to capture the spirit of the enterprise. Since it also comprises the penultimate line of Bishop's "The Bight,"[3] and flows directly into its final line, "awful but cheerful," I felt that in my choice of motto, I may have gotten something right.

In the fall of 1994, the next significant Bishop symposium took place, a scholarly conference hosted at another of Bishop's worlds: her alma mater, Vassar College. *CBS News Sunday Morning* arrived with journalists and cameras to report on this occasion, because the program deemed the rise of Bishop's literary reputation to be an event worthy of note. Along with several of my colleagues at the conference, I was surprised to learn that Bishop's side of her parents' gravestone had never been inscribed. It remained completely blank. The truth came out when three young poets and Bishop devotees, Jeffrey Harrison, Robert Cording, and Peter Schmitt, who had been inspired by the closing line of Millier's biography, made a pilgrimage to Bishop's burial place in Worcester. There they made the unsettling discovery that her grave remained unmarked, an event memorialized in Schmitt's poem "Hope Cemetery (Worcester, 1994)." Biographer Millier, who was present at the Vassar conference, explained to her fellow Bishop scholars that in closing her work with that carefully worded sentence, she hoped to nudge Methfessel into following Bishop's wishes and inscribing her epitaph. Millier was not sure why, but she knew that something in Bishop's request was causing Methfessel to balk. Harrison made an inquiry to James Merrill, and Merrill passed along the inquiry to Frank Bidart. When Bidart called Methfessel to ask why, she admitted she'd been "caught red-handed,"[4] but would explain her motives no further, and thus the gravestone continued to remain uninscribed.

In May 1996, I was invited to Worcester, Massachusetts, to consult with Laura Menides, Carle Johnson, and Angela Dorenkamp about organizing an Elizabeth Bishop Conference and Poetry Festival in Worcester in October 1997. Professor Dorenkamp was tasked with working out certain details of the conference scheduling with Bishop's executor, Alice Methfessel. The conference organizers had naturally planned a pilgrimage to Bishop's gravestone in nearby Hope Cemetery. If Bishop's side of the monument continued to remain blank, this might cause a minor scandal. Dorenkamp explained that she had at length extracted an explanation for the impasse; in Methfessel's mind, Bishop's requested epitaph, those words "awful but cheerful," simply seemed too stark or raw. Methfessel couldn't bring herself to put those three words, by themselves, under Bishop's name and dates. Yet she also felt uncomfortable inscribing Bishop's name without the epitaph, and so the stone had remained blank for all these years.

With the *Bishop Bulletin*'s motto fresh in my mind, I suggested inserting the line "All the untidy activity continues" ahead of "awful but cheerful." This might take some of the edge off of Bishop's phrase, and turn it into an appealing and characteristic comment on life. The organizing committee endorsed this suggestion, and when Dorenkamp passed it along to Meth-fessel, she immediately accepted it as well, authorizing the inscription of Bishop's gravestone with the final *two* lines of Bishop's "The Bight."[5] The carver's work was promptly executed, and the summer 1996 *Bulletin* reported that Bishop's gravestone was now "newly inscribed." Dorenkamp offered a judiciously compressed version of the story, "Inscribing the Stone: Notes from Worcester's Hope Cemetery," in the winter 1996 *Bulletin*. Surely all would now be well for that planned pilgrimage to Bishop's gravestone.

But all was not *quite* well. When the journey at last took place in Octo-ber 1997, more than one sharp-eyed observer recognized that a comma had been omitted from the end of the line "All the untidy activity continues." This caused no little perturbation among certain pilgrims, and vocal pro-tests were addressed to the conference organizers. Even so—*a kerfuffle over a comma! The New Yorker* would have been proud.

At last, even this note of discord was resolved, and in a short piece for the summer 1998 *Bulletin* titled "A Comma for a Bishop," Dorenkamp de-clared, "After waiting for proper weather and the availability of the stone-cutter, the comma has been restored to its rightful place in the pantheon of punctuation. Rest easy!" The poet's inscription now reads:

ELIZABETH BISHOP

1911–1979

"ALL THE UNTIDY ACTIVITY CONTINUES,

AWFUL BUT CHEERFUL"

And so, in the city of her birth, under the revised, expanded, and copy-edited epitaph inscribed on her gravestone, the ashes of Elizabeth Bishop now rest, reunited with the parents she had lost so long before.

ACKNOWLEDGMENTS

The creation of this biography would have been impossible without the ongoing support and encouragement of my friends and colleagues in the Elizabeth Bishop Society over the past three decades. Much of the scholarship on Bishop has had a biographical turn, and while the character of this biography has precluded the extensive citation of previous scholarship, that does not mean that I value the work of my colleagues any the less. In recent years, the unflagging support of society members kept me going through some of the challenging moments I have encountered during the course of this biographical enterprise, and I only hope that *Love Unknown* will prove worthy of this consistent support. I have also been frequently informed, encouraged, and inspired by the previous biographical efforts of Brett Millier, Gary Fountain, and Megan Marshall.

Sandra Barry, whose expertise on Bishop's early years in Nova Scotia is unparalleled, generously shared her vast fund of knowledge with myself and many others. Frank Bidart has similarly shared his knowledge and understanding of his mentor Elizabeth Bishop's later years, when she was teaching at Harvard and inspiring the work of a younger generation of poets. Neil Besner has shared his knowledge of Brazilian culture and of Bishop's life in Brazil. He also read and provided invaluable commentary on several of my Brazilian chapters. Lorrie Goldensohn read the entire manuscript and provided many vital suggestions, insights, and corrections. David Hoak also read the entire manuscript, including some chapters in numerous drafts. He served as an ongoing sounding board as my thoughts evolved, offered numerous fruitful research leads, and encouraged me to take a closer look at Bishop's important relationship with May Swenson. Laura Menides shared her knowledge of Bishop's early years in her birthplace, Worcester, Massachusetts. Monica Stearns Morse provided vital perspectives on Bishop's years in Rio and at Samambaia, on Bishop's relationship with Monica's adoptive mother, Mary Morse, and on her relationship with Lota de Macedo Soares. Mildred Nash shared her experiences as Bishop's student and also shared her personal trove of clippings from Bishop's years at Harvard. Ron Patkus, Head of Special Collections at Vassar College, and Dean Rogers, Special Collections Assistant, provided unflagging support for my ongoing exploration of Bishop's major archival collection. My former student Danielle Pelloquin, in her role as archivist at Walnut Hill School for the Arts, provided vital manuscript material documenting Bishop's time at Walnut Hill. Francesco Rognoni drew my attention to the importance of Bishop's correspondence with Ilse and Kit Barker, and shared with me a transcript he had made of that correspondence. Lloyd Schwartz, Bishop's friend and editor, submitted to a series of interviews, and over the course of more than thirty years he shared his deep knowledge of Bishop's character and of her Harvard years. Fiona Sheehan provided vital insights and manuscript materials illuminating Bishop's friendship with her grandmother, Rhoda Wheeler Sheehan. My agent, Wendy Strothman, helped me hone my book proposal and find, in Viking/Penguin the ideal publisher for my biography. Penguin's publisher Kathryn Court, who acquired the manuscript, and Victoria Savanh, who along with Court edited it through several drafts, helped to polish the volume into its current shape. My biographical efforts received further support from a Guggenheim Fellowship, a National Endowment for the Humanities Summer Stipend, a Franklin Research Grant, and a Key West Literary Seminars residency. Hartwick College provided a Wandersee Scholar-in-Residence award, an early sabbatical, and numerous faculty research grants that helped to fund my travel and research and provide release time from teaching.

Additional encouragement and assistance were provided by, among many others, Linda Anderson, Steven Gould Axelrod, Jacqueline Vaught Brogan, Brewster Chamberlin, Angus Cleghorn, Bonnie Costello, Roxanne Cumming, Jonathan Ellis, Richard Flynn, Gary Fountain, Dave Gonzales, Kenneth Gordon, Ann Grifalconi, Saskia Hamilton, Jeffrey Harrison, Arlo Haskell, Bethany Hicok, Carle Johnson, Bessel van der Kolk, Brian Loughlin, Megan Marshall, Gary Methfessel, Brett Millier, George Monteiro, Carmen Oliveira, Gregory Orr, Barbara Page, Robert Pinsky, Susan Rosenbaum, Jane Shore, Kathleen Spivack, David Staines, Joan Thompson, Zuleika Torrealba, Michael and Emily Travisano, Heather Treseler, Eric M. Van, and Bessie Weiss.

Words cannot express the debt of gratitude I owe to my wife, Elsa, who has been not only the soul of patience during my six years of work on this biography, but also my help and supporter through my three decades and more of exploration into the life and work of Elizabeth Bishop. On top of that, Elsa's listening ear, her keen editorial eye, and her command—as a computer support professional—of all matters relating to Apple's electronic devices have proved indispensable, as always.

NOTES

PROLOGUE

1. Adrienne Rich, "The Eye of the Outsider," *Boston Review* 8 (April 1983): 16.
2. James Merrill, *Poetry Pilot,* Academy of American Poets, December 1979.
3. James Merrill, *Poetry Pilot.*
4. Book jacket blurb, Gary Fountain and Peter Brazeau, *Remembering Elizabeth Bishop: An Oral Biography* (New Brunswick, N.J.: Rutgers University Press, 1994). Hereafter, *Remembering EB.*
5. David Orr, "Rough Gems," *New York Times Book Review*, April 2, 2006. Web. Accessed March 12, 2013.
6. Swenson to Bishop, August 24 & 29, 1955. Washington University Library.

CHAPTER ONE. BETWEEN TWO WORLDS

1. Elizabeth Bishop, *Poems* (New York: Farrar, Straus & Giroux, 2011), 317–19. Hereafter, *Poems.*
2. Elizabeth Bishop, *Prose,* ed. Lloyd Schwartz (New York: Farrar, Straus & Giroux, 2011), 62. Hereafter, *Prose.*
3. Bishop to Lowell, August 15, 1957. *Words in Air: The Complete Correspondence Between Elizabeth Bishop and Robert Lowell,* ed. Thomas Travisano with Saskia Hamilton (New York: Farrar, Straus & Giroux, 2008), 225. Hereafter, *WIA.*
4. Kathleen Spivack, *With Robert Lowell and His Circle* (Lebanon, N.H.: Northeastern University Press, 2012), 98–99.
5. *Remembering EB*, 285.
6. *Remembering EB*, 278.
7. *Prose*, 414.
8. Sam Leith, "Love Between the Lines," *The Spectator*, November 19, 2008.
9. *Prose*, 392.
10. *Prose*, 427.
11. *Prose*, 427.
12. Ellery Crane Bicknell, *Historic Homes* (New York: Lewis Publishing, 1907), 174.
13. *Prose*, 400–401.
14. Along with public buildings and churches in Boston and New York, and substantial structures at Harvard, Brown, and Dartmouth, the family business also erected numerous buildings in Worcester, including the Worcester Armory, the Curtis Chapel, the Public Library, and Pilgrims' Congregational Church. The *Architectural Record* observed in 1895 that Pilgrims' Congregational Church, where John W. himself at least nominally worshipped, and which his wife attended faithfully, was "said to be the finest church in New England."
15. *Architectural Record: Great American Architects Series*, no. 1 (1895): 113.
16. "A Brief History of the American Antiquarian Society," American Antiquarian Society. Web. Accessed May 12, 2015.

17. Nancy Hall Burkett and John B. Hench, *Under Its Generous Dome: The Collections and Program of the American Antiquarian Society* (Worcester, Mass.: American Antiquarian Society, 1992).
18. *American Antiquarian Society Proceedings* 27 (1917): 284.
19. Brett C. Millier, *Elizabeth Bishop: Life and the Memory of It* (Berkeley: University of California Press, 1993), 3.
20. *Prose*, 438.
21. *Prose*, 438.
22. Sandra Barry, "The Art of Remembering: The Influence of Great Village, Nova Scotia, on the Life and Works of Elizabeth Bishop," *Nova Scotia Historical Review* 1, no. 1 (1991): 12.
23. *Prose*, 427.
24. A word must be said about Elizabeth's maternal family surname, which was often spelled "Bulmer" but just as often spelled—and always pronounced—"Boomer." The family treated these spellings almost interchangeably. Where close kin lie beneath adjacent graves in Mahon Cemetery, Great Village, one stone might read "Bulmer" and the next "Boomer." This biography will use the Bulmer spelling, because Bishop preferred it in her later years, and because her maternal grandparents in Great Village and her mother in Worcester are buried under the Bulmer name. Yet where quoted sources give the name as Boomer, that spelling will not be altered.
25. *Prose*, 425–26.
26. *Edgar Allan Poe & The Juke-Box*, ed. Alice Quinn (New York: Farrar, Straus & Giroux, 2006), 154. Hereafter, *EAP*.
27. "Poem," *Poems*, 197.
28. *EAP*, 170.
29. *Remembering EB*, 2–3.
30. *Prose*, 429.
31. *Prose*, 428.
32. *Remembering EB*, 13.
33. This volume may be found, along with the bulk of her papers, in the archives and special collections at the library of her alma mater, Vassar College. Although *The Biography of Our Baby* was often published with a plain blue cover, Elizabeth's was a deluxe edition. Over the course of a century and more, its once-elegant scarlet cloth cover has badly weathered, bleached, and frayed, and the ornate gilt letters that proudly proclaim its title have sadly eroded around the edges.
34. *EAP*, 155.
35. *EAP*, 156.
36. Grace Bulmer, "Statement" for the Nova Scotia Hospital, 1916. Acadia University, Wolfville, Nova Scotia. Hereafter, "Statement."
37. *Poems*, 123–24.

CHAPTER TWO. THE COUNTRY MOUSE

1. Notes by Ruby Willis, "Confidential Information Given by Elizabeth Bishop's Guardian, 27 July 1926." *Remembering EB*, 29–30.
2. Joelle Biele, ed., *Elizabeth Bishop and* The New Yorker: *The Complete Correspondence* (New York: Farrar, Straus & Giroux, 2011), 319. Hereafter, *EBNYR*.
3. *Prose*, 62.
4. *Prose*, 151.
5. Bishop to Bradley, August 5, 1925. Wylie House Museum, Indiana University.
6. *Prose*, 62–63.
7. *Prose*, 62–63.
8. "Statement."
9. "Statement."
10. "Statement."
11. "Statement."
12. Bishop to Lowell, December 11, 1957. *WIA*, 243.
13. *EAP*, 150.
14. *Prose*, 62.
15. Richard Famularo, *Harvard Mental Health Letter* 13 (January 1997): 8.
16. *Prose*, 62.

17. Bishop to Foster, February 1947. Vassar College Library, Archives and Special Collections, f. 118.33. Hereafter, VCL for first reference.
18. *EAP*, 156 and 347.
19. *Prose*, 70.
20. *Prose*, 71.
21. *Remembering EB*, 9.
22. *Prose*, 77.
23. *Poems*, 121.
24. *Poems*, 122.
25. *Prose*, 79.
26. *Prose*, 82.
27. *Prose*, 84.
28. *Prose*, 85.
29. *Prose*, 84.
30. *Prose*, 81.
31. *Barry*, "Art of Remembering," 33.
32. *Prose*, 85.
33. *Prose*, 85.
34. *Prose*, 89.
35. *EAP*, 102.
36. *Prose*, 91.
37. *Prose*, 95.
38. *Prose*, 95.
39. Bishop to Foster, February 1947.
40. Bishop to Foster, February 1947.
41. *Prose*, 98.
42. *Prose*, 98.
43. *Prose*, 99.

CHAPTER THREE. WERE WE ALL TOUCHED BY MIDAS?

1. *EAP*, 198.
2. *EAP*, 198.
3. Elizabeth Spires, "The Art of Poetry, XXVII: Elizabeth Bishop," in *Conversations with Elizabeth Bishop*, ed. George Montiero (Jackson, Miss.: University Press of Mississippi, 1996), 114. Hereafter, *Conversations*.
4. *EAP*, 197.
5. *Prose*, 428–29.
6. *EAP*, 197.
7. Bishop to Lowell, August 27, 1964. *WIA*, 553.
8. Bishop's aunt's name was spelled alternately "Maud" and "Maude" by members of her family, with no apparent concern for consistency. Bishop scholars have largely settled on "Bulmer" (rather than "Boomer") as the spelling of Bishop's maternal family surname, but they have so far failed to reach consensus on the spelling of her eldest maternal aunt's given name. Since in later years Bishop preferred "Maud," this biography will also prefer that spelling, allowing the alternate form when it appears in quotations.
9. *EAP*, 203.
10. Bishop to Foster, February 24, 1947. *VCL*.
11. *EAP*, 203.
12. Bishop to Bradley, October 16, 1926.
13. *EAP*, 203.
14. *EAP*, 197.
15. *Prose*, 428.
16. Interview with Dr. Bessel van der Kolk, May 22, 2015. Thanks are due to Lorrie Goldensohn for arranging this interview. Van der Kolk is the founder and medical director of the Trauma Center in Brookline, Massachusetts, and the director of the National Complex Trauma Treatment Network.
17. Alice Miller, *Drama of the Gifted Child*, trans. Ruth Ward (New York: Basic Books, 1981), 74.
18. *EAP*, 164. Edited with an introduction by the author in the *Georgia Review* (Winter 1992).
19. *EAP*, 164.

20. *EAP*, 164.
21. *EAP*, 165.
22. December 1, 1923, letter from the municipal clerk of Truro, Nova Scotia, to Dr. F. E. Lawlor, superintendent of the Nova Scotia Hospital. Acadia University, Wolfville, Nova Scotia.
23. *Prose*, 438.
24. Bishop to Lowell, December 14, 1957. *WIA*, 247.
25. I am grateful to Dr. Kenneth Gordan, MD, for his consultation over diagnoses of Gertrude Bulmer Bishop.
26. *Prose*, 438.
27. *Prose*, 437–38.
28. The Dartmouth Hospital's "Clinical Record" is now on file in the Bulmer-Bowers-Hutchinson-Sutherland family fonds at the library at Acadia University in Wolfville, Nova Scotia.
29. "Clinical Record of Gertrude Bulmer Bower, Nova Scotia Hospital." Unpaginated. Archive at Acadia University in Wolfville, Nova Scotia. Hereafter, "Clinical Record."
30. "Clinical Record."
31. *Prose*, 98.
32. "Clinical Record."
33. "Clinical Record."
34. *EAP*, 281.
35. *EAP*, 281.
36. *Prose*, 62.
37. *Poems*, 196–97.
38. *Poems*, 189.
39. *EAP*, 98.
40. *Prose*, 427.
41. *Prose*, 63.
42. *Conversations*, 71.
43. *Poems*, 87.
44. *Poems*, 59.
45. *Poems*, 37.
46. Bishop to Foster, February 1947.
47. Bishop to Foster, February 1947.
48. Bishop to Foster, February 1947.
49. Famularo, *Harvard Mental Health Letter*, 8.
50. Bessel van der Kolk, *The Body Keeps the Score* (Viking, 2014), 127.
51. Randall Jarrell, "An Unread Book," in *Third Book of Criticism* (New York: Farrar, Straus & Giroux, 1969), 51–52.
52. *EAP*, 5.
53. *EAP*, 7.

CHAPTER FOUR. WADING IN THE MUD OF THE CELESTIAL GARDENS

1. Bishop to Bradley, October 26, 1926.
2. Bishop to Foster, February 1947. VCL.
3. *Prose*, 429.
4. Bishop to Foster, February 1947.
5. William Logan, "Elizabeth Bishop at Summer Camp," *Virginia Quarterly Review* 88, no. 2 (Spring 2012).
6. Bishop to Bradley, August 5, 1925.
7. Bishop, "The Call," *Camp Chequesset Log* 18 (Fall 1925).
8. Bishop to Bradley, September 17, 1925.
9. Bishop to Bradley, January 5, 1926.
10. Michael Hood, "The Revere and Saugus, Massachusetts, Experience," *Worcester Review* 21 (2000).
11. Bishop to Bradley, March 30, 1926.
12. Bishop to Bradley, January 14, 1926.
13. Bishop to Bradley, January 14, 1926.

14. Bishop to Bradley, July 1926.
15. Bishop to Bradley, July 1926.
16. Bishop to Bradley, August 29, 1926.
17. Bishop to Bradley, December 5, 1926.
18. Bishop to Bradley, November 16, 1926.
19. Bishop to Bradley, October 16, 1926.
20. Bishop to Bradley, March 30, 1926.
21. Bishop to Foster, February 1947.
22. Elizabeth Bishop, *Poems, Prose, and Letters* (New York: Library of America, 2008). Hereafter, *PPL*, 183.

CHAPTER FIVE. WALNUT HILL

1. Walnut Hill is now an independent school for the arts. Its most recently constructed dormitory is named after Elizabeth Bishop '30.
2. Walnut Hill admissions pamphlet, undated, circa 1930.
3. Rhoda Wheeler Sheehan to her mother, September 28, 1927. Courtesy of Fiona Sheehan.
4. Rhoda Wheeler Sheehan to her mother, October 6, 1927.
5. *PPL*, 321.
6. Walnut Hill admissions pamphlet, undated, circa 1930.
7. "Introduction," in Elizabeth Bishop, *Collected Prose*, ed. Robert Giroux (New York: Farrar, Straus & Giroux, 1984), xii.
8. *Remembering EB*, 27.
9. "Introduction," *Collected Prose*, xiii.
10. *Conversations*, 21.
11. *PPL*, 639.
12. *PPL*, 639.
13. Bishop to Bradley, April 19, 1927.
14. "English 285, TAKE-HOME EXAMINATION," May 1975. Provided to the author by Dana Gioia.
15. *PPL*, 640.
16. *Remembering EB*, 22.
17. *Remembering EB*, 22.
18. *Remembering EB*, 23.
19. *Remembering EB*, 24.
20. *Remembering EB*, 27.
21. Rhoda Wheeler Sheehan to her mother, October 25, 1927.
22. *Remembering EB*, 28.
23. *Remembering EB*, 21.
24. *Remembering EB*, 21.
25. *Remembering EB*, 25.
26. *Prose*, 431.
27. *Remembering EB*, 25.
28. Rhoda Wheeler Sheehan to her mother, January 22, 1930.
29. *Prose*, 431.
30. Recorded in 1935. See Boris Berman, *Prokofiev's Piano Sonatas: A Guide for the Listener and the Performer* (New Haven: Yale University Press, 2008).
31. Recital program, Spring 1930, Walnut Hill School.
32. Bishop to Bradley, January 3, 1928.
33. Bishop to Bradley, January 3, 1928.
34. Bishop to Bradley, January 3, 1928.
35. Bishop to Bradley, March 5, 1928.
36. *PPL*, 186.
37. Bishop to Bradley, January 3, 1928.
38. Bishop to Bradley, July 17, 1928.
39. Robert Boucheron, "Elizabeth Bishop at Harvard," *Talking Writing*, January 21, 2013. Web. Accessed March 3, 2018.

40. Bishop to Bradley, June 27, 1928.
41. Bishop to Bradley, August 1929.
42. Bishop to Foster, February 1947. VCL.
43. Notebook, July 1 or 2, 1935. *EAP*, 247–48.
44. Elizabeth Bishop, *One Art: Letters*, ed. Robert Giroux (New York: Farrar, Straus & Giroux, 1994), 320. Hereafter, *OA*.
45. Bishop to Foster, February 1947.
46. Bishop to Foster, February 1947.
47. Bishop to Foster, February 1947.
48. Bishop to Foster, February 1947.
49. Bishop to Blough, January 22, 1975. *OA*, 594.
50. Bishop to Blough, January 22, 1975. *OA*, 594.
51. *EAP*, 244.
52. *Remembering EB*, 29.
53. Bishop to Foster, February 1947.
54. "Dead" was overlooked in Candace MacMahon's meticulous *Elizabeth Bishop: A Bibliography*, whose list of Bishop's Walnut Hill publications formed the basis for the section "Poems Written in Early Youth" in Bishop's 1983 *Complete Poems*. It was discovered by this author and first published in the *Gettysburg Review* in 1992.
55. *Prose*, 455–56.
56. *Prose*, 456.
57. Bishop to Bradley, July 17, 1928.
58. *PPL*, 456.
59. *PPL*, 458.

CHAPTER SIX. CON SPIRITO

1. "Jenny Holzer's Granite Ode to Elizabeth Bishop Honors Vassar President," Vassar Office of Communications, May 5, 2006. Web. Accessed February 10, 2017.
2. "Interview with Jenny Holzer." Web. Accessed February 10, 2017.
3. *Conversations*, 128.
4. Bishop to Bradley, undated, summer of 1930.
5. Bishop to Bradley, undated, summer of 1930.
6. *Conversations*, 127.
7. "Elizabeth Bishop: One Art," *Voices and Visions*, New York Center for Visual History, 1988. Web.
8. *Conversations*, 128.
9. *Remembering EB*, 40.
10. *Remembering EB*, 39.
11. *Remembering EB*, 39.
12. *Remembering EB*, 39–40
13. Interview with Dr. Bessel van der Kolk, May 22, 2015.
14. *Remembering EB*, 39–40.
15. Bishop to Foster, February 1947. VCL.
16. Eunice Clark Jessup, "Memoirs of Literatae and Socialists, 1929–1933," *Vassar Quarterly* (Winter 1979): 17.
17. May Swenson, "Her Early Work," in *Collected Poems* (New York: Library of America, 2013), 471.
18. Jessup, "Memoirs," 17.
19. Jessup, "Memoirs," 17.
20. Bishop to Bradley, September 15, 1931.
21. Bishop to Bradley, dated "Monday morning." Posted in late August or early September 1931, based on handwriting, ink color, and external evidence.
22. Bishop to Bradley, August–September 1931.
23. Bishop to Bradley, September 15, 1931.
24. Bishop to Bradley, September 15, 1931.
25. "Elizabeth Bishop: One Art," *Voices and Visions*.
26. Recited from memory by Mary McCarthy, "Elizabeth Bishop: One Art," *Voices and Visions*.

27. "Elizabeth Bishop: One Art," *Voices and Visions*.
28. Bishop to Foster, February 1947.
29. *Remembering EB*, 41.
30. *Remembering EB*, 43.
31. Millier, *Elizabeth Bishop*, 47–48.
32. Bishop to Blough, August 20, 1932. *OA*, 6–7.
33. "Elizabeth Bishop: One Art," *Voices and Visions*.
34. Bishop to Bradley, December 30, 1932.
35. "Informal Interview with Mary McCarthy," *Vassar Encyclopedia*, February 12, 1982. Web. Accessed October 12, 2017.
36. "T. S. Eliot Reads and Comments on His Poetry," *Miscellany News*, May 10, 1933, 1.
37. *Conversations*, 108.
38. "Eliot Favors Short-Lived Spontaneous Publications," *Miscellany News*, May 10, 1933, 1.
39. *Poems*, 217.
40. *Conversations*, 128–29.
41. Bethany Hicok, *Degrees of Freedom: American Women Poets and the Women's College, 1905–1955* (Cranbury, N.J.: Bucknell Uninersity Press, 2008), 110.
42. *Miscellany News*, November 29, 1933. Unsigned, like all "Campus Chat" contributions. Bishop claimed authorship in a December 12, 1933, letter to Frani Blough, *OA*, 14–15.
43. These eighteen publications appeared in *Con Spirito* and the *Vassar Review*, as well as the *Vassar Journal of Undergraduate Studies*. This accounting considers "Three Sonnets for the Eyes" as individual poems. Cf. MacMahon, *Bibliography*, 140–41. This count does *not* include the many items Bishop produced for the *Miscellany*, most of them anonymous.
44. Spires, *Conversations*, 129.
45. Bishop to Foster, February 1947.
46. Bishop to Foster, February 1947.
47. Christopher Ricks, "The Art and Faith of Gerard Manley Hopkins," *New Criterion* (September 1991).
48. *Prose*, 472.
49. *Prose*, 473.
50. *Conversations*, 26.
51. *Poems*, 220.
52. Marianne Moore, *The Poems of Marianne Moore*, ed. Grace Shulman (New York: Viking, 2003), 155.
53. Moore, *Poems*, 155.
54. Bishop to Blough, April 1, 1934. *OA*, 21.
55. *Prose*, 120.
56. Bishop to Foster, February 1947.
57. Bishop to Blough, June 4, 1934. *OA*, 24.
58. Bishop to Foster, February 1947.
59. Bishop to Blough, May 27, 1934. *OA*, 24.
60. Bishop to Blough, July 29, 1934. *OA*, 25.
61. Bishop to Blough, November 1, 1934. *OA*, 28.
62. Marianne Moore, "Archaically New," in *Trial Balances*, ed. Ann Winslow (New York: Macmillan, 1935).
63. Berryman to Bishop, December 22, 1969. VCL 1.13.
64. *Remembering EB*, 64.

CHAPTER SEVEN. THIS STRANGE WORLD OF TRAVEL

1. Bishop to Blough, November 1, 1934. *OA*, 28.
2. *Remembering EB*, 63.
3. *EAP*, 3.
4. Bishop to Blough, August 27, 1935. Passage omitted from *OA*.
5. *Remembering EB*, 63.
6. Bishop to Bradley, September 18, 1935.
7. Bishop to Blough, August 3, 1935.
8. Bishop to Blough, August 27, 1935. *OA*, 35.

9. *Remembering EB*, 63.
10. Bishop to Moore, August 21, 1935. *OA*, 34.
11. *Remembering EB*, 63.
12. Bishop to Blough, August 27, 1935. *OA*, 35.
13. Bishop to Blough, August 27, 1935. *OA*, 35.
14. Bishop to Moore, August 27, 1935. *OA*, 34.
15. Bishop to Bradley, September 18, 1935.
16. Bishop to Bradley, September 18, 1935.
17. Bishop to Blough, October 20, 1935. *OA*, 37.
18. Louise Crane to Josephine Crane, November 12, 1935. Beinecke Library, Yale University.
19. Bishop to Blough, October 20, 1935. *OA*, 38–39.
20. *Remembering EB*, 64.
21. Despite diligent research, the actual misprint has yet to be found.
22. Robert Lowell, "Interview with Frederick Seidel," *Paris Review* (Winter/Spring 1961).
23. *Poems*, 12.
24. *Poems*, 28.
25. *Remembering EB*, 65.
26. Louise Crane to Josephine Crane, December 10, 1935.
27. *Prose*, 10.
28. Bishop to Moore, May 12, 1936 (*OA*, 41, mistakenly gives the date as May 21)—Hotel Costa Brava, Puerto de Sóller, Mallorca.
29. *Prose*, 121.
30. *Prose*, 121.
31. Millier, *Elizabeth Bishop*, 112.
32. Bishop to Moore, January 5, 1937. *OA*, 53.
33. Bishop to Moore, February 4, 1937. *OA*, 58.
34. Bishop to Moore, February 4, 1937. *OA*, 59.
35. Bishop to Humphries, April & May 1937. *OA*, 60.
36. George Herbert, "Love Unknown," in *The Temple* (1633).
37. *Poems*, 23.
38. Millier, *Elizabeth Bishop*, 121–23.
39. Bishop to Blough, July 28, 1937.
40. Bishop to Blough, August 1937.
41. *Remembering EB*, 41.
42. Bishop to Blough, August 21, 1937.
43. Bishop to Blough, August 21, 1937.
44. Bishop to Blough, October 7, 1937.
45. Bishop to Blough, November 21, 1937.
46. Bishop to Blough, November 24, 1937. *OA*, 64.
47. Bishop to Blough, December 10, 1937. *OA*, 65.
48. Bishop to Gregory, December 27, 1937. *OA*, 66.

CHAPTER EIGHT. THE STATE WITH THE PRETTIEST NAME

1. Bishop to Blough, January 4, 1937.
2. *Conversations*, 27.
3. Bishop to Moore, February 19, 1939. *OA*, 80.
4. Lynn Mitsuko Kaufelt, *Key West Writers and Their Houses* (Sarasota, Fla.: Pineapple Press, 1991).
5. Interview with Dave Gonzales, March 17, 2013.
6. Maureen Ogle, *Key West: History of an Island of Dreams* (Gainesville, Fla.: University Press of Florida, 2006).
7. Ogle, *Key West*.
8. Bishop to Blough, January 4, 1937.
9. *Poems*, 45.
10. Bishop to Moore, January 31, 1938.
11. David Kalstone, *Becoming a Poet* (Ann Arber, Mich.: University of Michigan Press, 2001), 56.

12. *Prose*, 18.
13. Bishop to Moore, February 13, 1939. *OA*, 80.
14. Louise Crane to Josephine Crane, March 20, 1938.
15. Bishop to Moore, June 2, 1938. *OA*, 74.
16. Bishop to Blough and Miller, June 3, 1938. *OA*, 75.
17. *Prose*, 27–28.
18. Ogle, *Key West*.
19. *Prose*, 31.
20. *Conversations*, 27.
21. *Conversations*, 27.
22. Ogle, *Key West*.
23. *Remembering EB*, 75.
24. *Remembering EB*, 75.
25. *Remembering EB*, 104.
26. *Prose*, 412.
27. Bishop to Moore, May 21, 1940. *OA*, 90.
28. Milton Trexler, "Elizabeth Bishop's Private Love: Thomas Edwards Wanning," December 21, 2014. Web. Accessed September 8, 2015.
29. Trexler, "Elizabeth Bishop's Private Love."
30. Elizabeth Wanning Harries, email to author, September 12, 2015.
31. *Poems*, 42.
32. Bishop to Blough, May 2, 1938. *OA*, 71.
33. Bishop to Blough, May 2, 1938. *OA*, 71.
34. Louise Crane to Josephine Crane, dated "Saturday" in 1939.
35. James Merrill, "Elizabeth Bishop (1911–1979)," *New York Review of Books*, December 6, 1979.
36. Ogle, *Key West*.
37. Louise Crane to Josephine Crane, December 14, 1939.
38. Louise Crane to Josephine Crane, January 3, 1939.
39. Louise Crane to Josephine Crane, January 3, 1939.
40. Bishop to Stevenson, January 8, 1964. *Prose*, 413.
41. Bishop to Stevenson, January 8, 1964. *Prose*, 413.
42. Bishop to Moore, February 5, 1940. *OA*, 87.
43. Ernest Hemingway, *Death in the Afternoon* (New York: Scribner's, 1932), 192.
44. *Conversations*, 99.
45. Bishop to Moore, January 31, 1938. *OA*, 68.
46. *Poems*, 35.
47. *Prose*, 414.

CHAPTER NINE. AS OUR KISSES ARE CHANGING

1. Elizabeth Bishop, *Poems*, 40.
2. *Prose*, 328.
3. Bishop to Moore, February 5, 1940. *OA*, 87.
4. *Remembering EB*, 93.
5. *Prose*, 146.
6. *Prose*, 151.
7. *Prose*, 160.
8. *Remembering EB*, 85.
9. *EAP*, 44.
10. Lorrie Goldensohn, "Elizabeth Bishop: An Unpublished, Untitled Poem," *American Poetry Review* (January/February 1988): 35–36.
11. Bishop to Charlotte Russell [June 1941]. *OA*, 100.
12. Ogle, *Key West*, Chapter 9.
13. *EAP*, 59.
14. Ronald Christ, "Elizabeth Bishop's Doctor," *New York Times*, May 8, 1994. *New York Times* digital archive. Accessed April 26, 2019.

15. Millier asserts that Bishop began seeing Baumann in spring 1947, but Bishop's February 1947 letters to Foster make clear that she had begun as Baumann's patient, and subsequently as a patient of Foster's, some months before she made her August 1946 trip to Great Village.

16. Randall Jarrell, *Poetry and the Age* (New York: Vintage, 1953), 235.

CHAPTER TEN. THE PRODIGAL

1. Mizener to Bishop, January 14, 1947. Cited in footnote, *OA*, 144.
2. Bishop to Joseph and U. T. Summers, July 18, 1955. *OA*, 308.
3. Bishop to Summers, July 18, 1955. *OA*, 308.
4. Bishop to Swenson, September 6, 1955.
5. Bishop to Swenson, September 6, 1955.
6. *Poems*, 73.
7. Bishop to Summers, July 18, 1955. *OA*, 308.
8. Bishop to Swenson, September 6, 1955.
9. *Poems*, 79.
10. White to Bishop, February 17, 1947. *EBNYR*, 28.
11. *Poems*, 63.
12. *Poems*, 64.
13. Interview with Frank Bidart, May 20, 2015.
14. Bishop to Foster, February 1947. VCL.
15. Bishop to White, February 13, 1947. *EBNYR*, 28.
16. Lowell to Bishop, December 18, 1974. *WIA*, 776.
17. Lowell to Bishop, December 18, 1974. *WIA*, 778–79.
18. "Elizabeth Bishop on Robert Lowell," *WIA*, 810.
19. Bishop to Lowell, January 16, 1975. *WIA*, 778.
20. "Elizabeth Bishop on Robert Lowell," *WIA*, 810.
21. Lowell to Bishop, March 11, 1970, *WIA*, 669.
22. Bishop to Lowell, January 16, 1975. *WIA*, 778.
23. *Poems*, 62.
24. Bishop to Lowell, August 14, 1947. *WIA*, 6.
25. *Poems*, 63.
26. Bishop to Lowell, November 18, 1947. *WIA*, 13.
27. Bishop to Lowell, November 18, 1947. *WIA*, 14.
28. Millier mistakenly suggests that the poem is describing the larger and more elegant Garrison Bight, which stood at some distance from Bishop's current Dey Street lodging and which was not a working harbor for fishing boats, as was Key West Bight.
29. *Poems*, 60.
30. *EBNYR*, 37.
31. *Remembering EB*, 105–6.
32. Lowell to Bishop, August 15, 1957. *WIA*, 225.
33. Lowell to Bishop, August 15, 1957. *WIA*, 226.
34. Lowell to Bishop, November 11, 1948. *WIA*, 66.
35. Millier, *Elizabeth Bishop*, 215.
36. *Poems*, 58.
37. *Poems*, 58.
38. *Remembering EB*, 108.
39. James Merrill, "Overdue Pilgrimage to Nova Scotia," in *A Scattering of Salts* (New York: Alfred A. Knopf, 1995).
40. *Remembering EB*, 115–16.
41. *Conversations*, 3.
42. *Conversations*, 5.
43. *PPL*, 686.
44. *PPL*, 687.
45. Bishop to Bradley, January 14, 1926.
46. *Poems*, 69.
47. Swenson to Hanson, November 7, 1951.

48. *Poems*, 55.
49. *Poems*, 56.

CHAPTER ELEVEN. TOO MANY WATERFALLS

1. Bishop to McBride, October 8, 1951. *OA*, 224.
2. IFC brochure. Web. Accessed August 12, 2015.
3. Bishop to Hanson, January 29, 1952. The relationship between Mary Morse and Lota de Macedo Soares was characterized in a presentation by Monica Stearns Morse, Vassar College, May 11, 2016.
4. Bishop to Lowell, November 26, 1951. *WIA*, 131.
5. IFC brochure. Web. Accessed August 12, 2015.
6. Bishop to Hanson, November 12, 1951.
7. Bishop to Hanson, November 12, 1951.
8. Lowell to Bishop, November 26, 1951. *WIA*, 129.
9. Bishop to Hanson, November 12, 1951.
10. Lowell to Bishop, November 26, 1951. *WIA*, 129.
11. Bishop to Hanson, November 12, 1951.
12. Lowell to Bishop, November 26, 1951. *WIA*, 130.
13. Millier, *Elizabeth Bishop*, 238.
14. "'Silk Stocking' Gang Leader Suspect Seized," *Detroit Free Press*, January 29, 1928, 1–2.
15. "Ex-Policewoman Mary Breen Dies," *Detroit Free Press*, January 3, 1967.
16. "Lt. Mary Breen to Quit Force After 25 Years," *Detroit Free Press*, September 19, 1946.
17. "Suicide Guard for Schweitzer," *Detroit Free Press*, July 3, 1935.
18. "Profile: Miss Mary Breen," *Detroit Free Press*, August 7, 1932.
19. Bishop to Hanson, November 12, 1951.
20. "It's News of Detroit in Brief," *Detroit Free Press*, September 20, 1946.
21. "2 Policewomen Raid Hotels, Arrest Eight," *Detroit Free Press*, May 7, 1928, 24.
22. "Outstate Prejudice . . . ," *Detroit Free Press*, December 24, 1939, 5.
23. Millier, *Elizabeth Bishop*, 239.
24. *Poems*, 87.
25. Pearl K[azin] Bell, "Dona Elizabetchy: A Memoir of Elizabeth Bishop," *Partisan Review* (Winter 1991).
26. Bishop to Swenson, September 1953.
27. Bishop to Alfred Kazin, December 1951. *OA*, 227.
28. Bishop to Hanson, January 19, 1952.
29. Bishop to Hanson, January 19, 1952.
30. Bishop to Baumann, January 8, 1952. *OA*, 231.
31. Bishop to Baumann, January 8, 1952. *OA*, 231.
32. Bishop to Hanson, January 19, 1952.
33. Bishop to Moore, February 14, 1952. *OA, 236.*
34. Bishop to MacIver, January 26, 1952. *OA*, 233.
35. Bishop to Hanson, January 19, 1952.
36. Bishop to Barkers, February 7, 1952. *OA*, 233.
37. Bishop to Barkers, February 7, 1952. *OA*, 234.
38. Bishop to Barkers, February 7, 1952. *OA*, 234.
39. Bishop to Barkers, February 7, 1952. *OA*, 233.
40. Bishop to Moore, February 14, 1952. *OA*, 236.
41. *Remembering EB*, 128.
42. Bishop to Barkers, February 7, 1952. *OA*, 234.
43. Bishop to Moore, February 14, 1952. *OA*, 236.
44. Bishop to Moore, March 3, 1952. *OA*, 238.
45. *Remembering EB*, 128.
46. Bell, "Dona Elizabetchy."
47. Bell, "Dona Elizabetchy."
48. Lowell to Bishop, February 26, 1952. *WIA*, 133.
49. Bishop to Lowell, March 21, 1952. *WIA*, 136.
50. Bishop to Lowell, March 21, 1952. *WIA*, 136.

51. Elizabeth Bishop, *Exchanging Hats: Paintings*, ed. William Benton (New York: Farrar, Straus & Giroux, 1996), 61.
52. *Poems*, 227–28.
53. Rich, "The Eye of the Outsider," 16.
54. *Poems*, 82.
55. *EBNYR*, 112.
56. Bishop to Pearl K. Bell, 1953. *OA*, 241. *OA*'s date is mistaken.
57. Swenson to Bishop, September 14, 1953. WU Library.
58. *Poems, 82.*
59. Bishop to Swenson, September 19, 1953.
60. Swenson to Bishop, September 14, 1953.
61. *Remembering EB, 142.*
62. Rich, "The Eye of the Outsider," 16.

CHAPTER TWELVE. SAMAMBAIA

1. Bishop to Barkers, October 12, 1952. *OA*, 249.
2. Bell, "Dona Elizabetchy," 31.
3. *WIA*, xv.
4. Bell, "Dona Elizabetchy," 34.
5. Bishop to Swenson, June 1, 1956.
6. Bishop to Lowell, December 5, 1953. *WIA*, 147.
7. Bishop to Barkers, October 12, 1952. *OA*, 249.
8. Bishop to Barkers, October 12, 1951. *OA*, 250.
9. Bishop to Swenson, February 5, 1956.
10. Bishop to Barkers, October 12, 1952. *OA*, 249.
11. Bishop to Hanson, March 25, 1953.
12. Bishop to Barkers, July 13, 1953. *OA*, 266.
13. Bishop to Bradley, April 19, 1927. Wylie House.
14. Bishop to Sargent, October 4, 1952.
15. Bishop to Hanson, March 25, 1953.
16. Bishop to Hanson, March 25, 1953.
17. Bishop to Hanson, March 25, 1953.
18. Bishop to Hanson, March 25, 1953.
19. Bishop to Barkers, May 24, 1953. *OA*, 265.
20. Bishop to Swenson, March 17, 1955.
21. Bishop to Swenson, March 17, 1955.
22. Bishop to Barkers, June 17, 1953.
23. Bishop to Barkers, November 23, 1953. *OA*, 278.
24. Bishop to Barkers, July 13, 1953. *OA*, 266.
25. Bishop to Barkers, October 8, 1953. *OA*, 273.
26. Bishop to Hanson, July 27, 1953.
27. Bishop to Hanson, July 27, 1953.
28. Bishop, *Exchanging Hats*, 64–65.
29. Bishop to Barkers, May 24, 1953. *OA*, 265.
30. Bishop to Lowell, April 1, 1958. *WIA*, 253.
31. Bishop to Barkers, January 26, 1956.
32. Bishop to Barkers, August 29, 1953. *OA, 271.*
33. Bishop to Swenson, March 17, 1955.
34. Bishop to Swenson, March 17, 1955.
35. Bishop to Lowell, March 21, 1952. *WIA*, 134.
36. Bishop to Barkers, June 17, 1953.
37. Bishop to Barkers, February 26, 1954. *OA*, 292
38. Bishop to Lowell, December 11, 1957. *WIA*, 242.
39. Lowell to Bishop, March 10, 1963. *WIA*, 452.
40. Bishop to Lowell, July 28, 1953. *WIA*, 142–43.
41. Bishop to Lowell, July 28, 1953. *WIA*, 143.

42. Bishop to Lowell, July 28, 1953. *WIA*, 143.
43. Lowell to Bishop, November 29, 1953. *WIA*, 145.
44. Lowell to Bishop, October 24, 1956. *WIA*, 187.
45. Lowell, *Collected Prose* (New York: Farrar, Straus & Giroux, 1987), 76.
46. Bishop to Lowell, December 5, 1953. *WIA*, 147.
47. Bishop to Pearl Kazin, November 16, 1953. *OA*, 276–77.
48. *Remembering EB*, 75.
49. Bishop to Lowell, December 5, 1953. *WIA*, 146.
50. Bishop to Barkers, October 22, 1954.
51. Bishop to Barkers, February 28, 1955.
52. Bishop to McKenna, November 19, 1956. *OA*, 329.
53. *Prose*, 52.
54. *Prose*, 54.
55. *Prose*, 59.
56. *Prose*, 61.
57. *Prose*, 78.
58. Elizabeth Bishop, "Introduction," in *The Diary of "Helena Morley"* (New York: Farrar, Straus & Giroux, 1957), ix–x.
59. Bishop to Barkers, August 7, 1954.
60. *PPL*, 238.
61. Bishop to Barkers, February 5, 1954.
62. Randall Jarrell, "The Year in Poetry," first published in *Harper's*, October 1955. Cited from *Kipling, Auden & Co.* (New York: Farrar, Straus & Giroux, 1980), 244–45.
63. Bishop to Jarrell, December 26, 1955. *OA*, 312.
64. Bishop to White, February 28, 1947. *EBNYR*, 28.
65. Bishop to White, January 12, 1949. *EBNYR*, 38.
66. White to Bishop, January 20, 1949. *EBNYR*, 39.

CHAPTER THIRTEEN. "O PRÊMIO PULITZER!"

1. Bishop, "Introduction," in *Diary of "Helena Morley,"* xv.
2. Bishop, "Foreword," in *Diary of "Helena Morley,"* vii.
3. Bishop, "Foreword," in *Diary of "Helena Morley,"* xxxiii. This edifice is now known as Hotel Tijuco Turismo.
4. Bishop to Barkers, June 5, 1956.
5. Bishop to Swenson, May 10, 1956.
6. Bishop to Barkers, June 5, 1956.
7. Bishop to Lowell, June 7, 1956. *WIA*, 176.
8. Bishop to Swenson, May 10, 1956.
9. Bishop to Barkers, June 5, 1956.
10. Bishop to Merrill, June 5, 1956.
11. Bishop to Barkers, June 5, 1956.
12. Bishop to Kazin, May 21, 1956. *OA*, 318.
13. Bishop to Lowell, June 7, 1956. *WIA*, 176.
14. Bishop to Barkers, June 5, 1956.
15. "Pulitzer Prize Poet Lives in Petrópolis," *O Globo*, May 1956. Cited in translation from *Conversations*, 8–11.
16. Bishop to Baumann, May 10, 1956. *OA*, 317.
17. Bishop to Barkers, June 5, 1956.
18. Bishop to Lowell, July 17, 1955. *WIA*, 166.
19. Bishop to Barkers, March 23, 1956.
20. Bishop to Swenson, November 25, 1956. *OA*, 331.
21. Bishop to Barkers, June 5, 1956.
22. Bishop to Barkers, June 14, 1956.
23. Bishop to Grace Bulmer Bowers, July 5, 1956. *OA*, 322.
24. Bishop to Barkers, June 14, 1956.
25. Bishop to Gold and Fizdale, May 5, 1953. *OA*, 263.

26. *Poems*, 90.
27. *Poems*, 91.
28. Lowell to Bishop, June 10, 1957. *WIA*, 204.
29. Lowell to Bishop, April 28, 1960. *WIA*, 324.
30. Bishop to Lowell [February 1959]. *WIA*, 289.
31. Bishop to Barkers, January 26, 1957.
32. Bishop to Swenson, February 10, 1957. *OA*, 336.
33. *Remembering EB*, 153–54.
34. Bishop to Moss, January 25, 1957. *EBNYR*, 193.
35. Bishop to Barkers, June 28, 1957.
36. Bishop to Lowell, August 11, 1957. *WIA*, 216.
37. Bishop to Lowell, August 11, 1957. *WIA*, 217.
38. Bishop to Barkers, November 2, 1957.
39. Bishop to Lowell, September 29, 1957. *WIA*, 233.
40. Bishop to Barkers, November 2, 1957.
41. Bishop to Lowell, August 28, 1958. *WIA*, 264.
42. Bishop to Moss, September 8, 1959. *EBNYR*, 215.

CHAPTER FOURTEEN. APARTMENT IN LEME

1. *Poems*, 90.
2. *Poems*, 91.
3. Lowell to Bishop, January 4, 1960. *WIA*, 307.
4. The Portuguese "Flamengo" is not to be confused with the English "flamingo," a bird name spelled identically in both languages. "Flamengo" in Portuguese means "Flemish" and refers to Flemish or Dutch colonial associations with this sector of Rio. A literal translation of this site would be "Flemish Park." The park is also frequently referred to as the "Aterro" (or "Fill"), given its associations with the landfill on which the park was built.
5. Bishop to Merrill, April 25, 1961.
6. Bishop to Lowell, dated "March?? [1962]." *WIA*, 392.
7. Bishop to Barkers, June 20, 1961.
8. Robert Lowell, "Elizabeth Bishop 4," in *Selected Poems* (New York: Farrar, Straus & Giroux, 2006), 230.
9. Lowell to Bishop, September 10, 1952. *WIA*, 429.
10. See Bishop to Lowell, September [2]1, 1962. *WIA*, 418.
11. Bishop to Lowell, December 19, 1962. *WIA*, 429.
12. Bishop to Merrill, January 1964.
13. Bishop to Lowell, May 26, 1963. *WIA*, 460.
14. Bishop to Lowell, May 26, 1963. *WIA*, 458.
15. Bishop to Barkers, April 13, 1964.
16. Bishop to Barkers, April 27, 1964.
17. Bishop to Lowell, June 13, 1964. *WIA*, 540.
18. *Remembering EB*, 187.
19. Bishop to Lowell, August 27, 1964. *WIA*, 554.
20. Bishop to Lowell, July 30, 1964. *WIA*, 546.
21. *EAP*, 126.
22. *EAP*, 126.
23. Bishop to Barkers, November 24, 1965.
24. *Poems*, 212.
25. *Poems*, 213.
26. Footnote, *WIA*, 559.
27. Bishop to Swenson, November 5, 1964.
28. *Remembering EB*, 192.
29. *EAP*, 135.
30. *EAP*, 134.
31. Bishop to Lowell, August 2, 1965. *WIA*, 583.
32. Lowell to Bishop, November [22], 1964. *WIA*, 560.
33. *Poems*, 111.

34. *Poems*, 114.
35. Bishop to Lowell, December 11, 1964. *WIA*, 562.
36. Bishop to Lowell, March 11, 1965. *WIA*, 574.
37. Bishop to Swenson, November 10, 1965.
38. *Remembering EB*, 196–97.
39. Bishop to Swenson, November 10, 1965.
40. Translation courtesy of David Hoak.
41. Translation by George Monteiro, *The Presence of Camões* (Lexington, Ky.: University Press of Kentucky, 1996), 106.
42. Lowell to Bishop, November 22, 1964. *WIA*, 560.
43. Lowell, blurb for Bishop, *Questions of Travel* (New York: Farrar, Straus & Giroux, 1965).
44. Lowell to Bishop, October 28, 1965. *WIA*, 591.
45. Bishop to Lowell, November 18, 1965. *WIA*, 596.
46. Lowell to Bishop, November 24, 1965. *WIA*, 597.

CHAPTER FIFTEEN. NO COFFEE CAN WAKE YOU

1. Tom Robbins, "Now Playing: A Touch of the Poetess," in *Conversations*, 33.
2. *Conversations*, 33.
3. *Conversations*, 34.
4. *Conversations*, 36.
5. *Conversations*, 33–34.
6. *Conversations*, 34.
7. *Remembering EB*, 202.
8. Bishop to Lowell, May 19, 1960. *WIA*, 328.
9. Bishop to Barkers, February 8, 1966.
10. Bishop to Baumann, March 19, 1966. *OA*, 446.
11. Bishop to Barkers, February 8, 1966.
12. *Remembering EB*, 203.
13. Bishop to Barkers, February 8, 1966.
14. Bishop to Lowell, February 23, 1966. *WIA*, 600.
15. Lowell to Bishop, May 23, 1965. *WIA*, 575.
16. *PPL*, 469.
17. *Conversations*, 40.
18. *Conversations*, 40.
19. Interview with Roxanne Cumming, January 19, 2019.
20. Delores Tarzan Ament, "Cumming, William (1917–2010, Painter)," February 15, 2003. Web. Accessed November 10, 2018.
21. Interview with Cumming, January 19, 2019.
22. Cumming, email to author, November 22, 2018.
23. Bishop to Bowie, August 13, 1966.
24. Bishop to Baumann, September 1, 1966. *OA*, 449.
25. Bishop to Baumann, September 1, 1966. *OA*, 449.
26. Interview with Monica Morse, January 12, 2019.
27. Bishop to Magú and Rosinha Leão, August 27, 1967.
28. Lota to Bishop, September 7, 1967. VCL 118.28.
29. Dr. Decio Soares de Souza to Bishop, October 18, 1967. VCL 117.14.
30. Lota to Bishop, September 15, 1967.
31. Bishop to Rosinha Leão, September 23, 1967.
32. Bishop to Rosinha Leão, September 23, 1967.
33. Bishop to Rosinha Leão, September 25, 1967. *OA*, 469.
34. Lota to Bishop, September 7, 1967. VCL 118.28.
35. Bishop to Barkers, October 18, 1967.
36. Bishop to Barkers, October 18, 1967.
37. Monica Morse, presentation at Vassar College, May 11, 2016.
38. Bishop to Barkers, October 18, 1967.
39. Bishop to Barkers, September 28, 1967. *OA*, 470.

40. *EAP*, 149.
41. Decio de Souza to Bishop, October 18, 1967.
42. Bishop to Bowie, letters of November 10 & 14, 1967.
43. Interview with Morse, January 12, 2018.
44. Bishop to Bowie, November 14, 1967.
45. Bishop to Osser, January 4, 1968. *OA*, 488–91.
46. Bishop to Lowell, January 9, 1968. *WIA*, 635.
47. Interview with Morse, January 12, 2018.
48. Bishop to Muser, January 4, 1968. *OA*, 487.
49. Bishop to Osser, January 4, 1968. *OA*, 488–91.
50. Bishop to Muser, January 4, 1968. This passage omitted from *OA*.
51. Bishop to Muser, January 4, 1968. Passage omitted from *OA*.
52. Interview with Cumming, January 18, 2019.
53. Bishop to Barkers, March 31, 1969.
54. Interview with Cumming, January 18, 2019.
55. Bishop to Barkers, August 10, 1969.
56. Bishop to Barkers, August 25, 1969.
57. Bishop to Barkers, August 25, 1969.
58. Bishop to Barkers, October 3, 1969.
59. Lowell to Bishop, December 6, 1959. *WIA*, 656.
60. Bishop to Lowell, December 15 or 16, 1969. *WIA*, 661.
61. Bishop to Barkers, December 1, 1969.
62. Bishop to Barkers, January 2, 1970.
63. Bishop to Barkers, March 7, 1970.
64. Bishop to Barkers, May 13, 1970.
65. Bishop to Bowie, May 28, 1970.
66. Bishop to Bowie, June 14, 1970.
67. Bishop to Bowie, June 19, 1970.
68. Merrill, *Poetry Pilot*.
69. Merrill, *Poetry Pilot*.
70. Bishop to Barkers, August 28 or 29, 1970.
71. Bishop to Barkers, August 28 or 29, 1970.
72. Bishop to Bowie, September 15, 1970.

CHAPTER SIXTEEN. BREAKFAST SONG

1. Methfessel to Bishop, November 24, 1970.
2. Methfessel to Bishop, December 28, 1970.
3. Interview with Gary Methfessel, December 2018.
4. Bishop to Methfessel, [December] 29, [1970].
5. *Remembering EB*, 270.
6. Bishop to Muser, October 1, 1970. *OA*, 532.
7. *Remembering EB*, 270.
8. Bishop to MacIver, October 6, 1970. *OA*, 535.
9. Bishop to Bowie, November 2, 1970.
10. Bishop to Bowie, November 7, 1970.
11. *Remembering EB*, 270.
12. Bishop to Bowie, February 23, 1971.
13. Interview with Bidart, May 20, 2015.
14. Bishop to Bowie, February 23, 1971.
15. Bishop to Barkers, June 25, 1971.
16. Bishop to Baumann, September 9, 1971. *OA*, 547.
17. Bishop to Methfessel, typed note addressed to "my darling darling" and dated only "4 PM."
18. Bishop to Gold and Fizdale, July 8, 1971. *OA*, 544.
19. Bishop to Barkers, August 29, 1953. *OA*, 273.
20. Tom Paulin, "Newness and Nowness: The Extraordinary Brilliance of Elizabeth Bishop's Letters," *Times Literary Supplement*, April 29, 1994, 3.

21. Review in *The Week*, November 7, 2008.
22. Jonathan Ellis, ed., *Letter Writing Among Poets: From William Wordsworth to Elizabeth Bishop* (Edinburgh, U.K.: University of Edinburgh Press, 2015).
23. U. T. Summers, "Surprised by *One Art*," *Elizabeth Bishop Bulletin* (Summer 1994): 2–4.
24. Bishop to Muser, January 8, 1972. *OA*, 553.
25. Bishop to Brown, January 25, 1972. *OA*, 556.
26. Swenson to Bishop, December 2, 1971.
27. *Poems*, 183.
28. *Poems*, 184.
29. *Poems*, 184.
30. *Poems*, 185.
31. *Poems*, 186.
32. Lowell to Bishop, July 31, 1973. *WIA*, 754.
33. *Remembering EB*, 333.
34. See discussion of "Crusoe in England," *EBNYR*, 273–80.
35. *Poems*, 189–90.
36. Bishop to Foster, February 1947. VCL.
37. Bishop to Foster, February 1947.
38. *Remembering EB*, 291.
39. Millier, *Elizabeth Bishop*, 466.
40. Bishop to Lowell, June 30, 1948. *WIA*, 39.
41. Bishop to Lowell, February 10, 1972. *WIA*, 708.
42. Hardwick to Bishop, August 16, 1978. *VCL*.
43. Lowell to Bishop, July 12, 1973. *WIA*, 752.
44. Moss to Bishop, March 28, 1972. *EBNYR*, 339.
45. *Poems*, 196.
46. *Poems*, 197.

CHAPTER SEVENTEEN. THE RAINBOW-BIRD

1. Megan Marshall, *Elizabeth Bishop: A Miracle for Breakfast* (New York: Houghton Mifflin Harcourt), 261.
2. Bishop to Bowie, September 11, 1974.
3. Bishop to Barkers, September 11, 1974.
4. Bishop to Barkers, August 5, 1974.
5. Moss to Bishop, January 4, 1975. *EBNYR*, 356.
6. Bishop to Barkers, April 7, 1975.
7. Bishop to Bowie, April 27, 1974.
8. Bishop to Bowie, April 27, 1974.
9. Bishop to Barkers, November 11, 1974.
10. Bishop to Barkers, April 7, 1975.
11. Elizabeth Spires, "An Afternoon with Elizabeth Bishop," *Vassar Quarterly* (Winter 1979): 5.
12. *Remembering EB*, 322.
13. *Remembering EB*, 322.
14. *Remembering EB*, 322.
15. Bishop to MacIver and Frankenberg, July 30, 1974. *OA*, 587.
16. *Remembering EB*, 63.
17. *Remembering EB*, 319–20.
18. *Remembering EB*, 320.
19. Schwartz, email to author, February 26, 2019.
20. Bishop indicated in a letter to *The New Yorker* that neither Brinnin nor Read had been on the walk she describes in the poem (*EBNYR*, 361). Her companion must surely have been Methfessel.
21. Bishop to Lowell, September 3, 1974. *WIA*, 767.
22. *Poems*, 200.
23. Bishop to Moss, July 18, 1974. *EBNYR*, 360.
24. Harold Bloom, "Geography III," *New Republic*, February 5, 1977, 29.
25. *The New Yorker* lost track of the revised ending Bishop sent them, but it was later restored in book publication.

26. Bishop to Henderson, August 15, 1974. *EBNYR*, 361.
27. Moss to Bishop, July 28, 1975. *EBNYR*, 372.
28. Bishop to MacIver, October 6, 1970. *OA*, 535.
29. *Remembering EB*, 280.
30. *Remembering EB*, 298.
31. Notes shared with the author by Mildred Nash.
32. Interview with Eric M. Van, January 13, 2019.
33. Boucheron, "Elizabeth Bishop at Harvard," Web. Accessed March 3, 2018.
34. *Remembering EB*, 327.
35. *Remembering EB*, 298.
36. *Remembering EB*, 311.
37. Interview with Mildred Nash, April 30, 2015.
38. Mildred Nash, "Elizabeth Bishop's Library: A Reminiscence," *Massachusetts Review* 24, no. 2 (1983): 436.
39. Nash, "Elizabeth Bishop's Library," 437.
40. Interview with Nash, April 30, 2015.
41. *Remembering EB*, 326.
42. *Remembering EB*, 327.
43. *Remembering EB*, 330.
44. Charles P. Elliot, "Minor Poet with a Major Fund of Love," *Life*, July 4, 1969, 13.
45. Bishop to Summers, March 1, 1979.
46. Nash, "Elizabeth Bishop's Library."
47. *Remembering EB, 330.*
48. Rich, "The Eye of the Outsider," 16.
49. Marilyn May Lombardi, ed., *Elizabeth Bishop: The Geography of Gender* (Charlottesville, Va.: University of Virginia Press, 1993), 5.
50. Lowell to Bishop, December 18, 1974. *WIA*, 776.
51. Bishop to Lowell, January 16, 1975. *WIA*, 778.
52. Bishop to Barkers, April 7, 1975.
53. Interview with Bidart, May 20, 2015.
54. Gregory Orr, email to the author, June 16, 2013.
55. Interview with Bidart, May 20, 2015.
56. *Conversations*, 329.
57. *Remembering EB*, 320.
58. Bishop to Barkers, April 19, 1976.
59. Email exchange with Fiona Sheehan, February 24, 2019.
60. Moss to Bishop, November 4, 1975. *EBNYR*, 373.
61. *Poems*, 198.
62. *Poems*, 198.
63. *Remembering EB*, 334.
64. *Remembering EB*, 334.
65. Interview with Bidart, May 20, 2015.
66. Bloom, "*Geography III* by Elizabeth Bishop." *New Republic*, February 5, 1977, 29–30.
67. *Remembering EB*, 290.
68. *Remembering EB*, 341.
69. *Remembering EB*, 341.
70. *Poems*, 210.
71. *Remembering EB*, 344.
72. *Poems*, 211.
73. Hardwick to Bishop, August 16, 1978.
74. *Remembering EB*, 346.
75. Robert Taylor, "Book-Making," *Boston Globe*, October 14, 1979, C2. Clipping from the collection of Mildred Nash.
76. *Remembering EB*, 350.
77. Taylor, "Book-Making."
78. Lloyd Schwartz, "Annals of Poetry: Elizabeth Bishop and Brazil," *The New Yorker*, September 30, 1991, 85–97.

79. Lloyd Schwartz, "Elizabeth Bishop's 'Sonnet,'" *Atlantic*, March 29, 2000.
80. Swenson, "In the Bodies of Words: For Elizabeth Bishop (1911–1979)."

CODA: ALL THE UNTIDY ACTIVITY CONTINUES

1. John Malcolm Brinnin, Sound Recording, Key West Literary Seminar, January 1993.
2. Millier, *Elizabeth Bishop*, 550. In an August 23, 2013, email to the author, Millier explained, "The language in my book was carefully worded—because Alice told me that Elizabeth had asked her to inscribe the stone, but she, Alice, had decided against it."
3. *Poems*, 59.
4. Merrill to Jeffrey Harrison, July 25, 1994. Transcribed for the author by Harrison in a March 14, 2013, email.
5. Email exchange with Carle Johnson, June 11, 2014.

Letters from Elizabeth Bishop to Louise Bradley, courtesy of the Louise Bradley and Elizabeth Bishop Correspondence Collection, Wylie House Museum, Indiana University Libraries, Bloomington.

Letter from May Swenson to Pauline Hanson, courtesy of The Literary Estate of May Swenson.

Letters from Louise Crane to Josephine Crane, courtesy of the Crane Foundation and the Louise Crane and Victoria Kent papers, Yale Collection of American Literature, Beinecke Rare Book and Manuscript Library.

All photographs are courtesy of Archives and Special Collections, Vassar College, unless noted below.

Insert page 1 (*bottom*): Courtesy of Esther Clark Wright Archives, Acadia University

Insert page 4 (*top left*): Courtesy of Louise Crane and Victoria Kent Papers; Yale Collection of American Literature, Beinecke Rare Book and Manuscript Library

Insert page 4 (*top right*): Courtesy of DeWolfe and Wood Collection, Florida Keys Public Libraries

Insert page 4 (*bottom*): Photograph by Josef Breitenbach © The Josef and Yaye Breitenbach Charitable Foundation

Insert page 5 (*top*): Courtesy of The Literary Estate of May Swenson

Insert page 5 (*center*): Courtesy of Monica Stearns Morse

Insert page 6 (*top left*): J. L. Castel, courtesy of Archives and Special Collections, Vassar College Library.

Insert page 8 (*top*): Courtesy of the author's private collection

INDEX